NAOKI URASAWA'S
20th CENTURY BOYS

Naoki Urasawa's
20th Century Boys
Volume 11

VIZ Signature Edition

STORY AND ART BY NAOKI URASAWA

20 SEIKI SHONEN 11 by Naoki URASAWA/Studio Nuts
© 2003 Naoki URASAWA/Studio Nuts
With the cooperation of Takashi NAGASAKI
All rights reserved. Original Japanese
edition published in 2003 by Shogakukan Inc., Tokyo.

English Adaptation/Akemi Wegmüller
Touch-up Art & Lettering/Freeman Wong
Cover & Interior Design/Sam Elzway
Editor/Kit Fox

VP, Production/Alvin Lu
VP, Sales & Product Marketing/Gonzalo Ferreyra
VP, Creative/Linda Espinosa
Publisher/Hyoe Narita

Printed in the U.S.A.

Published by VIZ Media, LLC
P.O. Box 77010
San Francisco, CA 94107

10 9 8 7 6 5 4 3 2 1
First printing, October 2010

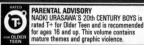

VIZ SIGNATURE
www.vizsignature.com

www.viz.com

NAOKI URASAWA'S
20th CENTURY BOYS

VOL 11
LIST OF INGREDIENTS

Story & Art by

NAOKI URASAWA

With the cooperation of

Takashi NAGASAKI

NAOKI URASAWA'S 20th CENTURY BOYS PROFILES

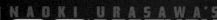

Her father is the Friend?! This incredible irony of fate plunges Kanna into the depths of despair. Will she be able to fight her way out of it?! Meanwhile, Koizumi and Sadakiyo are on the run, but where can they escape to? It's the year 2014, and history is about to be changed!!

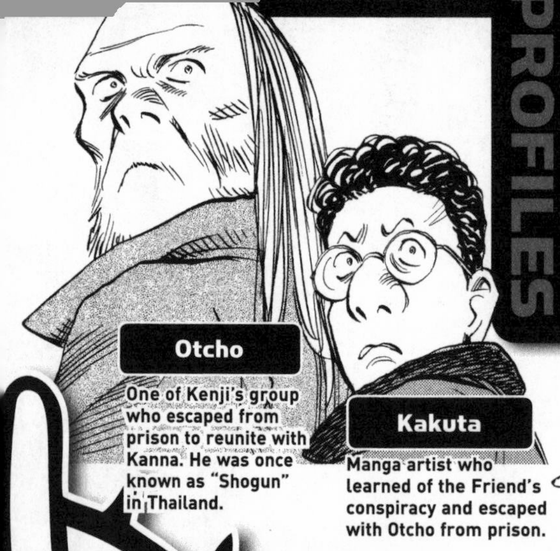

Otcho

One of Kenji's group who escaped from prison to reunite with Kanna. He was once known as "Shogun" in Thailand.

Kakuta

Manga artist who learned of the Friend's conspiracy and escaped with Otcho from prison.

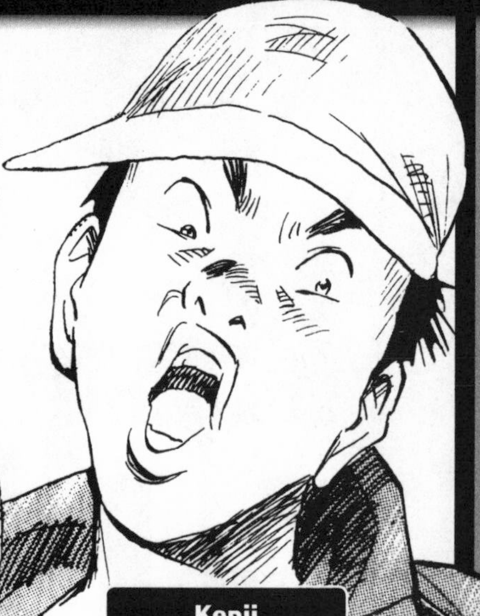

Kenji

Kanna's uncle, who lost his life battling the Friend on Bloody New Year's Eve, 2000.

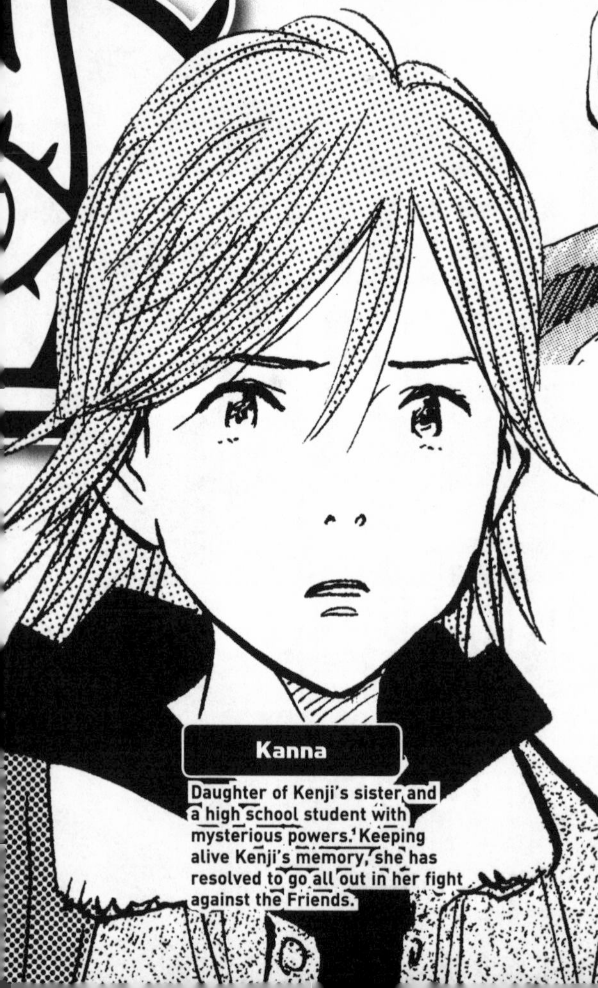

Kanna

Daughter of Kenji's sister and a high school student with mysterious powers. Keeping alive Kenji's memory, she has resolved to go all out in her fight against the Friends.

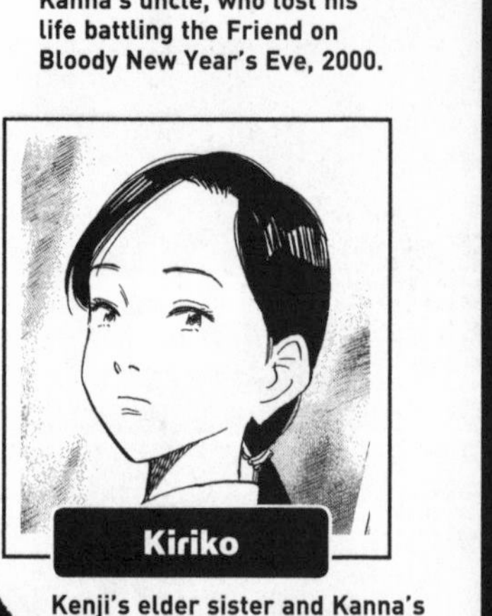

Kiriko

Kenji's elder sister and Kanna's mother, she has never been seen again since she left the infant Kanna with her family.

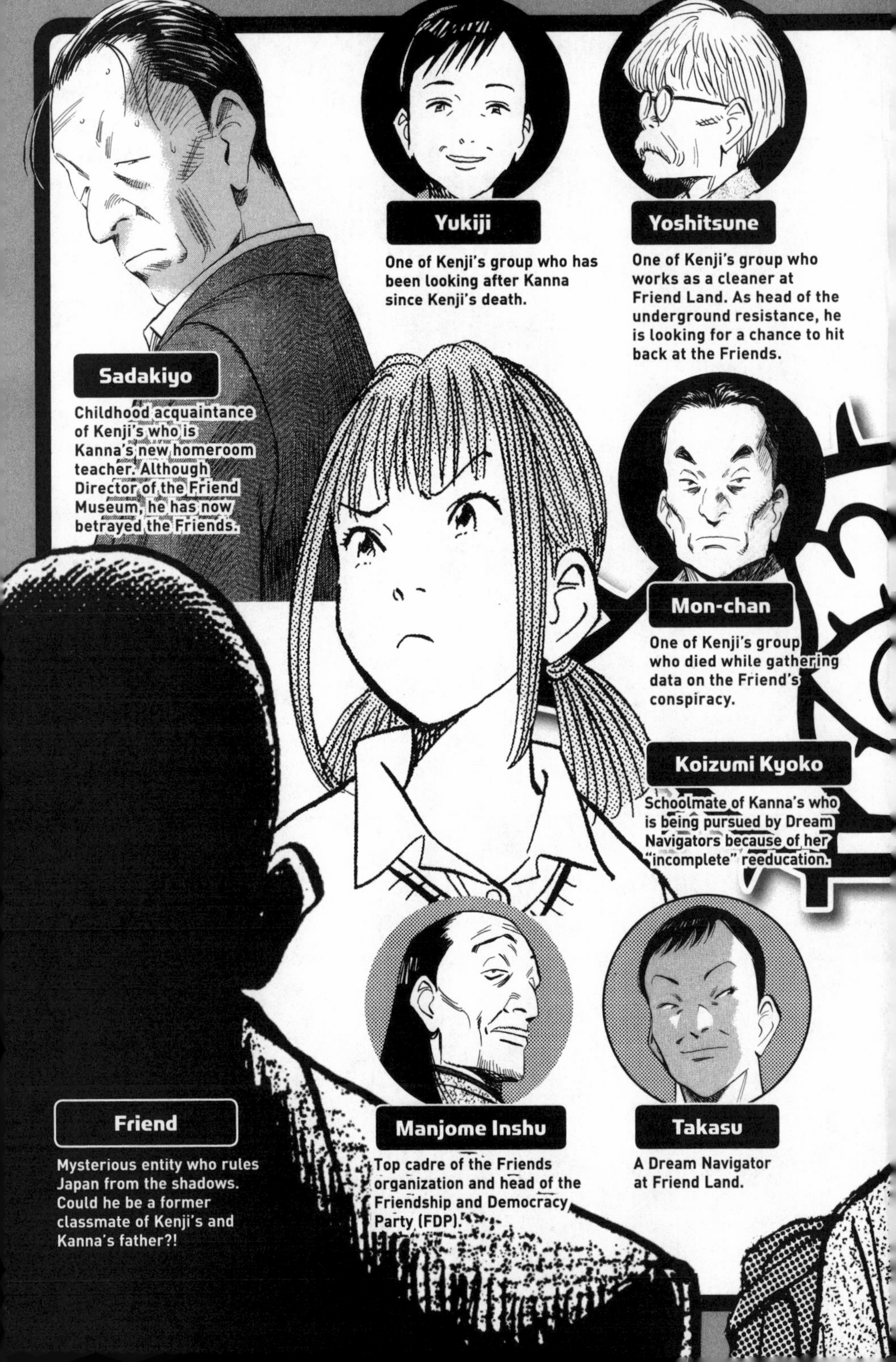

Yukiji
One of Kenji's group who has been looking after Kanna since Kenji's death.
Yoshitsune
One of Kenji's group who works as a cleaner at Friend Land. As head of the underground resistance, he is looking for a chance to hit back at the Friends.
Sadakiyo
Childhood acquaintance of Kenji's who is Kanna's new homeroom teacher. Although Director of the Friend Museum, he has now betrayed the Friends.
Mon-chan
One of Kenji's group who died while gathering data on the Friend's conspiracy.
Koizumi Kyoko
Schoolmate of Kanna's who is being pursued by Dream Navigators because of her "incomplete" reeducation.
Friend
Mysterious entity who rules Japan from the shadows. Could he be a former classmate of Kenji's and Kanna's father?!
Manjome Inshu
Top cadre of the Friends organization and head of the Friendship and Democracy Party (FDP).
Takasu
A Dream Navigator at Friend Land.

NAOKI URASAWA'S

20th CENTURY BOYS

CONTENTS

VOL 11

LIST OF INGREDIENTS

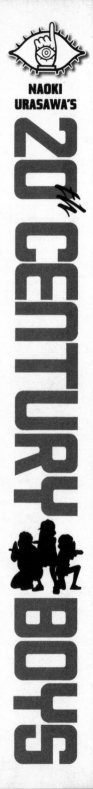

Chapter 1 Depths of Despair

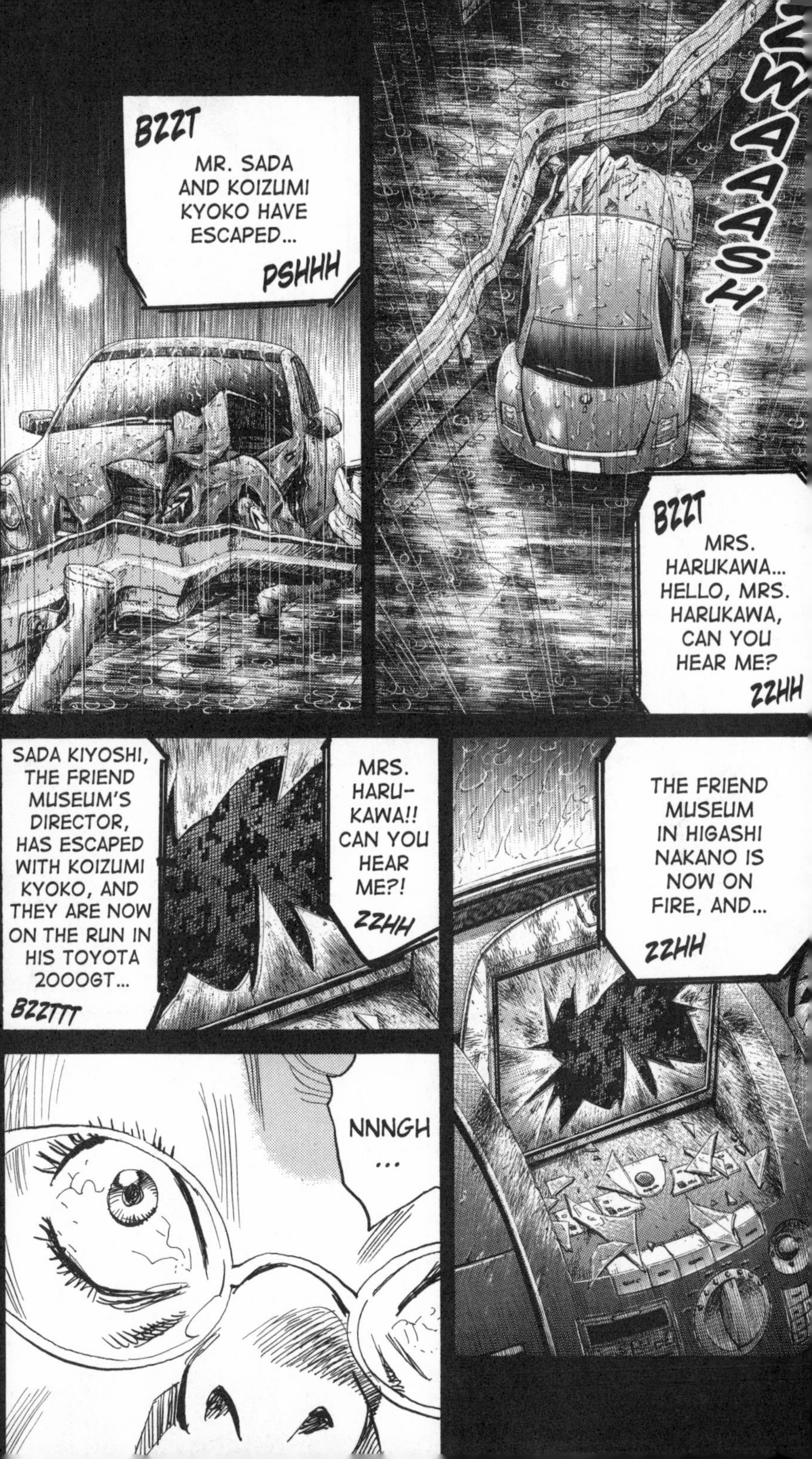
WAAAASH
BZZT
MRS. HARUKAWA... HELLO, MRS. HARUKAWA, CAN YOU HEAR ME?
ZZHH
BZZT
MR. SADA AND KOIZUMI KYOKO HAVE ESCAPED...
PSHHH
THE FRIEND MUSEUM IN HIGASHI NAKANO IS NOW ON FIRE, AND...
ZZHH
MRS. HARU-KAWA!! CAN YOU HEAR ME?!
ZZHH
SADA KIYOSHI, THE FRIEND MUSEUM'S DIRECTOR, HAS ESCAPED WITH KOIZUMI KYOKO, AND THEY ARE NOW ON THE RUN IN HIS TOYOTA 2000GT...
BZZTTT
NNNGH...

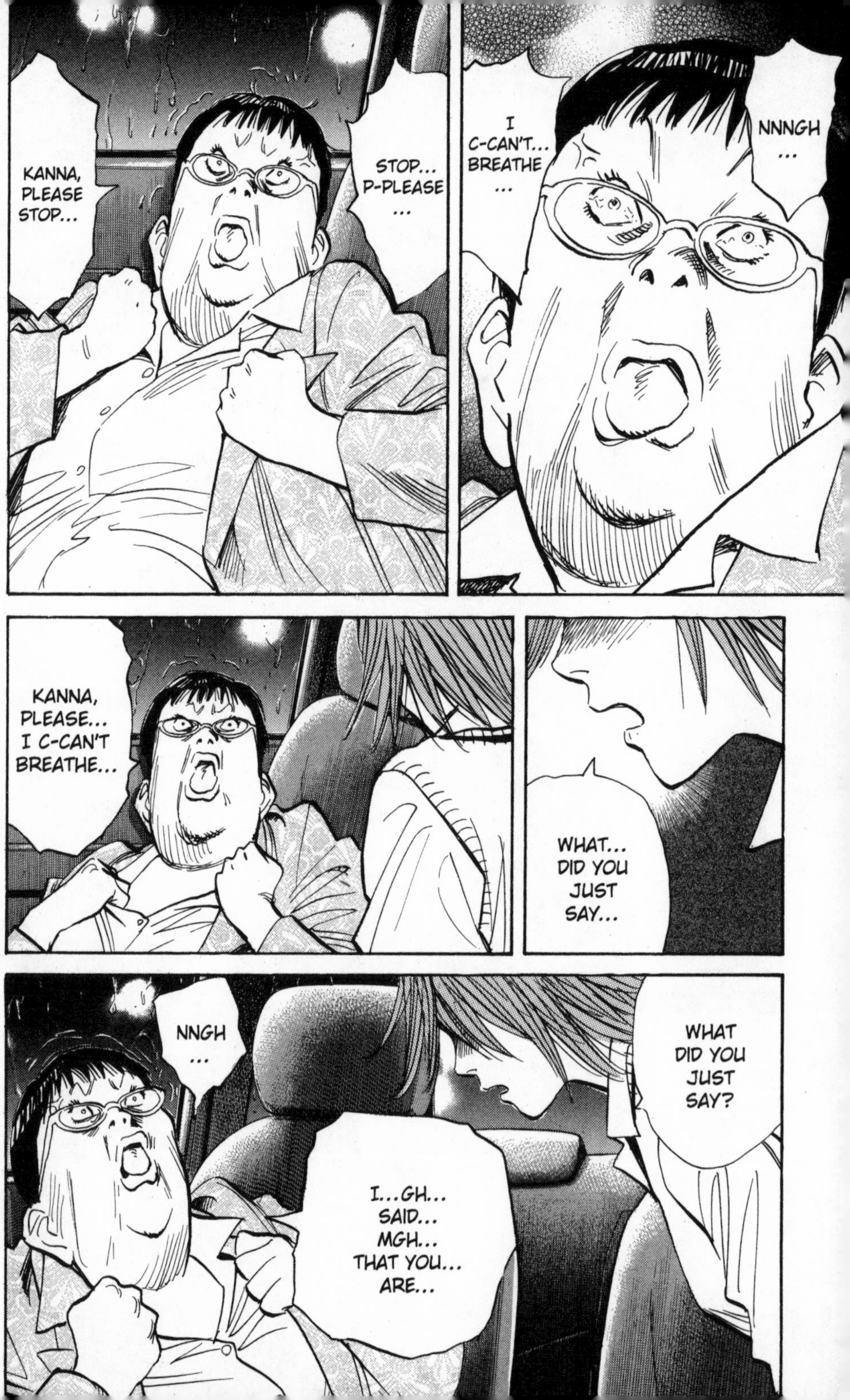
NNNGH ...
I C-CAN'T... BREATHE ...
STOP... P-PLEASE ...
KANNA, PLEASE STOP...
WHAT... DID YOU JUST SAY...
KANNA, PLEASE... I C-CAN'T BREATHE...
WHAT DID YOU JUST SAY?
NNGH ...
I...GH... SAID... MGH... THAT YOU... ARE...

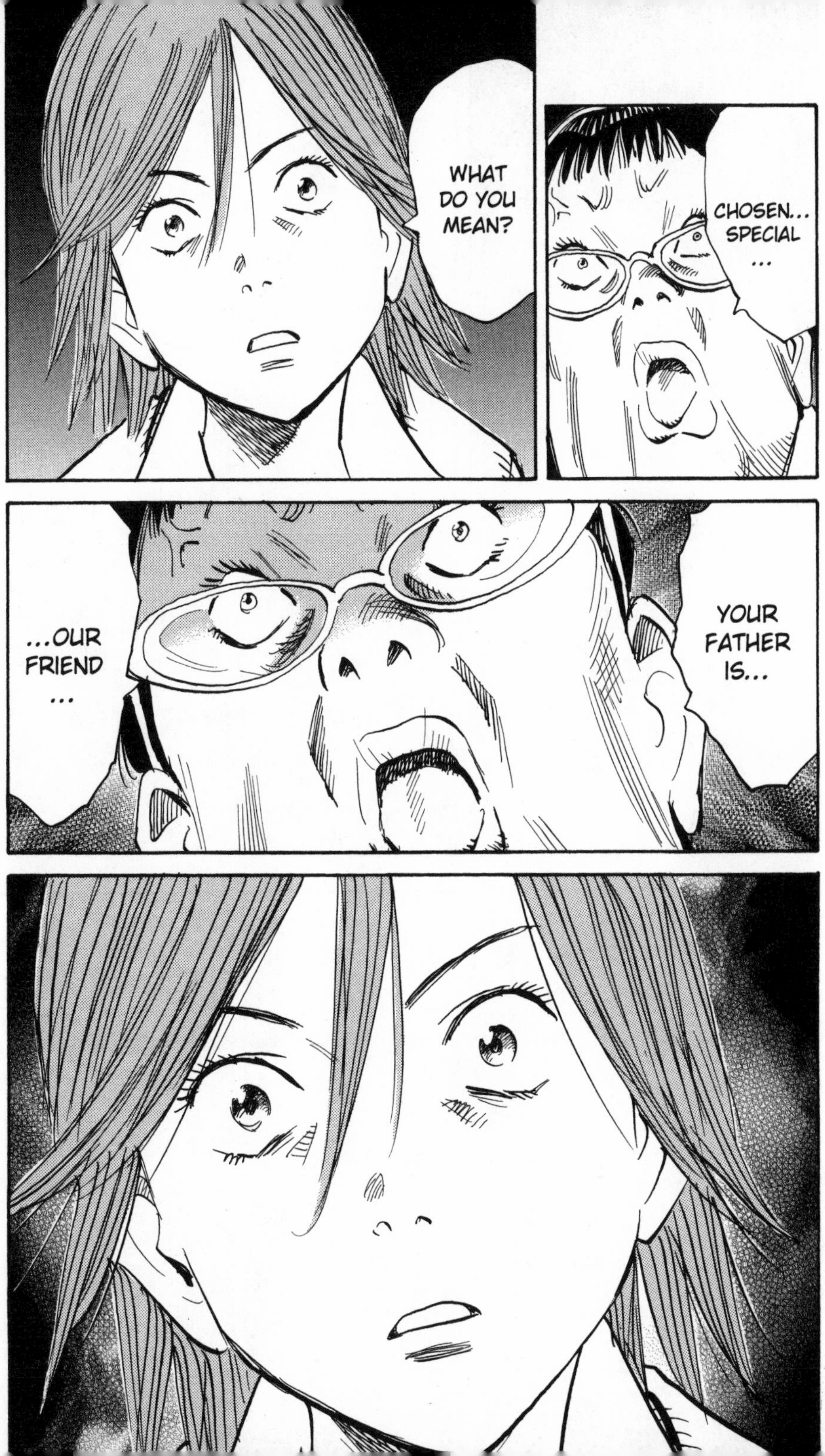
CHOSEN... SPECIAL ...
WHAT DO YOU MEAN?
YOUR FATHER IS...
...OUR FRIEND ...

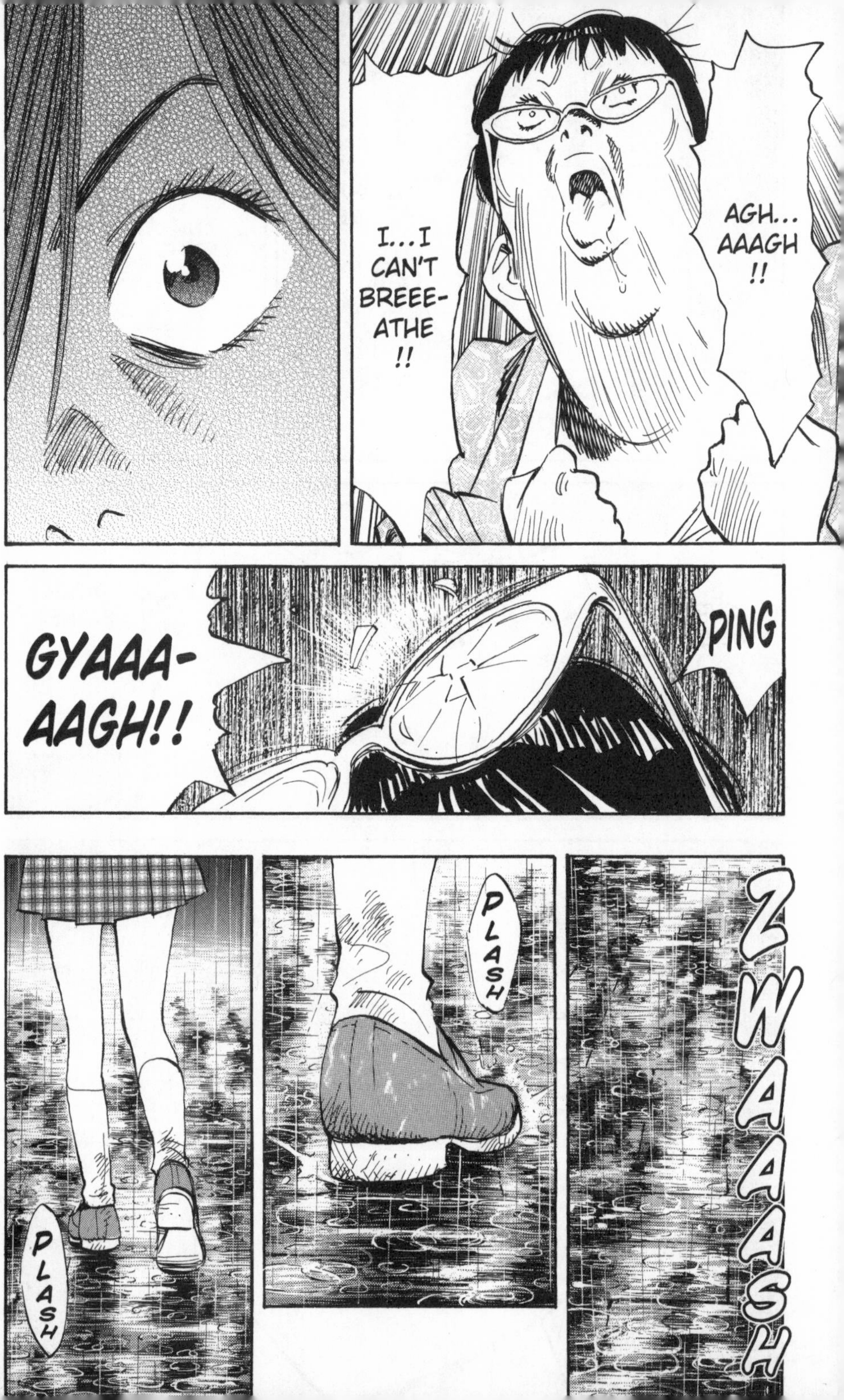
AGH... AAAGH!!
I...I CAN'T BREEE-ATHE!!
PING
GYAAA-AAGH!!
ZWAAAASH
PLASH
PLASH

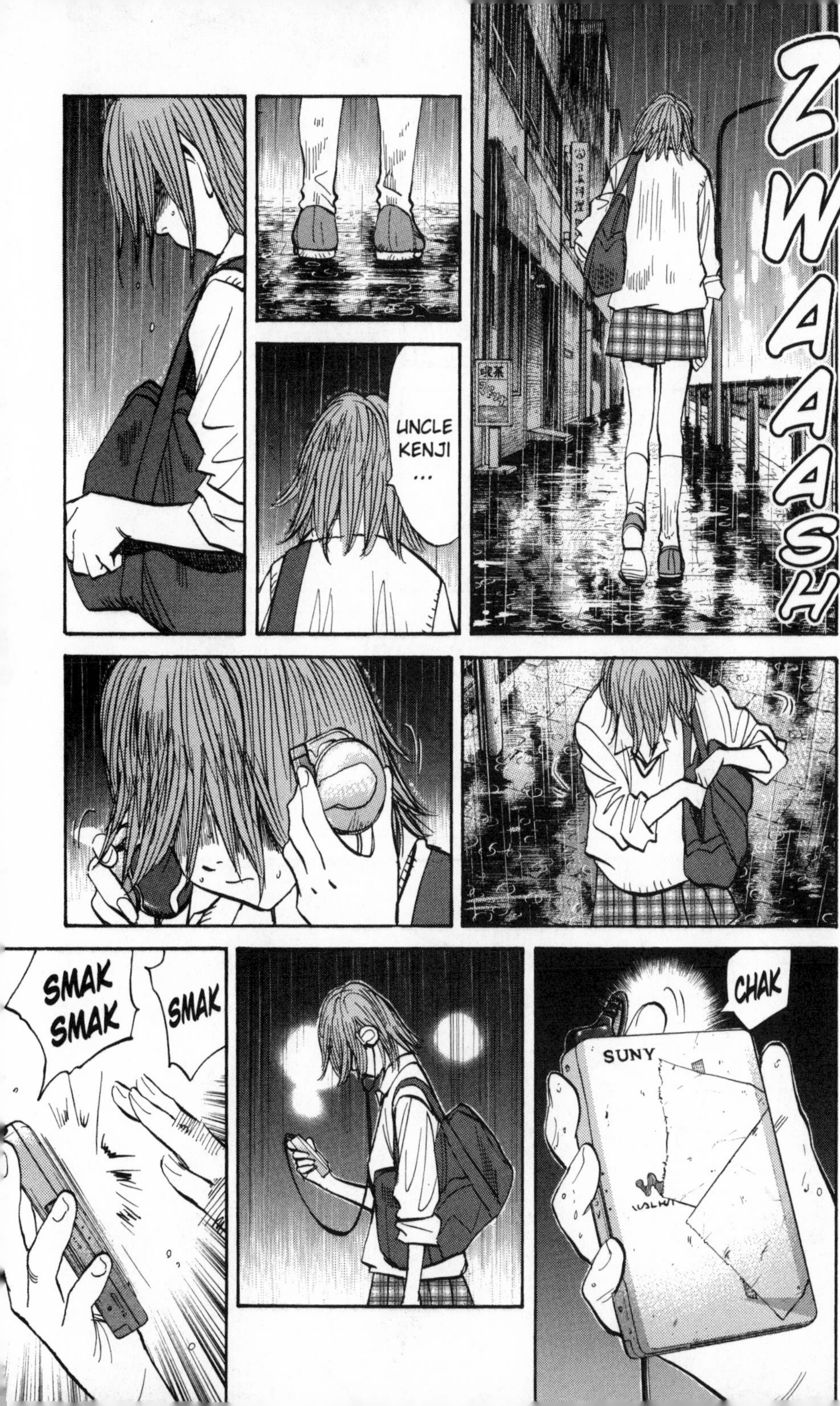
ZWAAASH
UNCLE KENJI ...
CHAK
SMAK
SMAK SMAK

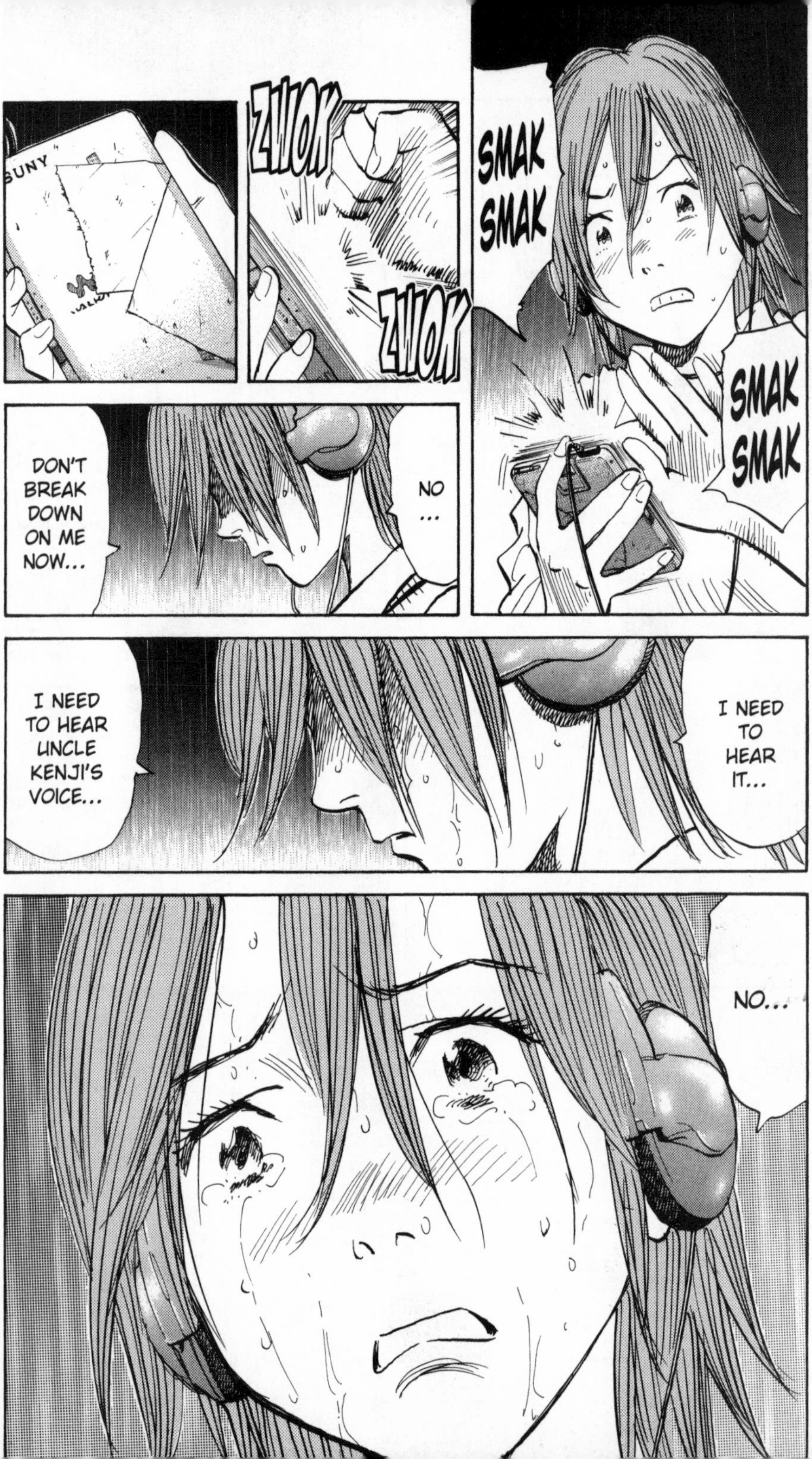
SMAK SMAK
SMAK SMAK
ZWOK
ZWOK
SUNY
NO ...
DON'T BREAK DOWN ON ME NOW...
I NEED TO HEAR IT...
I NEED TO HEAR UNCLE KENJI'S VOICE...
NO...

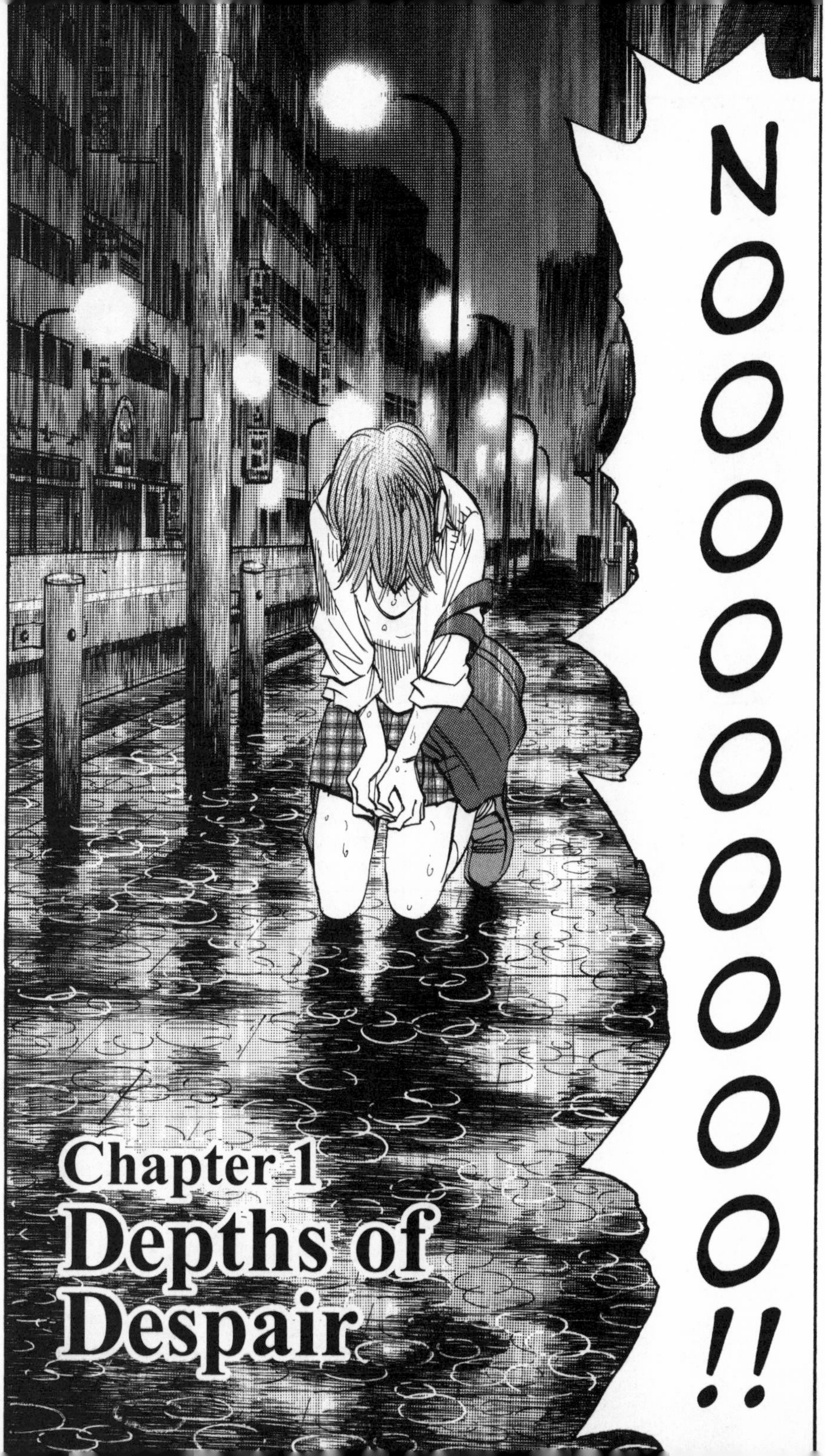
NOOOOOOOOO!!
Chapter 1
Depths of Despair

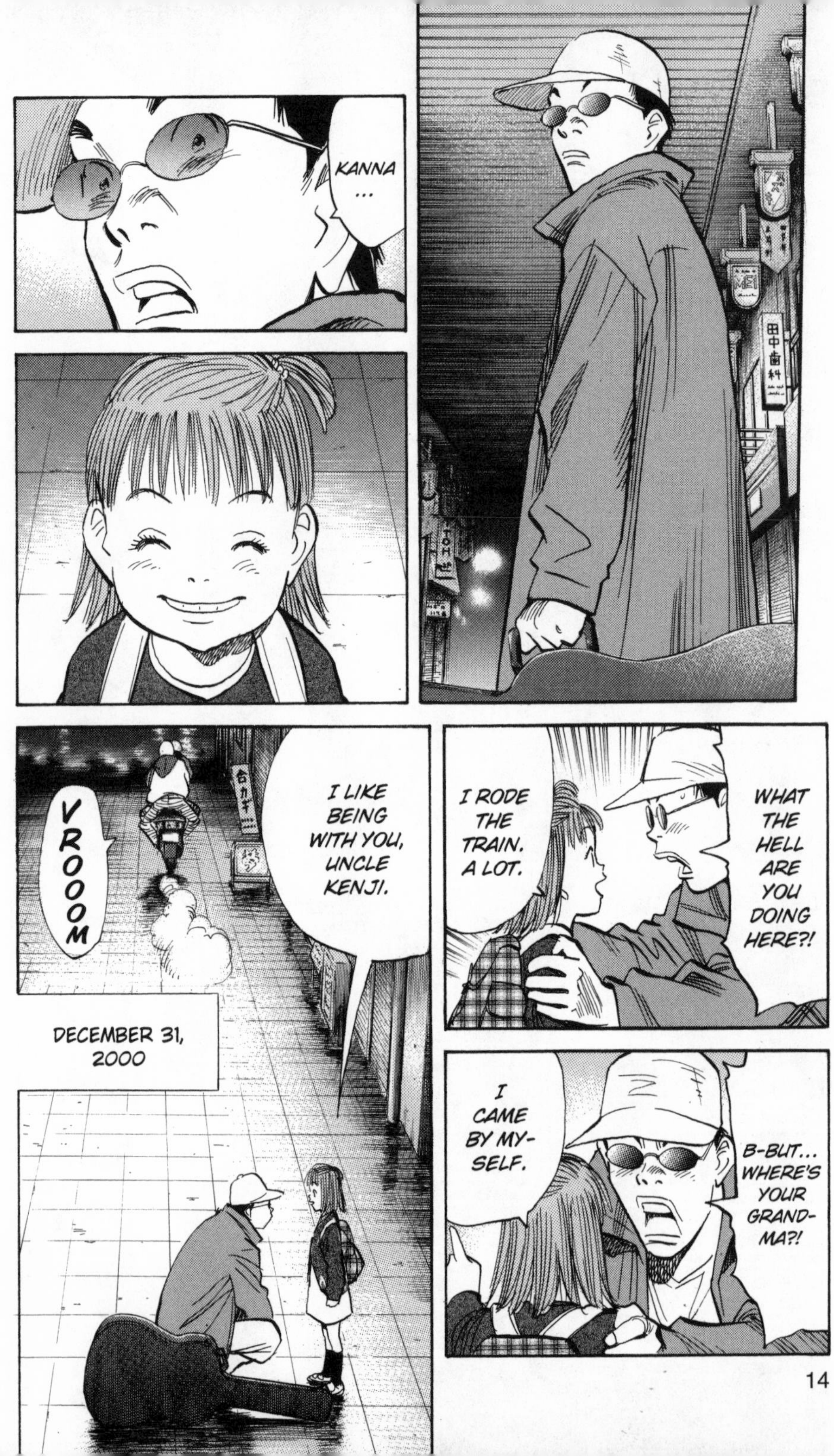
KANNA ...
WHAT THE HELL ARE YOU DOING HERE?!
I RODE THE TRAIN. A LOT.
B-BUT... WHERE'S YOUR GRANDMA?!
I CAME BY MY-SELF.
I LIKE BEING WITH YOU, UNCLE KENJI.
VROOOM
DECEMBER 31, 2000

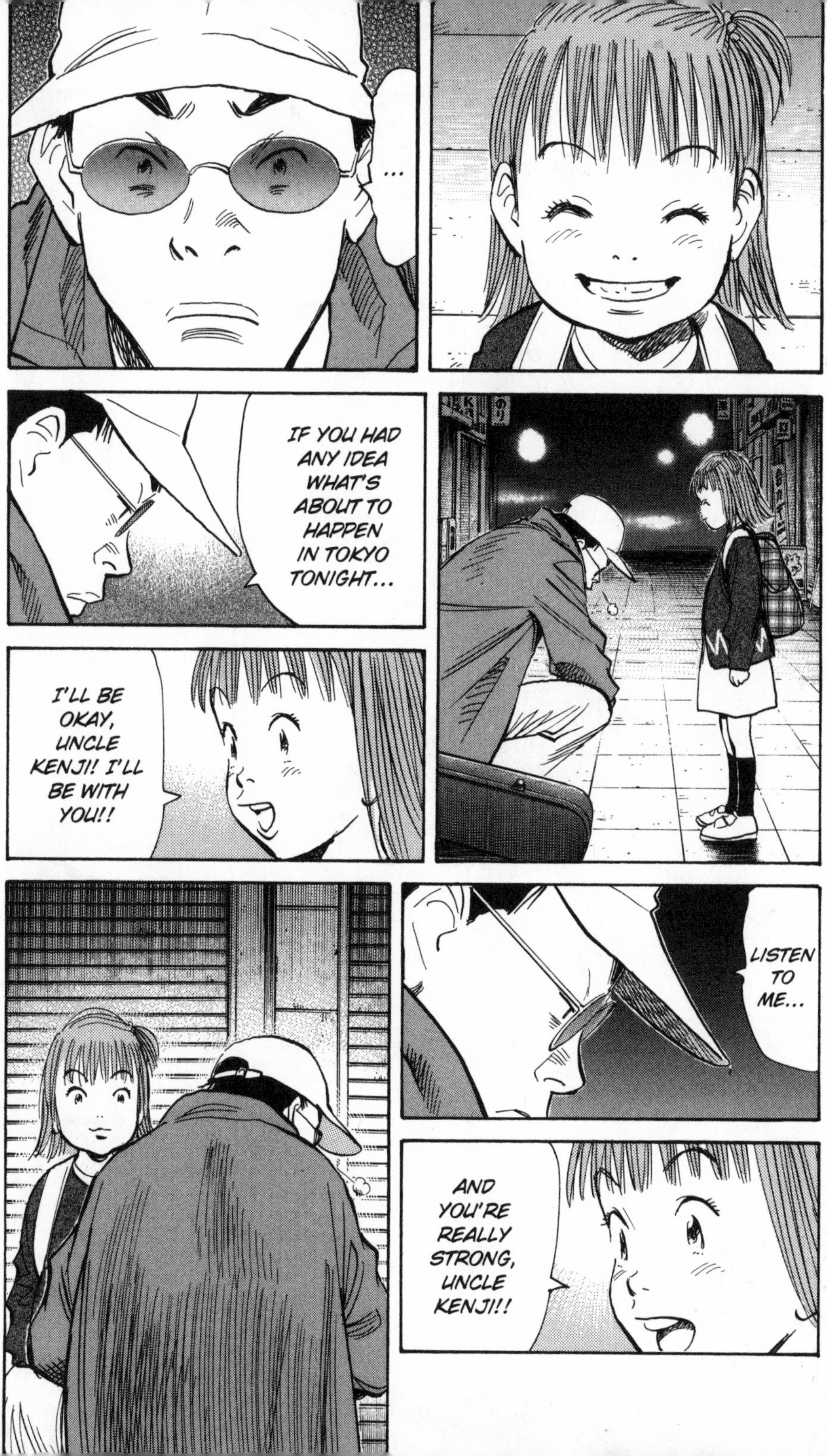
...
IF YOU HAD ANY IDEA WHAT'S ABOUT TO HAPPEN IN TOKYO TONIGHT...
I'LL BE OKAY, UNCLE KENJI! I'LL BE WITH YOU!!
LISTEN TO ME...
AND YOU'RE REALLY STRONG, UNCLE KENJI!!

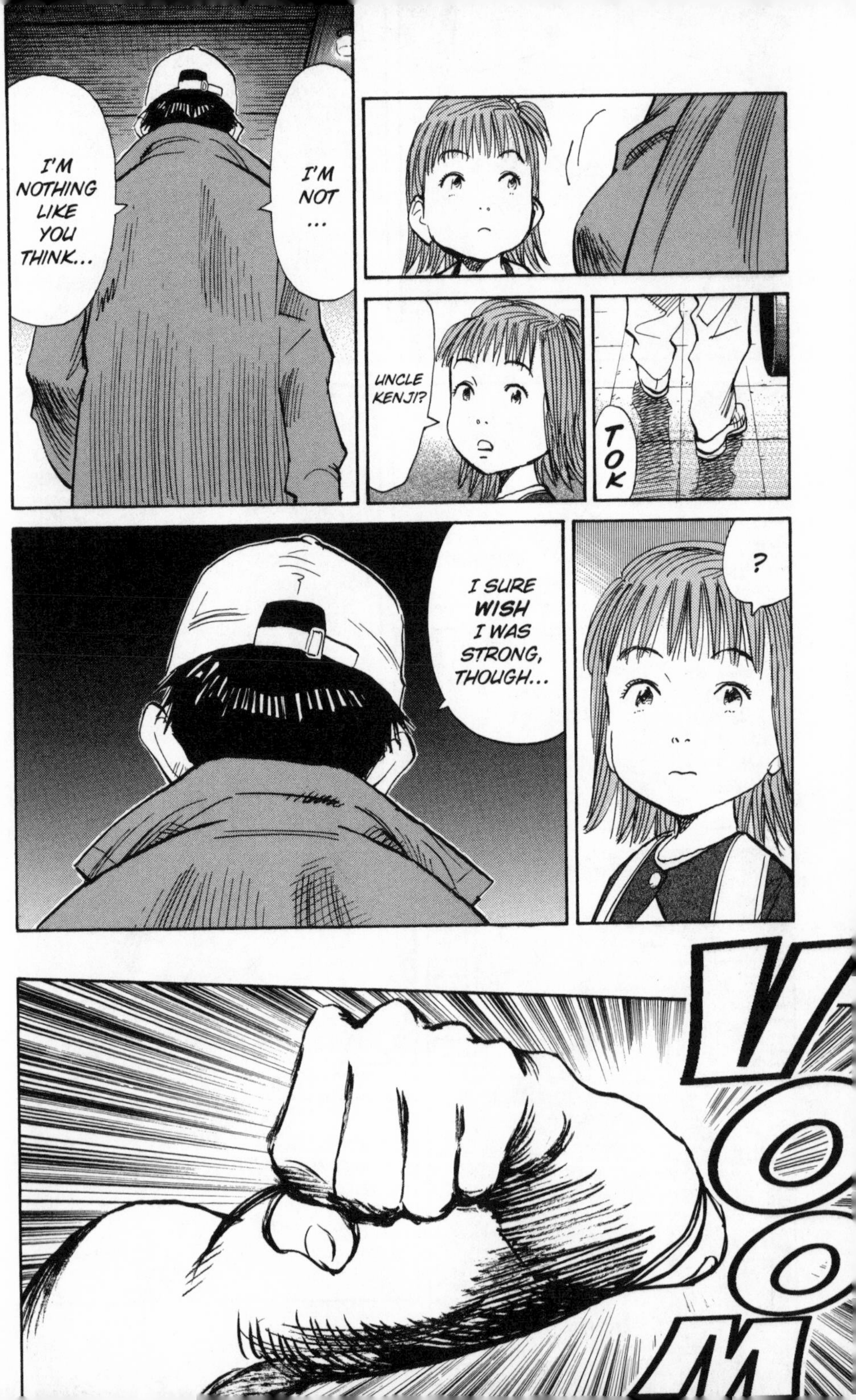
TOK
UNCLE KENJI?
I'M NOT...
I'M NOTHING LIKE YOU THINK...
?
I SURE **WISH** I WAS STRONG, THOUGH...
VOOOM

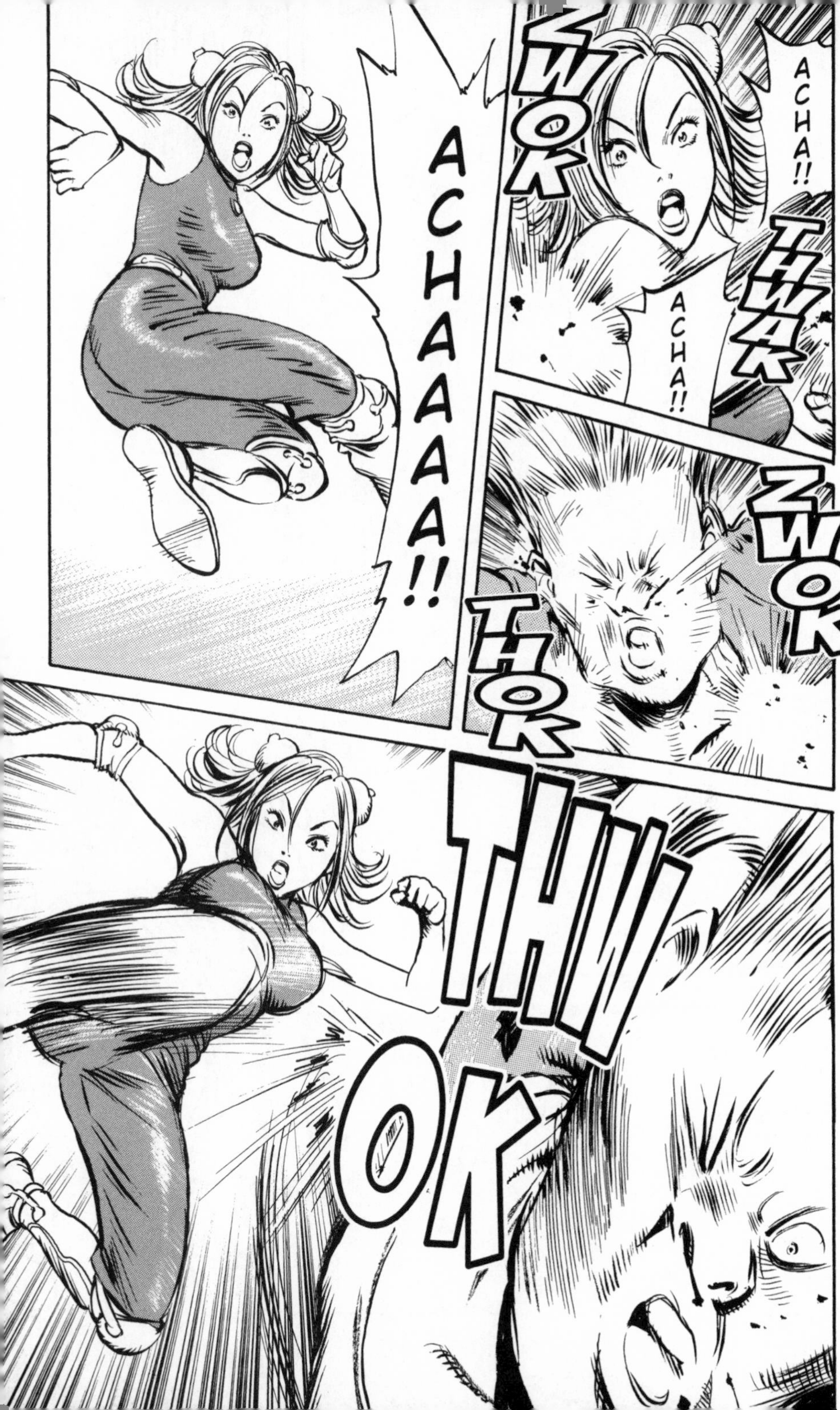
ACHA!!
ZWOK
THWAK
ACHA!!
ZWOK
THOK
ACHAAAAAA!!
THWOK

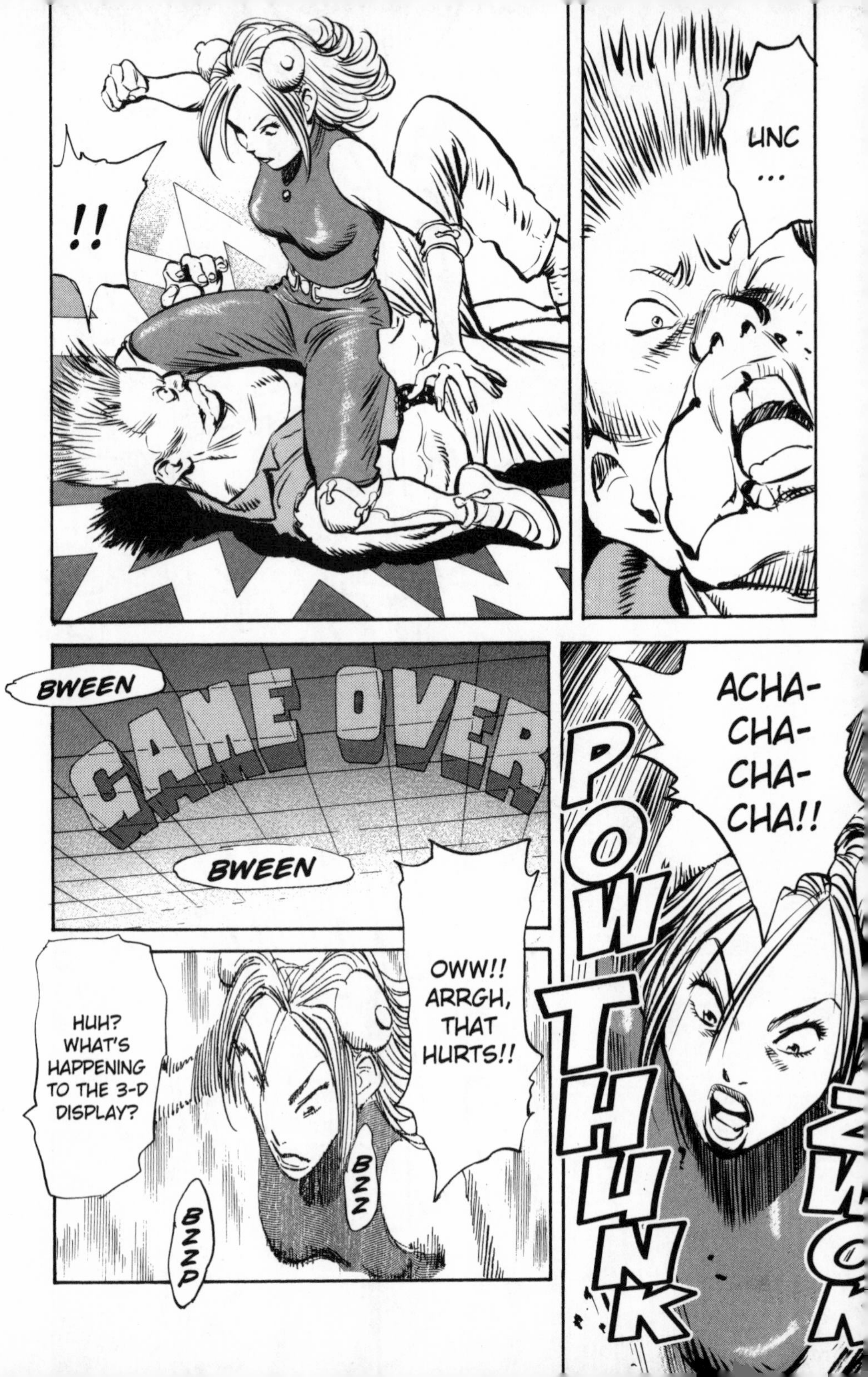
UNC ...
!!
ACHA-CHA-CHA-CHA!!
POW
THUNK
BWEEN
GAME OVER
BWEEN
OWW!! ARRGH, THAT HURTS!!
HUH? WHAT'S HAPPENING TO THE 3-D DISPLAY?
BZZ
BZZP

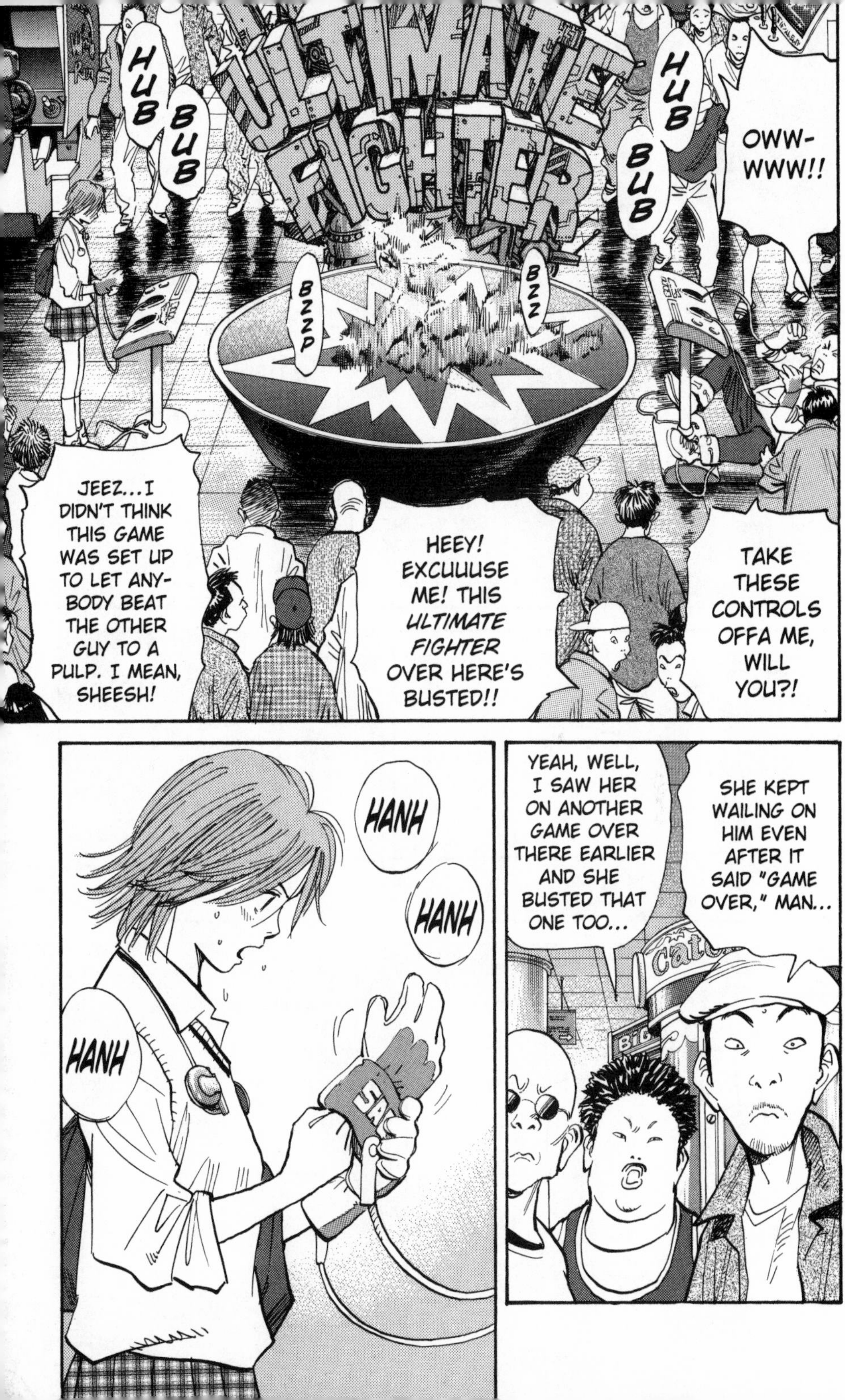
ULTIMATE FIGHTER
HUB BUB
OWW-WWW!!
HUB BUB
BZZ
BZZP
TAKE THESE CONTROLS OFFA ME, WILL YOU?!
HEEY! EXCUUUSE ME! THIS *ULTIMATE FIGHTER* OVER HERE'S BUSTED!!
JEEZ...I DIDN'T THINK THIS GAME WAS SET UP TO LET ANY-BODY BEAT THE OTHER GUY TO A PULP. I MEAN, SHEESH!
SHE KEPT WAILING ON HIM EVEN AFTER IT SAID "GAME OVER," MAN...
YEAH, WELL, I SAW HER ON ANOTHER GAME OVER THERE EARLIER AND SHE BUSTED THAT ONE TOO...
HANH
HANH
HANH

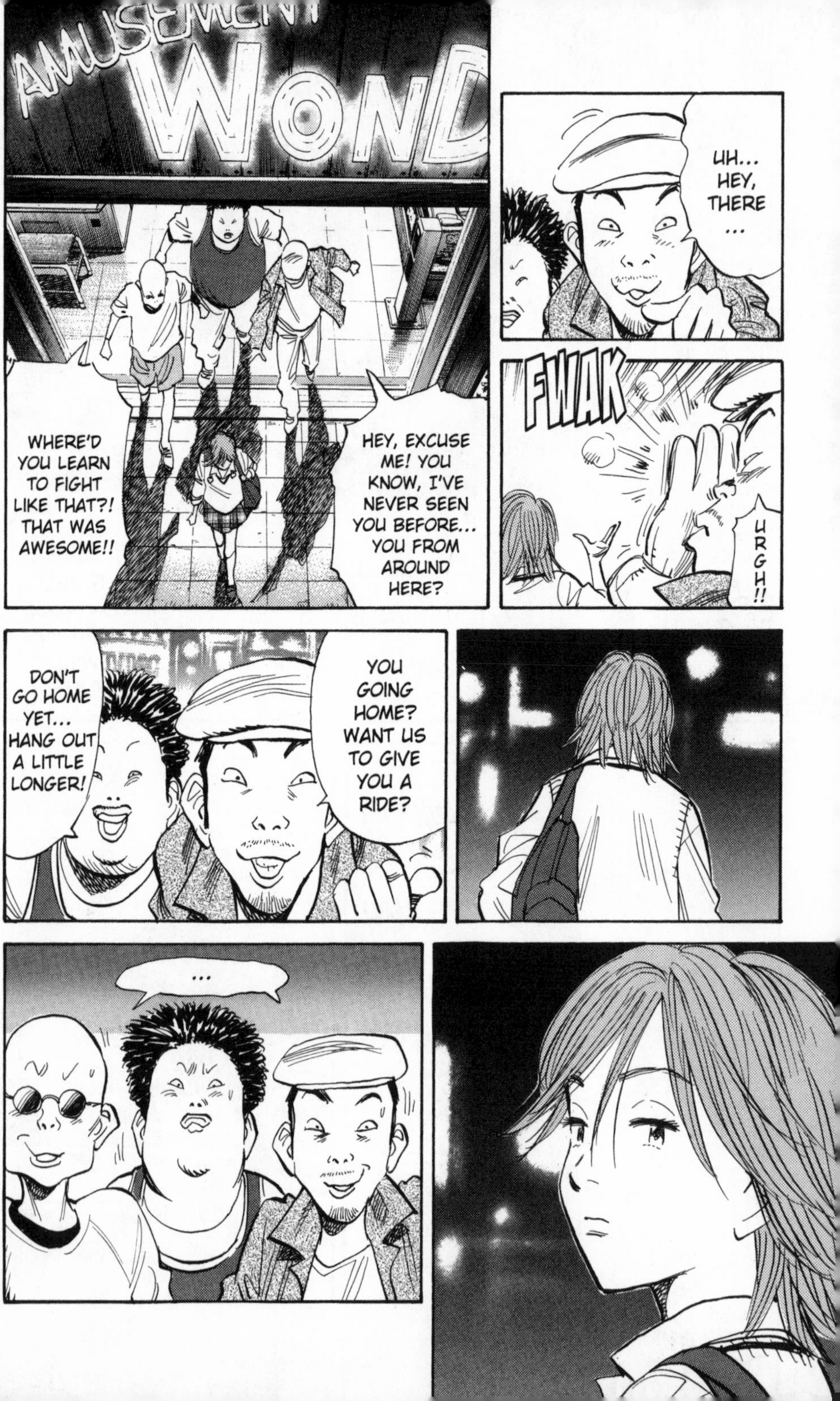
UH... HEY, THERE ...
FWAK
URGH!!
AMUSEMENT WOND
HEY, EXCUSE ME! YOU KNOW, I'VE NEVER SEEN YOU BEFORE... YOU FROM AROUND HERE?
WHERE'D YOU LEARN TO FIGHT LIKE THAT?! THAT WAS AWESOME!!
YOU GOING HOME? WANT US TO GIVE YOU A RIDE?
DON'T GO HOME YET... HANG OUT A LITTLE LONGER!
...

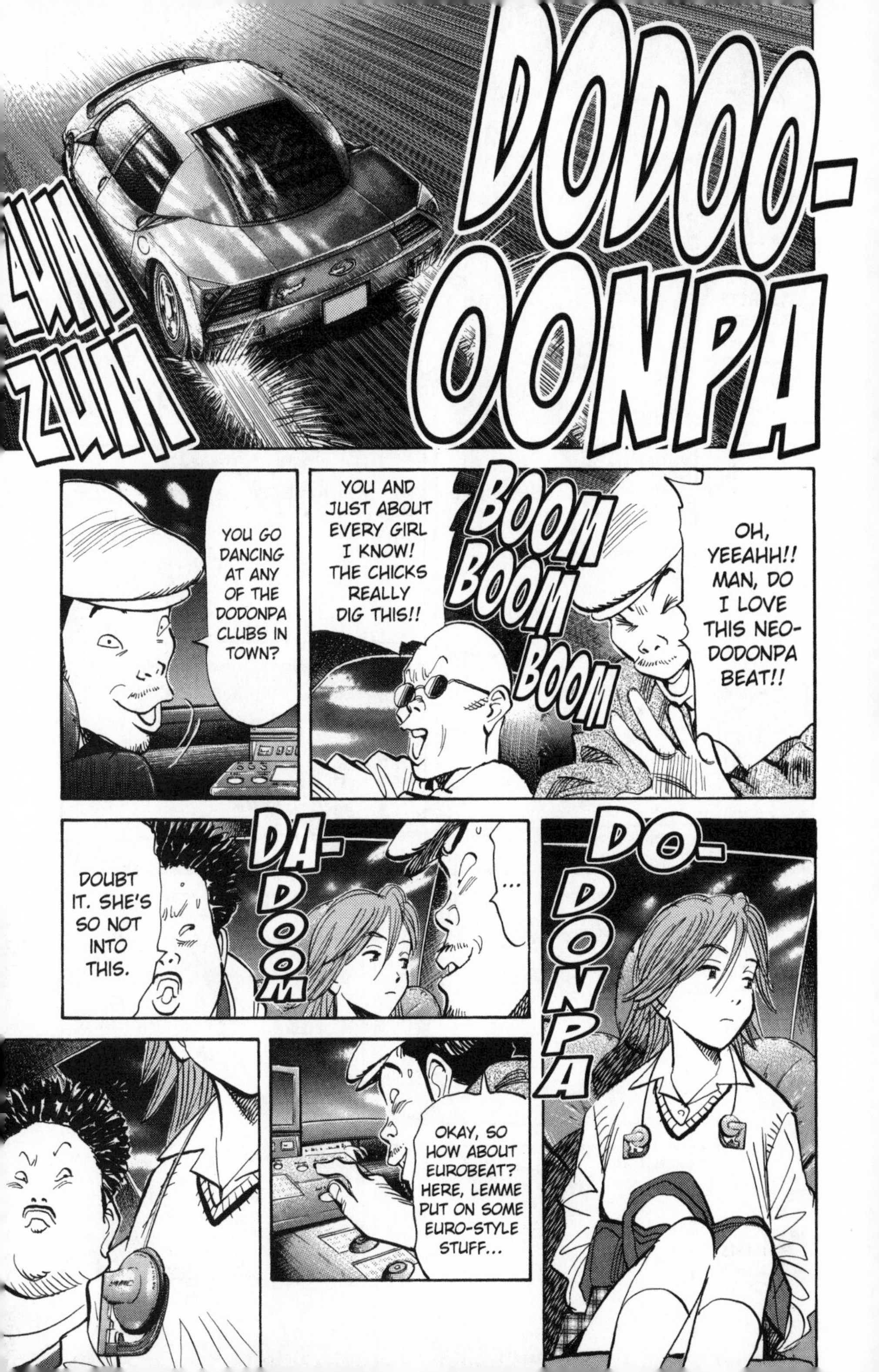
DODOO-OONPA
ZUM ZUM
OH, YEEAHH!! MAN, DO I LOVE THIS NEO-DODONPA BEAT!!
BOOM BOOM BOOM BOOM
YOU AND JUST ABOUT EVERY GIRL I KNOW! THE CHICKS REALLY DIG THIS!!
YOU GO DANCING AT ANY OF THE DODONPA CLUBS IN TOWN?
DO-DONPA
...
DA-DOOM
DOUBT IT. SHE'S SO NOT INTO THIS.
OKAY, SO HOW ABOUT EUROBEAT? HERE, LEMME PUT ON SOME EURO-STYLE STUFF...

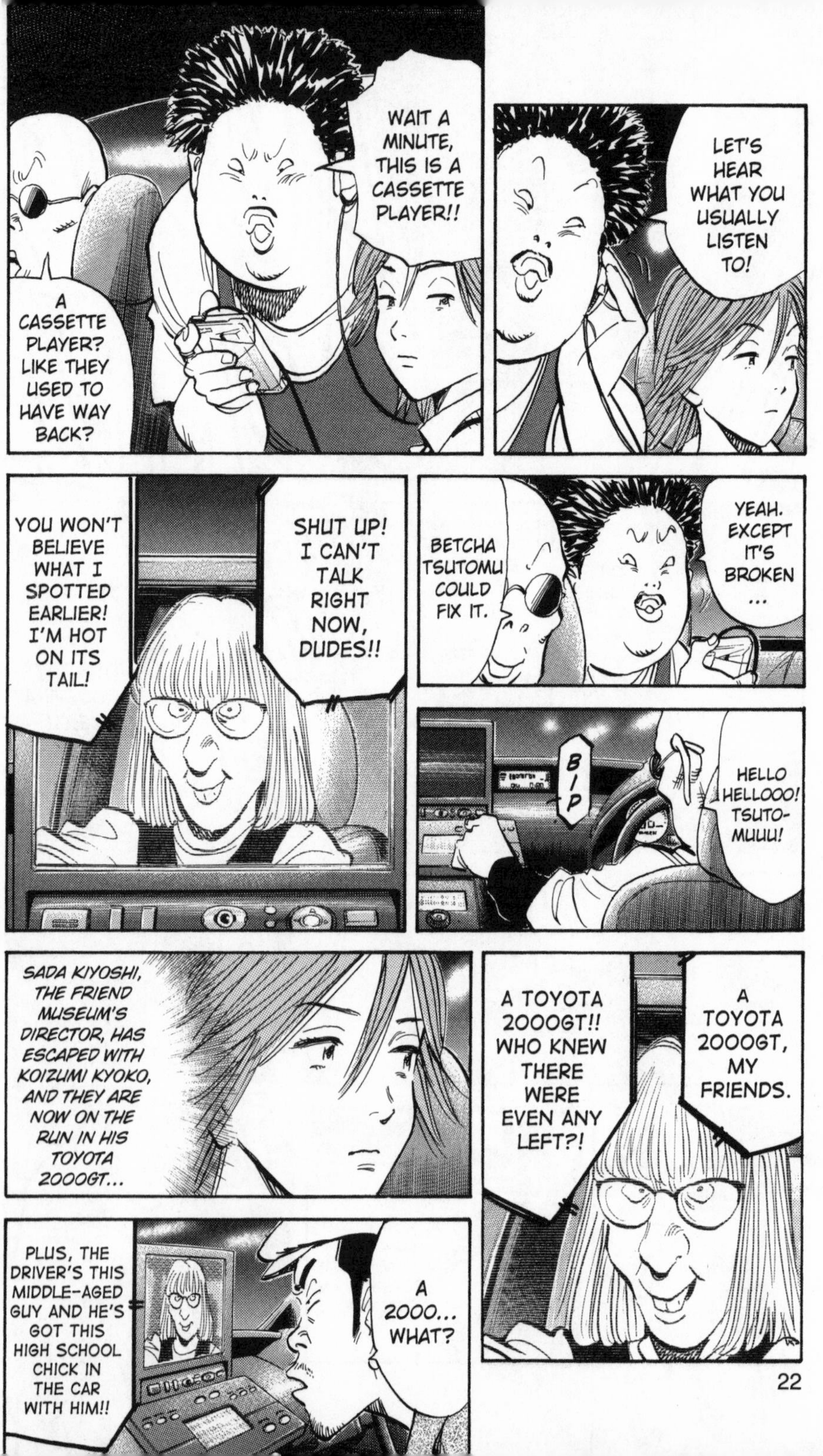
LET'S HEAR WHAT YOU USUALLY LISTEN TO!
WAIT A MINUTE, THIS IS A CASSETTE PLAYER!!
A CASSETTE PLAYER? LIKE THEY USED TO HAVE WAY BACK?
YEAH. EXCEPT IT'S BROKEN ...
BETCHA TSUTOMU COULD FIX IT.
HELLO HELLOOO! TSUTO-MUUU!
BIP
SHUT UP! I CAN'T TALK RIGHT NOW, DUDES!!
YOU WON'T BELIEVE WHAT I SPOTTED EARLIER! I'M HOT ON ITS TAIL!
A TOYOTA 2000GT, MY FRIENDS.
A TOYOTA 2000GT!! WHO KNEW THERE WERE EVEN ANY LEFT?!
SADA KIYOSHI, THE FRIEND MUSEUM'S DIRECTOR, HAS ESCAPED WITH KOIZUMI KYOKO, AND THEY ARE NOW ON THE RUN IN HIS TOYOTA 2000GT...
A 2000... WHAT?
PLUS, THE DRIVER'S THIS MIDDLE-AGED GUY AND HE'S GOT THIS HIGH SCHOOL CHICK IN THE CAR WITH HIM!!

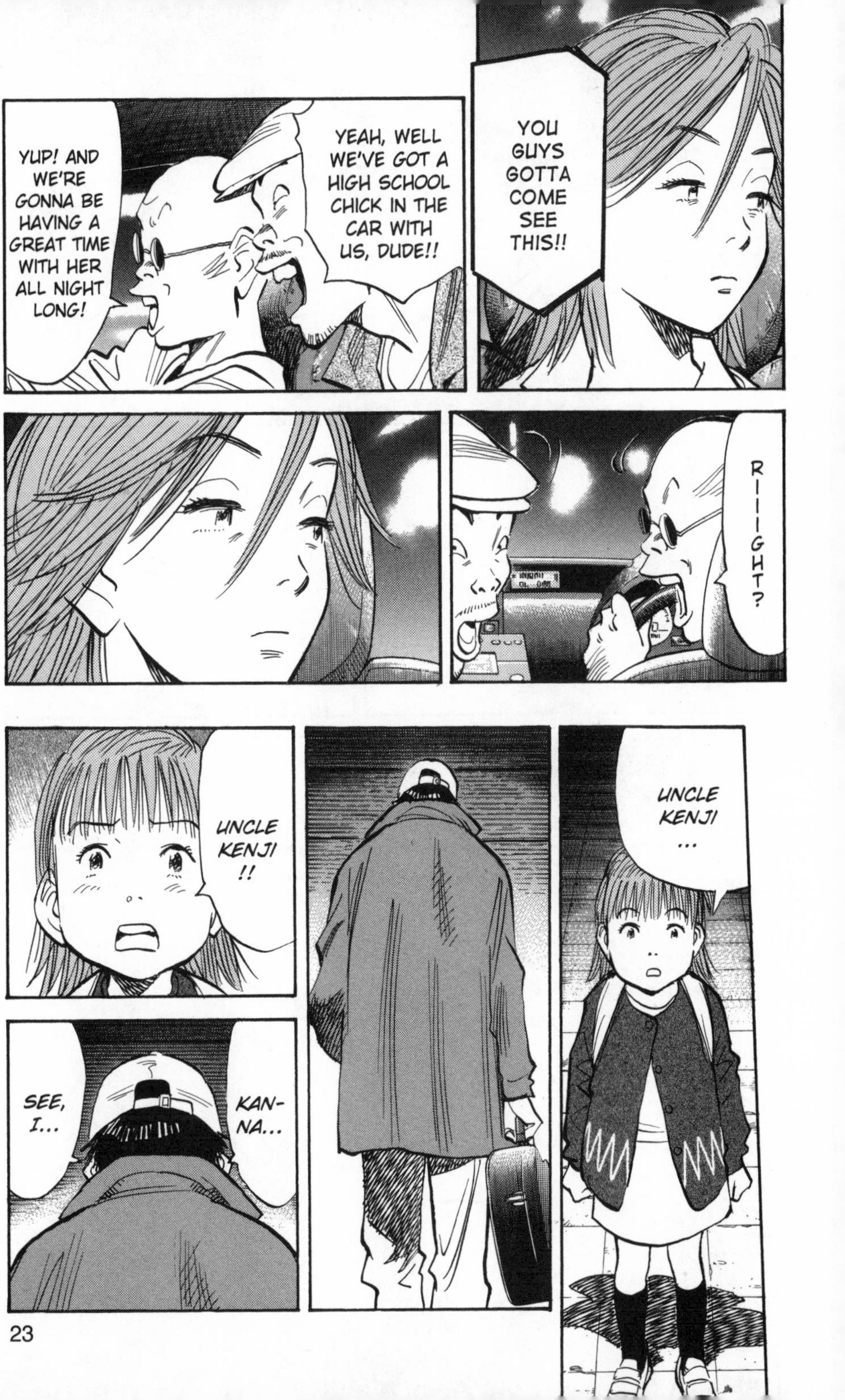
YOU GUYS GOTTA COME SEE THIS!!
YEAH, WELL WE'VE GOT A HIGH SCHOOL CHICK IN THE CAR WITH US, DUDE!!
YUP! AND WE'RE GONNA BE HAVING A GREAT TIME WITH HER ALL NIGHT LONG!
RIIIGHT?
UNCLE KENJI ...
UNCLE KENJI !!
KAN-NA...
SEE, I...

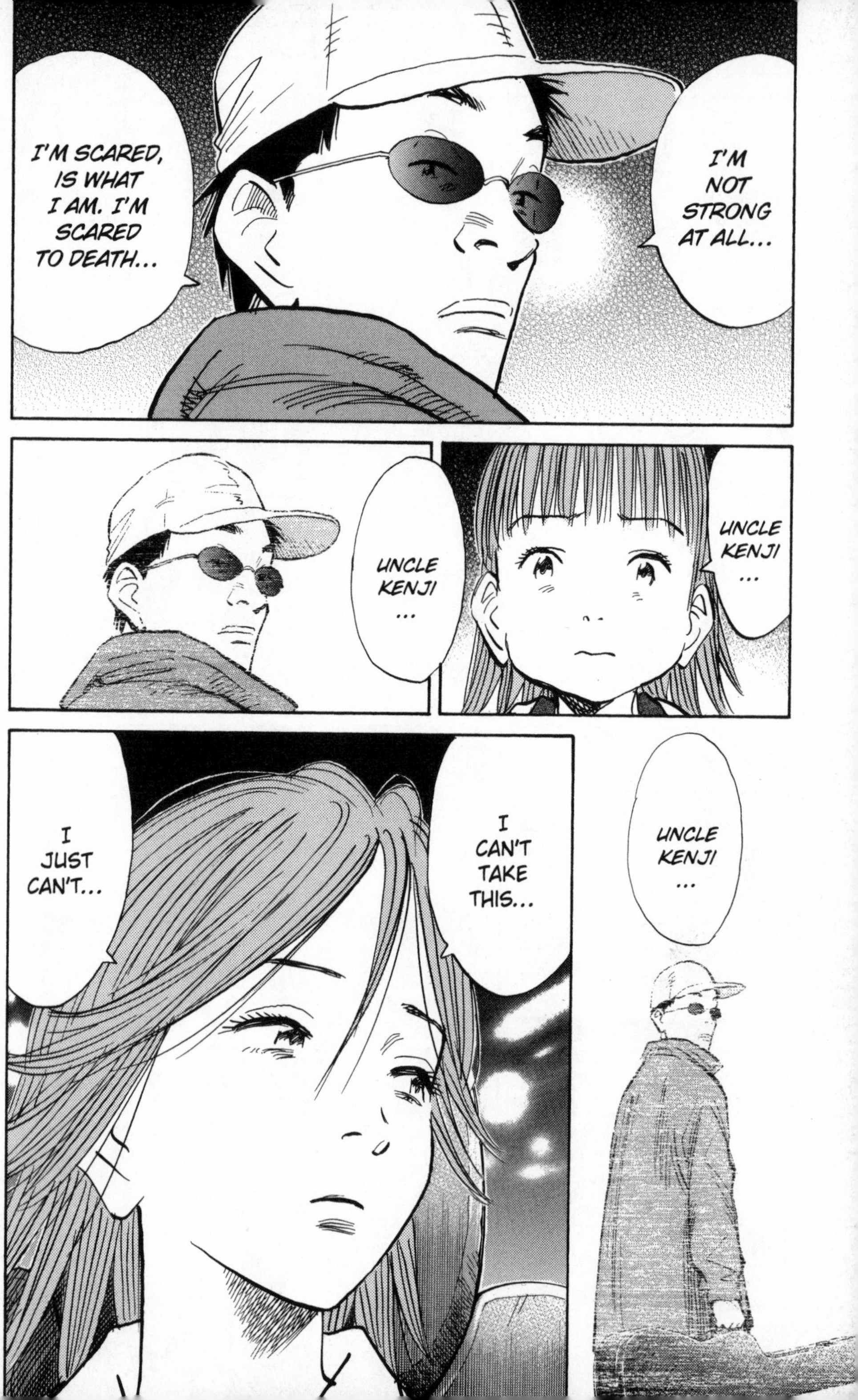
I'M NOT STRONG AT ALL...
I'M SCARED, IS WHAT I AM. I'M SCARED TO DEATH...
UNCLE KENJI ...
UNCLE KENJI ...
UNCLE KENJI ...
I CAN'T TAKE THIS...
I JUST CAN'T...

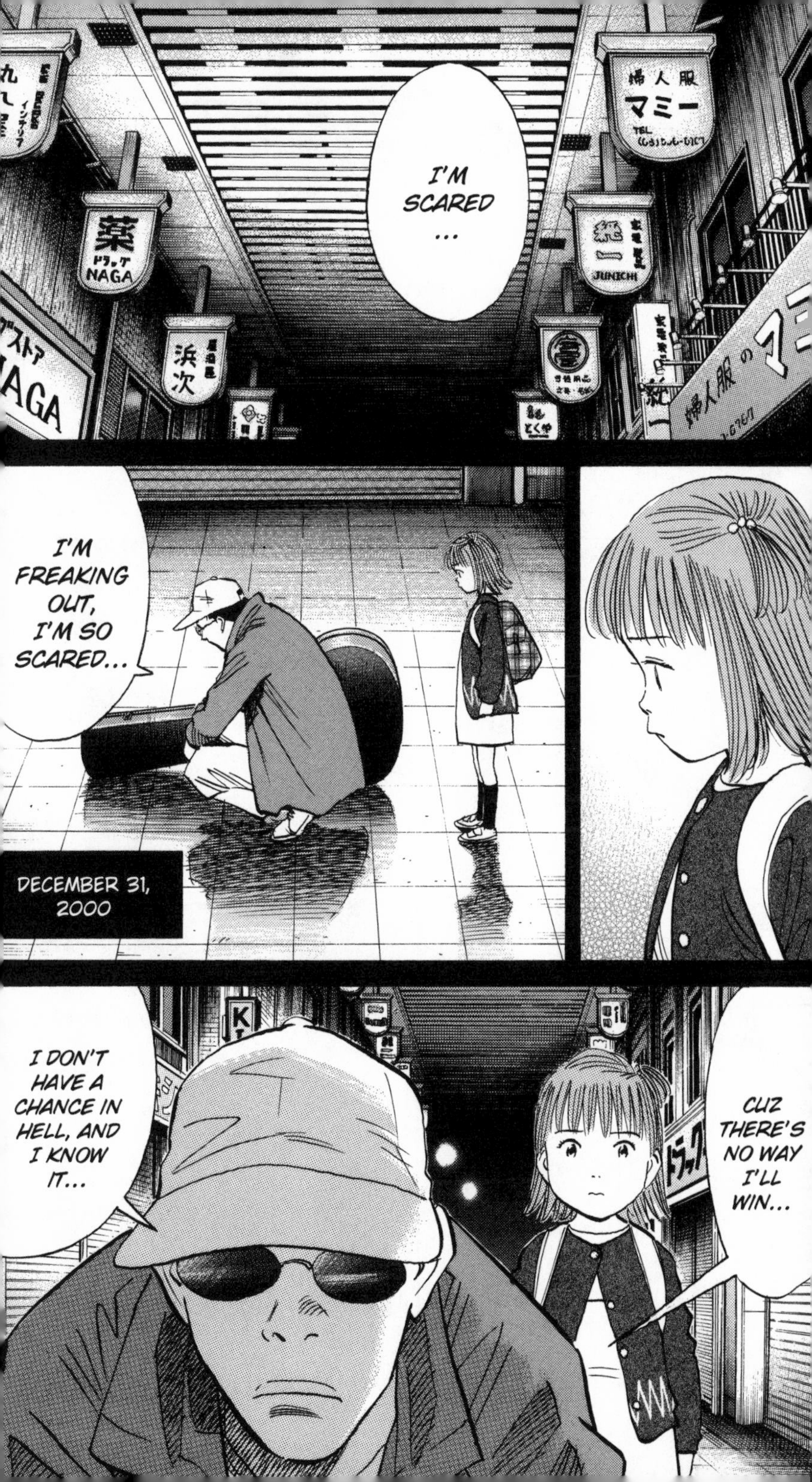
婦人服
マミー
JUNICHI
I'M SCARED...
浜次
薬
NAGA
I'M FREAKING OUT, I'M SO SCARED...
DECEMBER 31, 2000
CUZ THERE'S NO WAY I'LL WIN...
I DON'T HAVE A CHANCE IN HELL, AND I KNOW IT...

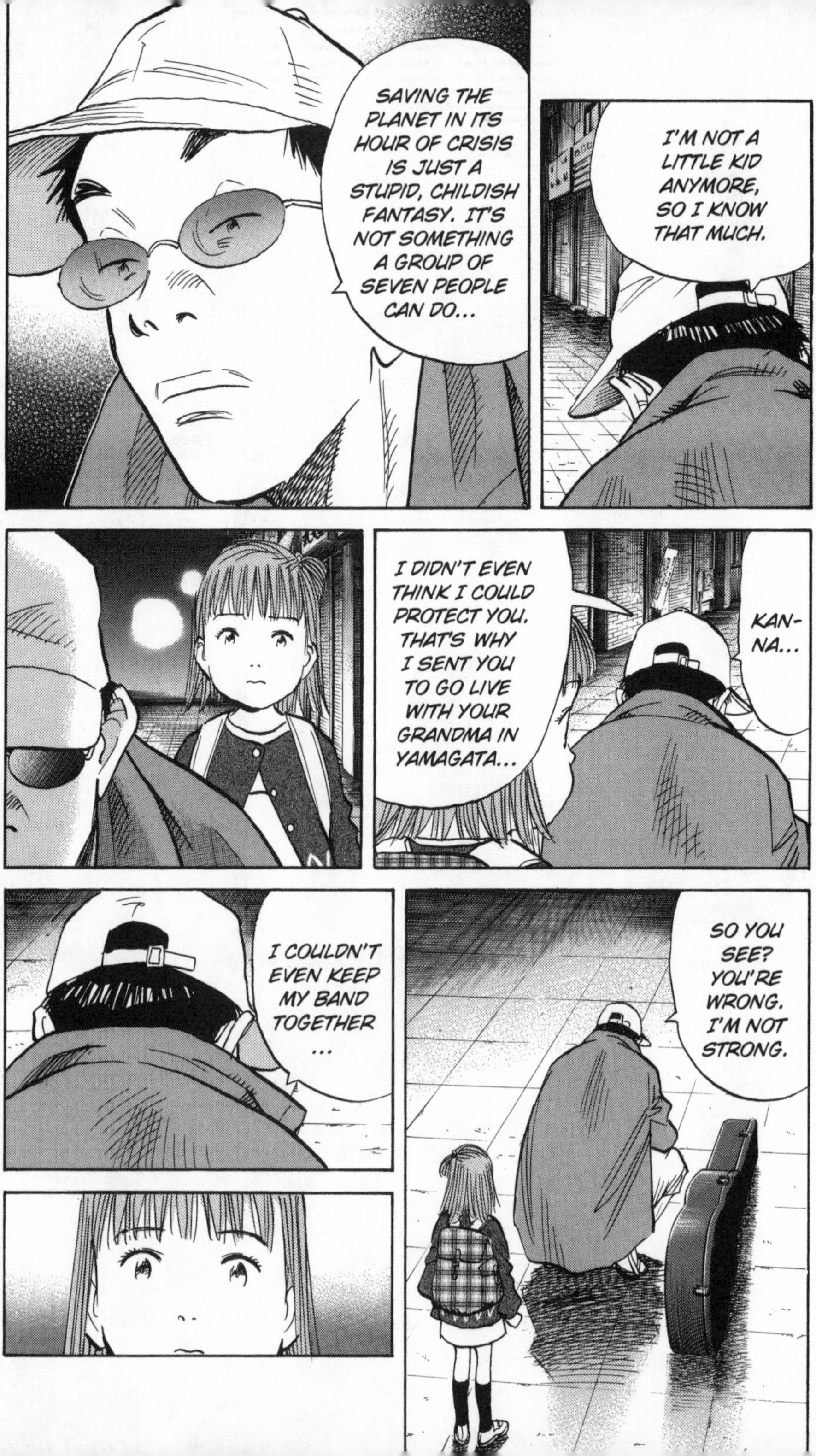
I'M NOT A LITTLE KID ANYMORE, SO I KNOW THAT MUCH.
SAVING THE PLANET IN ITS HOUR OF CRISIS IS JUST A STUPID, CHILDISH FANTASY. IT'S NOT SOMETHING A GROUP OF SEVEN PEOPLE CAN DO...
KAN-NA...
I DIDN'T EVEN THINK I COULD PROTECT YOU. THAT'S WHY I SENT YOU TO GO LIVE WITH YOUR GRANDMA IN YAMAGATA...
SO YOU SEE? YOU'RE WRONG. I'M NOT STRONG.
I COULDN'T EVEN KEEP MY BAND TOGETHER ...

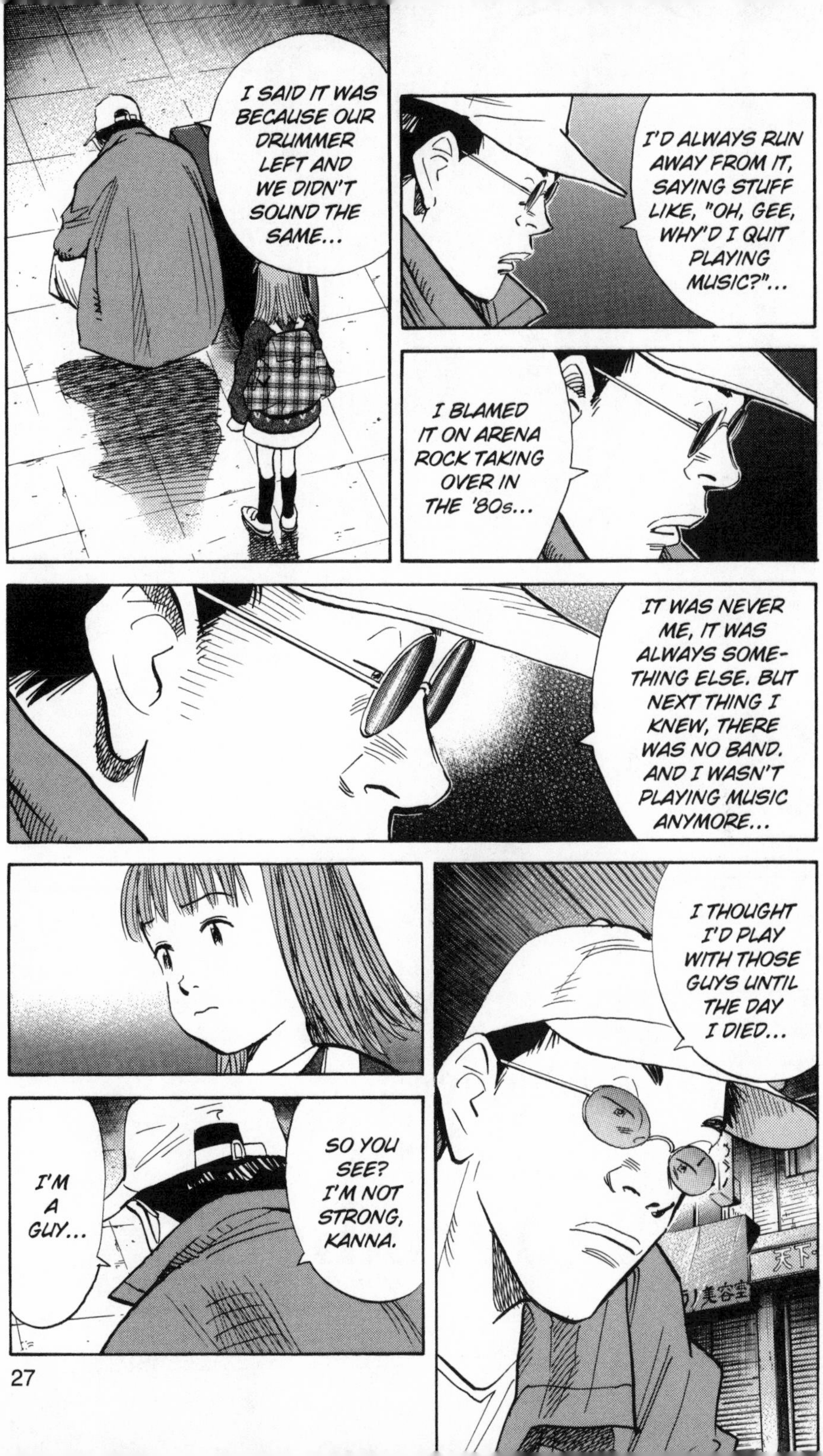
I'D ALWAYS RUN AWAY FROM IT, SAYING STUFF LIKE, "OH, GEE, WHY'D I QUIT PLAYING MUSIC?"...
I BLAMED IT ON ARENA ROCK TAKING OVER IN THE '80s...
I SAID IT WAS BECAUSE OUR DRUMMER LEFT AND WE DIDN'T SOUND THE SAME...
IT WAS NEVER ME, IT WAS ALWAYS SOME-THING ELSE. BUT NEXT THING I KNEW, THERE WAS NO BAND. AND I WASN'T PLAYING MUSIC ANYMORE...
I THOUGHT I'D PLAY WITH THOSE GUYS UNTIL THE DAY I DIED...
SO YOU SEE? I'M NOT STRONG, KANNA.
I'M A GUY...

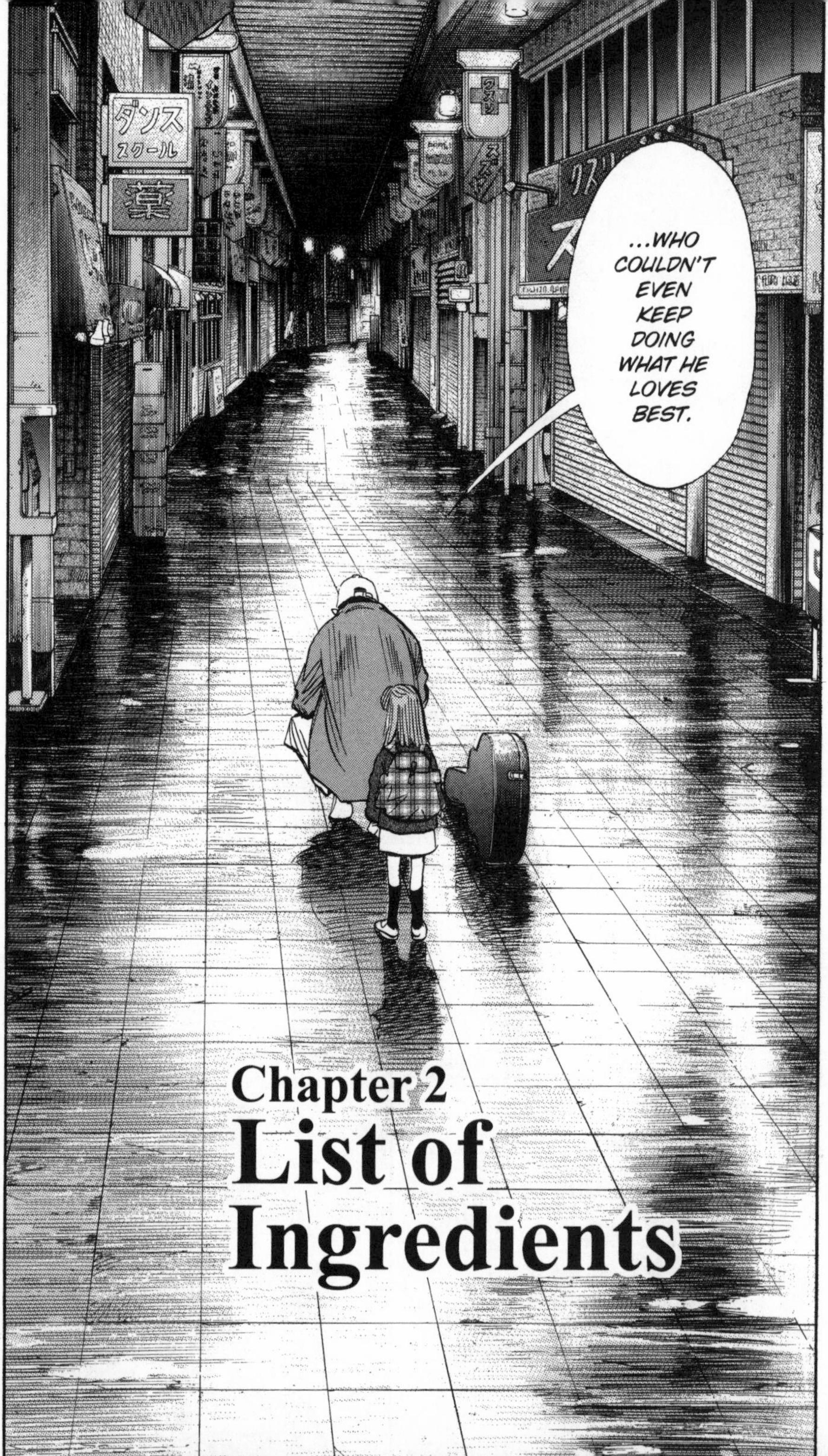
...WHO COULDN'T EVEN KEEP DOING WHAT HE LOVES BEST.
ダンス
スクール
薬

Chapter 2
List of Ingredients

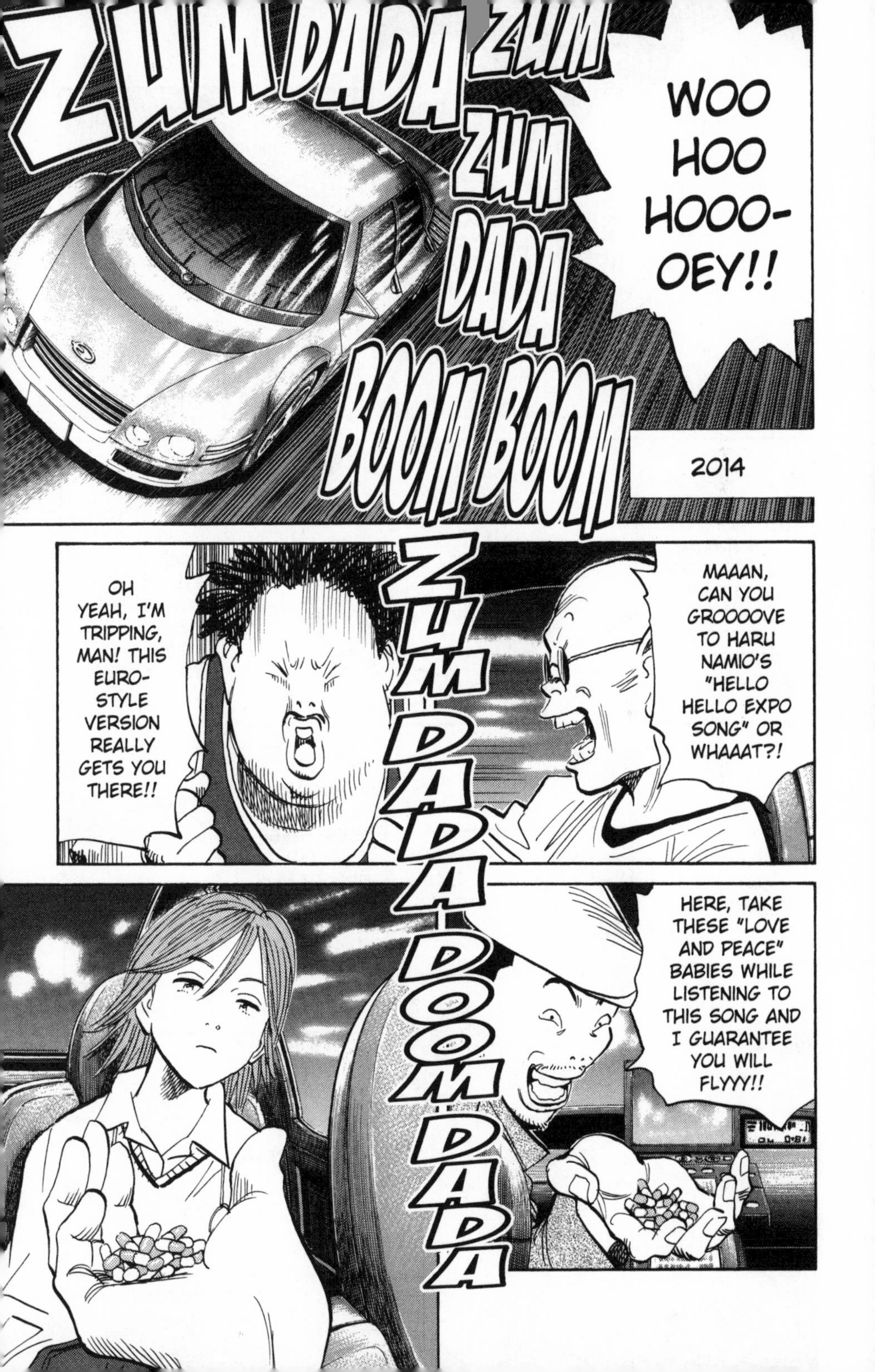
WOO HOO HOOOO-OEY!!
ZUM DADA ZUM
ZUM DADA
BOOM BOOM
2014
MAAAN, CAN YOU GROOOOVE TO HARU NAMIO'S "HELLO HELLO EXPO SONG" OR WHAAAT?!
OH YEAH, I'M TRIPPING, MAN! THIS EURO-STYLE VERSION REALLY GETS YOU THERE!!
ZUM DADA DADA DOOM DADA
HERE, TAKE THESE "LOVE AND PEACE" BABIES WHILE LISTENING TO THIS SONG AND I GUARANTEE YOU WILL FLYYY!!

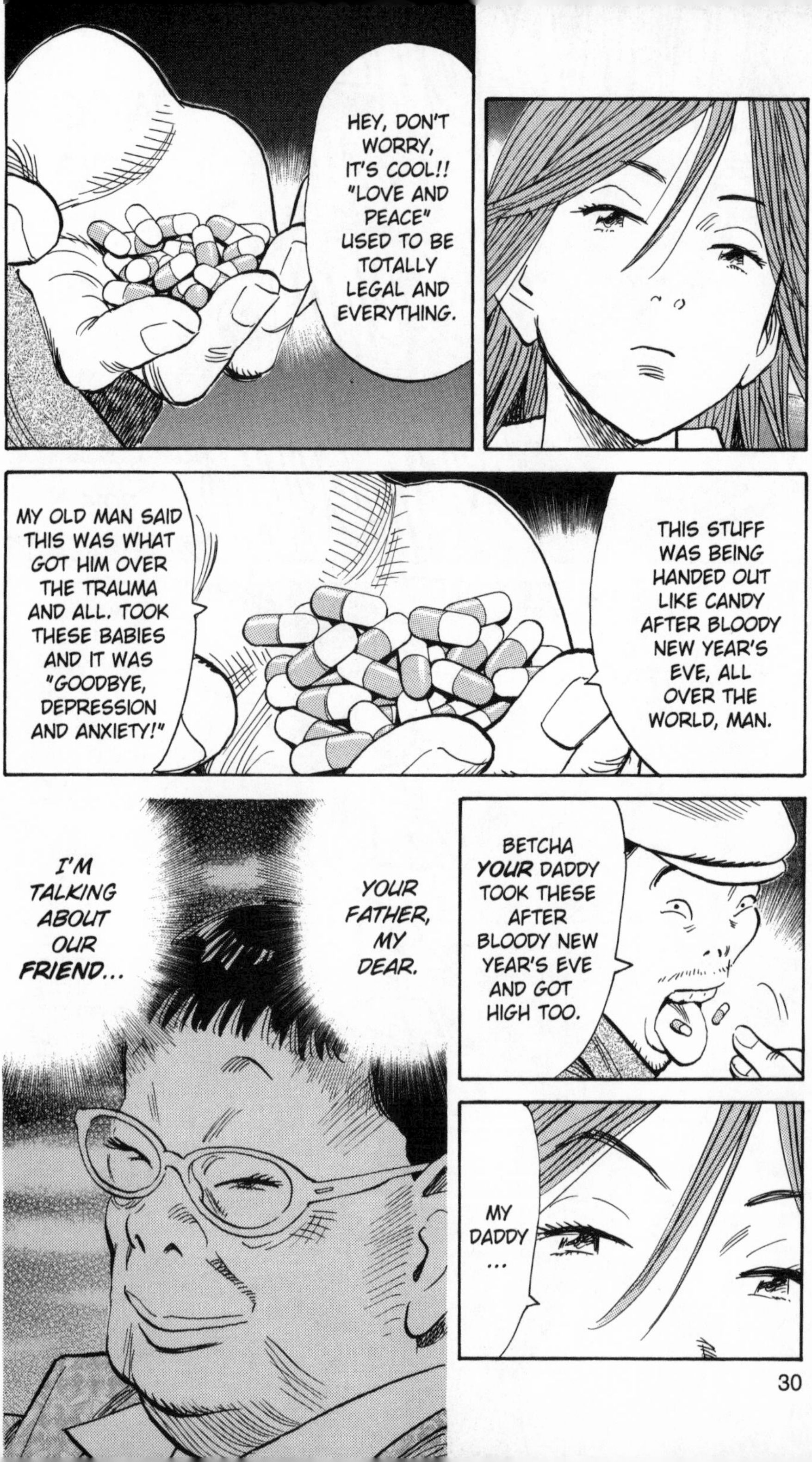
HEY, DON'T WORRY, IT'S COOL!! "LOVE AND PEACE" USED TO BE TOTALLY LEGAL AND EVERYTHING.
THIS STUFF WAS BEING HANDED OUT LIKE CANDY AFTER BLOODY NEW YEAR'S EVE, ALL OVER THE WORLD, MAN.
MY OLD MAN SAID THIS WAS WHAT GOT HIM OVER THE TRAUMA AND ALL. TOOK THESE BABIES AND IT WAS "GOODBYE, DEPRESSION AND ANXIETY!"
BETCHA **YOUR** DADDY TOOK THESE AFTER BLOODY NEW YEAR'S EVE AND GOT HIGH TOO.
MY DADDY ...
YOUR FATHER, MY DEAR.
*I'M TALKING ABOUT OUR **FRIEND**...*

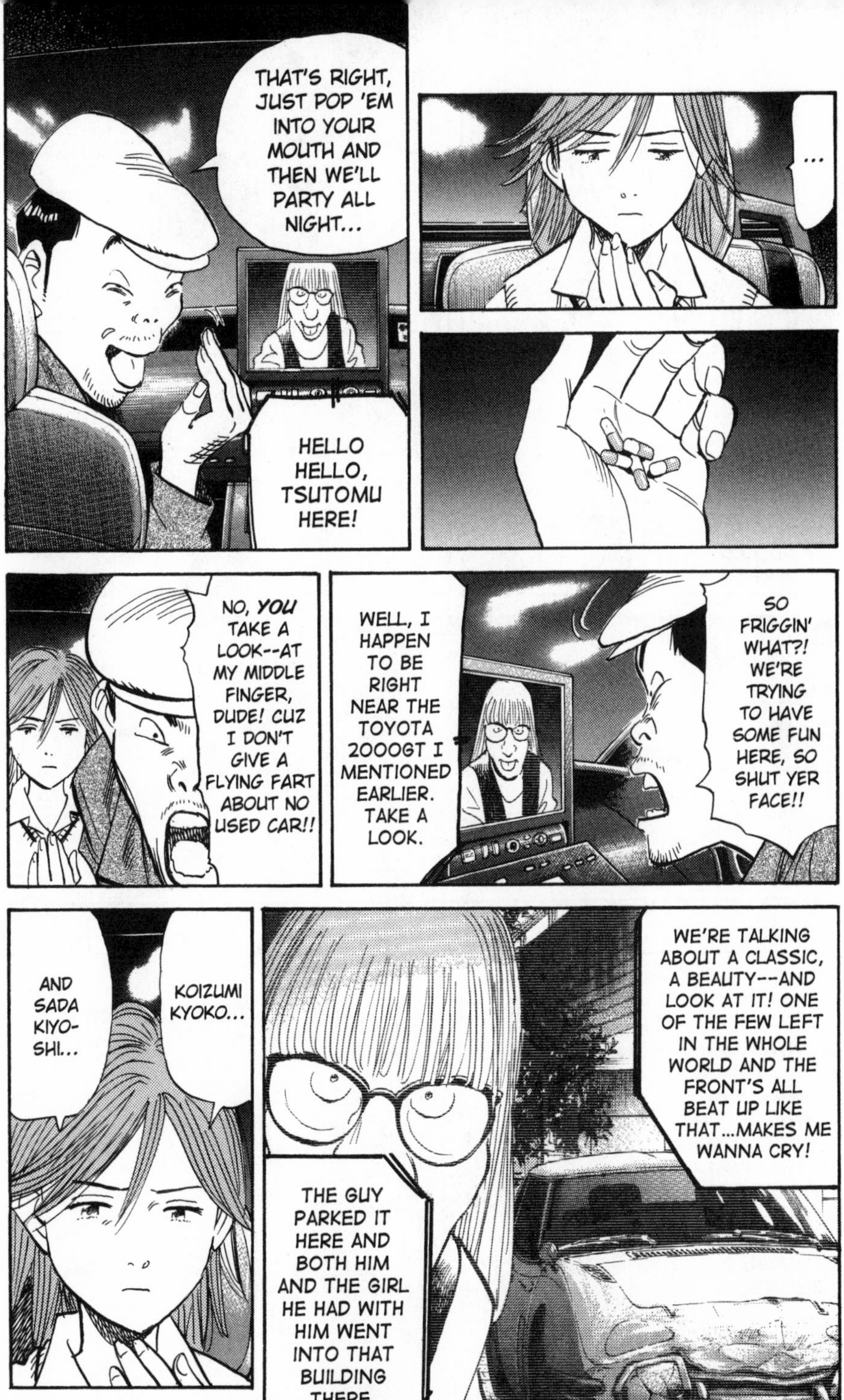
...
THAT'S RIGHT, JUST POP 'EM INTO YOUR MOUTH AND THEN WE'LL PARTY ALL NIGHT...
HELLO HELLO, TSUTOMU HERE!
SO FRIGGIN' WHAT?! WE'RE TRYING TO HAVE SOME FUN HERE, SO SHUT YER FACE!!
WELL, I HAPPEN TO BE RIGHT NEAR THE TOYOTA 2000GT I MENTIONED EARLIER. TAKE A LOOK.
NO, *YOU* TAKE A LOOK--AT MY MIDDLE FINGER, DUDE! CUZ I DON'T GIVE A FLYING FART ABOUT NO USED CAR!!
WE'RE TALKING ABOUT A CLASSIC, A BEAUTY--AND LOOK AT IT! ONE OF THE FEW LEFT IN THE WHOLE WORLD AND THE FRONT'S ALL BEAT UP LIKE THAT...MAKES ME WANNA CRY!
THE GUY PARKED IT HERE AND BOTH HIM AND THE GIRL HE HAD WITH HIM WENT INTO THAT BUILDING THERE.
KOIZUMI KYOKO...
AND SADA KIYO-SHI...

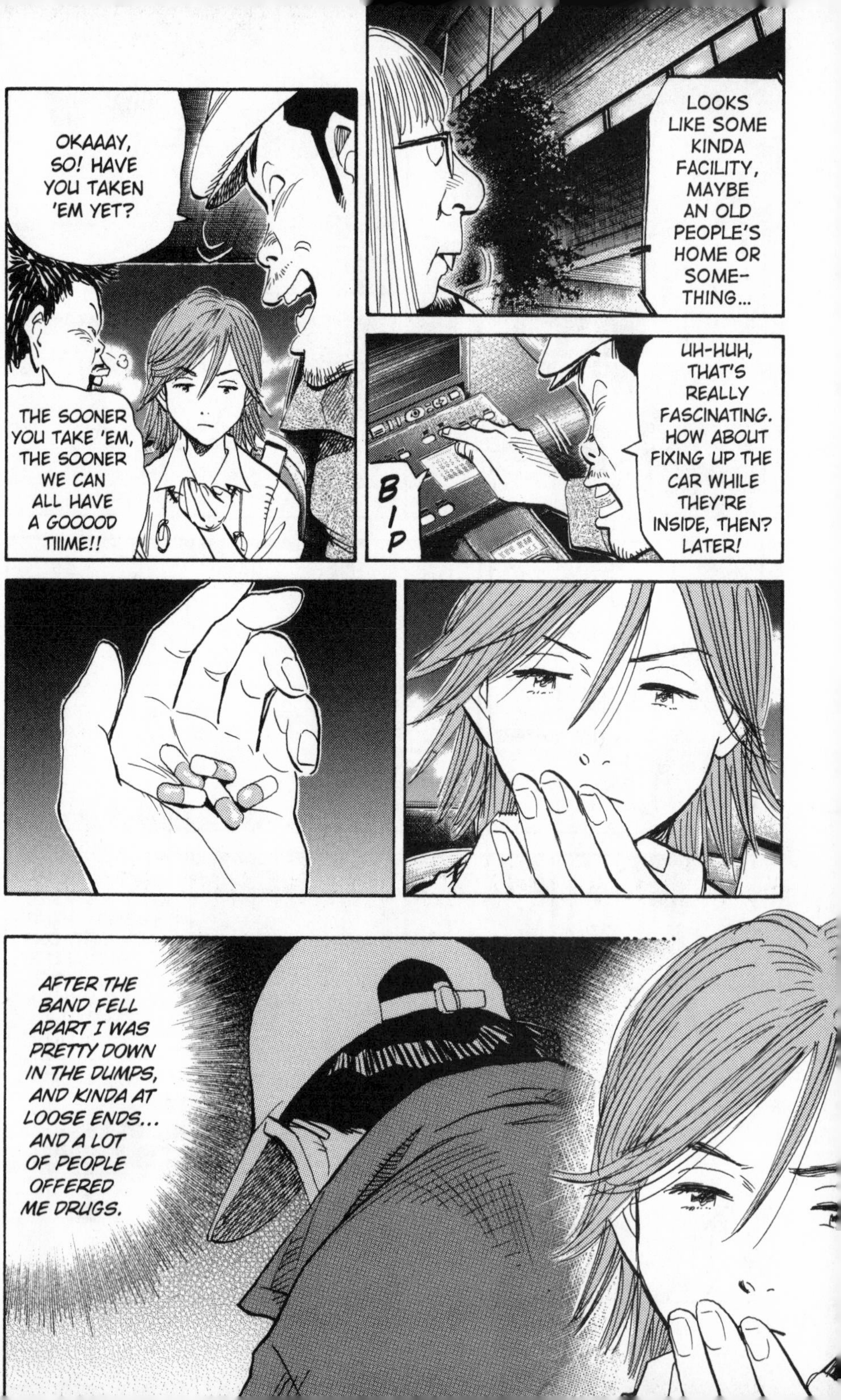
LOOKS LIKE SOME KINDA FACILITY, MAYBE AN OLD PEOPLE'S HOME OR SOME-THING...
UH-HUH, THAT'S REALLY FASCINATING. HOW ABOUT FIXING UP THE CAR WHILE THEY'RE INSIDE, THEN? LATER!
BIP
OKAAAY, SO! HAVE YOU TAKEN 'EM YET?
THE SOONER YOU TAKE 'EM, THE SOONER WE CAN ALL HAVE A GOOOOD TIIIME!!
AFTER THE BAND FELL APART I WAS PRETTY DOWN IN THE DUMPS, AND KINDA AT LOOSE ENDS... AND A LOT OF PEOPLE OFFERED ME DRUGS.

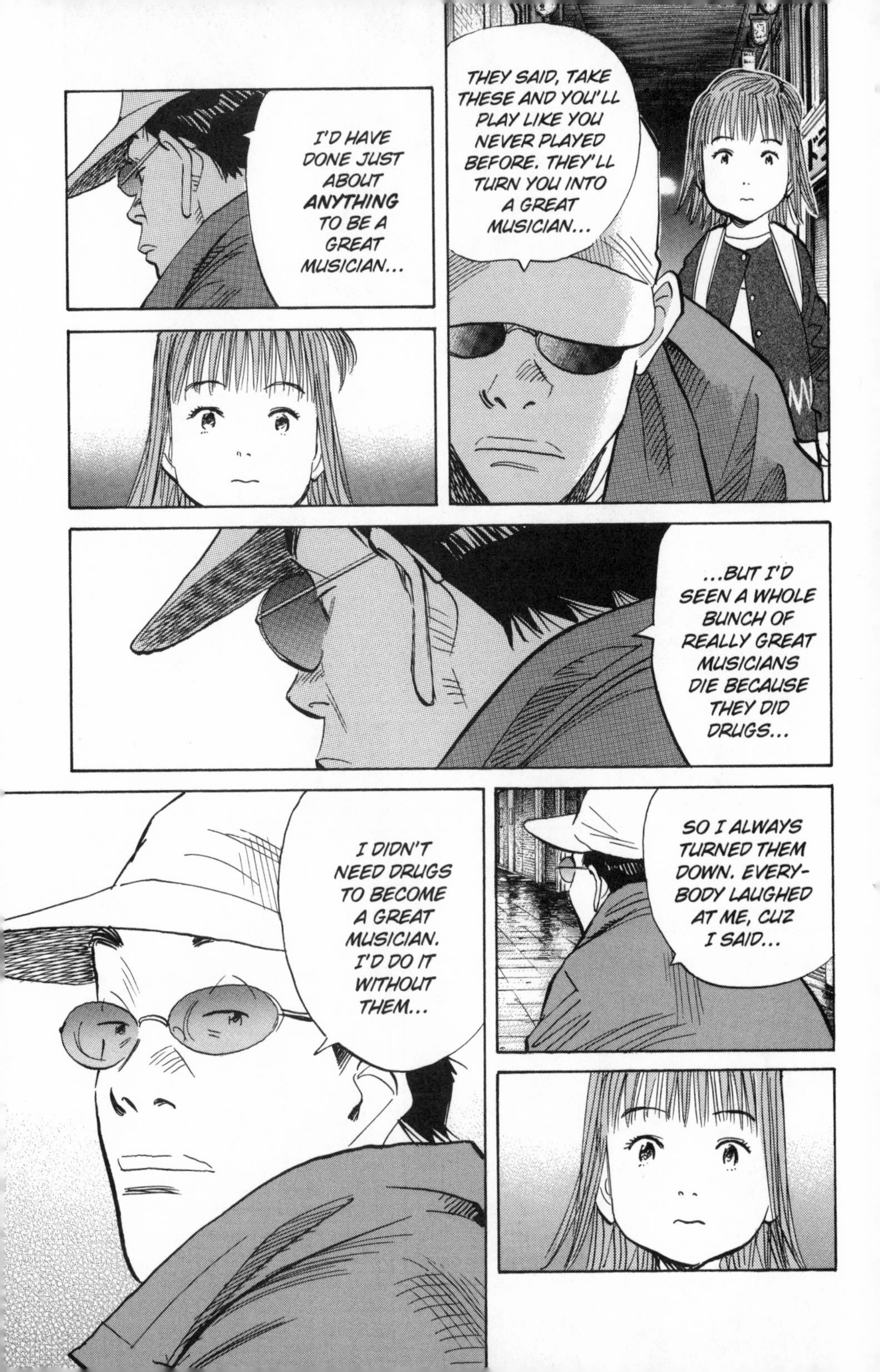
THEY SAID, TAKE THESE AND YOU'LL PLAY LIKE YOU NEVER PLAYED BEFORE. THEY'LL TURN YOU INTO A GREAT MUSICIAN...
I'D HAVE DONE JUST ABOUT **ANYTHING** TO BE A GREAT MUSICIAN...
...BUT I'D SEEN A WHOLE BUNCH OF REALLY GREAT MUSICIANS DIE BECAUSE THEY DID DRUGS...
SO I ALWAYS TURNED THEM DOWN. EVERY-BODY LAUGHED AT ME, CUZ I SAID...
I DIDN'T NEED DRUGS TO BECOME A GREAT MUSICIAN. I'D DO IT WITHOUT THEM...

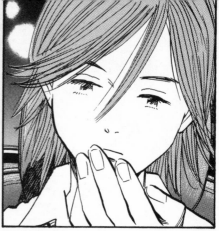

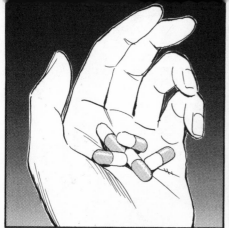

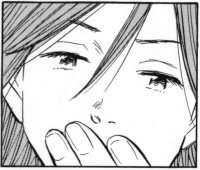

WHAT'RE YOU WAITING FOR?!
HELLO HELLO!
YOU AGAIN?! I THOUGHT I TOLD YOU TO LEAVE US THE HELL ALONE!!
WELL... IT'S JUST...
SOME-THING'S REALLY WEIRD.
YEAH, AND I'LL TELL YOU WHAT IT IS-- YOUR OBSESSION WITH JALOPIES!!
NO...IT'S LIKE, SOMETHING'S WRONG...LIKE, SOMETHING'S GOING ON HERE...

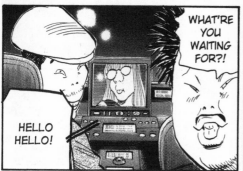

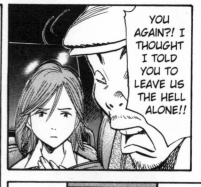

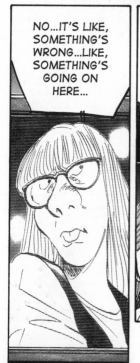

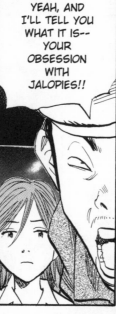

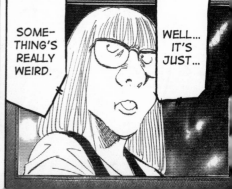

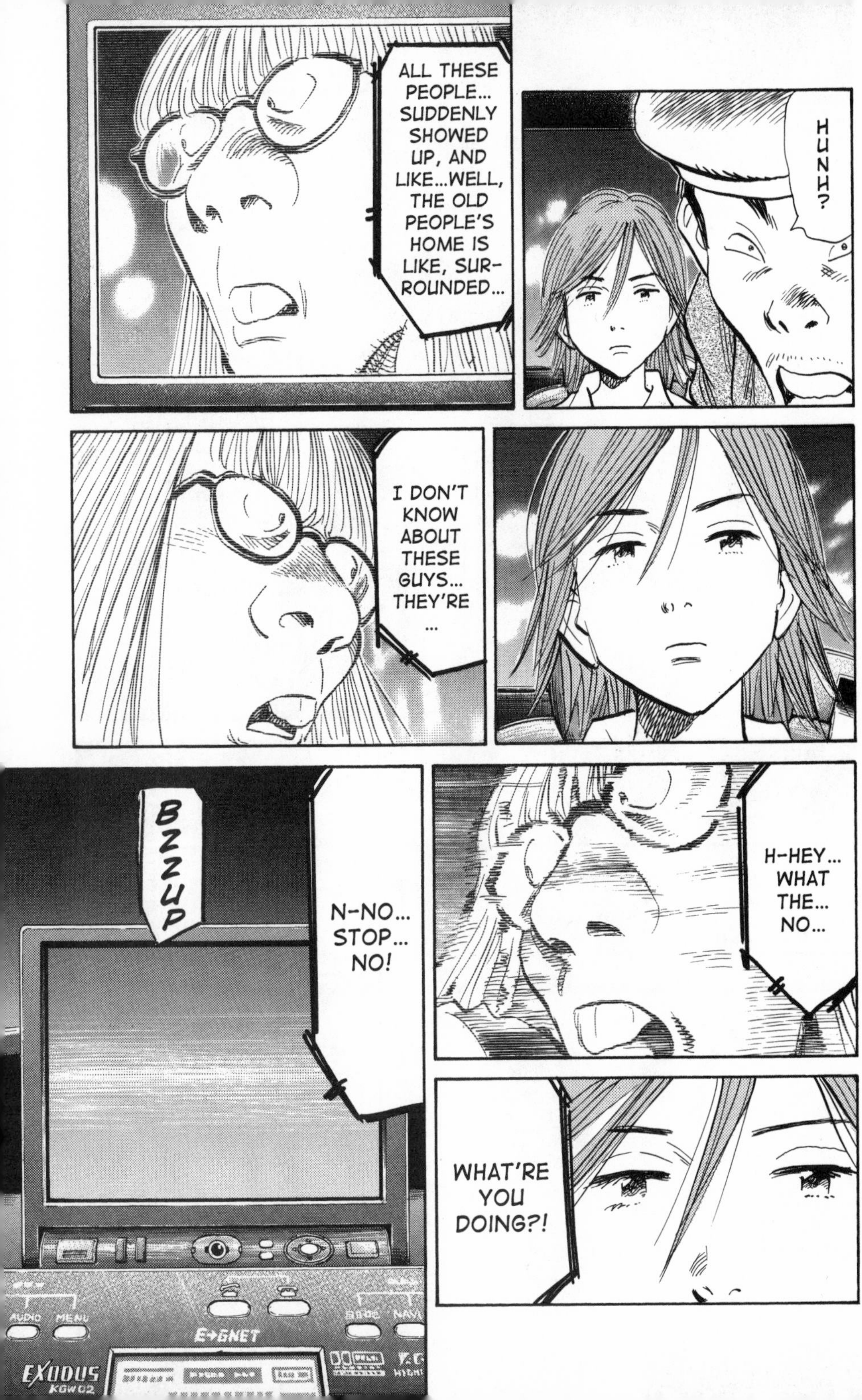
HUNH?
ALL THESE PEOPLE... SUDDENLY SHOWED UP, AND LIKE...WELL, THE OLD PEOPLE'S HOME IS LIKE, SUR-ROUNDED...
I DON'T KNOW ABOUT THESE GUYS... THEY'RE ...
H-HEY... WHAT THE... NO...
WHAT'RE YOU DOING?!
BZZUP
N-NO... STOP... NO!

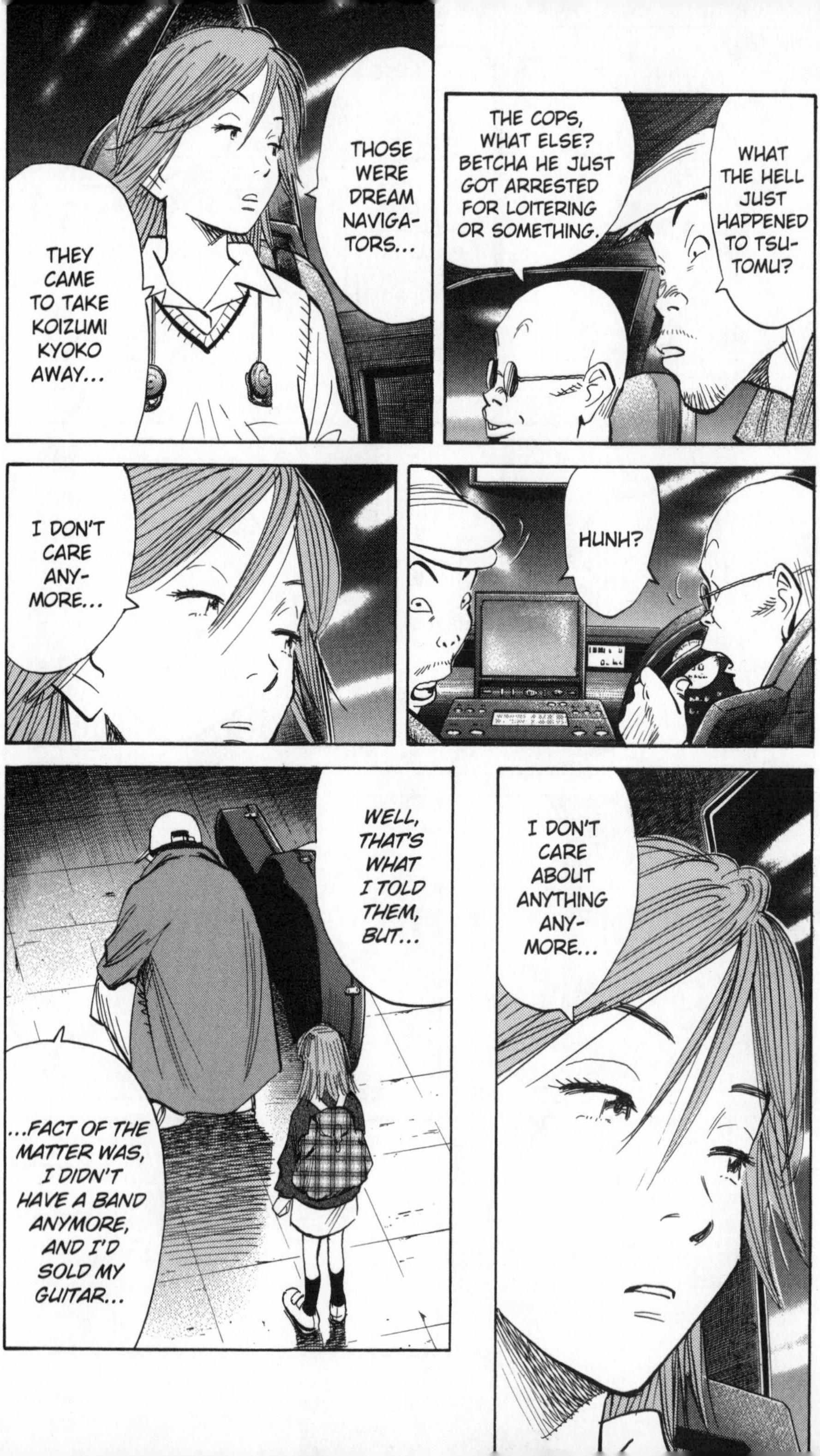
WHAT THE HELL JUST HAPPENED TO TSUTOMU?
THE COPS, WHAT ELSE? BETCHA HE JUST GOT ARRESTED FOR LOITERING OR SOMETHING.
THOSE WERE DREAM NAVIGATORS...
THEY CAME TO TAKE KOIZUMI KYOKO AWAY...
HUNH?
I DON'T CARE ANYMORE...
I DON'T CARE ABOUT ANYTHING ANYMORE...
WELL, THAT'S WHAT I TOLD THEM, BUT...
...FACT OF THE MATTER WAS, I DIDN'T HAVE A BAND ANYMORE, AND I'D SOLD MY GUITAR...

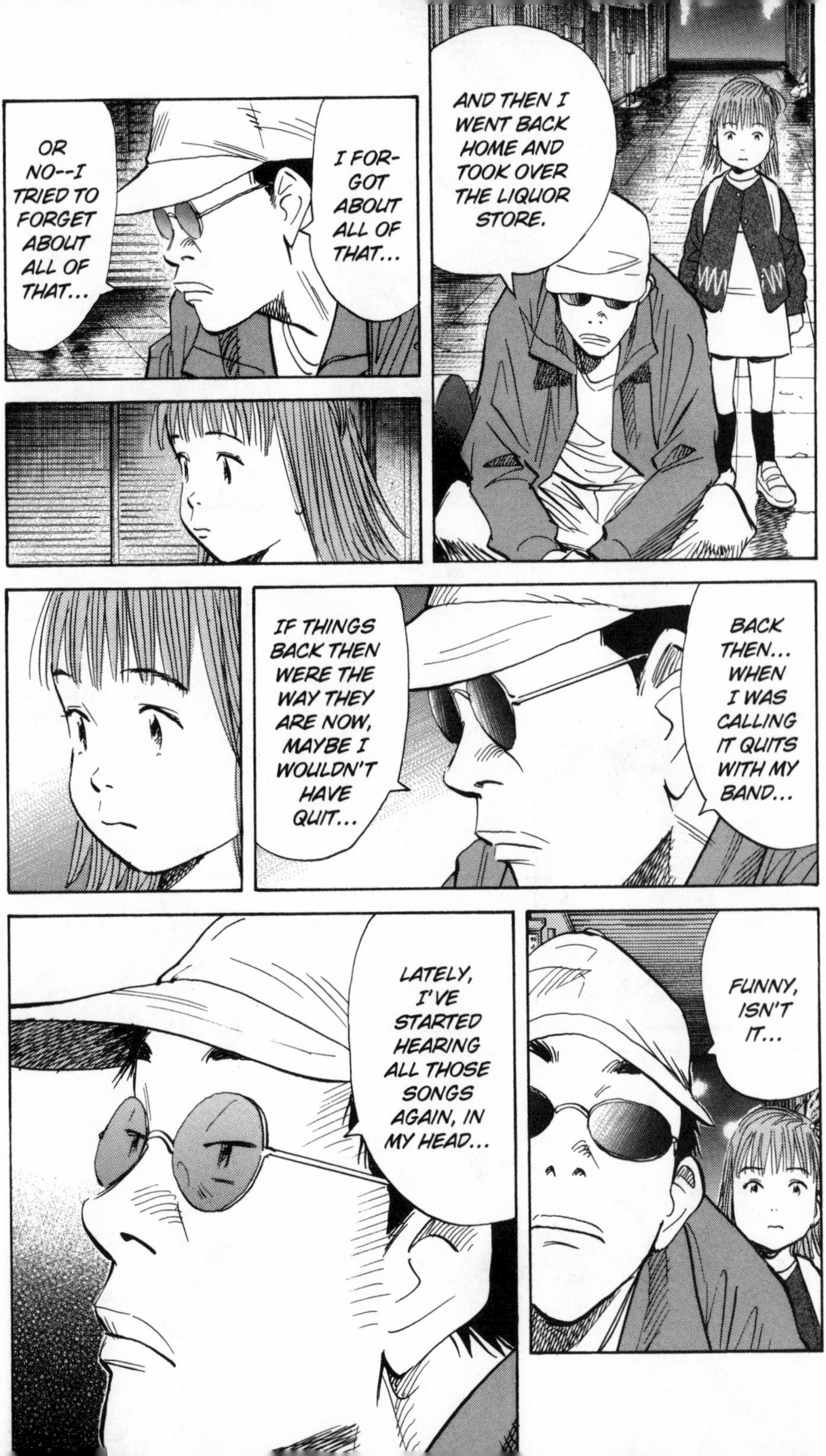
AND THEN I WENT BACK HOME AND TOOK OVER THE LIQUOR STORE.
I FOR-GOT ABOUT ALL OF THAT...
OR NO--I TRIED TO FORGET ABOUT ALL OF THAT...
BACK THEN... WHEN I WAS CALLING IT QUITS WITH MY BAND...
IF THINGS BACK THEN WERE THE WAY THEY ARE NOW, MAYBE I WOULDN'T HAVE QUIT...
FUNNY, ISN'T IT...
LATELY, I'VE STARTED HEARING ALL THOSE SONGS AGAIN, IN MY HEAD...

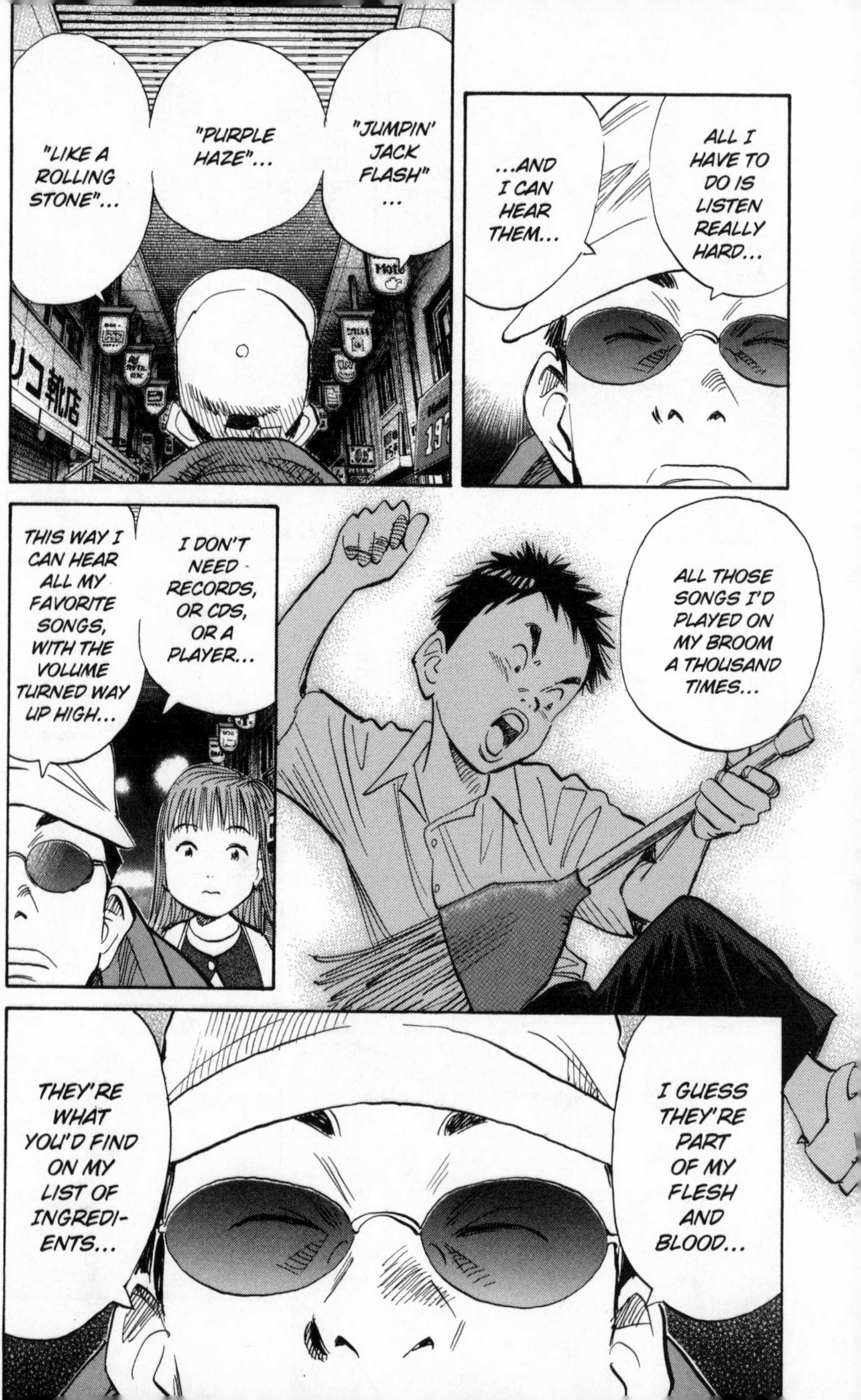
ALL I HAVE TO DO IS LISTEN REALLY HARD...
...AND I CAN HEAR THEM...
"JUMPIN' JACK FLASH"...
"PURPLE HAZE"...
"LIKE A ROLLING STONE"...
ALL THOSE SONGS I'D PLAYED ON MY BROOM A THOUSAND TIMES...
I DON'T NEED RECORDS, OR CDS, OR A PLAYER...
THIS WAY I CAN HEAR ALL MY FAVORITE SONGS, WITH THE VOLUME TURNED WAY UP HIGH...
I GUESS THEY'RE PART OF MY FLESH AND BLOOD...
THEY'RE WHAT YOU'D FIND ON MY LIST OF INGREDI-ENTS...

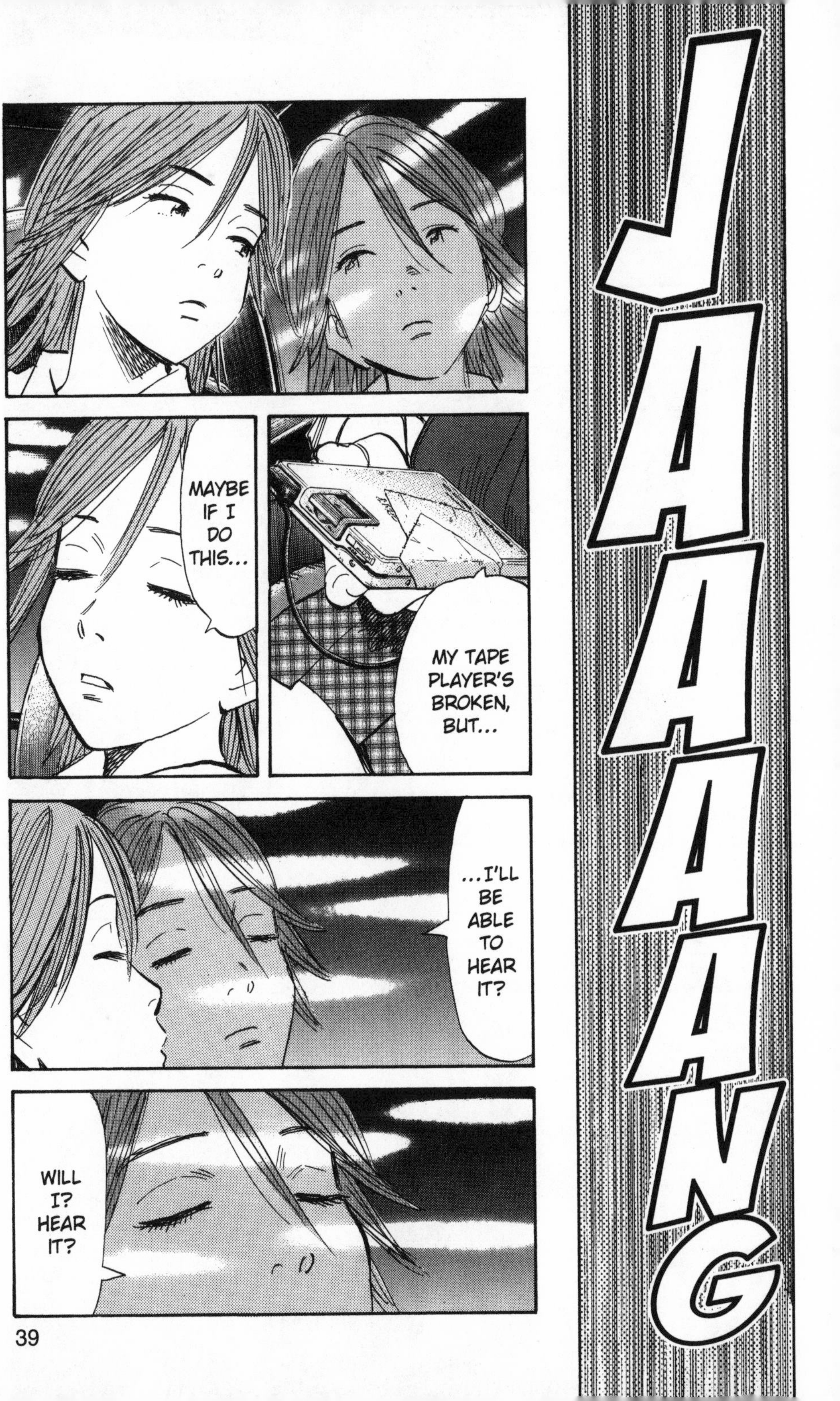
JAAAANG
MY TAPE PLAYER'S BROKEN, BUT...
MAYBE IF I DO THIS...
...I'LL BE ABLE TO HEAR IT?
WILL I? HEAR IT?

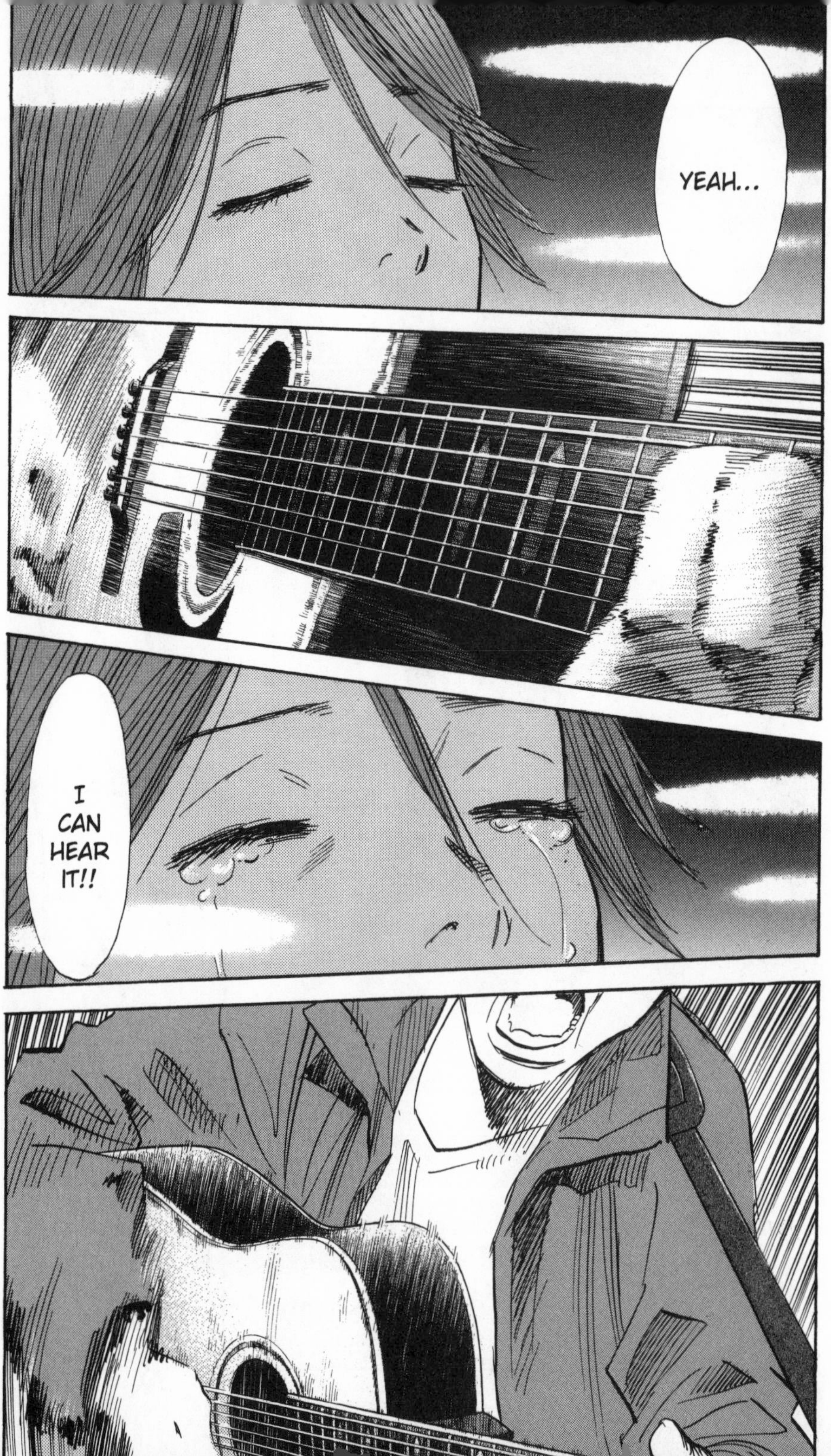
YEAH...
I CAN HEAR IT!!

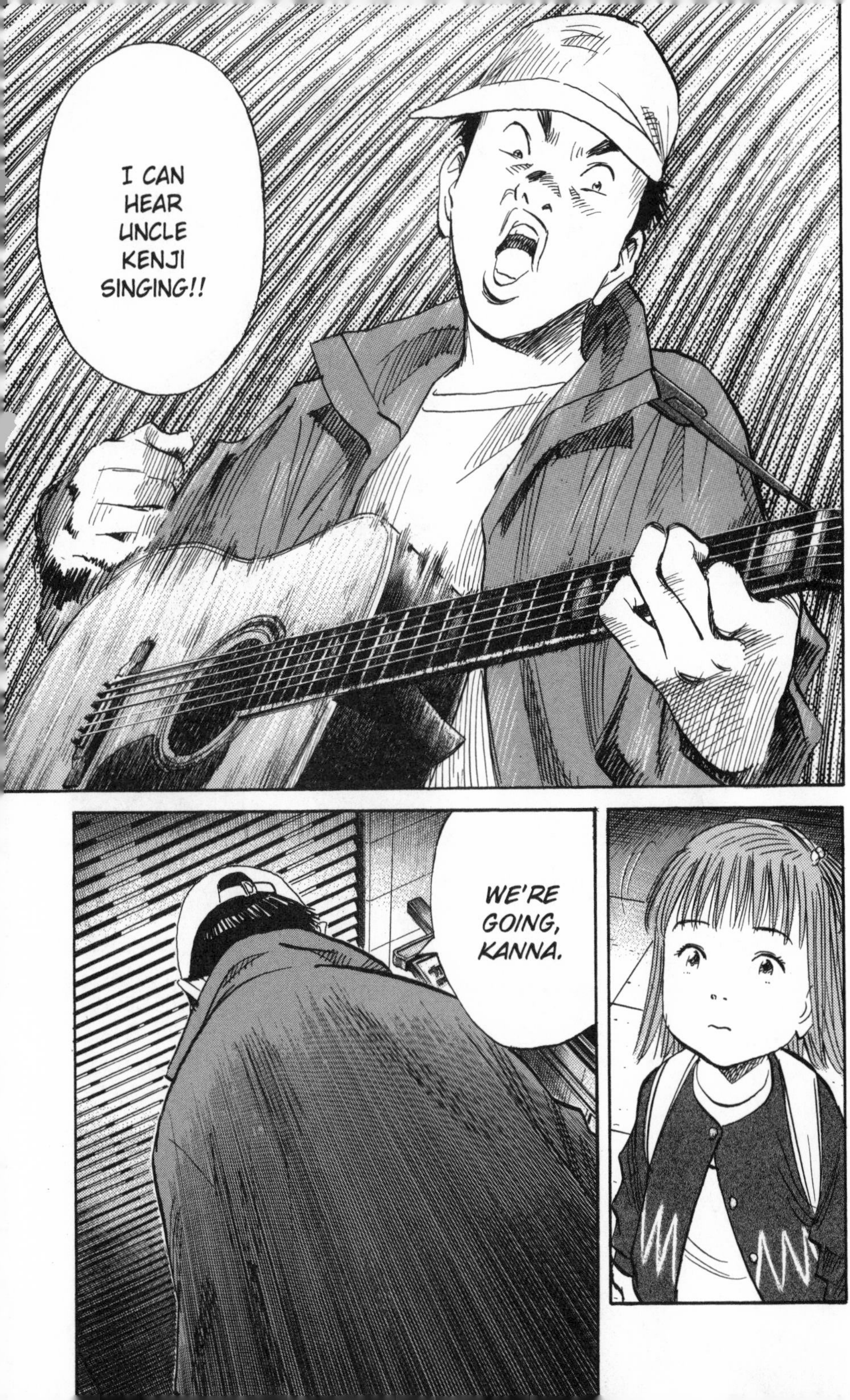
I CAN HEAR UNCLE KENJI SINGING!!
WE'RE GOING, KANNA.

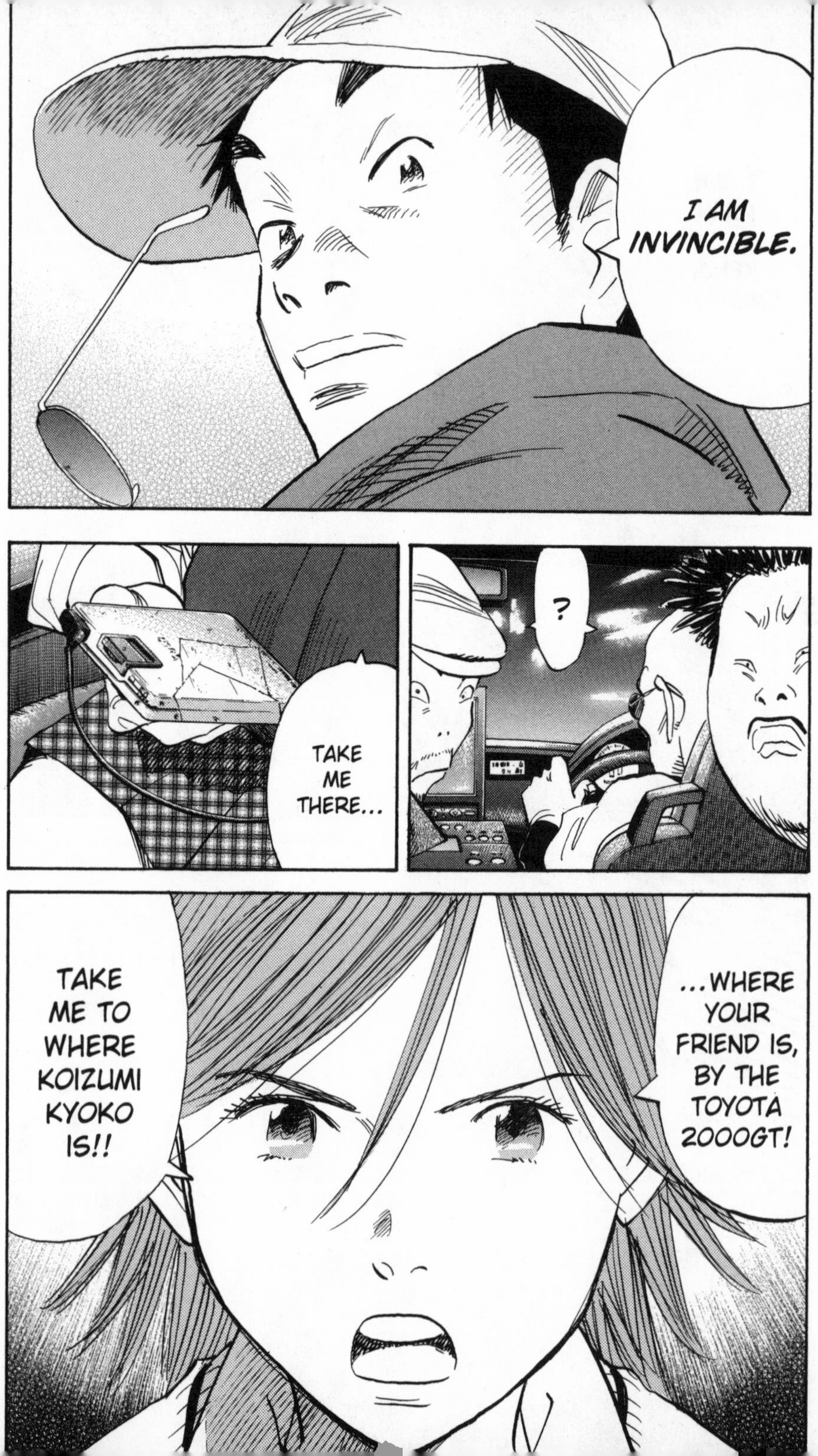
I AM INVINCIBLE.
?
TAKE ME THERE...
TAKE ME TO WHERE KOIZUMI KYOKO IS!!
...WHERE YOUR FRIEND IS, BY THE TOYOTA 2000GT!

Chapter 3 The Lie of 1970

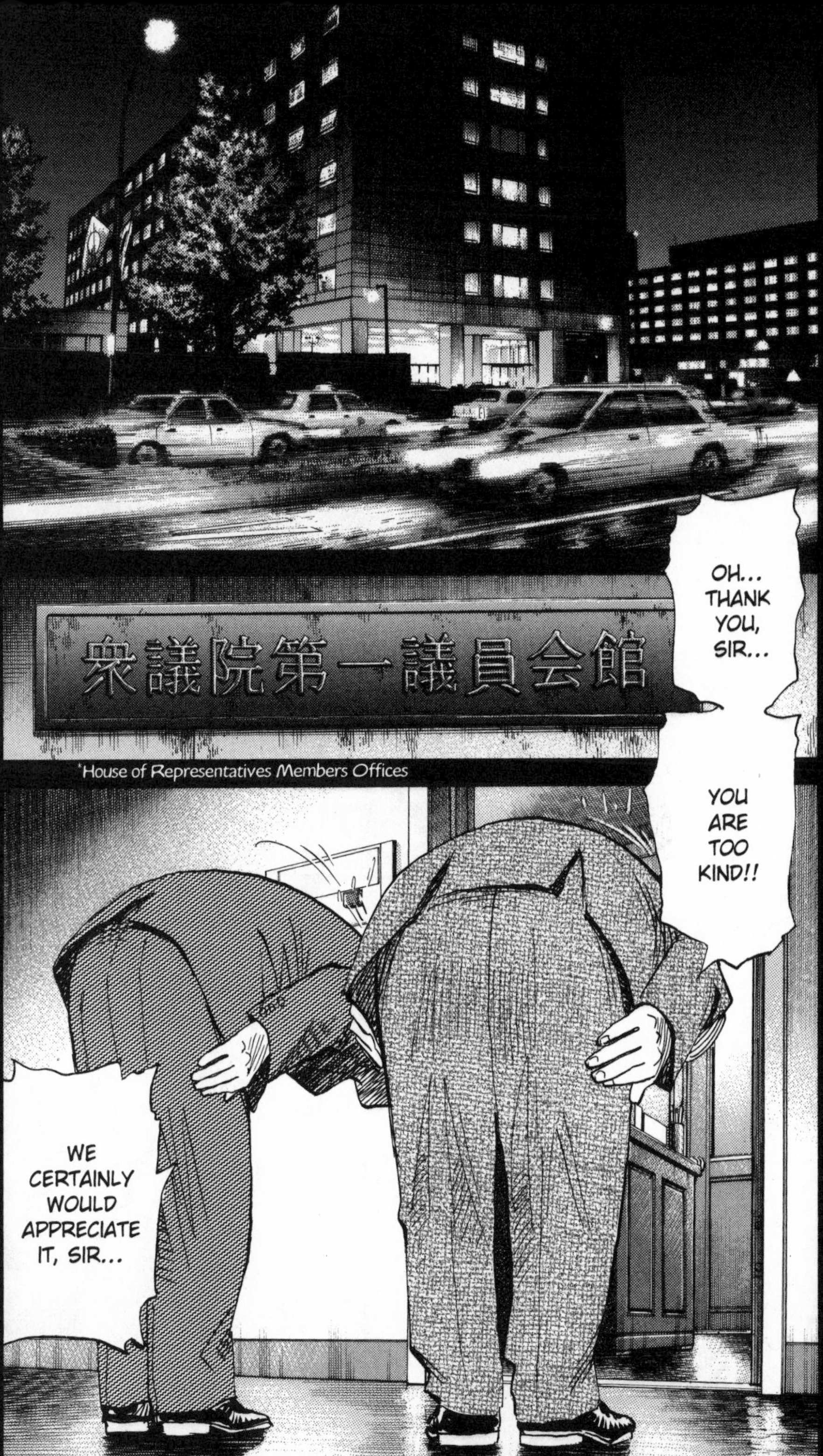
衆議院第一議員会館
*House of Representatives Members Offices
OH... THANK YOU, SIR...
YOU ARE TOO KIND!!
WE CERTAINLY WOULD APPRECIATE IT, SIR...

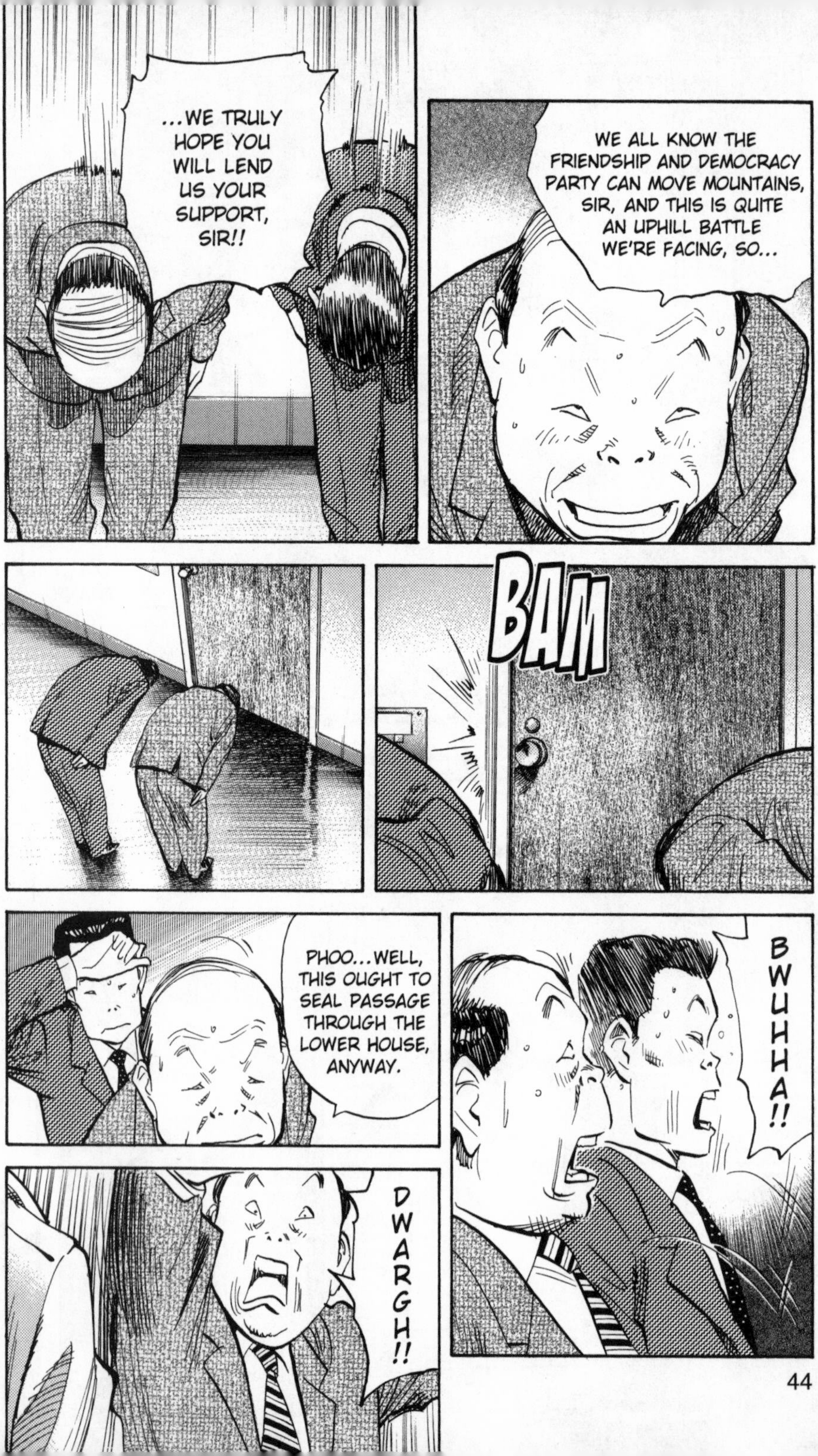
WE ALL KNOW THE FRIENDSHIP AND DEMOCRACY PARTY CAN MOVE MOUNTAINS, SIR, AND THIS IS QUITE AN UPHILL BATTLE WE'RE FACING, SO...
...WE TRULY HOPE YOU WILL LEND US YOUR SUPPORT, SIR!!
BAM
BWUHHA!!
PHOO...WELL, THIS OUGHT TO SEAL PASSAGE THROUGH THE LOWER HOUSE, ANYWAY.
DWARGH!!

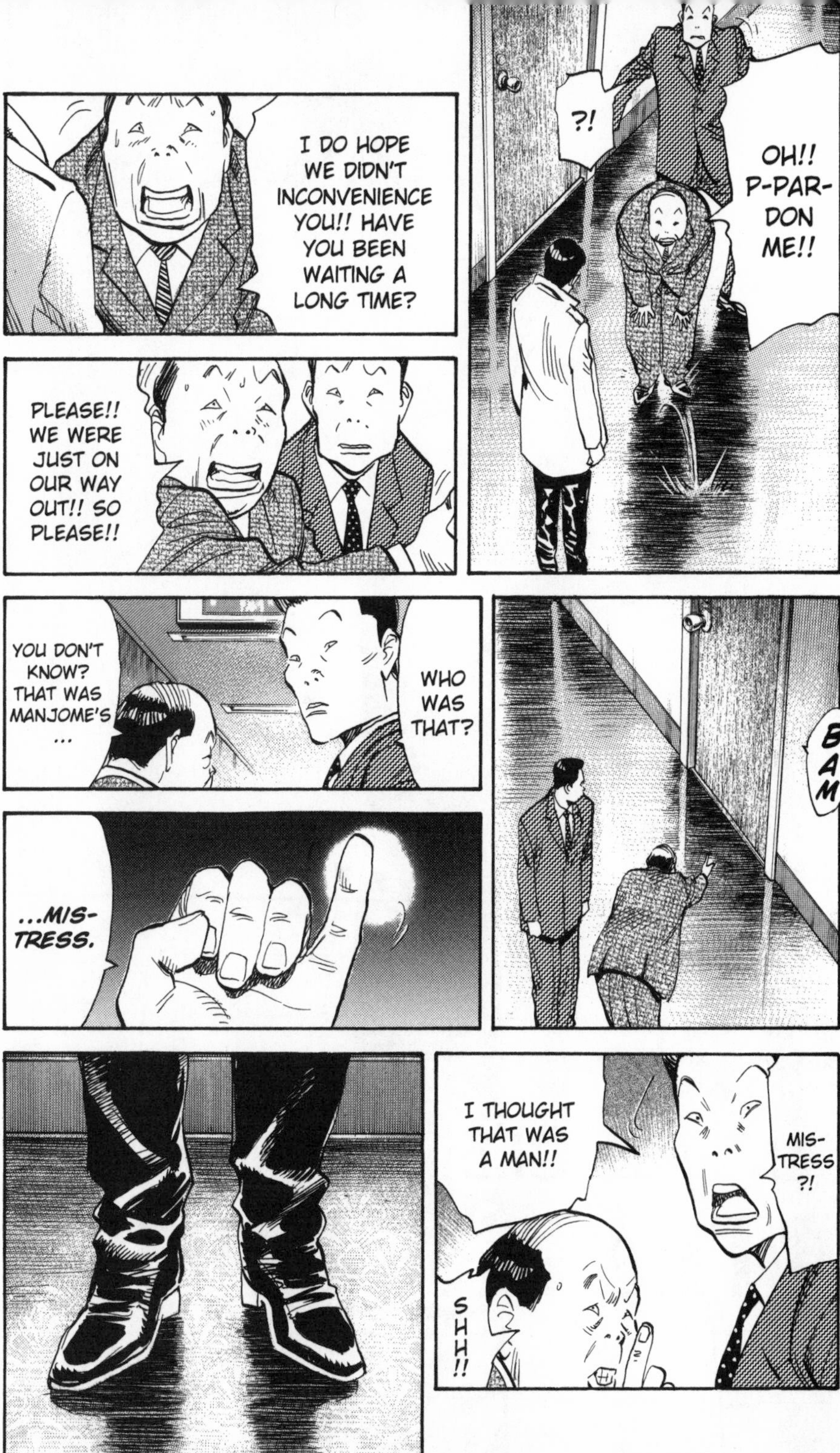

OH!! P-PARDON ME!!
?!
I DO HOPE WE DIDN'T INCONVENIENCE YOU!! HAVE YOU BEEN WAITING A LONG TIME?
PLEASE!! WE WERE JUST ON OUR WAY OUT!! SO PLEASE!!
BAM
WHO WAS THAT?
YOU DON'T KNOW? THAT WAS MANJOME'S ...
...MIS-TRESS.
MIS-TRESS?!
I THOUGHT THAT WAS A MAN!!
SHH!!

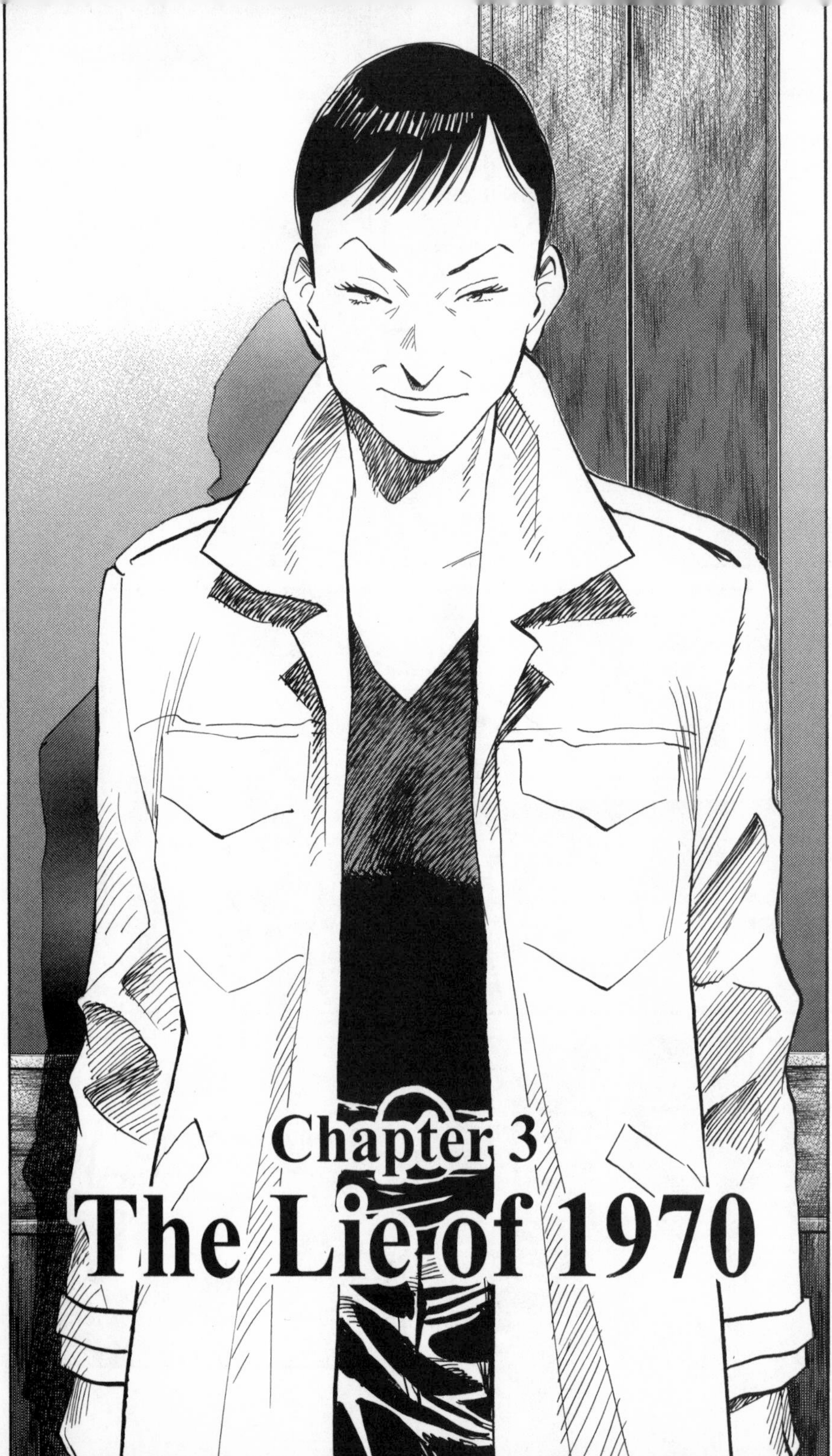

Chapter 3
The Lie of 1970

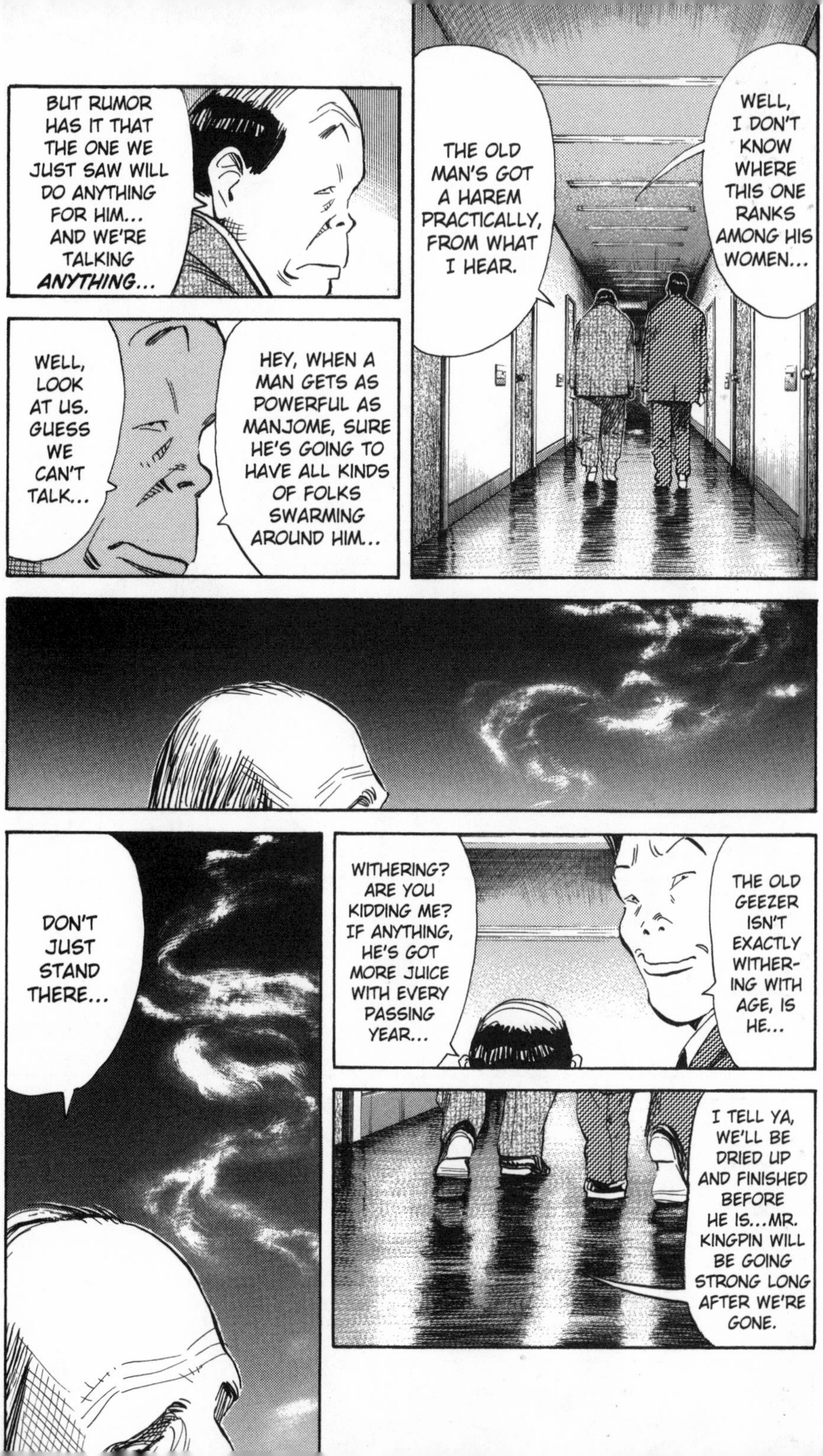
WELL, I DON'T KNOW WHERE THIS ONE RANKS AMONG HIS WOMEN...
THE OLD MAN'S GOT A HAREM PRACTICALLY, FROM WHAT I HEAR.
BUT RUMOR HAS IT THAT THE ONE WE JUST SAW WILL DO ANYTHING FOR HIM... AND WE'RE TALKING *ANYTHING*...
HEY, WHEN A MAN GETS AS POWERFUL AS MANJOME, SURE HE'S GOING TO HAVE ALL KINDS OF FOLKS SWARMING AROUND HIM...
WELL, LOOK AT US. GUESS WE CAN'T TALK...
THE OLD GEEZER ISN'T EXACTLY WITHER-ING WITH AGE, IS HE...
WITHERING? ARE YOU KIDDING ME? IF ANYTHING, HE'S GOT MORE JUICE WITH EVERY PASSING YEAR...
I TELL YA, WE'LL BE DRIED UP AND FINISHED BEFORE HE IS...MR. KINGPIN WILL BE GOING STRONG LONG AFTER WE'RE GONE.
DON'T JUST STAND THERE...

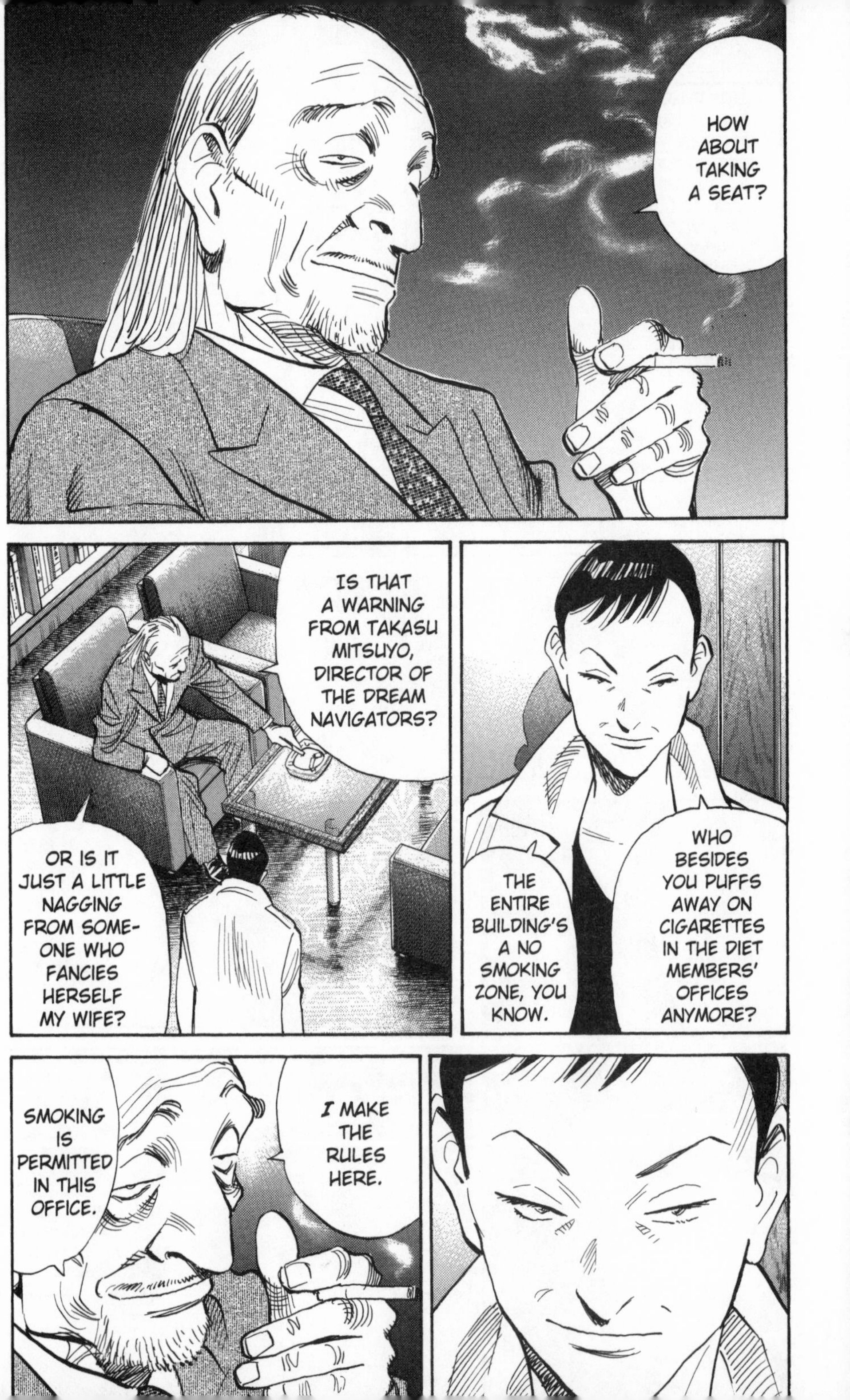
HOW ABOUT TAKING A SEAT?
WHO BESIDES YOU PUFFS AWAY ON CIGARETTES IN THE DIET MEMBERS' OFFICES ANYMORE?
THE ENTIRE BUILDING'S A NO SMOKING ZONE, YOU KNOW.
IS THAT A WARNING FROM TAKASU MITSUYO, DIRECTOR OF THE DREAM NAVIGATORS?
OR IS IT JUST A LITTLE NAGGING FROM SOME-ONE WHO FANCIES HERSELF MY WIFE?
I MAKE THE RULES HERE.
SMOKING IS PERMITTED IN THIS OFFICE.

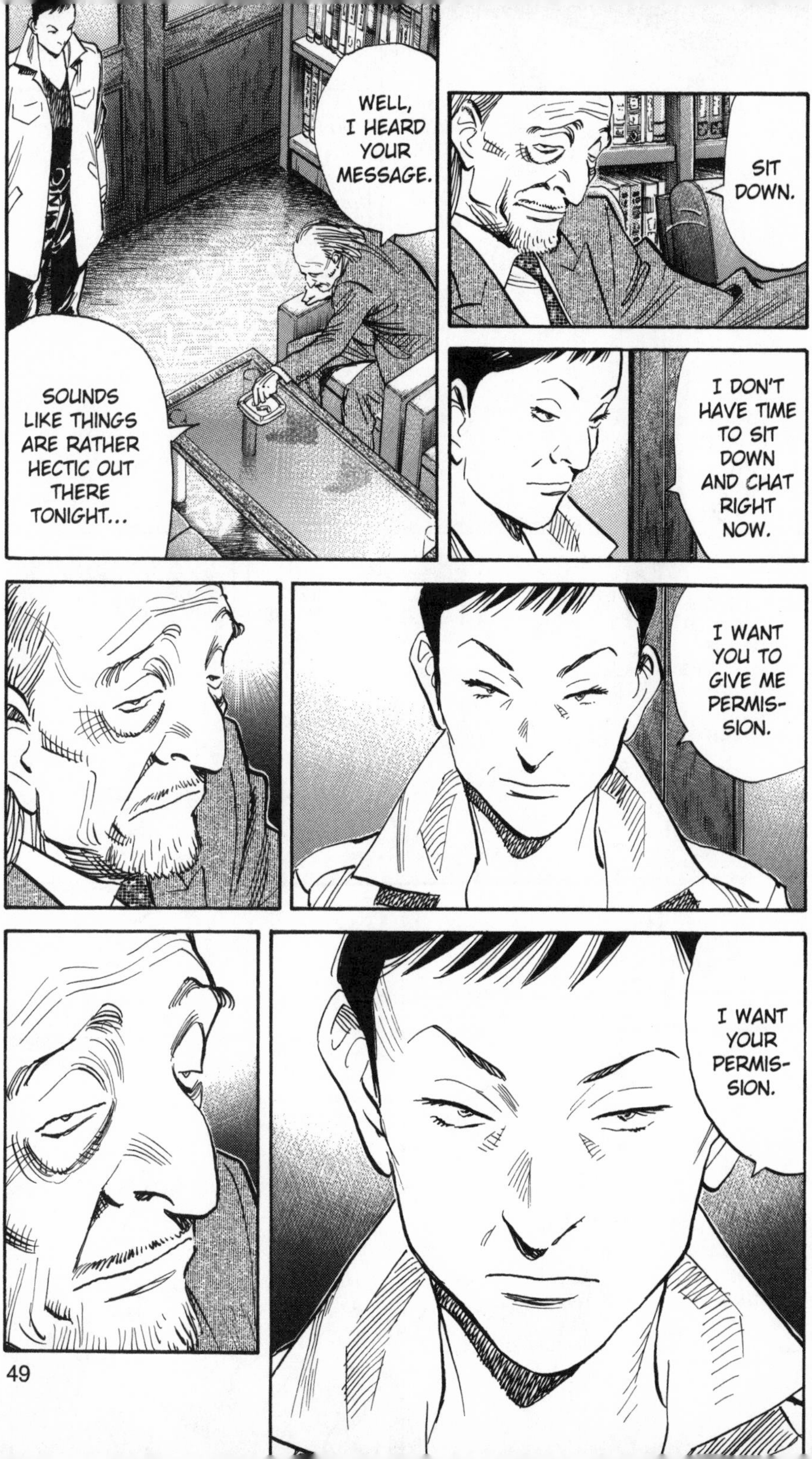
SIT DOWN.
I DON'T HAVE TIME TO SIT DOWN AND CHAT RIGHT NOW.
WELL, I HEARD YOUR MESSAGE.
SOUNDS LIKE THINGS ARE RATHER HECTIC OUT THERE TONIGHT...
I WANT YOU TO GIVE ME PERMIS-SION.
I WANT YOUR PERMIS-SION.

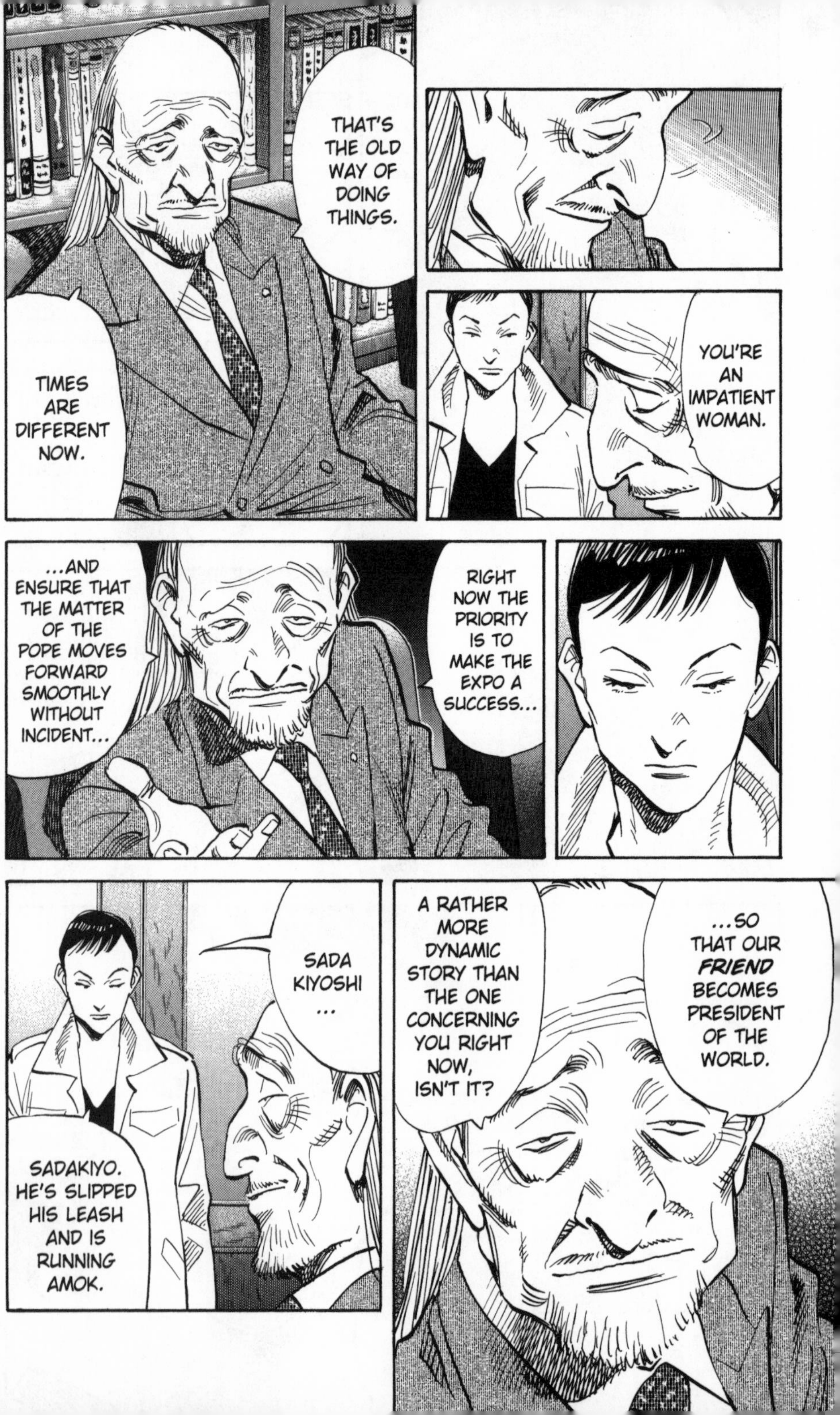
YOU'RE AN IMPATIENT WOMAN.
THAT'S THE OLD WAY OF DOING THINGS.
TIMES ARE DIFFERENT NOW.
RIGHT NOW THE PRIORITY IS TO MAKE THE EXPO A SUCCESS...
...AND ENSURE THAT THE MATTER OF THE POPE MOVES FORWARD SMOOTHLY WITHOUT INCIDENT...
...SO THAT OUR *FRIEND* BECOMES PRESIDENT OF THE WORLD.
A RATHER MORE DYNAMIC STORY THAN THE ONE CONCERNING YOU RIGHT NOW, ISN'T IT?
SADA KIYOSHI ...
SADAKIYO. HE'S SLIPPED HIS LEASH AND IS RUNNING AMOK.

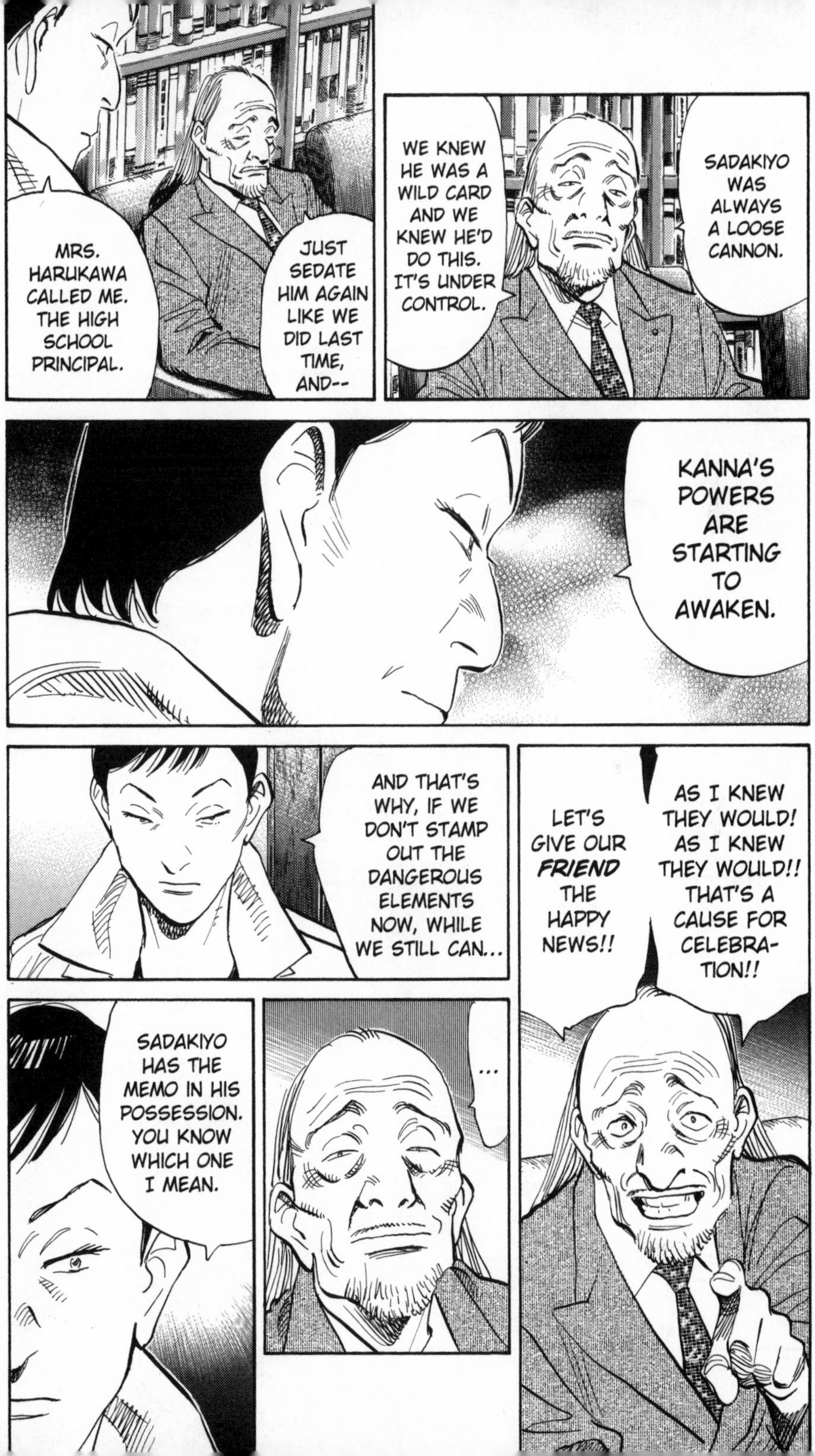
SADAKIYO WAS ALWAYS A LOOSE CANNON.
WE KNEW HE WAS A WILD CARD AND WE KNEW HE'D DO THIS. IT'S UNDER CONTROL.
JUST SEDATE HIM AGAIN LIKE WE DID LAST TIME, AND--
MRS. HARUKAWA CALLED ME. THE HIGH SCHOOL PRINCIPAL.
KANNA'S POWERS ARE STARTING TO AWAKEN.
AS I KNEW THEY WOULD! AS I KNEW THEY WOULD!! THAT'S A CAUSE FOR CELEBRA-TION!!
LET'S GIVE OUR *FRIEND* THE HAPPY NEWS!!
AND THAT'S WHY, IF WE DON'T STAMP OUT THE DANGEROUS ELEMENTS NOW, WHILE WE STILL CAN...
...
SADAKIYO HAS THE MEMO IN HIS POSSESSION. YOU KNOW WHICH ONE I MEAN.

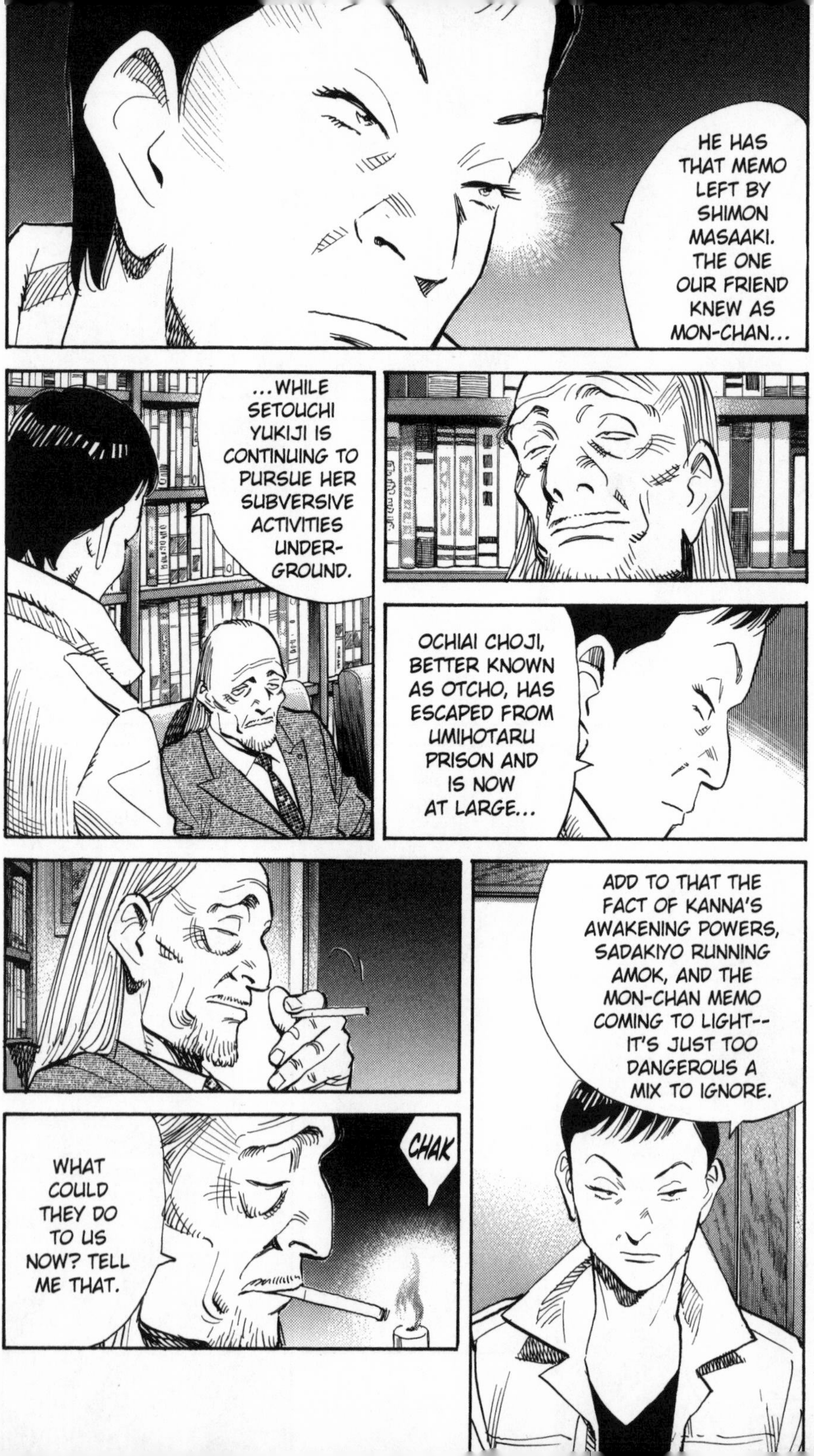
HE HAS THAT MEMO LEFT BY SHIMON MASAAKI. THE ONE OUR FRIEND KNEW AS MON-CHAN...
OCHIAI CHOJI, BETTER KNOWN AS OTCHO, HAS ESCAPED FROM UMIHOTARU PRISON AND IS NOW AT LARGE...
...WHILE SETOUCHI YUKIJI IS CONTINUING TO PURSUE HER SUBVERSIVE ACTIVITIES UNDER-GROUND.
ADD TO THAT THE FACT OF KANNA'S AWAKENING POWERS, SADAKIYO RUNNING AMOK, AND THE MON-CHAN MEMO COMING TO LIGHT-- IT'S JUST TOO DANGEROUS A MIX TO IGNORE.
CHAK
WHAT COULD THEY DO TO US NOW? TELL ME THAT.

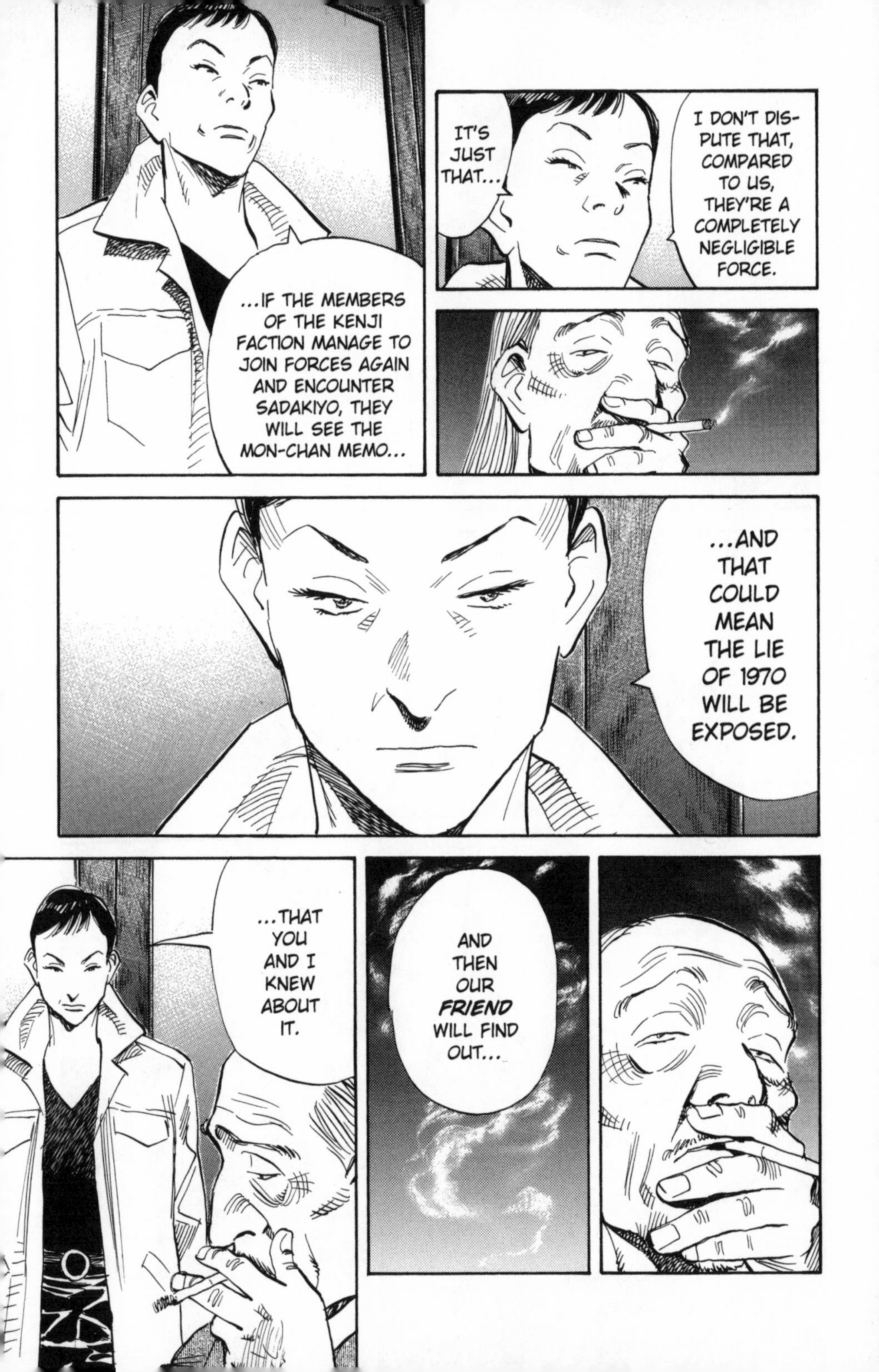
I DON'T DISPUTE THAT, COMPARED TO US, THEY'RE A COMPLETELY NEGLIGIBLE FORCE.
IT'S JUST THAT...
...IF THE MEMBERS OF THE KENJI FACTION MANAGE TO JOIN FORCES AGAIN AND ENCOUNTER SADAKIYO, THEY WILL SEE THE MON-CHAN MEMO...
...AND THAT COULD MEAN THE LIE OF 1970 WILL BE EXPOSED.
AND THEN OUR *FRIEND* WILL FIND OUT...
...THAT YOU AND I KNEW ABOUT IT.

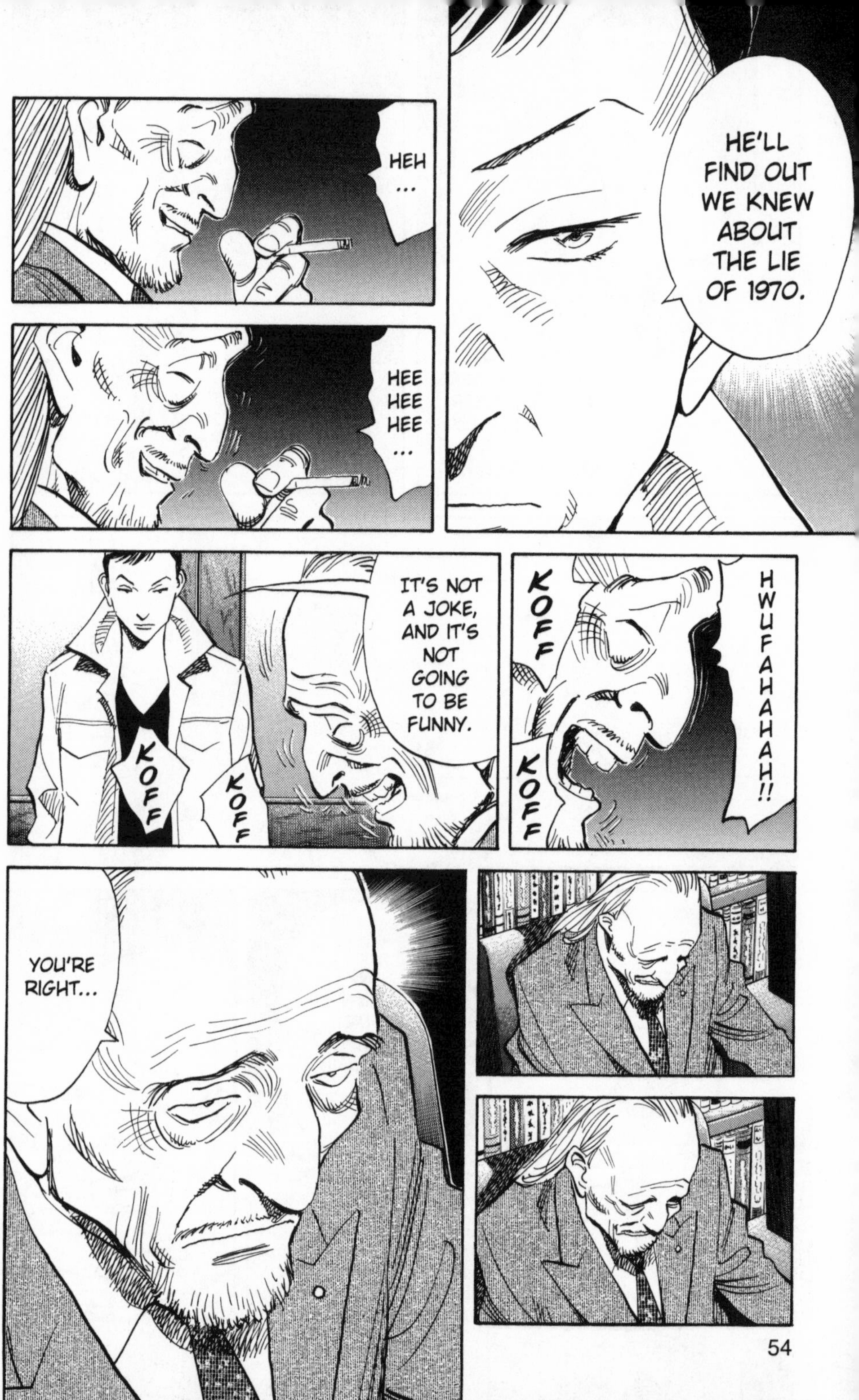
HE'LL FIND OUT WE KNEW ABOUT THE LIE OF 1970.
HEH ...
HEE HEE HEE ...
HWUFAHAHAH!!
KOFF
KOFF
IT'S NOT A JOKE, AND IT'S NOT GOING TO BE FUNNY.
KOFF
KOFF
YOU'RE RIGHT...

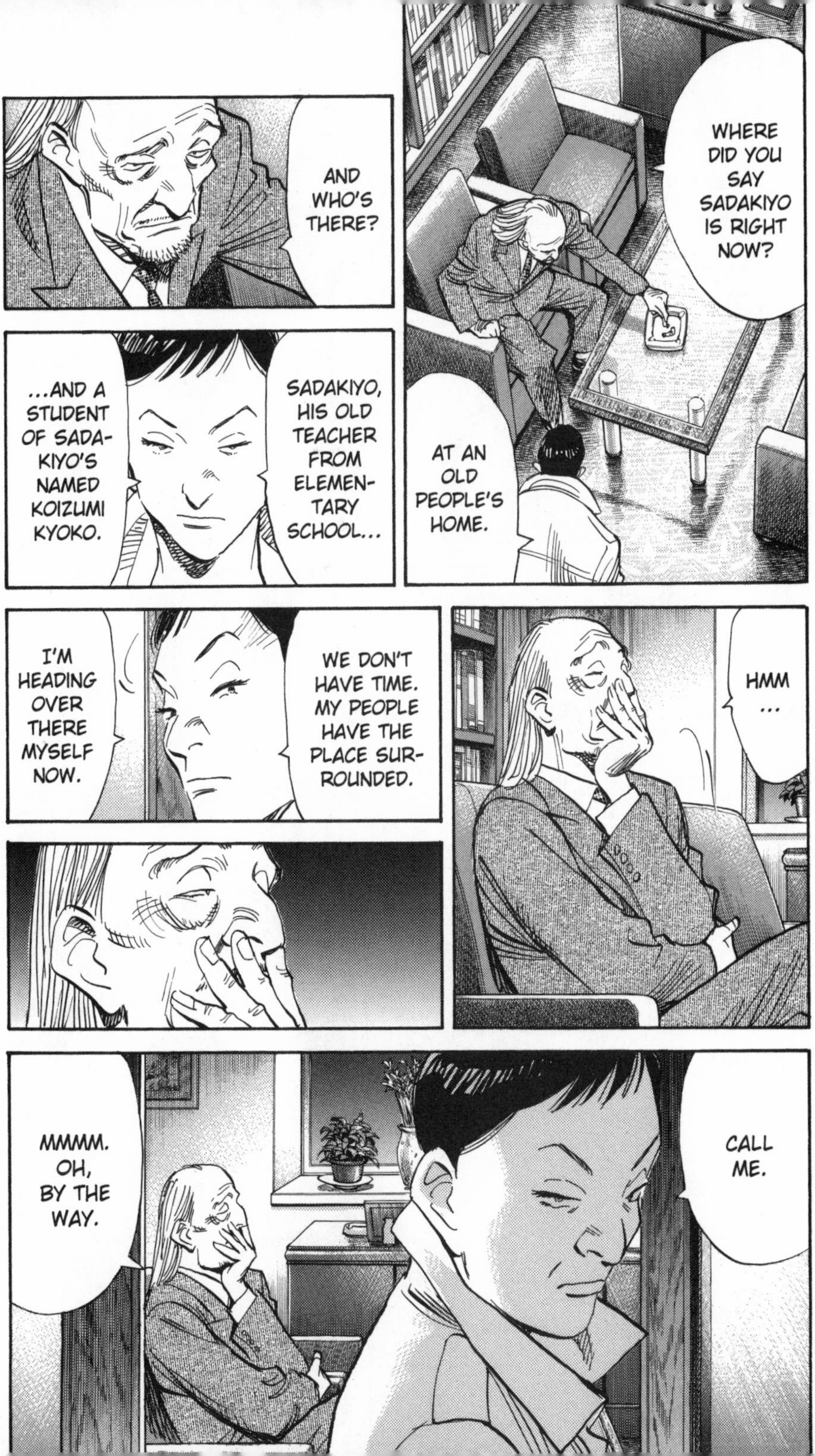
WHERE DID YOU SAY SADAKIYO IS RIGHT NOW?
AT AN OLD PEOPLE'S HOME.
AND WHO'S THERE?
SADAKIYO, HIS OLD TEACHER FROM ELEMENTARY SCHOOL...
...AND A STUDENT OF SADAKIYO'S NAMED KOIZUMI KYOKO.
HMM ...
WE DON'T HAVE TIME. MY PEOPLE HAVE THE PLACE SURROUNDED.
I'M HEADING OVER THERE MYSELF NOW.
CALL ME.
MMMM. OH, BY THE WAY.

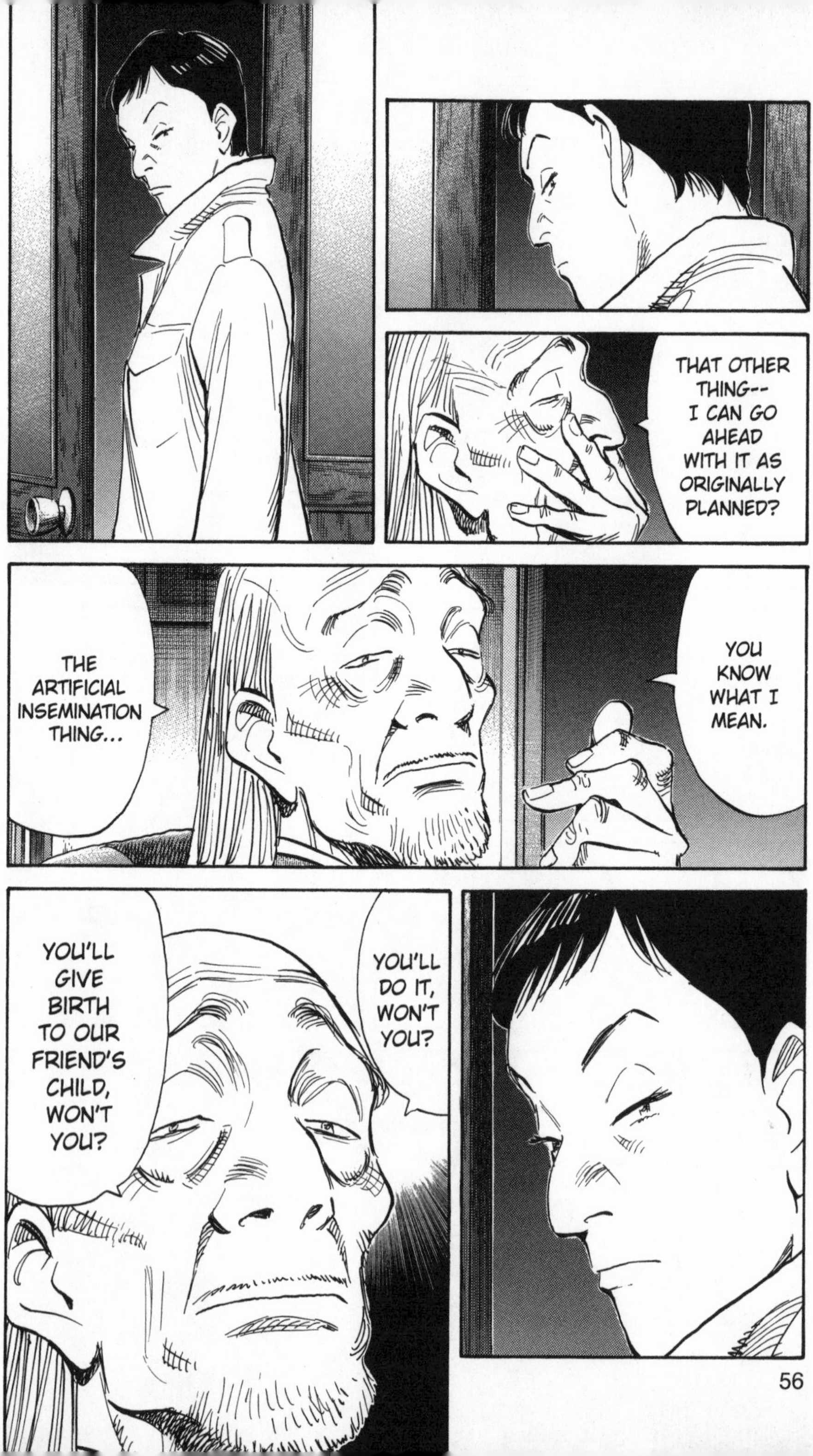
THAT OTHER THING-- I CAN GO AHEAD WITH IT AS ORIGINALLY PLANNED?
YOU KNOW WHAT I MEAN.
THE ARTIFICIAL INSEMINATION THING...
YOU'LL DO IT, WON'T YOU?
YOU'LL GIVE BIRTH TO OUR FRIEND'S CHILD, WON'T YOU?

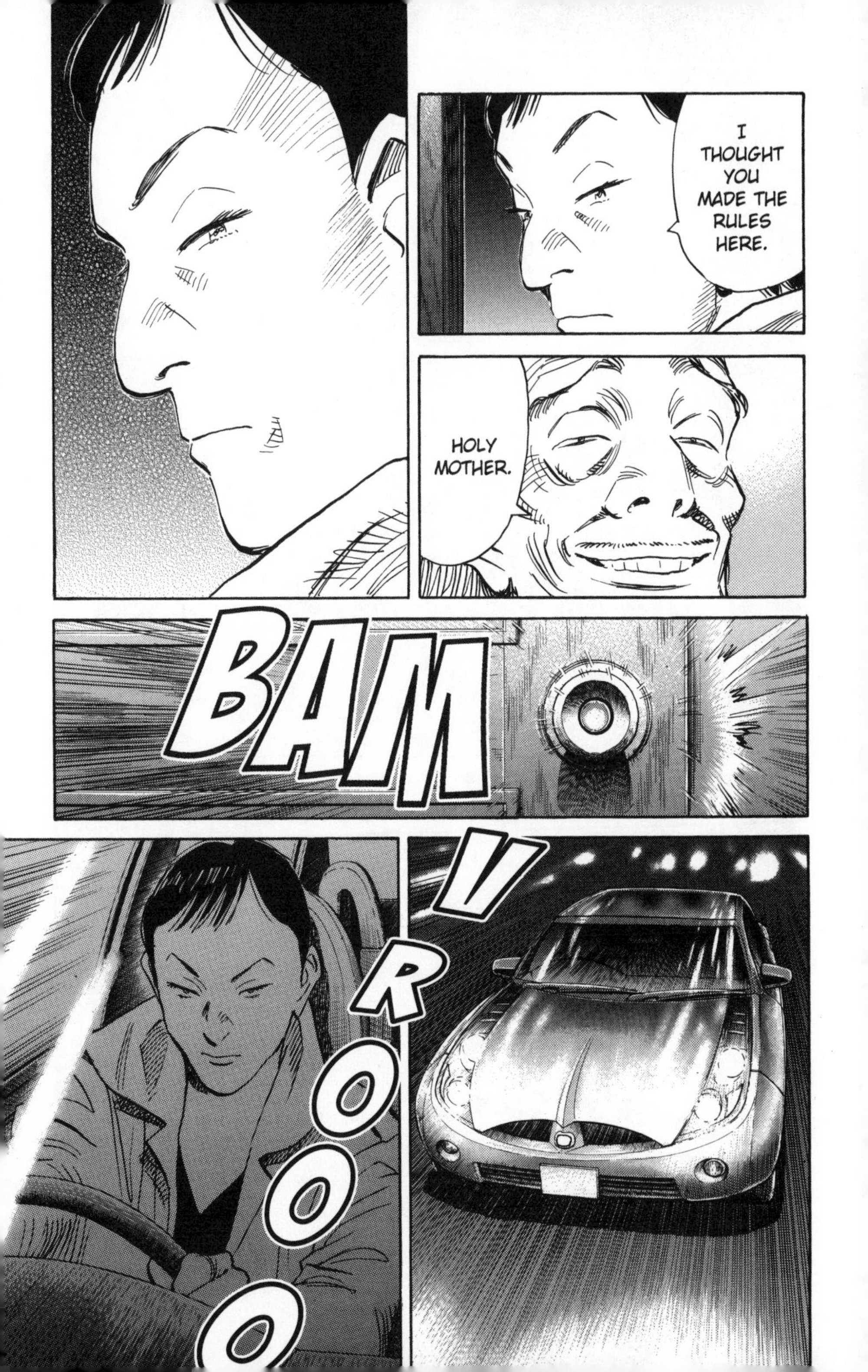
I THOUGHT YOU MADE THE RULES HERE.
HOLY MOTHER.
BAM
VROOOO

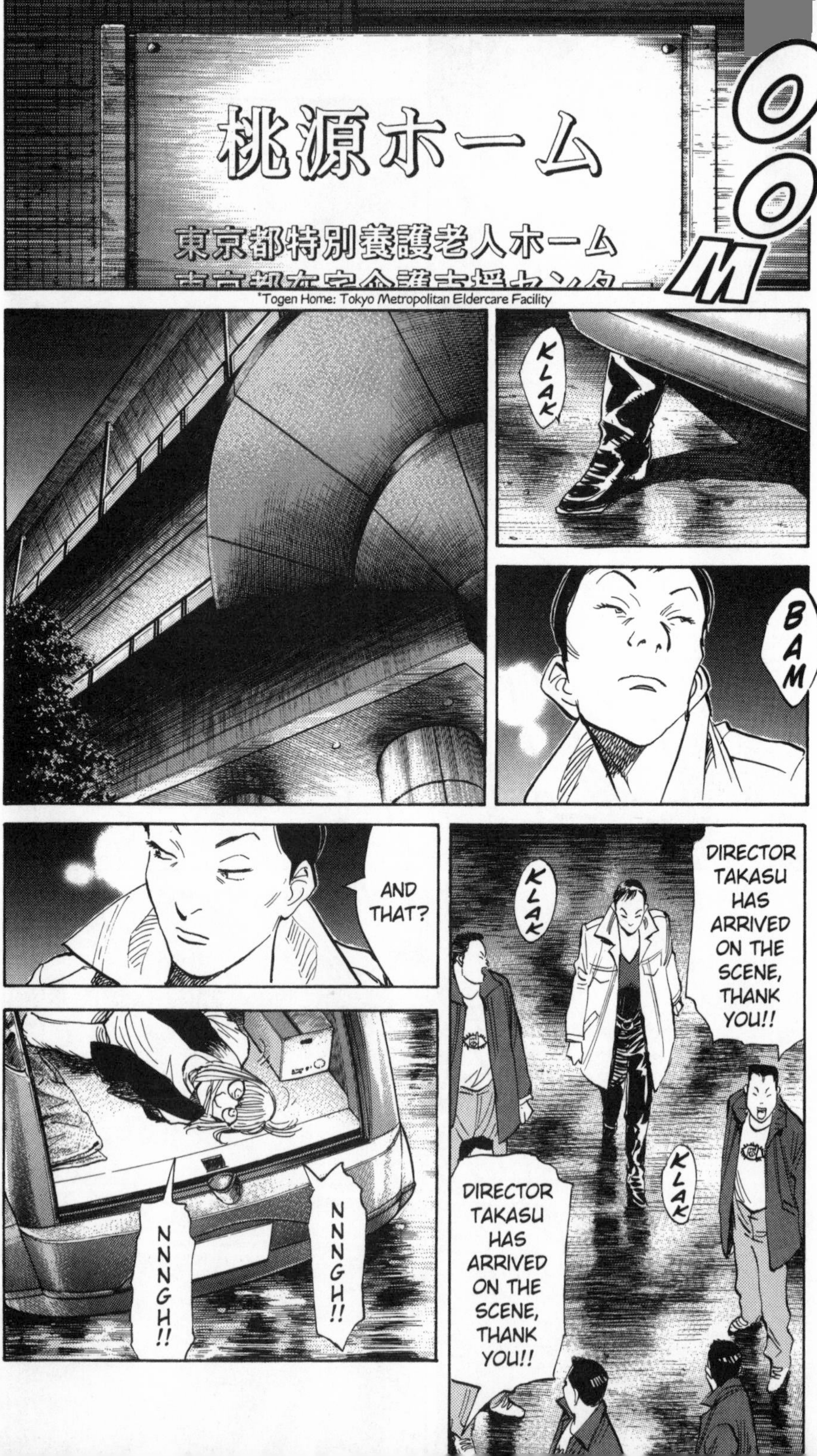
OOOM
桃源ホーム
東京都特別養護老人ホーム
*Togen Home: Tokyo Metropolitan Eldercare Facility
KLAK
BAM
DIRECTOR TAKASU HAS ARRIVED ON THE SCENE, THANK YOU!!
KLAK
KLAK
DIRECTOR TAKASU HAS ARRIVED ON THE SCENE, THANK YOU!!
AND THAT?
NNNGH!!
NNNGH!!

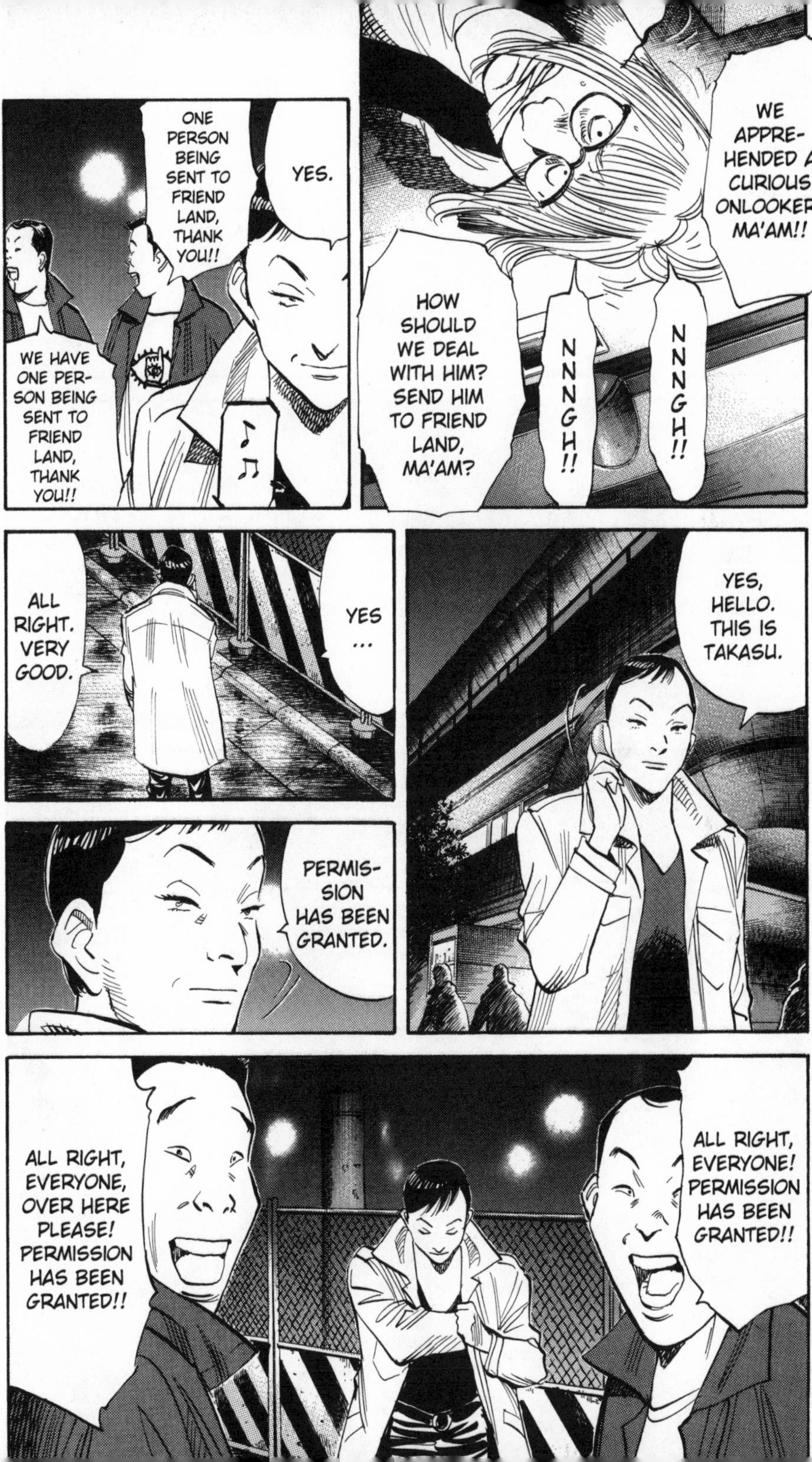
WE APPREHENDED A CURIOUS ONLOOKER, MA'AM!!
NNNGH!!
NNNGH!!
HOW SHOULD WE DEAL WITH HIM? SEND HIM TO FRIEND LAND, MA'AM?
YES.
ONE PERSON BEING SENT TO FRIEND LAND, THANK YOU!!
WE HAVE ONE PERSON BEING SENT TO FRIEND LAND, THANK YOU!!
YES, HELLO. THIS IS TAKASU.
YES ...
ALL RIGHT. VERY GOOD.
PERMISSION HAS BEEN GRANTED.
ALL RIGHT, EVERYONE! PERMISSION HAS BEEN GRANTED!!
ALL RIGHT, EVERYONE, OVER HERE PLEASE! PERMISSION HAS BEEN GRANTED!!

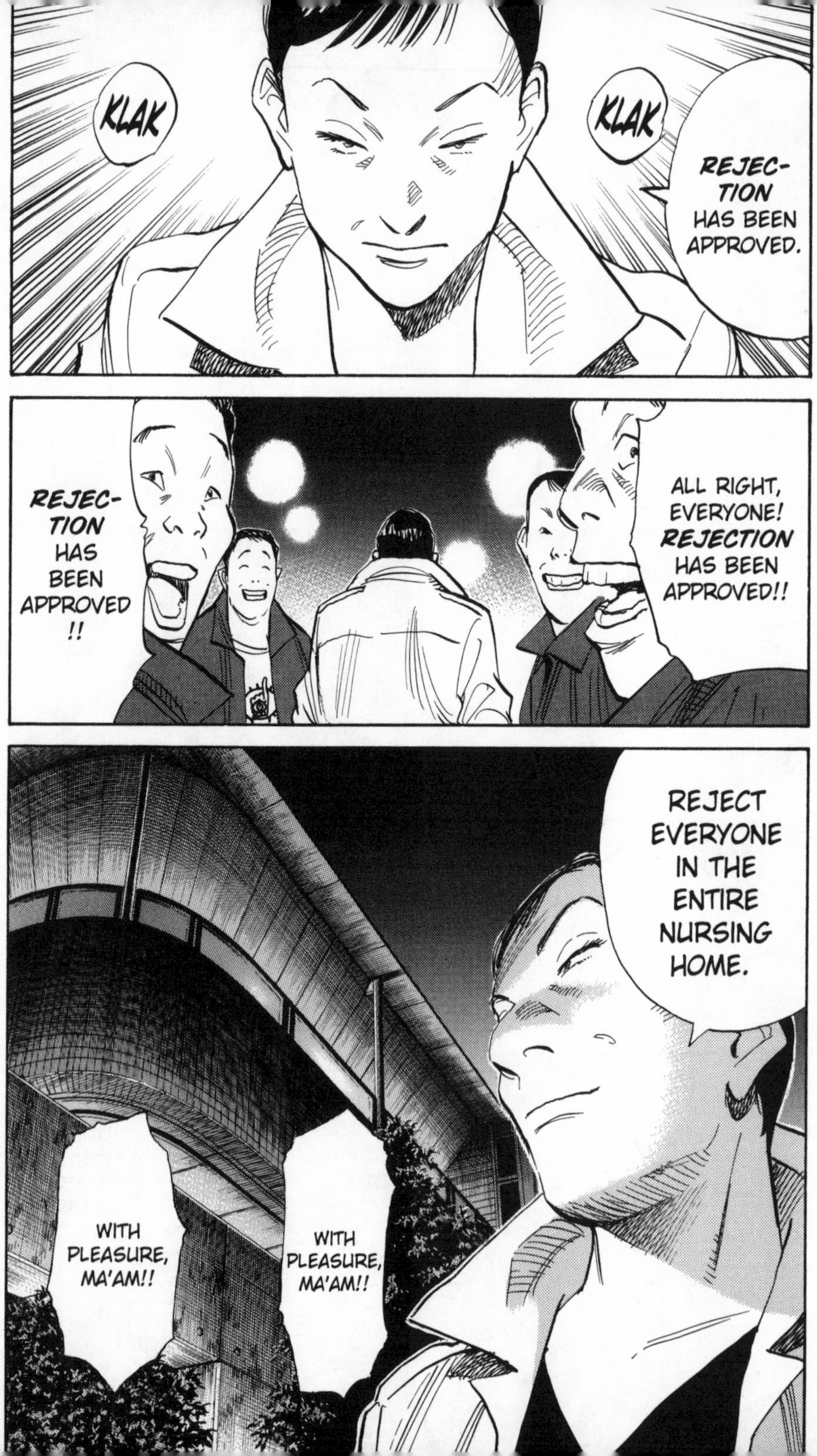

REJECTION HAS BEEN APPROVED.
KLAK
KLAK
ALL RIGHT, EVERYONE! REJECTION HAS BEEN APPROVED!!
REJECTION HAS BEEN APPROVED!!
REJECT EVERYONE IN THE ENTIRE NURSING HOME.
WITH PLEASURE, MA'AM!!
WITH PLEASURE, MA'AM!!

Chapter 4 Old Acquaintance

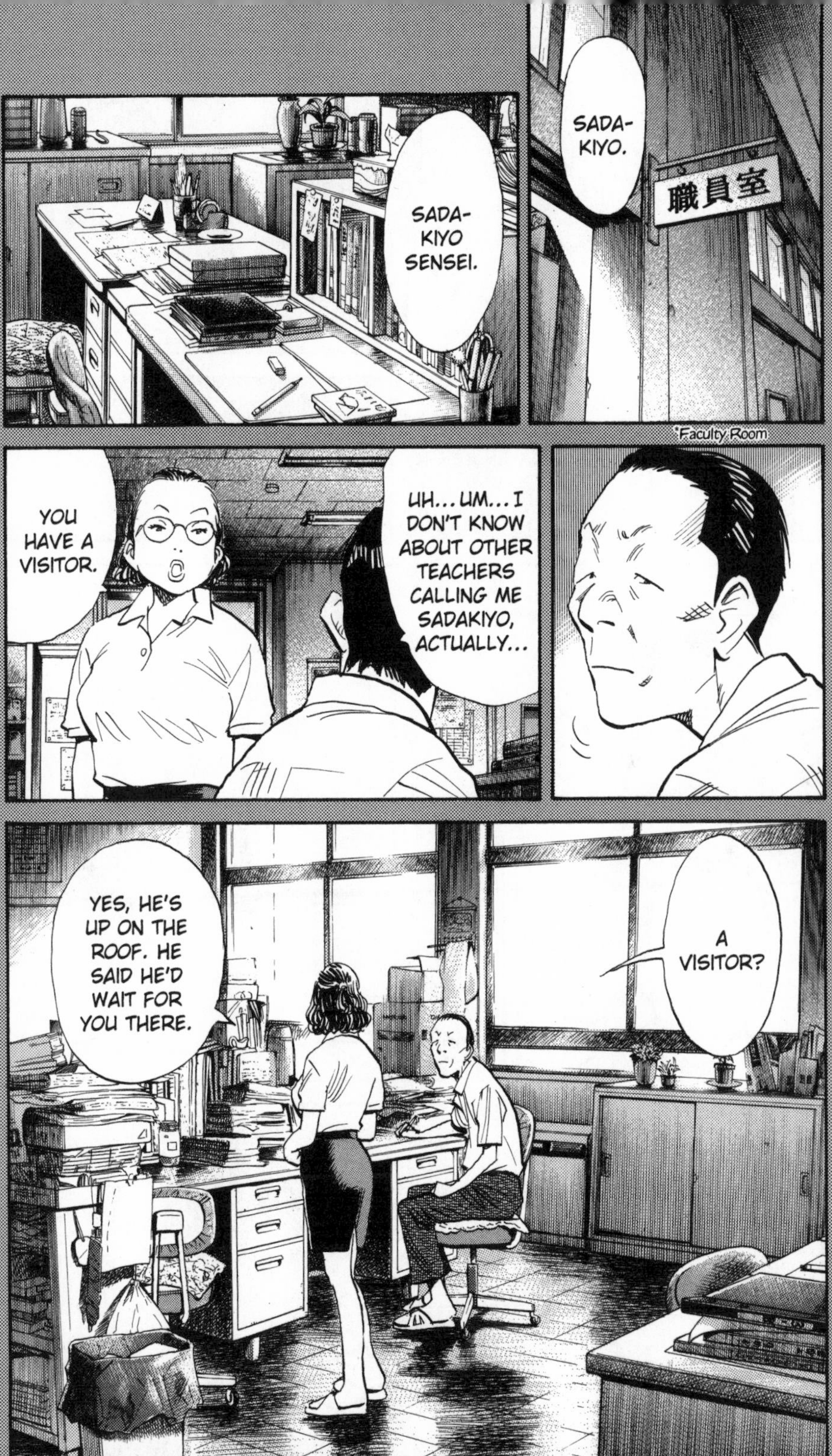
SADA-KIYO.
職員室
*Faculty Room
SADA-KIYO SENSEI.
UH… UM… I DON'T KNOW ABOUT OTHER TEACHERS CALLING ME SADAKIYO, ACTUALLY…
YOU HAVE A VISITOR.
A VISITOR?
YES, HE'S UP ON THE ROOF. HE SAID HE'D WAIT FOR YOU THERE.

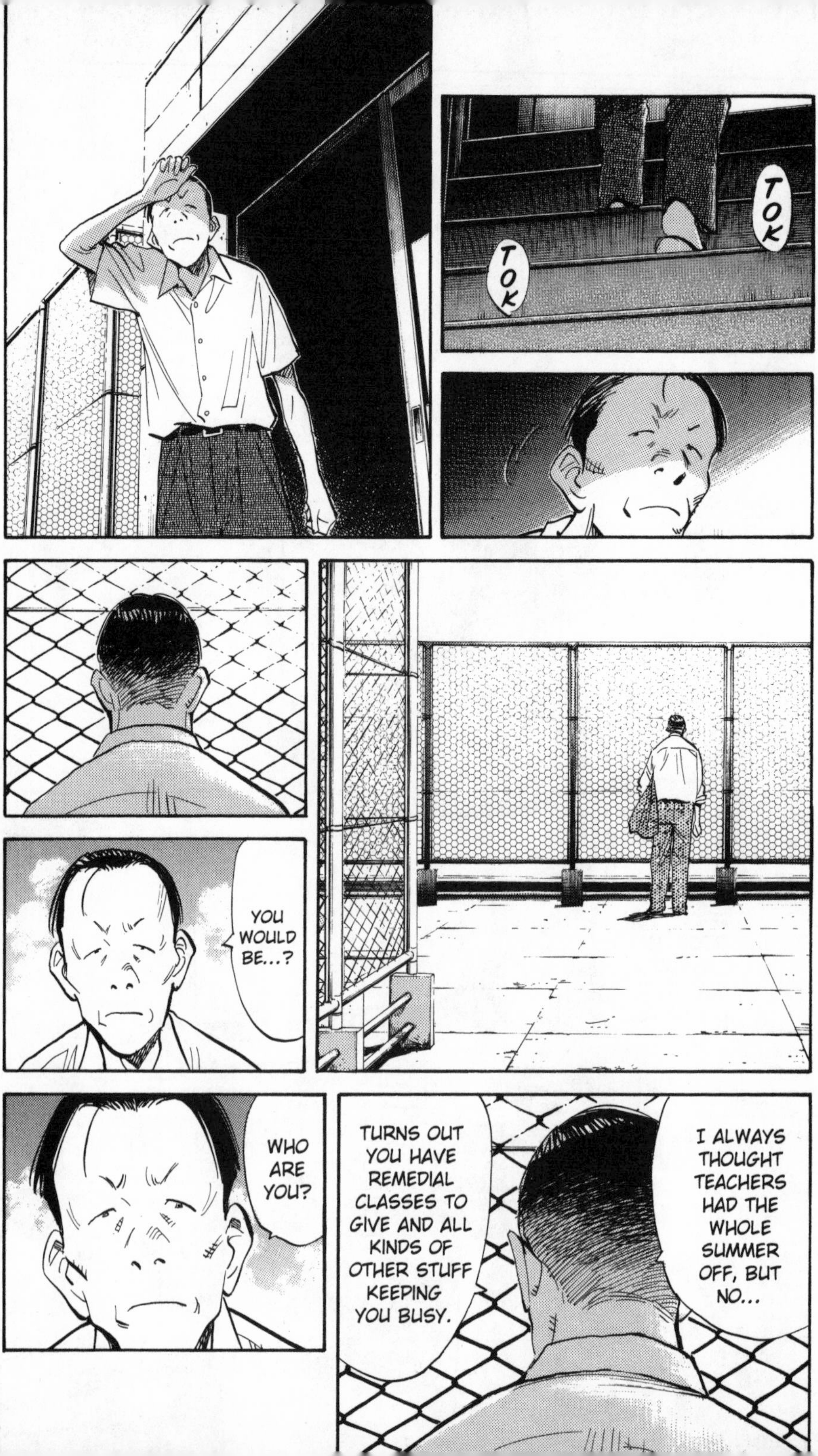
TOK
TOK
YOU WOULD BE...?
I ALWAYS THOUGHT TEACHERS HAD THE WHOLE SUMMER OFF, BUT NO...
TURNS OUT YOU HAVE REMEDIAL CLASSES TO GIVE AND ALL KINDS OF OTHER STUFF KEEPING YOU BUSY.
WHO ARE YOU?

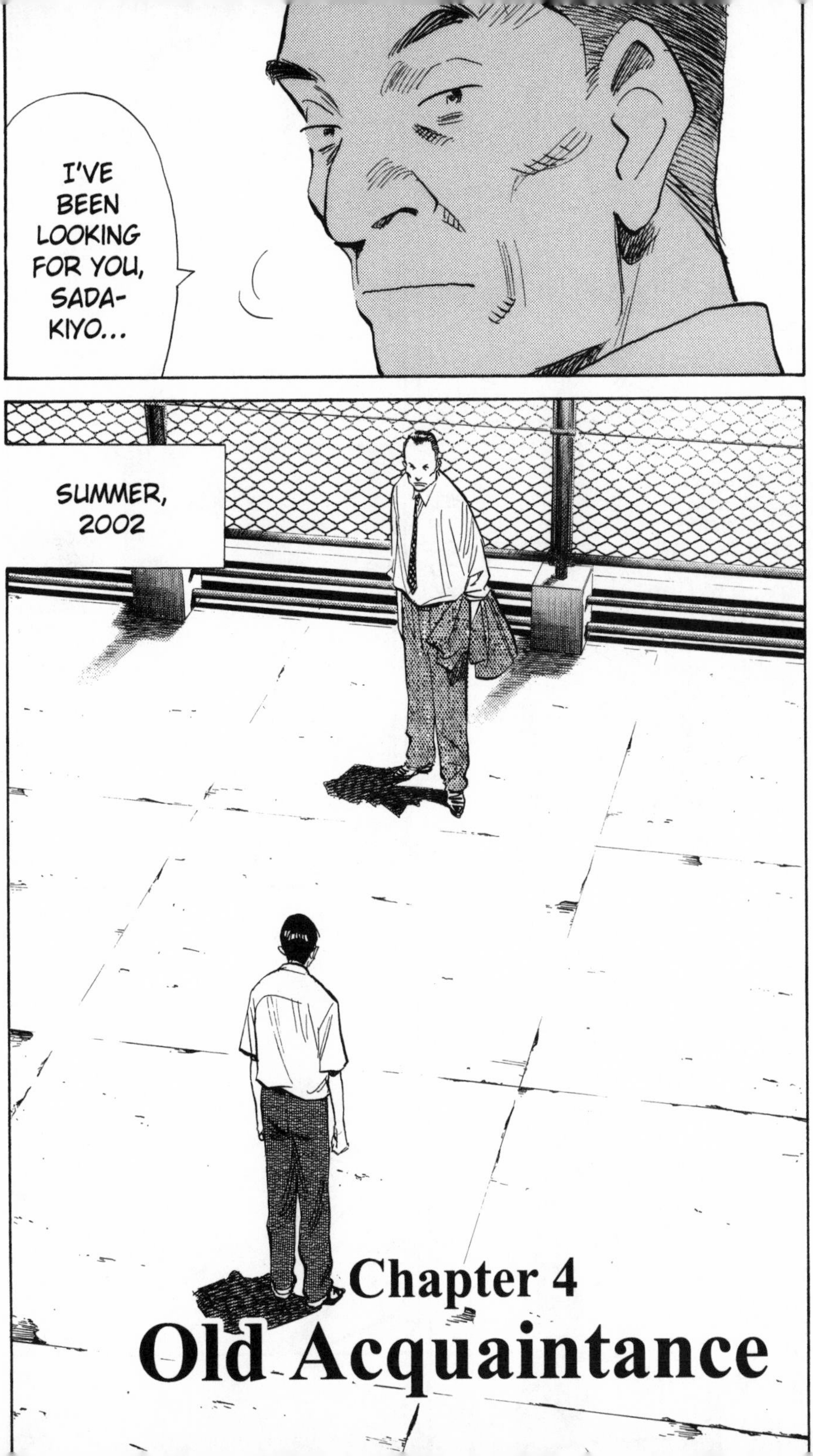
I'VE BEEN LOOKING FOR YOU, SADA-KIYO...
SUMMER, 2002
Chapter 4
Old Acquaintance

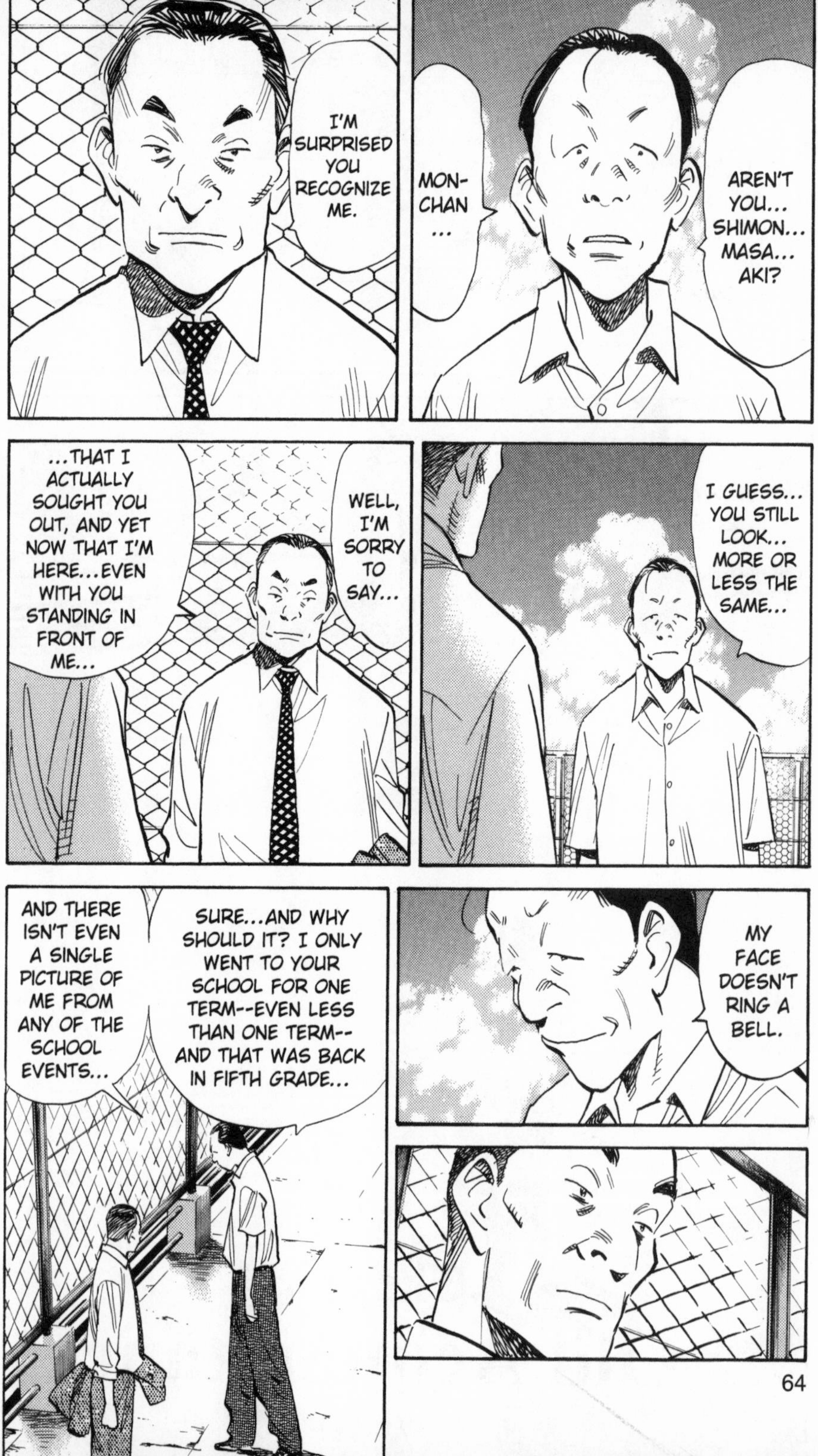
AREN'T YOU... SHIMON... MASA... AKI?
MON-CHAN...
I'M SURPRISED YOU RECOGNIZE ME.
I GUESS... YOU STILL LOOK... MORE OR LESS THE SAME...
WELL, I'M SORRY TO SAY...
...THAT I ACTUALLY SOUGHT YOU OUT, AND YET NOW THAT I'M HERE...EVEN WITH YOU STANDING IN FRONT OF ME...
MY FACE DOESN'T RING A BELL.
SURE...AND WHY SHOULD IT? I ONLY WENT TO YOUR SCHOOL FOR ONE TERM--EVEN LESS THAN ONE TERM--AND THAT WAS BACK IN FIFTH GRADE...
AND THERE ISN'T EVEN A SINGLE PICTURE OF ME FROM ANY OF THE SCHOOL EVENTS...

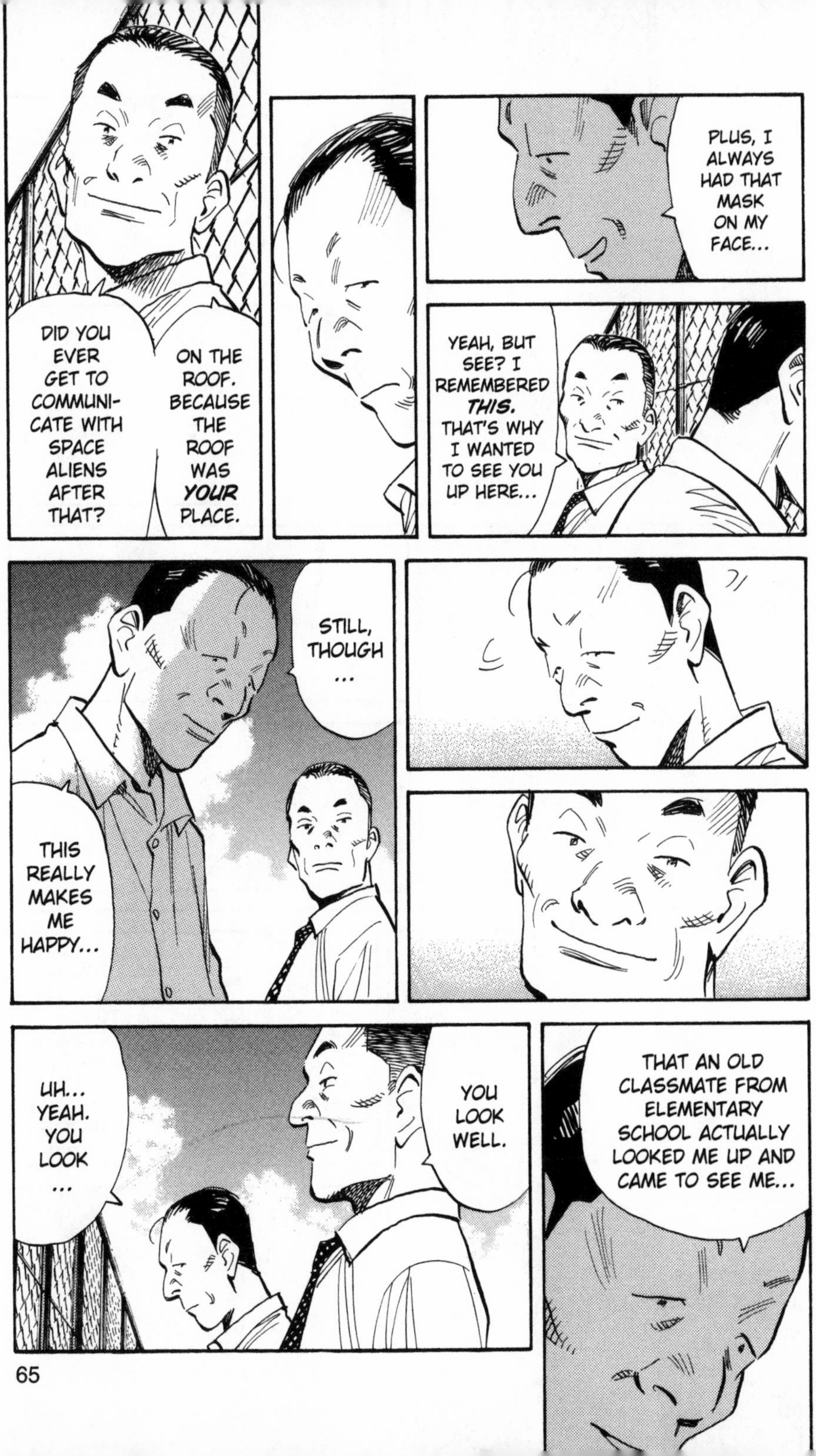
PLUS, I ALWAYS HAD THAT MASK ON MY FACE...
YEAH, BUT SEE? I REMEMBERED *THIS.* THAT'S WHY I WANTED TO SEE YOU UP HERE...
ON THE ROOF. BECAUSE THE ROOF WAS *YOUR* PLACE.
DID YOU EVER GET TO COMMUNI-CATE WITH SPACE ALIENS AFTER THAT?
STILL, THOUGH...
THIS REALLY MAKES ME HAPPY...
THAT AN OLD CLASSMATE FROM ELEMENTARY SCHOOL ACTUALLY LOOKED ME UP AND CAME TO SEE ME...
YOU LOOK WELL.
UH... YEAH. YOU LOOK ...

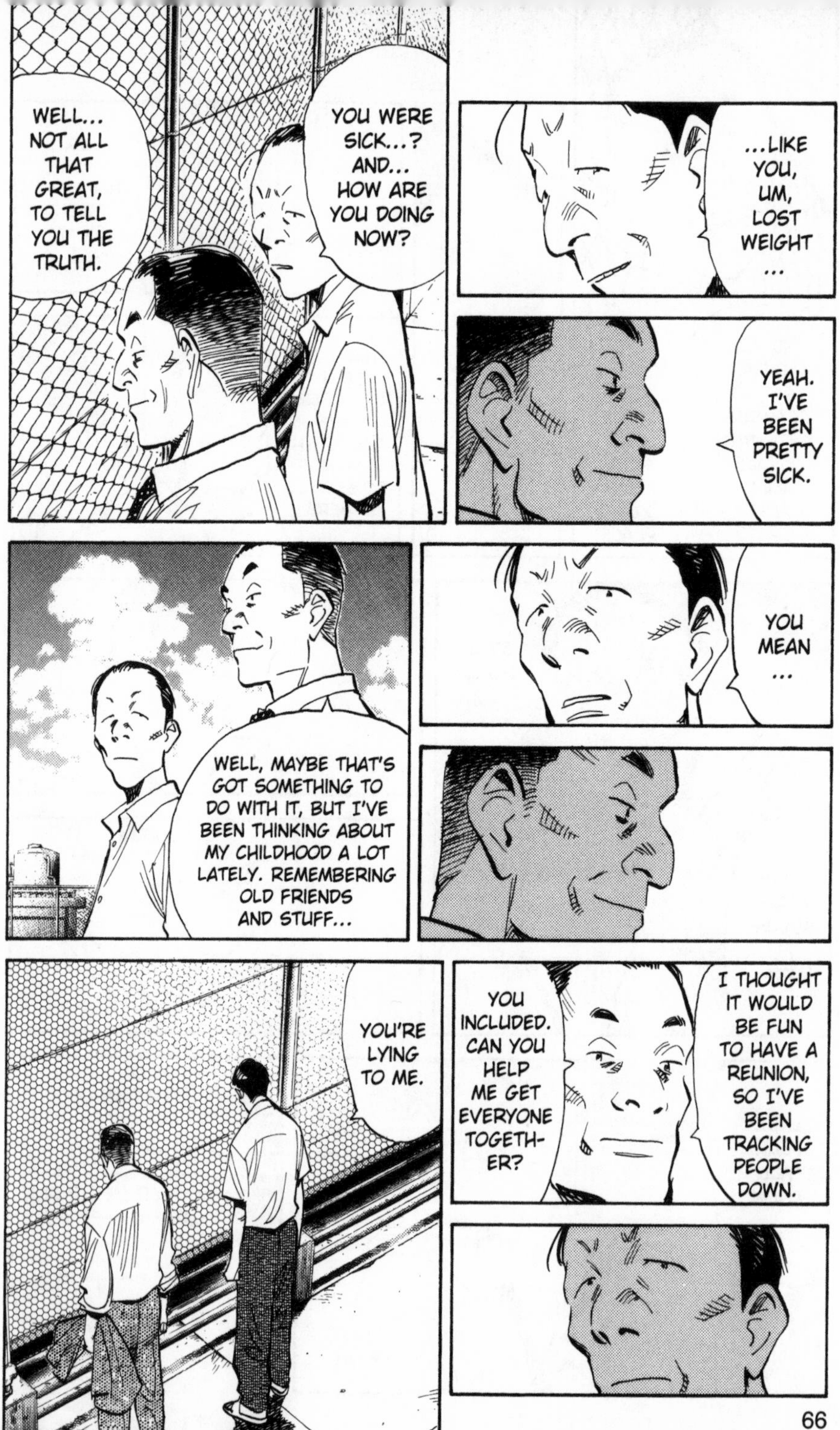
...LIKE YOU, UM, LOST WEIGHT...
YEAH. I'VE BEEN PRETTY SICK.
YOU WERE SICK...? AND... HOW ARE YOU DOING NOW?
WELL... NOT ALL THAT GREAT, TO TELL YOU THE TRUTH.
YOU MEAN...
WELL, MAYBE THAT'S GOT SOMETHING TO DO WITH IT, BUT I'VE BEEN THINKING ABOUT MY CHILDHOOD A LOT LATELY. REMEMBERING OLD FRIENDS AND STUFF...
I THOUGHT IT WOULD BE FUN TO HAVE A REUNION, SO I'VE BEEN TRACKING PEOPLE DOWN.
YOU INCLUDED. CAN YOU HELP ME GET EVERYONE TOGETH-ER?
YOU'RE LYING TO ME.

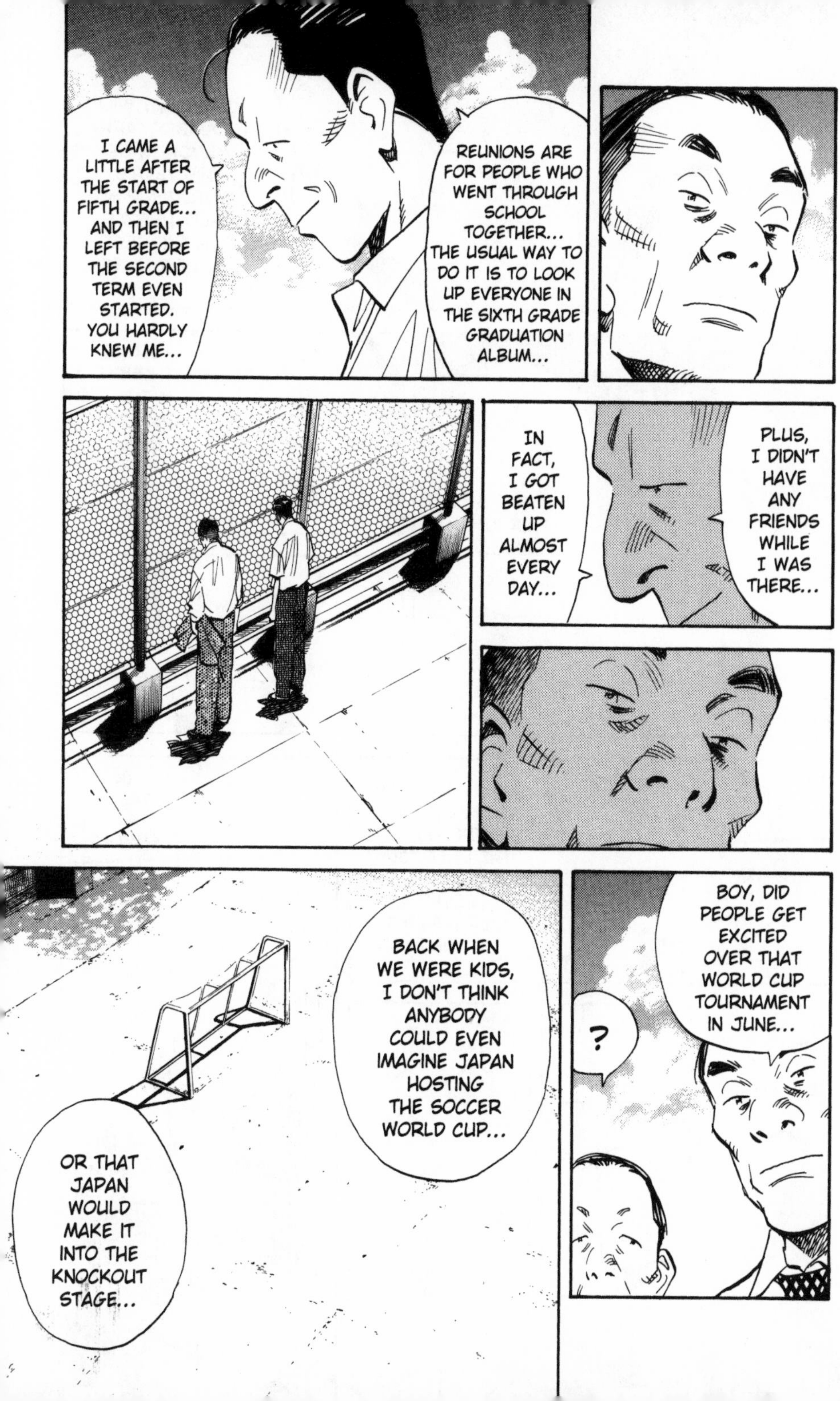
REUNIONS ARE FOR PEOPLE WHO WENT THROUGH SCHOOL TOGETHER... THE USUAL WAY TO DO IT IS TO LOOK UP EVERYONE IN THE SIXTH GRADE GRADUATION ALBUM...
I CAME A LITTLE AFTER THE START OF FIFTH GRADE... AND THEN I LEFT BEFORE THE SECOND TERM EVEN STARTED. YOU HARDLY KNEW ME...
PLUS, I DIDN'T HAVE ANY FRIENDS WHILE I WAS THERE...
IN FACT, I GOT BEATEN UP ALMOST EVERY DAY...
BOY, DID PEOPLE GET EXCITED OVER THAT WORLD CUP TOURNAMENT IN JUNE...
?
BACK WHEN WE WERE KIDS, I DON'T THINK ANYBODY COULD EVEN IMAGINE JAPAN HOSTING THE SOCCER WORLD CUP...
OR THAT JAPAN WOULD MAKE IT INTO THE KNOCKOUT STAGE...

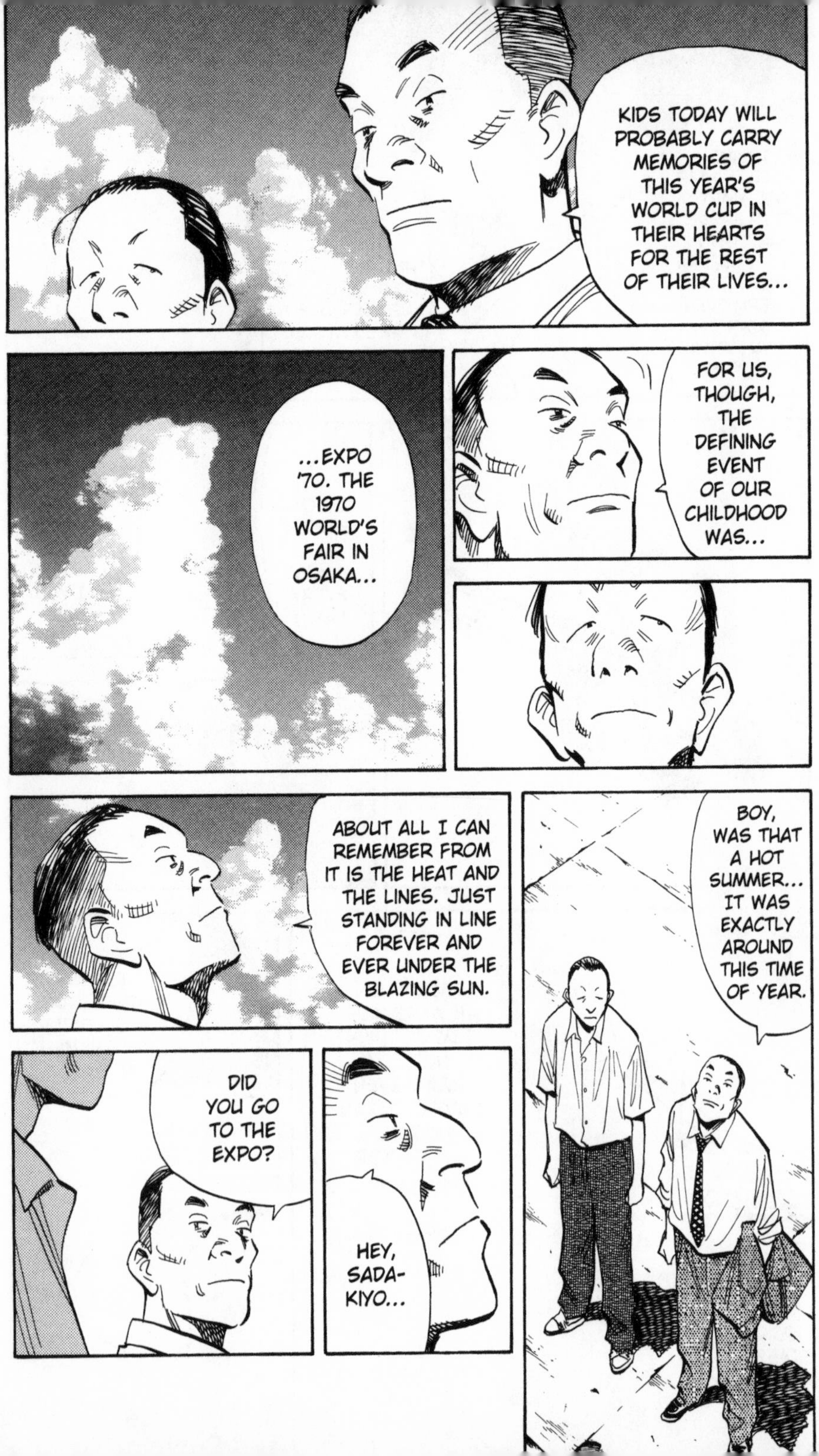
KIDS TODAY WILL PROBABLY CARRY MEMORIES OF THIS YEAR'S WORLD CUP IN THEIR HEARTS FOR THE REST OF THEIR LIVES...
FOR US, THOUGH, THE DEFINING EVENT OF OUR CHILDHOOD WAS...
...EXPO '70. THE 1970 WORLD'S FAIR IN OSAKA...
BOY, WAS THAT A HOT SUMMER... IT WAS EXACTLY AROUND THIS TIME OF YEAR.
ABOUT ALL I CAN REMEMBER FROM IT IS THE HEAT AND THE LINES. JUST STANDING IN LINE FOREVER AND EVER UNDER THE BLAZING SUN.
HEY, SADA-KIYO...
DID YOU GO TO THE EXPO?

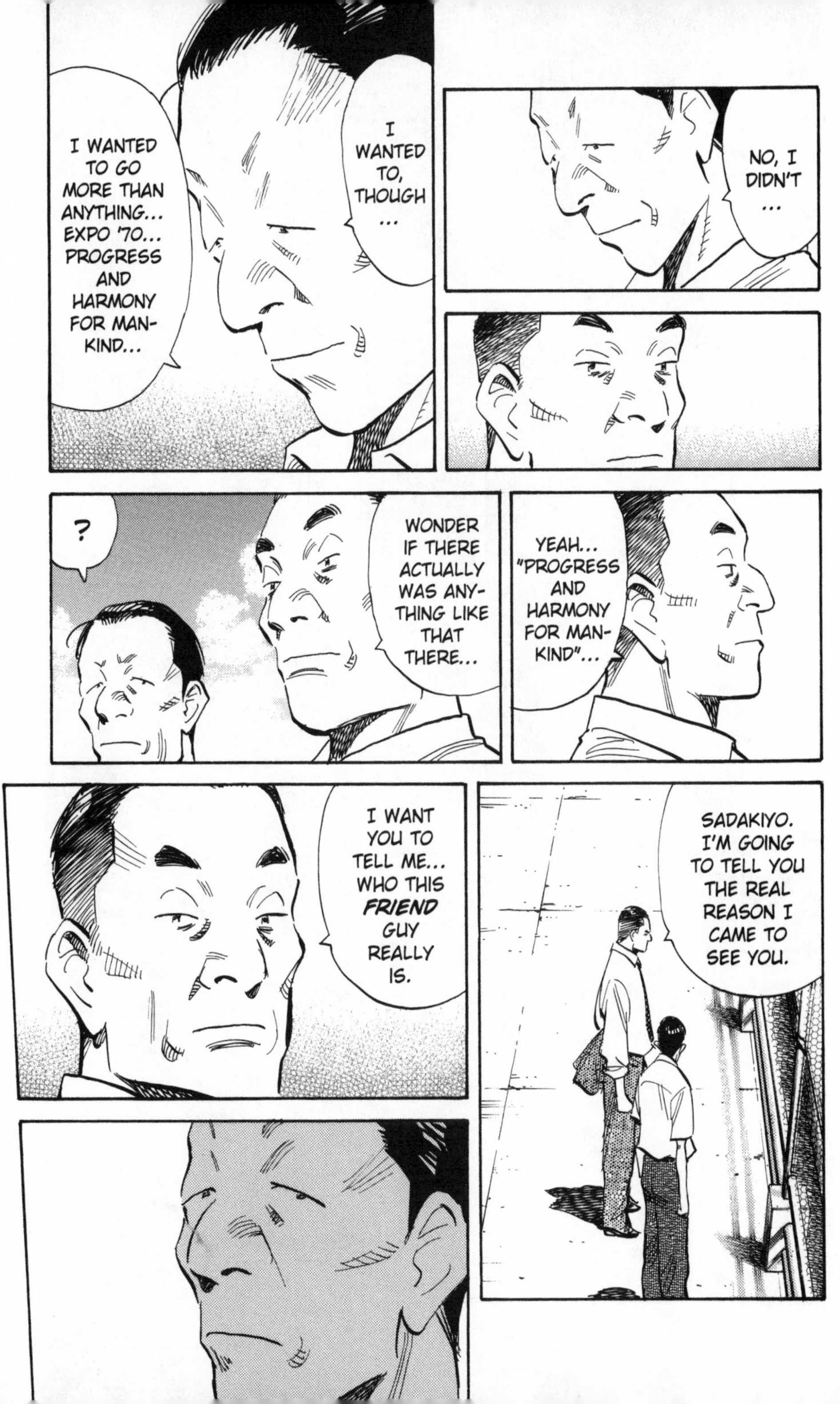
NO, I DIDN'T ...
I WANTED TO, THOUGH ...
I WANTED TO GO MORE THAN ANYTHING... EXPO '70... PROGRESS AND HARMONY FOR MAN-KIND...
YEAH... "PROGRESS AND HARMONY FOR MAN-KIND"...
WONDER IF THERE ACTUALLY WAS ANY-THING LIKE THAT THERE...
?
SADAKIYO. I'M GOING TO TELL YOU THE REAL REASON I CAME TO SEE YOU.
I WANT YOU TO TELL ME... WHO THIS *FRIEND* GUY REALLY IS.

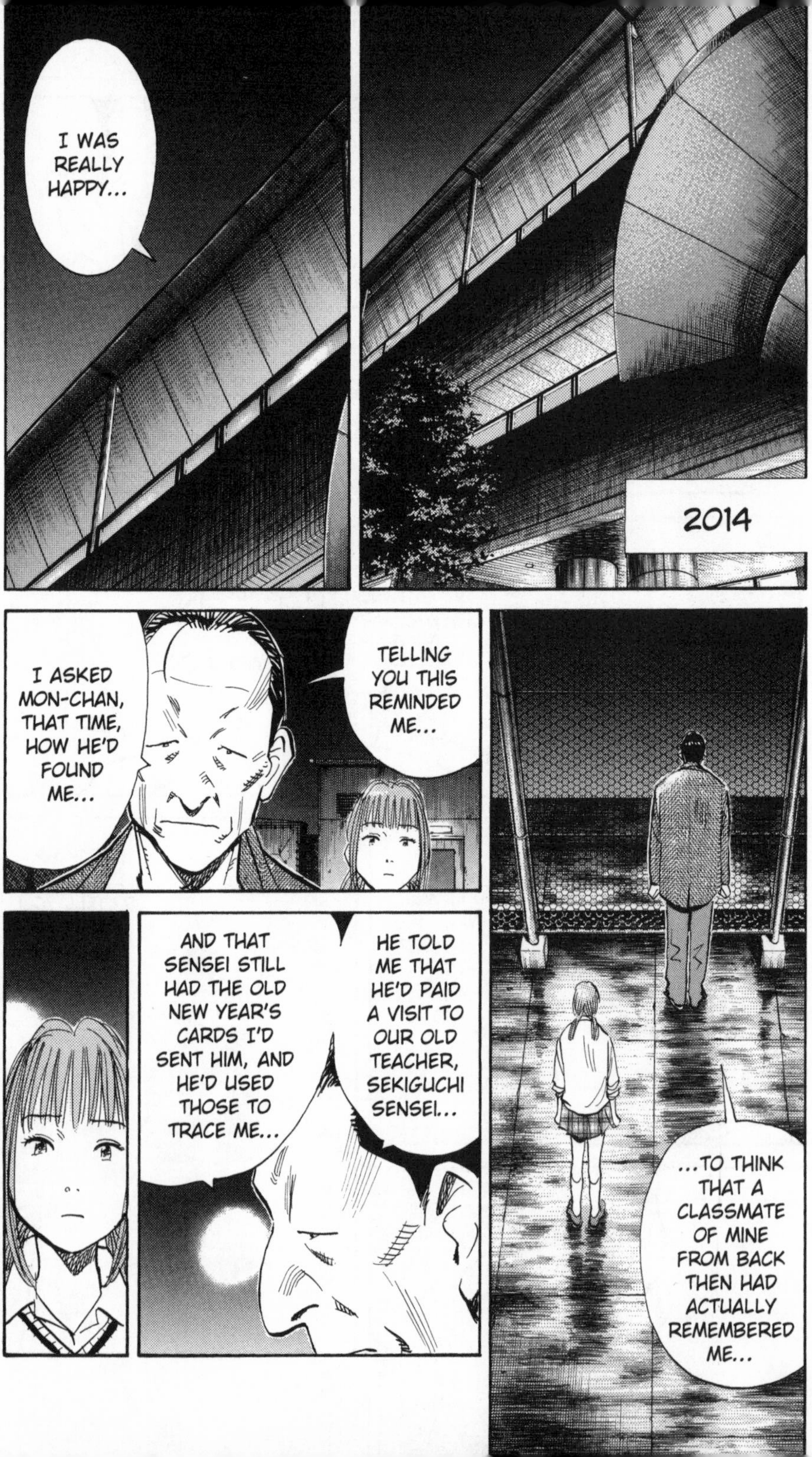
2014
I WAS REALLY HAPPY...
...TO THINK THAT A CLASSMATE OF MINE FROM BACK THEN HAD ACTUALLY REMEMBERED ME...
TELLING YOU THIS REMINDED ME...
I ASKED MON-CHAN, THAT TIME, HOW HE'D FOUND ME...
HE TOLD ME THAT HE'D PAID A VISIT TO OUR OLD TEACHER, SEKIGUCHI SENSEI...
AND THAT SENSEI STILL HAD THE OLD NEW YEAR'S CARDS I'D SENT HIM, AND HE'D USED THOSE TO TRACE ME...

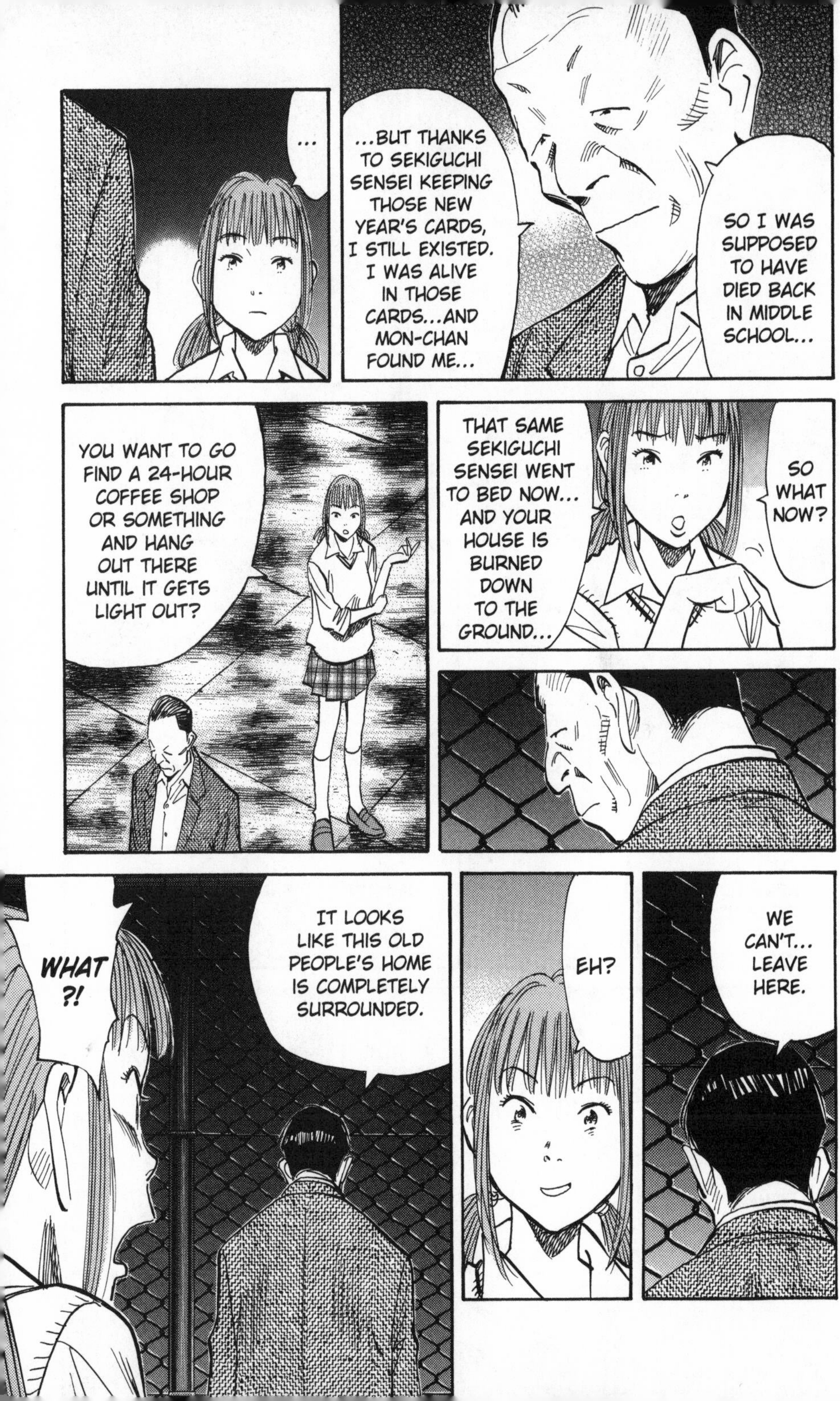
SO I WAS SUPPOSED TO HAVE DIED BACK IN MIDDLE SCHOOL...
...BUT THANKS TO SEKIGUCHI SENSEI KEEPING THOSE NEW YEAR'S CARDS, I STILL EXISTED. I WAS ALIVE IN THOSE CARDS...AND MON-CHAN FOUND ME...
...
SO WHAT NOW?
THAT SAME SEKIGUCHI SENSEI WENT TO BED NOW... AND YOUR HOUSE IS BURNED DOWN TO THE GROUND...
YOU WANT TO GO FIND A 24-HOUR COFFEE SHOP OR SOMETHING AND HANG OUT THERE UNTIL IT GETS LIGHT OUT?
WE CAN'T... LEAVE HERE.
EH?
IT LOOKS LIKE THIS OLD PEOPLE'S HOME IS COMPLETELY SURROUNDED.
WHAT ?!

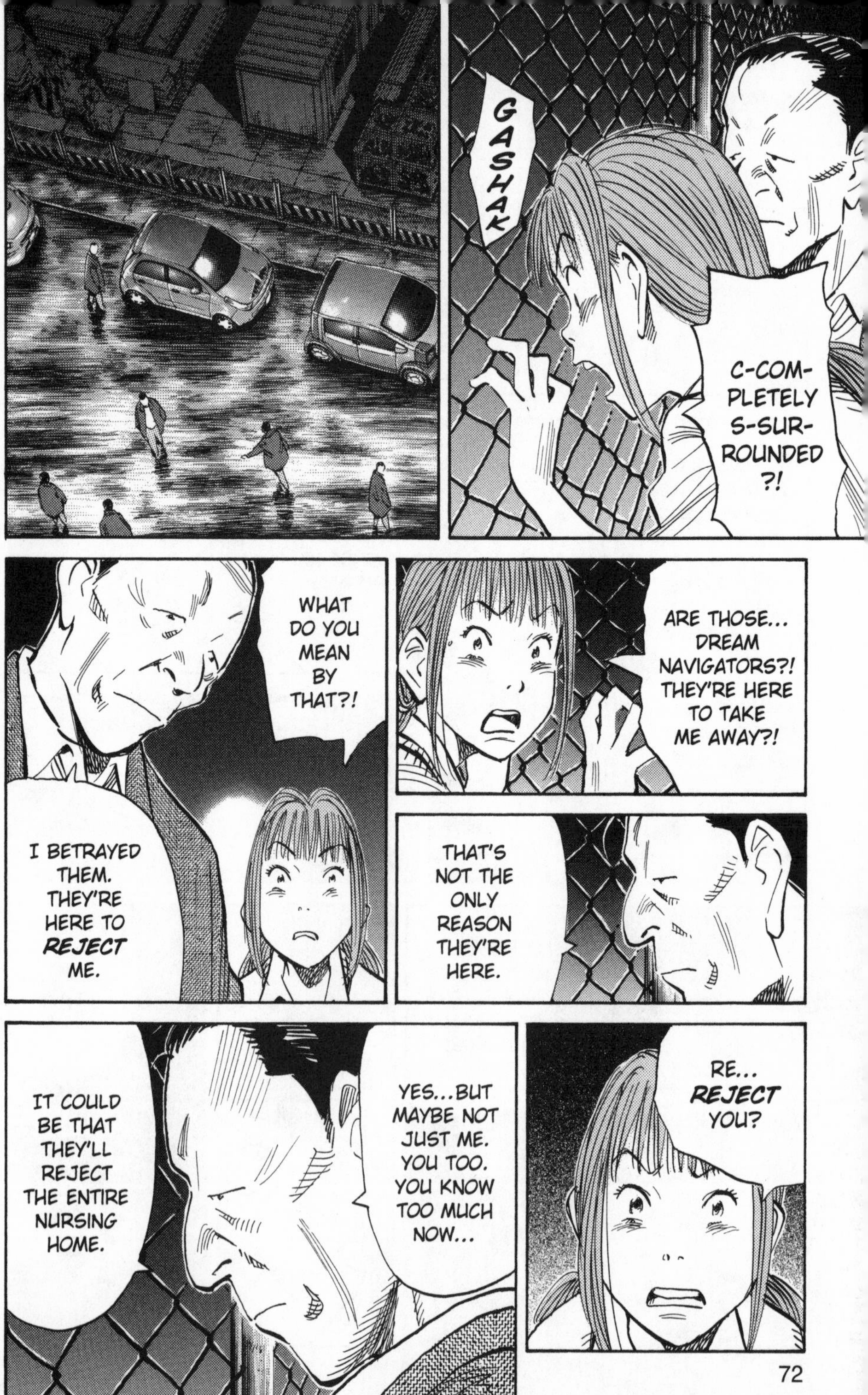
GASHAK
C-COMPLETELY S-SURROUNDED?!
ARE THOSE... DREAM NAVIGATORS?! THEY'RE HERE TO TAKE ME AWAY?!
THAT'S NOT THE ONLY REASON THEY'RE HERE.
WHAT DO YOU MEAN BY THAT?!
I BETRAYED THEM. THEY'RE HERE TO *REJECT* ME.
RE... *REJECT* YOU?
YES...BUT MAYBE NOT JUST ME. YOU TOO. YOU KNOW TOO MUCH NOW...
IT COULD BE THAT THEY'LL REJECT THE ENTIRE NURSING HOME.

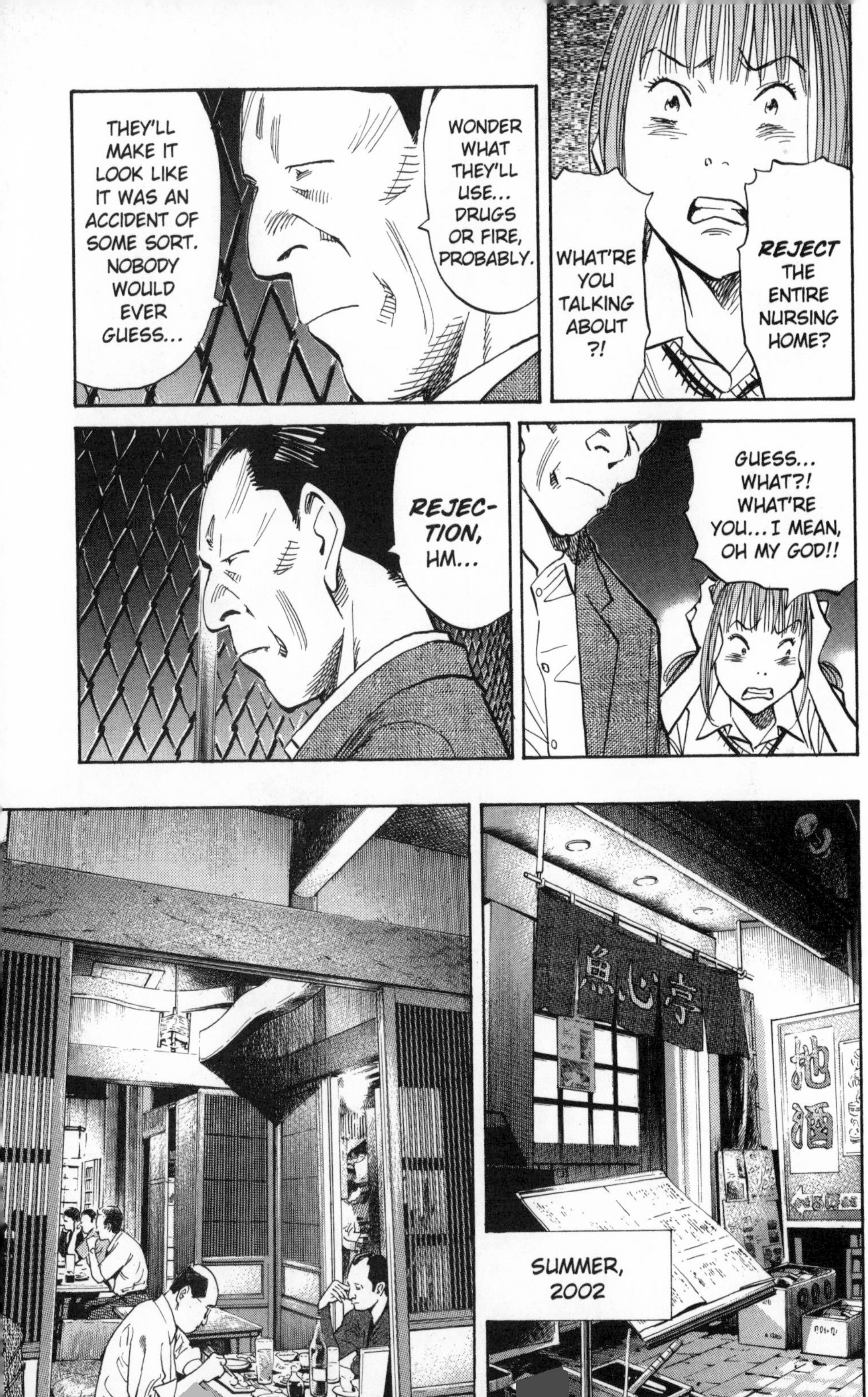
REJECT THE ENTIRE NURSING HOME?
WHAT'RE YOU TALKING ABOUT ?!
WONDER WHAT THEY'LL USE... DRUGS OR FIRE, PROBABLY.
THEY'LL MAKE IT LOOK LIKE IT WAS AN ACCIDENT OF SOME SORT. NOBODY WOULD EVER GUESS...
GUESS... WHAT?! WHAT'RE YOU... I MEAN, OH MY GOD!!
REJECTION, HM...
魚心亭
地酒
SUMMER, 2002

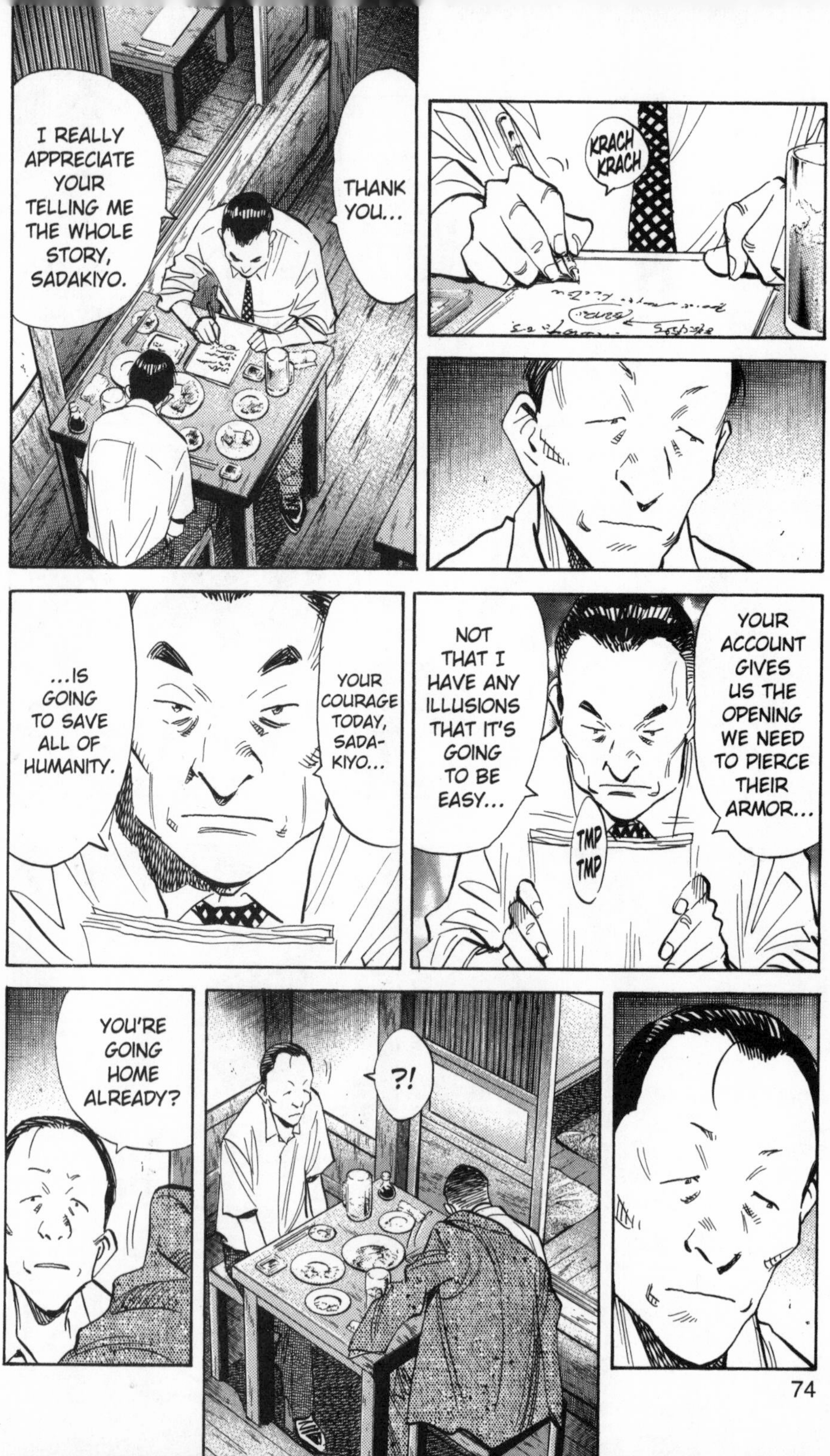
KRACH KRACH
I REALLY APPRECIATE YOUR TELLING ME THE WHOLE STORY, SADAKIYO.
THANK YOU...
YOUR ACCOUNT GIVES US THE OPENING WE NEED TO PIERCE THEIR ARMOR...
NOT THAT I HAVE ANY ILLUSIONS THAT IT'S GOING TO BE EASY...
TMP TMP
YOUR COURAGE TODAY, SADA-KIYO...
...IS GOING TO SAVE ALL OF HUMANITY.
?!
YOU'RE GOING HOME ALREADY?

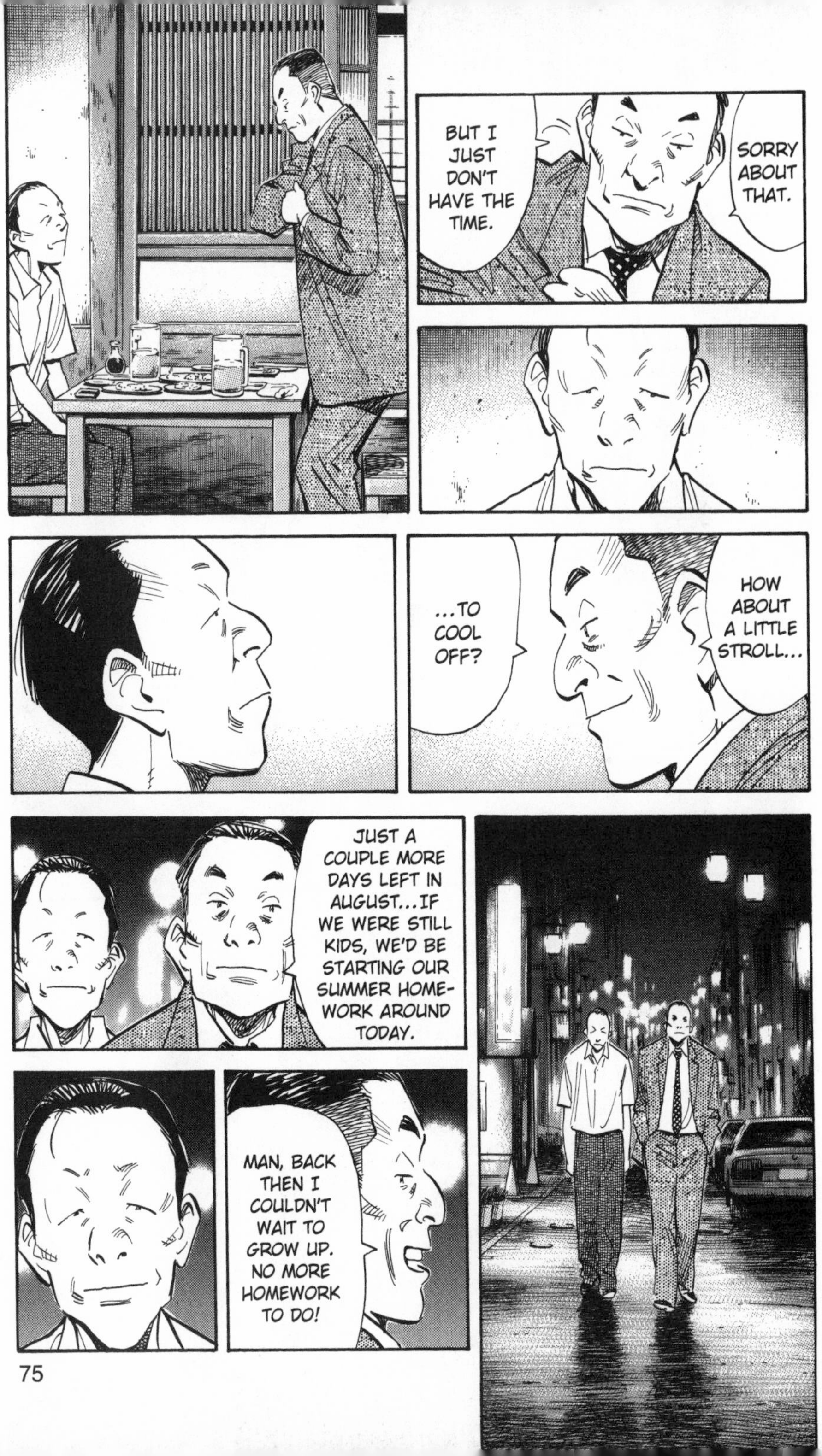
SORRY ABOUT THAT.
BUT I JUST DON'T HAVE THE TIME.
HOW ABOUT A LITTLE STROLL...
...TO COOL OFF?
JUST A COUPLE MORE DAYS LEFT IN AUGUST...IF WE WERE STILL KIDS, WE'D BE STARTING OUR SUMMER HOME-WORK AROUND TODAY.
MAN, BACK THEN I COULDN'T WAIT TO GROW UP. NO MORE HOMEWORK TO DO!

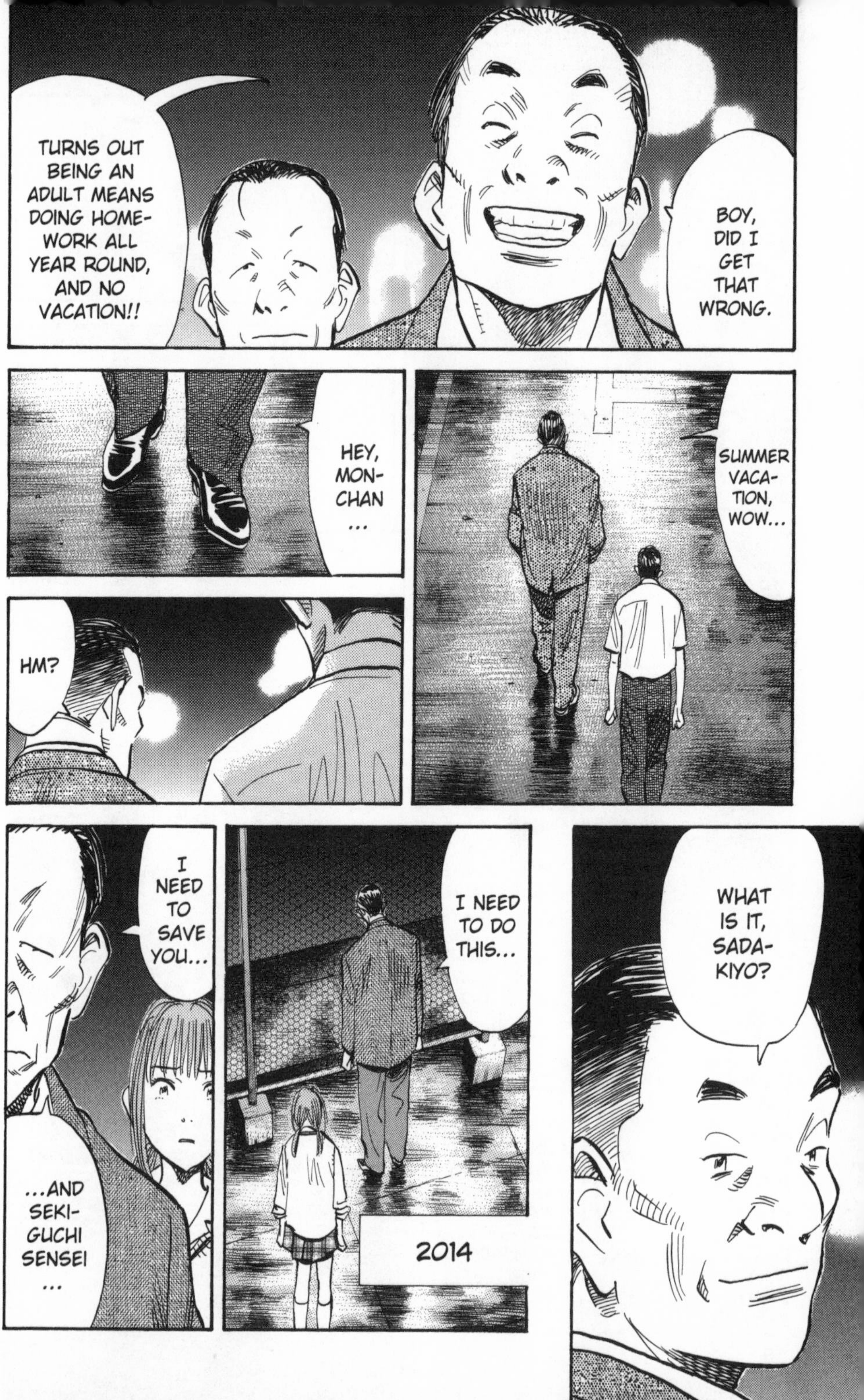
BOY, DID I GET THAT WRONG.
TURNS OUT BEING AN ADULT MEANS DOING HOME-WORK ALL YEAR ROUND, AND NO VACATION!!
SUMMER VACA-TION, WOW...
HEY, MON-CHAN...
HM?
WHAT IS IT, SADA-KIYO?
I NEED TO DO THIS...
2014
I NEED TO SAVE YOU...
...AND SEKI-GUCHI SENSEI...

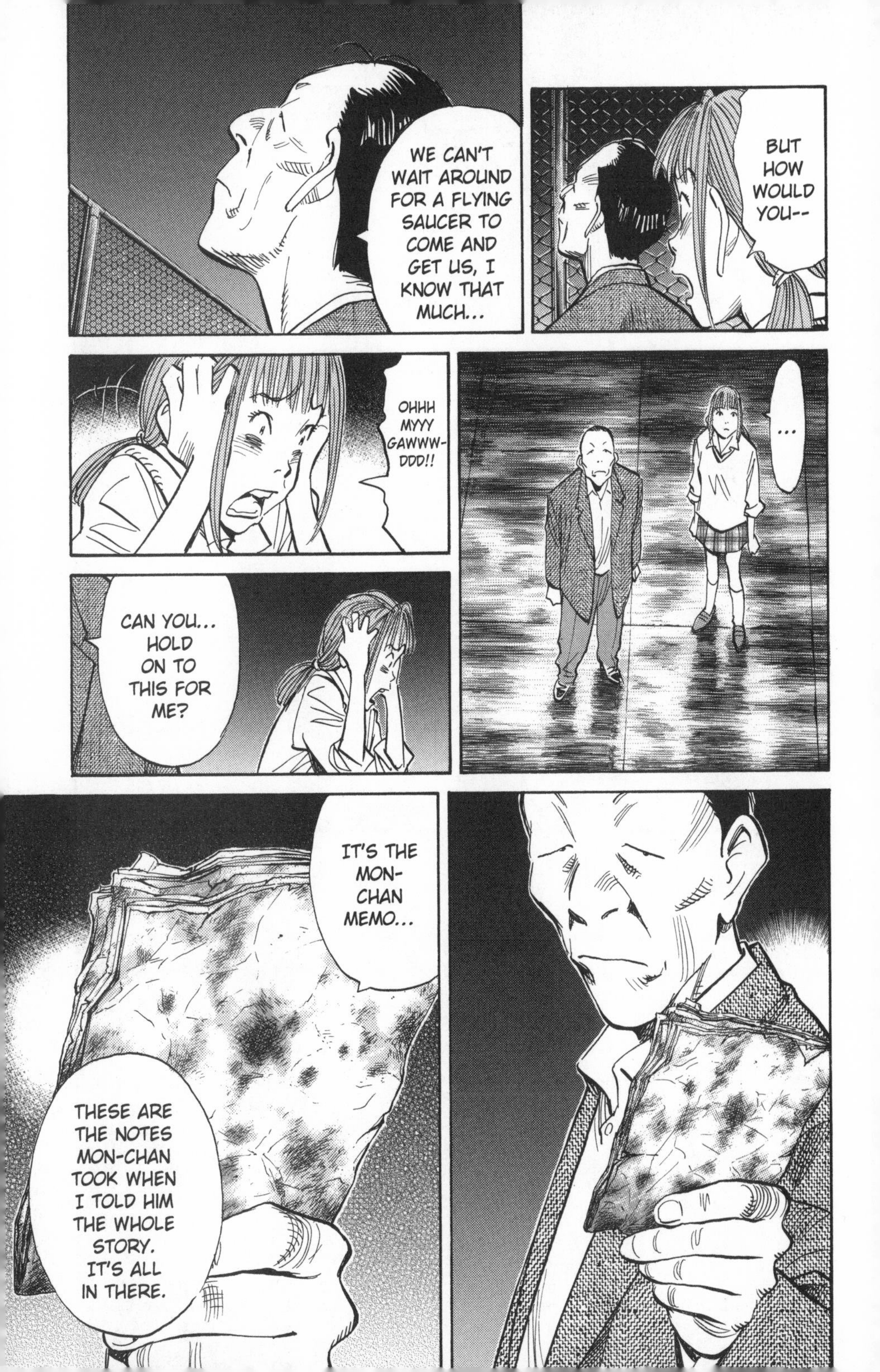
BUT HOW WOULD YOU--
WE CAN'T WAIT AROUND FOR A FLYING SAUCER TO COME AND GET US, I KNOW THAT MUCH...
...
OHHH MYYY GAWWW-DDD!!
CAN YOU... HOLD ON TO THIS FOR ME?
IT'S THE MON-CHAN MEMO...
THESE ARE THE NOTES MON-CHAN TOOK WHEN I TOLD HIM THE WHOLE STORY. IT'S ALL IN THERE.

WHAT?

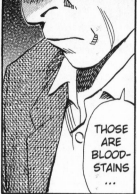

IT'S FALL-ING APART...

AND THERE'S ALL THESE DARK STAINS ALL OVER IT...

THOSE ARE BLOOD-STAINS...

YOU SEE...

I KILLED MON-CHAN THAT NIGHT.

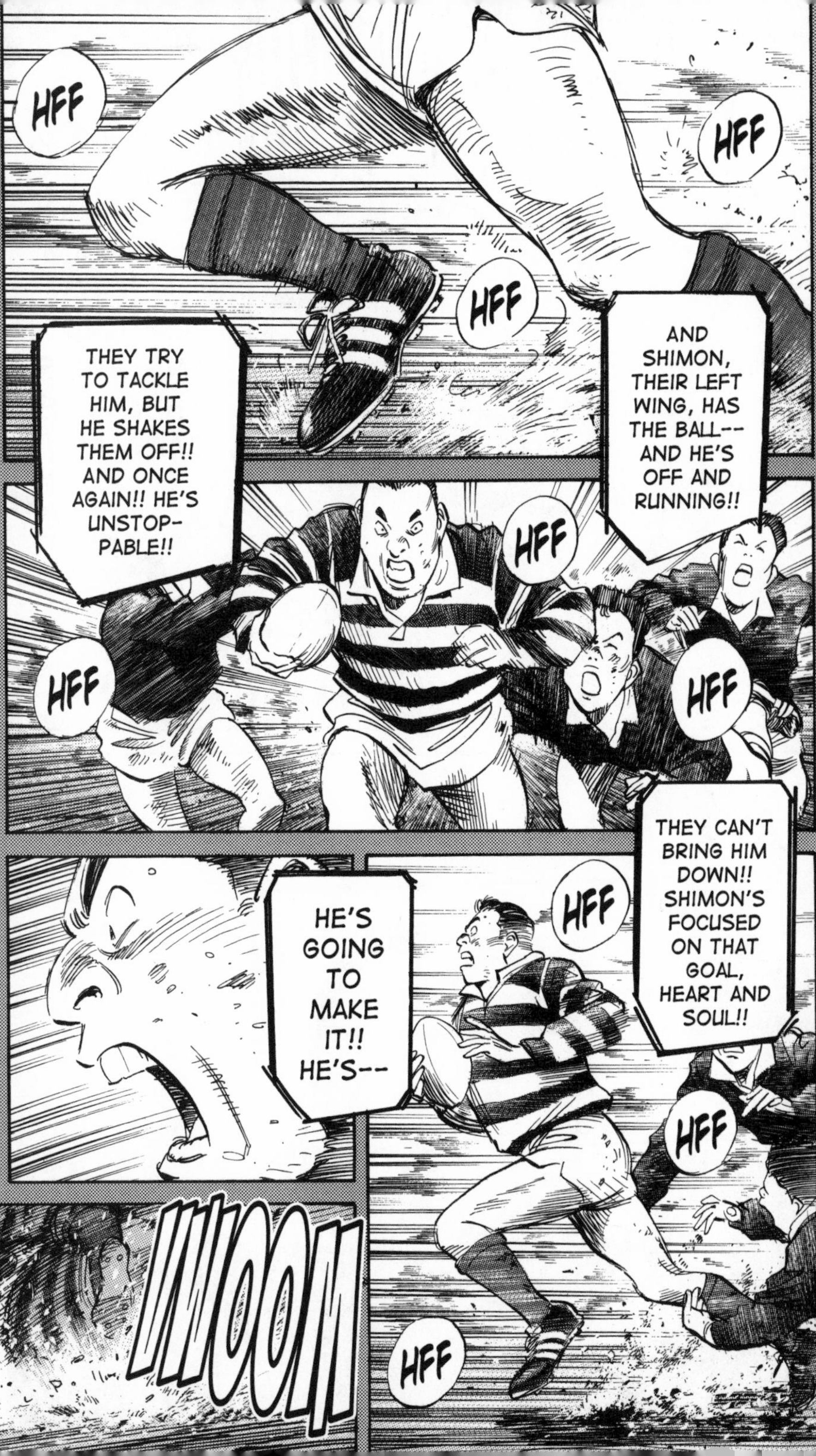
HFF
HFF
HFF
AND SHIMON, THEIR LEFT WING, HAS THE BALL-- AND HE'S OFF AND RUNNING!!
THEY TRY TO TACKLE HIM, BUT HE SHAKES THEM OFF!! AND ONCE AGAIN!! HE'S UNSTOP-PABLE!!
HFF
HFF
HFF
THEY CAN'T BRING HIM DOWN!! SHIMON'S FOCUSED ON THAT GOAL, HEART AND SOUL!!
HFF
HE'S GOING TO MAKE IT!! HE'S--
HFF
HFF
WOOOM

Chapter 5 Heart and Soul

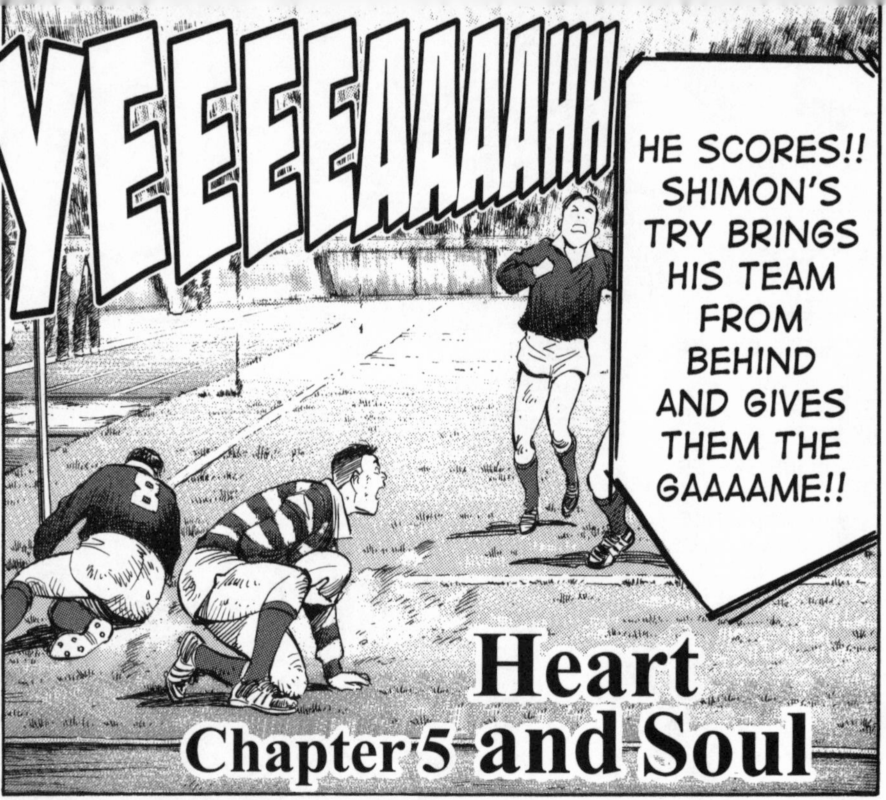
YEEEEAAAAAHH
HE SCORES!! SHIMON'S TRY BRINGS HIS TEAM FROM BEHIND AND GIVES THEM THE GAAAAME!!

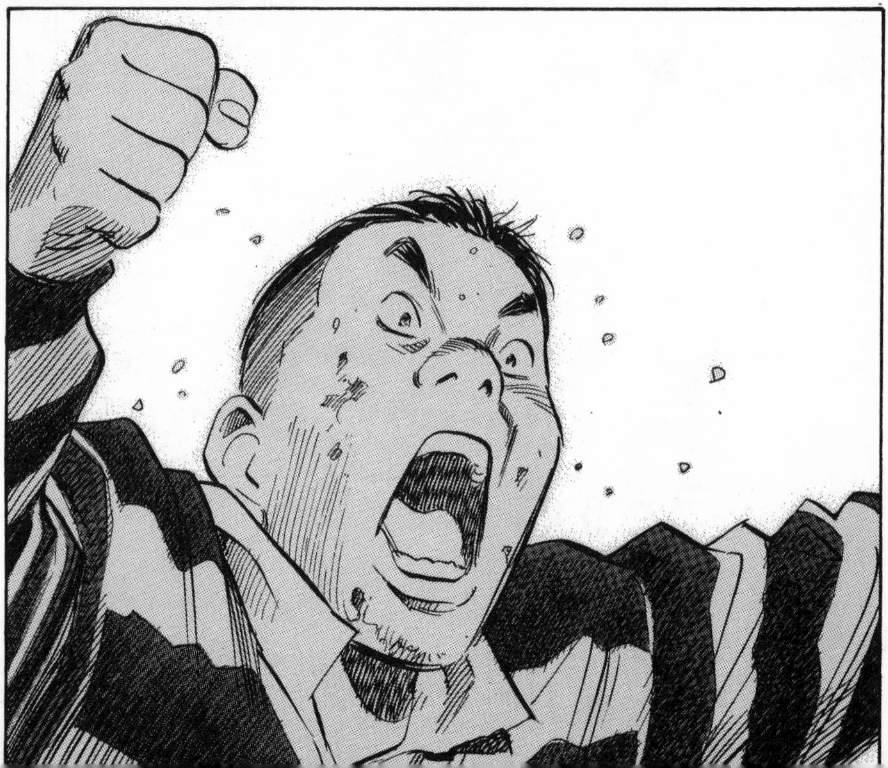

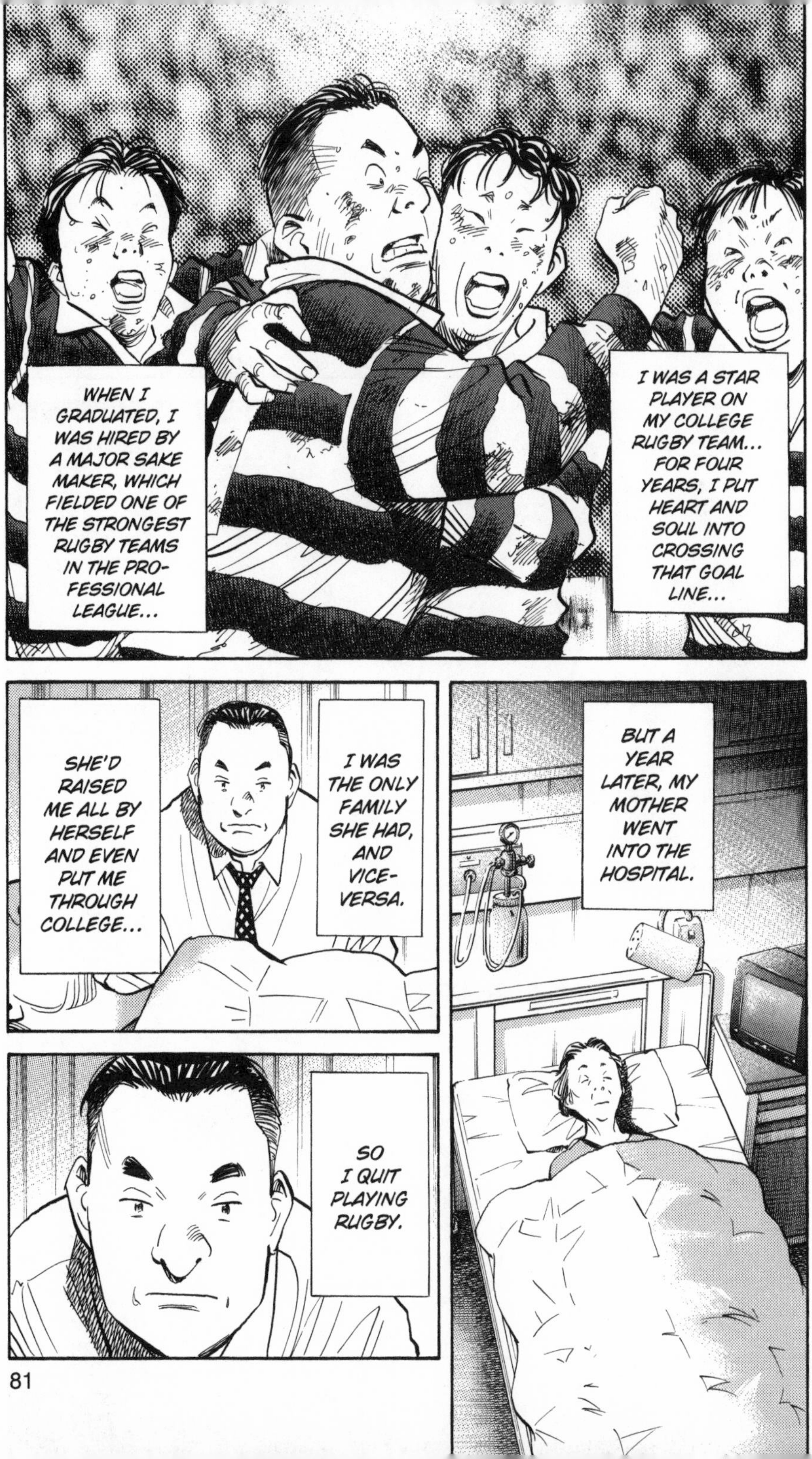
I WAS A STAR PLAYER ON MY COLLEGE RUGBY TEAM... FOR FOUR YEARS, I PUT HEART AND SOUL INTO CROSSING THAT GOAL LINE...
WHEN I GRADUATED, I WAS HIRED BY A MAJOR SAKE MAKER, WHICH FIELDED ONE OF THE STRONGEST RUGBY TEAMS IN THE PRO-FESSIONAL LEAGUE...
BUT A YEAR LATER, MY MOTHER WENT INTO THE HOSPITAL.
I WAS THE ONLY FAMILY SHE HAD, AND VICE-VERSA.
SHE'D RAISED ME ALL BY HERSELF AND EVEN PUT ME THROUGH COLLEGE...
SO I QUIT PLAYING RUGBY.

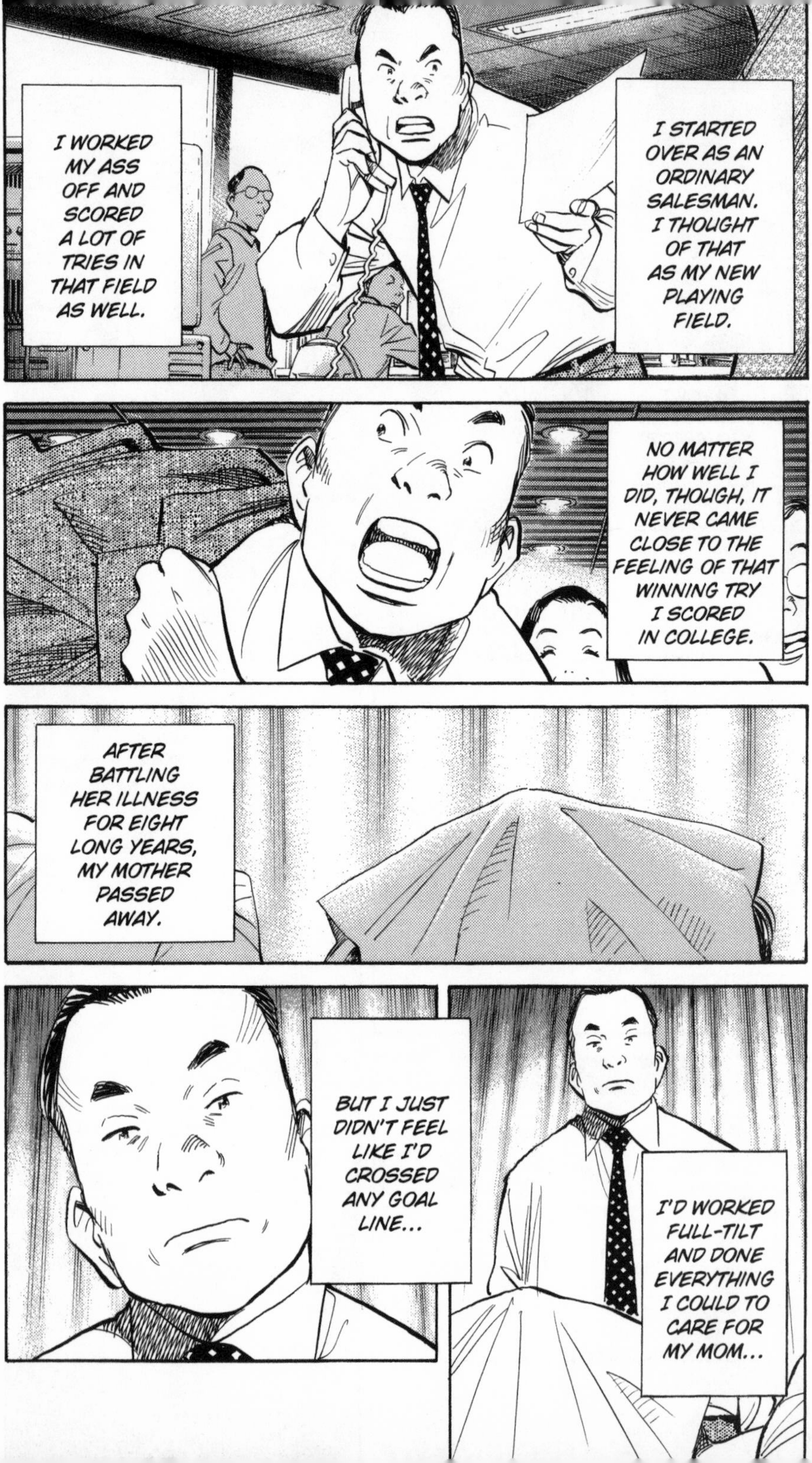
I STARTED OVER AS AN ORDINARY SALESMAN. I THOUGHT OF THAT AS MY NEW PLAYING FIELD.
I WORKED MY ASS OFF AND SCORED A LOT OF TRIES IN THAT FIELD AS WELL.
NO MATTER HOW WELL I DID, THOUGH, IT NEVER CAME CLOSE TO THE FEELING OF THAT WINNING TRY I SCORED IN COLLEGE.
AFTER BATTLING HER ILLNESS FOR EIGHT LONG YEARS, MY MOTHER PASSED AWAY.
I'D WORKED FULL-TILT AND DONE EVERYTHING I COULD TO CARE FOR MY MOM...
BUT I JUST DIDN'T FEEL LIKE I'D CROSSED ANY GOAL LINE...

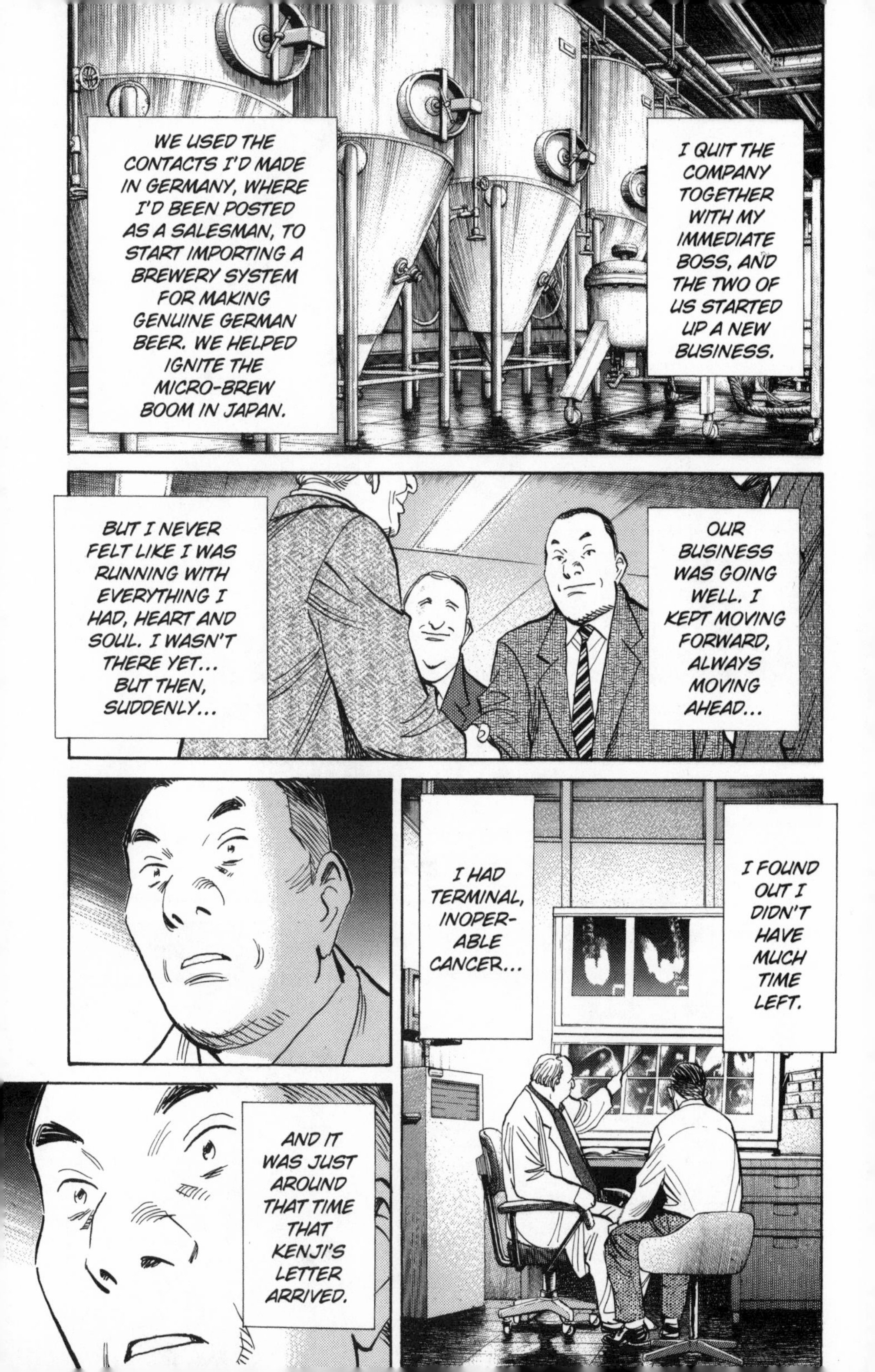
I QUIT THE COMPANY TOGETHER WITH MY IMMEDIATE BOSS, AND THE TWO OF US STARTED UP A NEW BUSINESS.
WE USED THE CONTACTS I'D MADE IN GERMANY, WHERE I'D BEEN POSTED AS A SALESMAN, TO START IMPORTING A BREWERY SYSTEM FOR MAKING GENUINE GERMAN BEER. WE HELPED IGNITE THE MICRO-BREW BOOM IN JAPAN.
OUR BUSINESS WAS GOING WELL. I KEPT MOVING FORWARD, ALWAYS MOVING AHEAD...
BUT I NEVER FELT LIKE I WAS RUNNING WITH EVERYTHING I HAD, HEART AND SOUL. I WASN'T THERE YET... BUT THEN, SUDDENLY...
I FOUND OUT I DIDN'T HAVE MUCH TIME LEFT.
I HAD TERMINAL, INOPER-ABLE CANCER...
AND IT WAS JUST AROUND THAT TIME THAT KENJI'S LETTER ARRIVED.

This is **our** emblem.
Let's take it back.

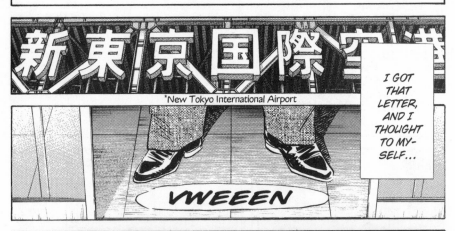

*New Tokyo International Airport

I GOT THAT LETTER, AND I THOUGHT TO MYSELF...

VWEEEN

NOW I'LL FINALLY BE ABLE TO RUN FULL-TILT, WITH ALL MY HEART AND SOUL. THIS WILL LET ME SCORE ANOTHER WINNING TRY.

TOK

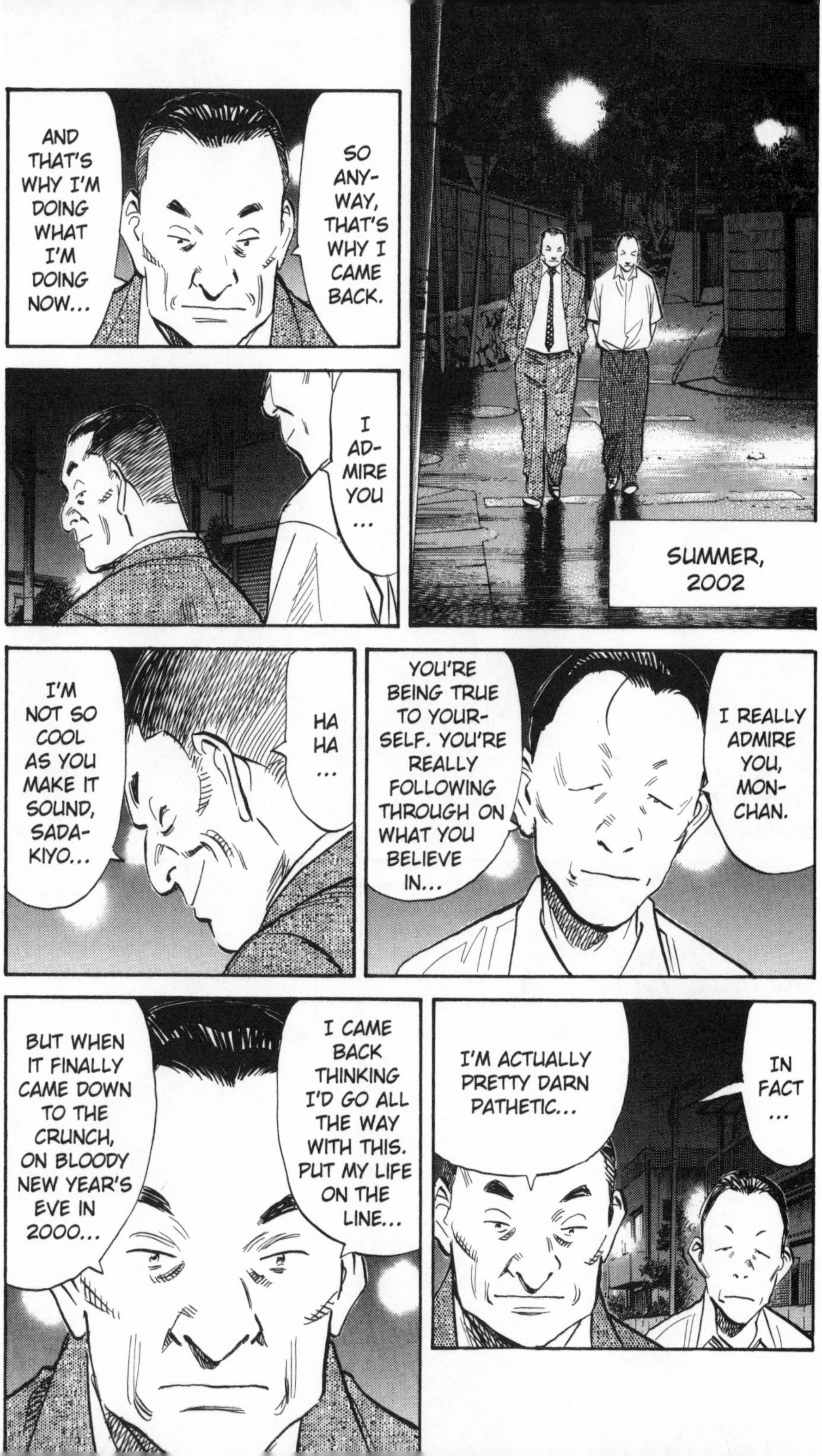
SUMMER, 2002
SO ANYWAY, THAT'S WHY I CAME BACK.
AND THAT'S WHY I'M DOING WHAT I'M DOING NOW...
I ADMIRE YOU...
I REALLY ADMIRE YOU, MON-CHAN.
YOU'RE BEING TRUE TO YOURSELF. YOU'RE REALLY FOLLOWING THROUGH ON WHAT YOU BELIEVE IN...
HA HA...
I'M NOT SO COOL AS YOU MAKE IT SOUND, SADAKIYO...
IN FACT...
I'M ACTUALLY PRETTY DARN PATHETIC...
I CAME BACK THINKING I'D GO ALL THE WAY WITH THIS. PUT MY LIFE ON THE LINE...
BUT WHEN IT FINALLY CAME DOWN TO THE CRUNCH, ON BLOODY NEW YEAR'S EVE IN 2000...

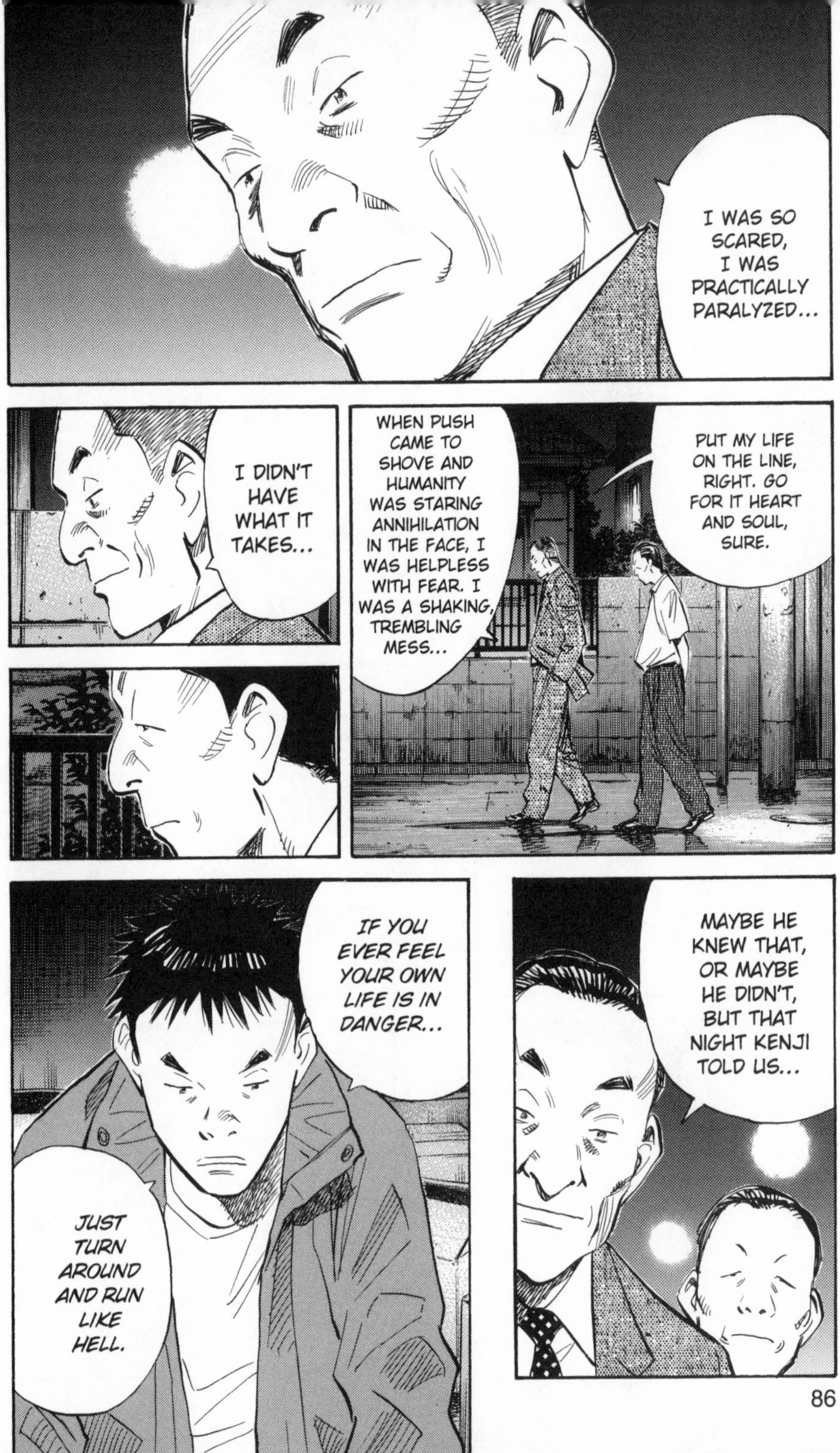
I WAS SO SCARED, I WAS PRACTICALLY PARALYZED...
PUT MY LIFE ON THE LINE, RIGHT. GO FOR IT HEART AND SOUL, SURE.
WHEN PUSH CAME TO SHOVE AND HUMANITY WAS STARING ANNIHILATION IN THE FACE, I WAS HELPLESS WITH FEAR. I WAS A SHAKING, TREMBLING MESS...
I DIDN'T HAVE WHAT IT TAKES...
MAYBE HE KNEW THAT, OR MAYBE HE DIDN'T, BUT THAT NIGHT KENJI TOLD US...
IF YOU EVER FEEL YOUR OWN LIFE IS IN DANGER...
JUST TURN AROUND AND RUN LIKE HELL.

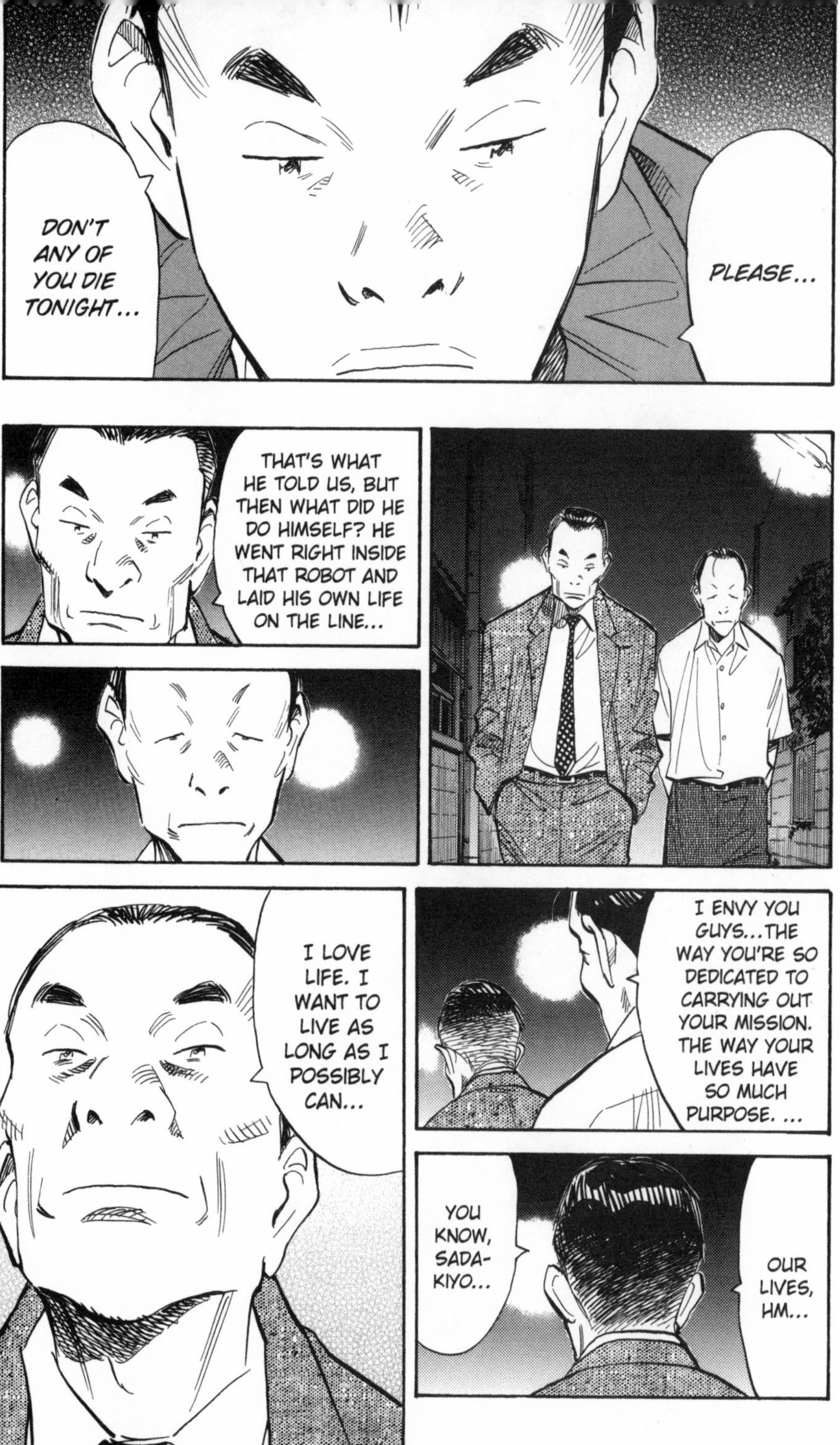
DON'T ANY OF YOU DIE TONIGHT...
PLEASE...
THAT'S WHAT HE TOLD US, BUT THEN WHAT DID HE DO HIMSELF? HE WENT RIGHT INSIDE THAT ROBOT AND LAID HIS OWN LIFE ON THE LINE...
I ENVY YOU GUYS...THE WAY YOU'RE SO DEDICATED TO CARRYING OUT YOUR MISSION. THE WAY YOUR LIVES HAVE SO MUCH PURPOSE. ...
OUR LIVES, HM...
YOU KNOW, SADA-KIYO...
I LOVE LIFE. I WANT TO LIVE AS LONG AS I POSSIBLY CAN...

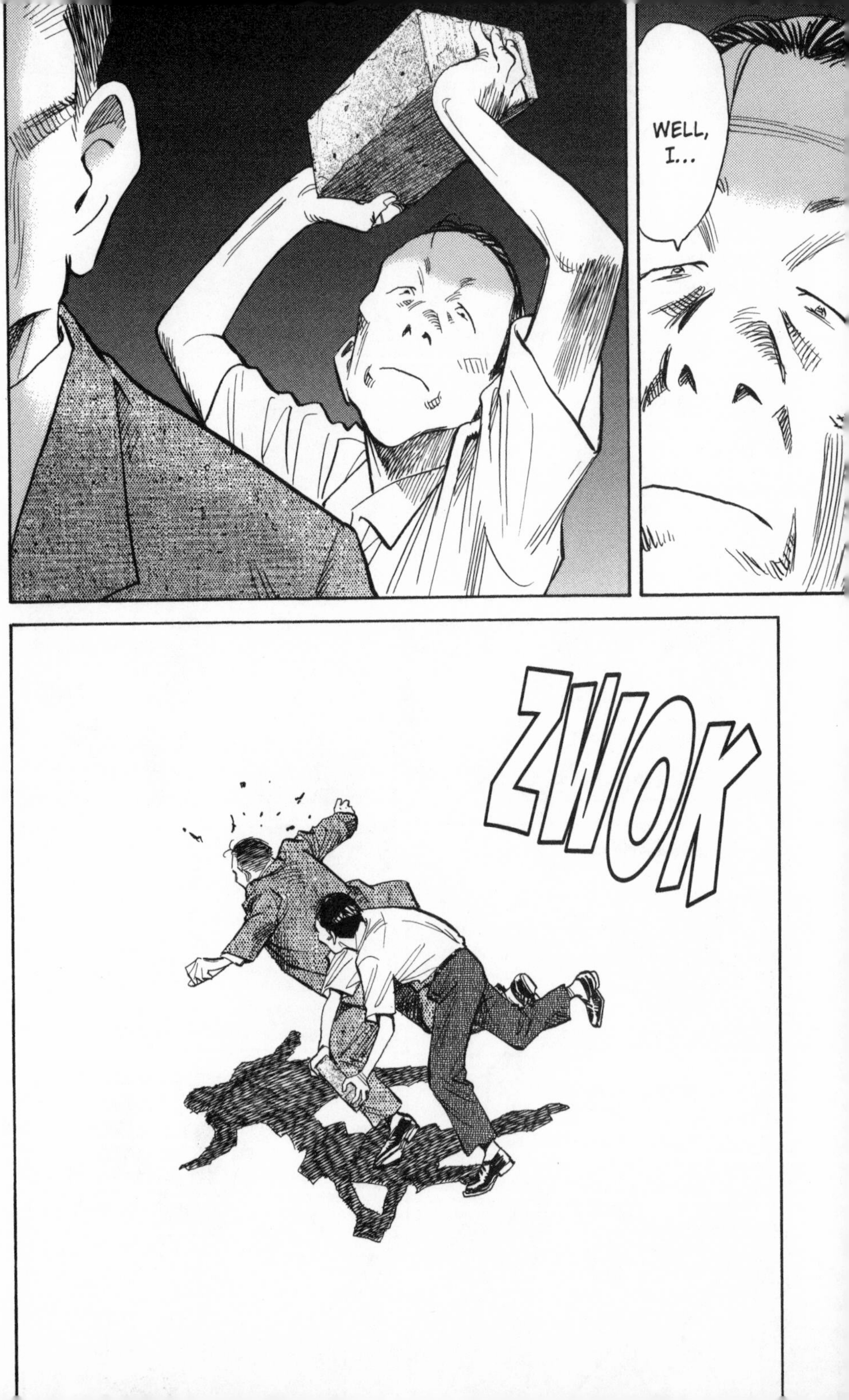
WELL, I...
ZWOK

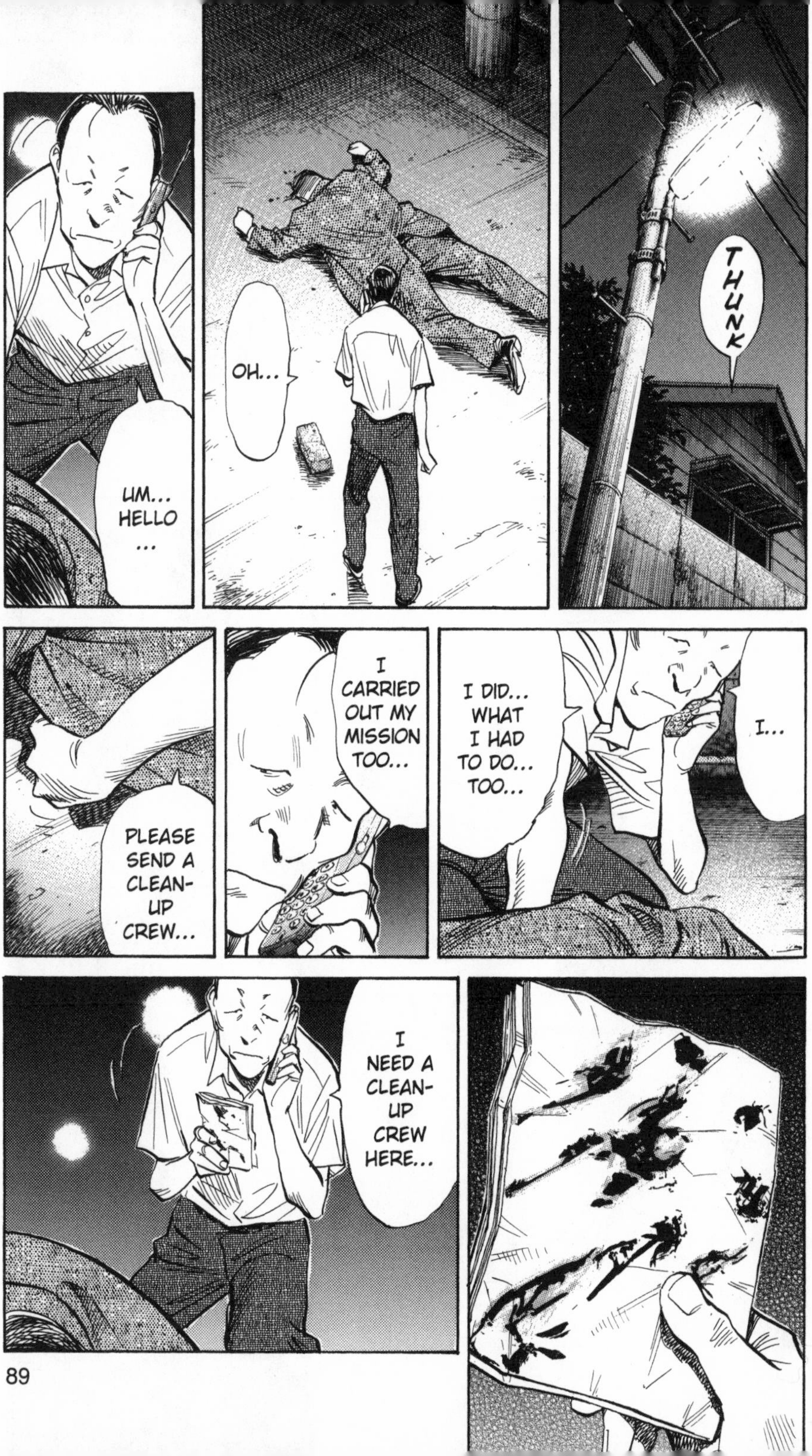
THUNK
OH...
UM... HELLO ...
I...
I DID... WHAT I HAD TO DO... TOO...
I CARRIED OUT MY MISSION TOO...
PLEASE SEND A CLEAN-UP CREW...
I NEED A CLEAN-UP CREW HERE...

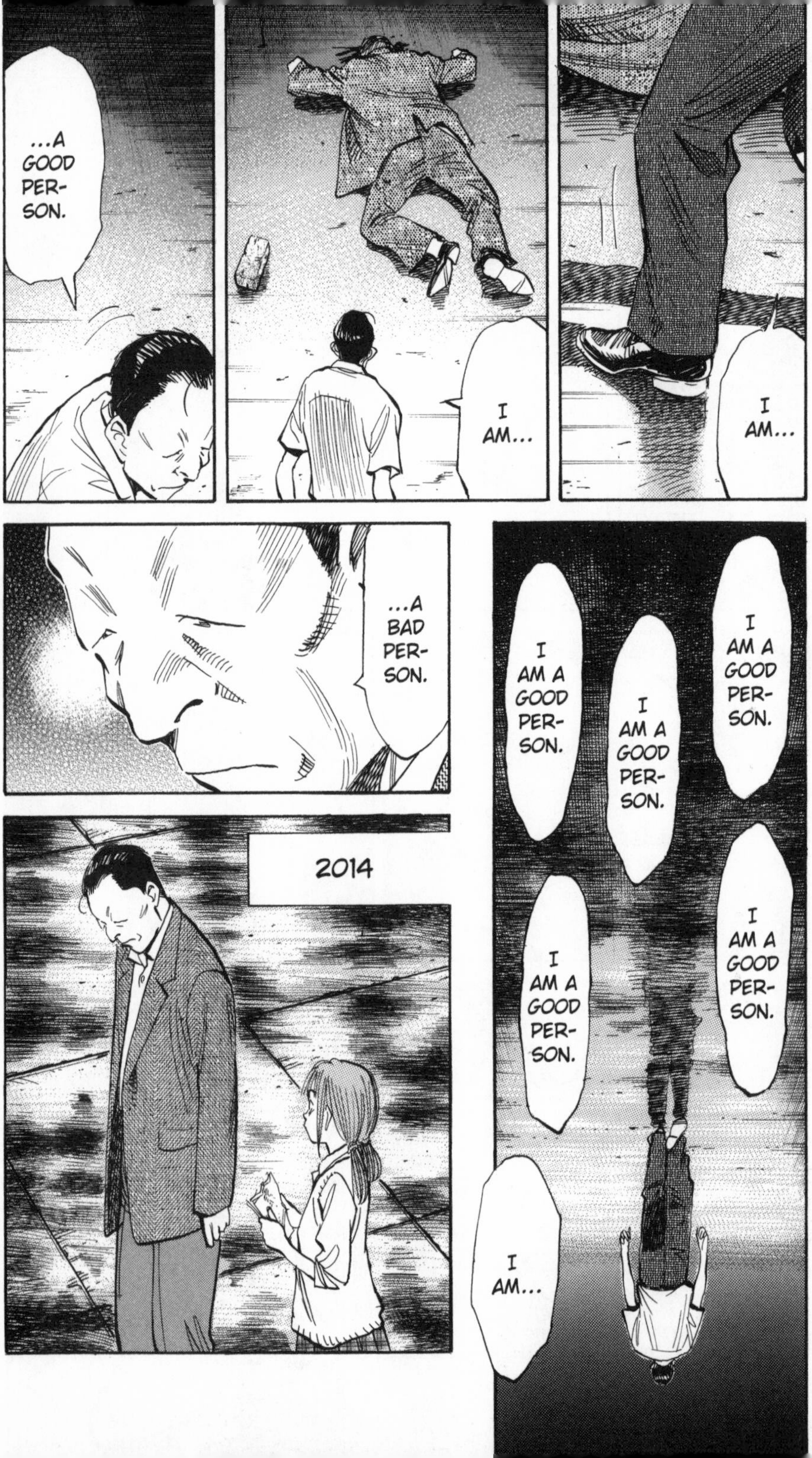
I AM...
I AM...
...A GOOD PER-SON.
I AM A GOOD PER-SON.
I AM A GOOD PER-SON.
I AM A GOOD PER-SON.
I AM A GOOD PER-SON.
I AM A GOOD PER-SON.
I AM...
...A BAD PER-SON.
2014

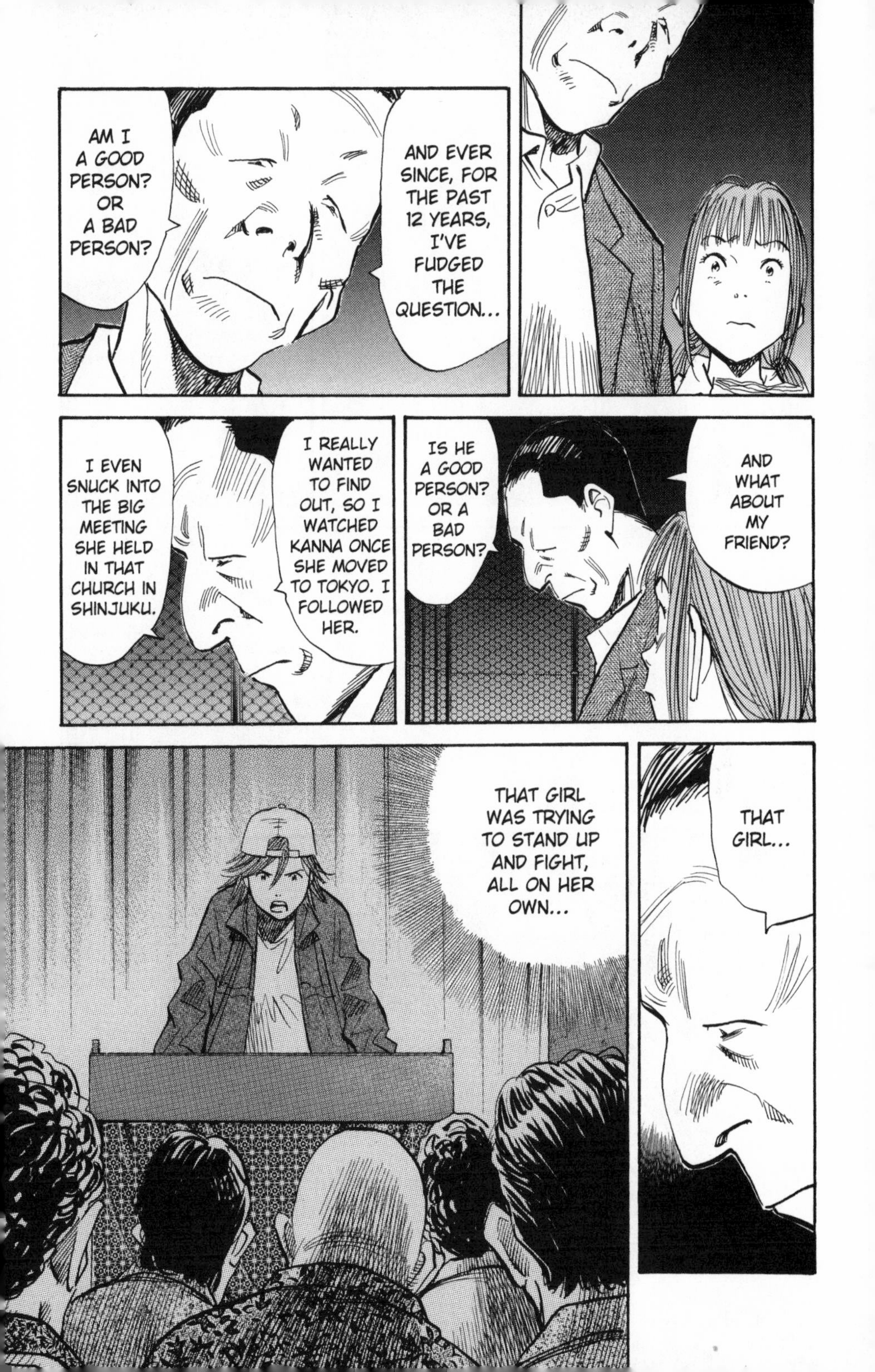
AND EVER SINCE, FOR THE PAST 12 YEARS, I'VE FUDGED THE QUESTION...
AM I A GOOD PERSON? OR A BAD PERSON?
AND WHAT ABOUT MY FRIEND?
IS HE A GOOD PERSON? OR A BAD PERSON?
I REALLY WANTED TO FIND OUT, SO I WATCHED KANNA ONCE SHE MOVED TO TOKYO. I FOLLOWED HER.
I EVEN SNUCK INTO THE BIG MEETING SHE HELD IN THAT CHURCH IN SHINJUKU.
THAT GIRL...
THAT GIRL WAS TRYING TO STAND UP AND FIGHT, ALL ON HER OWN...

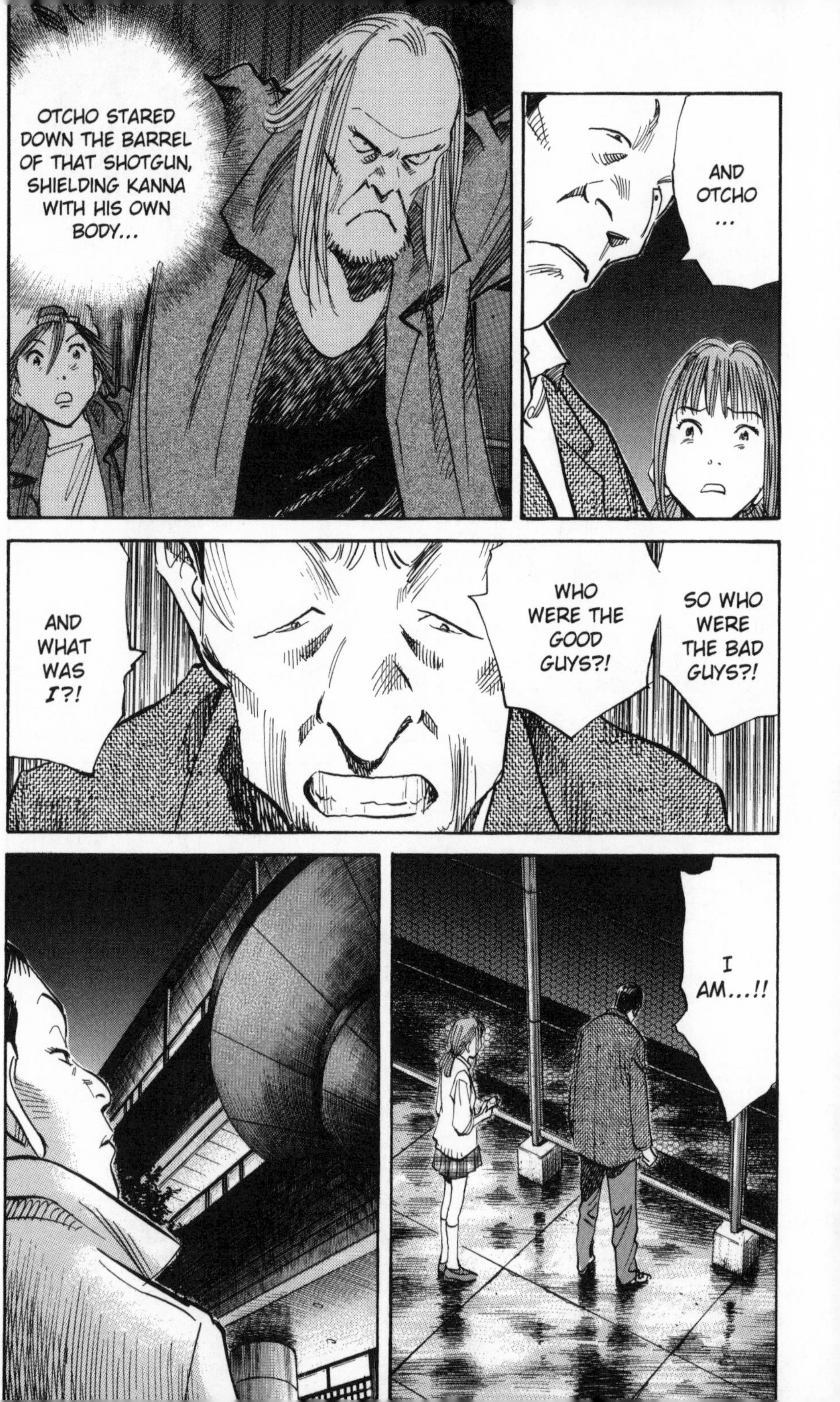
AND OTCHO ...
OTCHO STARED DOWN THE BARREL OF THAT SHOTGUN, SHIELDING KANNA WITH HIS OWN BODY...
SO WHO WERE THE BAD GUYS?!
WHO WERE THE GOOD GUYS?!
AND WHAT WAS *I*?!
I AM...!!

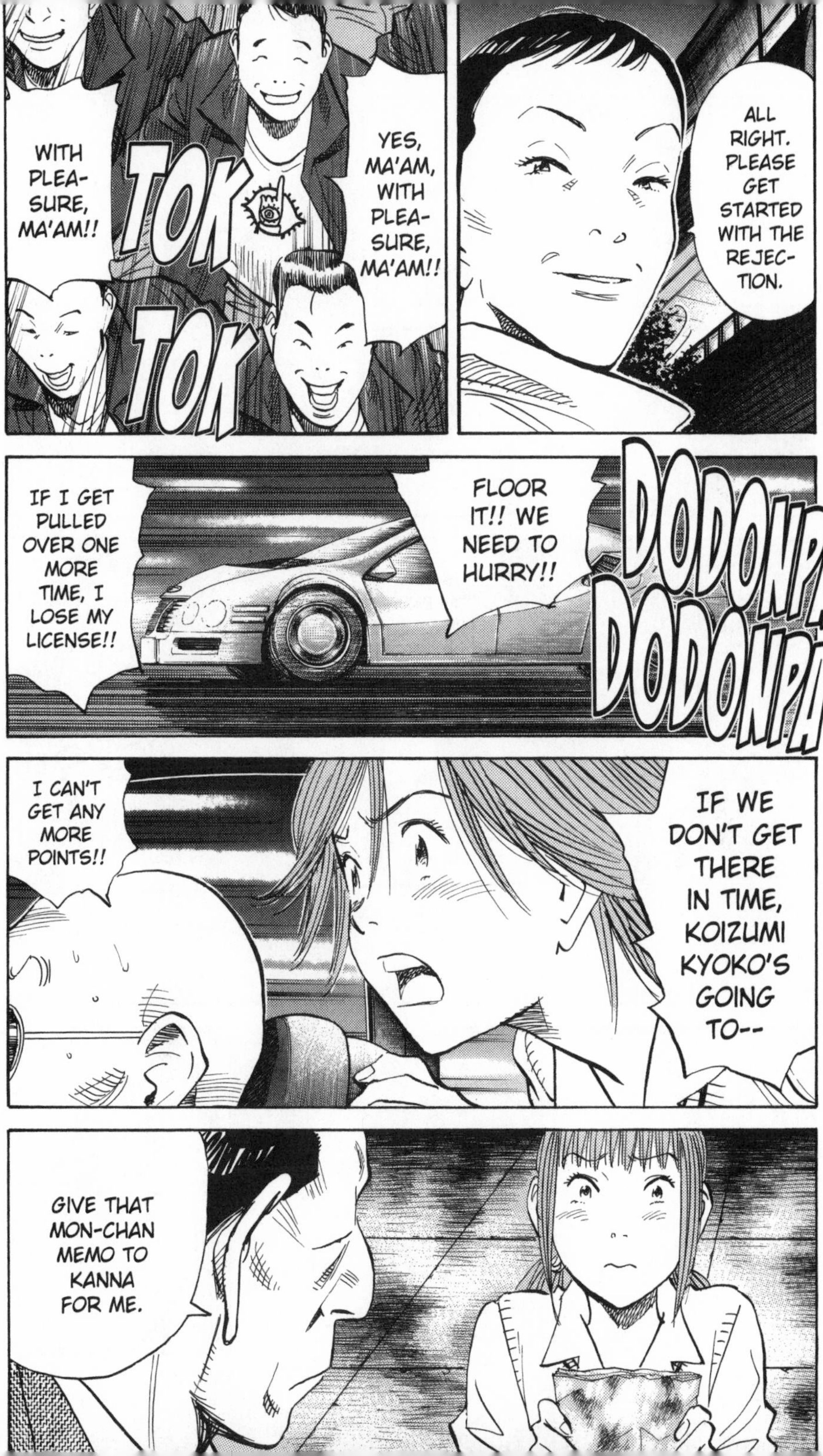
ALL RIGHT. PLEASE GET STARTED WITH THE REJECTION.
YES, MA'AM, WITH PLEASURE, MA'AM!!
TOK TOK
WITH PLEASURE, MA'AM!!
DODONPA DODONPA
FLOOR IT!! WE NEED TO HURRY!!
IF I GET PULLED OVER ONE MORE TIME, I LOSE MY LICENSE!!
IF WE DON'T GET THERE IN TIME, KOIZUMI KYOKO'S GOING TO--
I CAN'T GET ANY MORE POINTS!!
GIVE THAT MON-CHAN MEMO TO KANNA FOR ME.

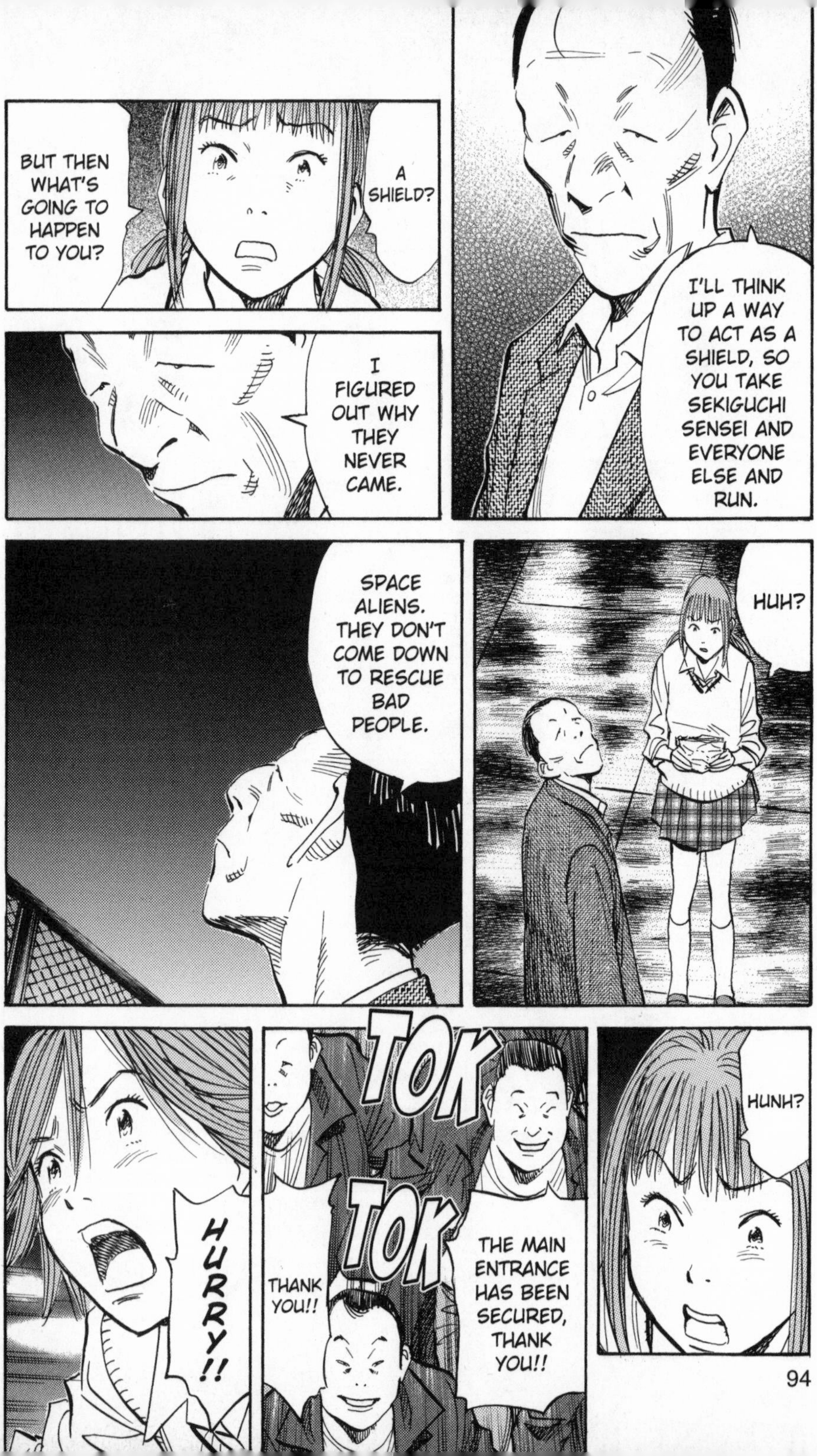
I'LL THINK UP A WAY TO ACT AS A SHIELD, SO YOU TAKE SEKIGUCHI SENSEI AND EVERYONE ELSE AND RUN.
A SHIELD?
BUT THEN WHAT'S GOING TO HAPPEN TO YOU?
I FIGURED OUT WHY THEY NEVER CAME.
HUH?
SPACE ALIENS. THEY DON'T COME DOWN TO RESCUE BAD PEOPLE.
HUNH?
TOK
TOK
THE MAIN ENTRANCE HAS BEEN SECURED, THANK YOU!!
THANK YOU!!
HURRY!!

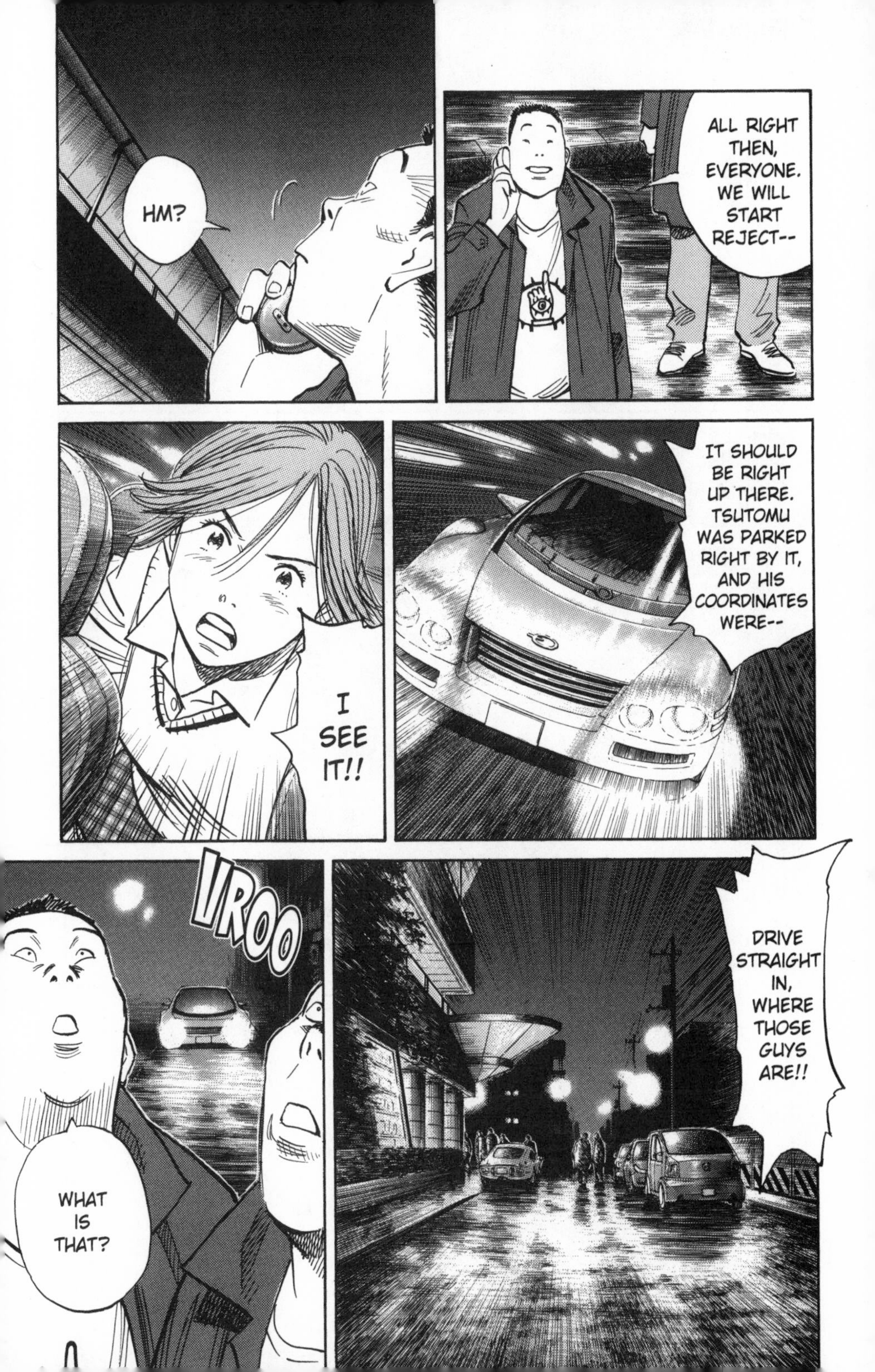
ALL RIGHT THEN, EVERYONE. WE WILL START REJECT--
HM?
IT SHOULD BE RIGHT UP THERE. TSUTOMU WAS PARKED RIGHT BY IT, AND HIS COORDINATES WERE--
I SEE IT!!
DRIVE STRAIGHT IN, WHERE THOSE GUYS ARE!!
VROO
WHAT IS THAT?

DON'T TELL ME...

NO WAY...

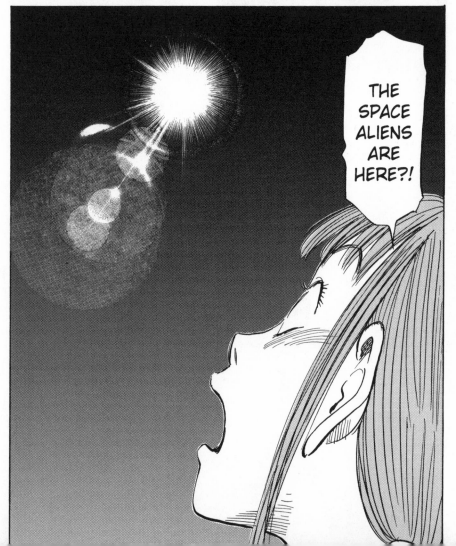

THE SPACE ALIENS ARE HERE?!

Chapter 6 Space Aliens

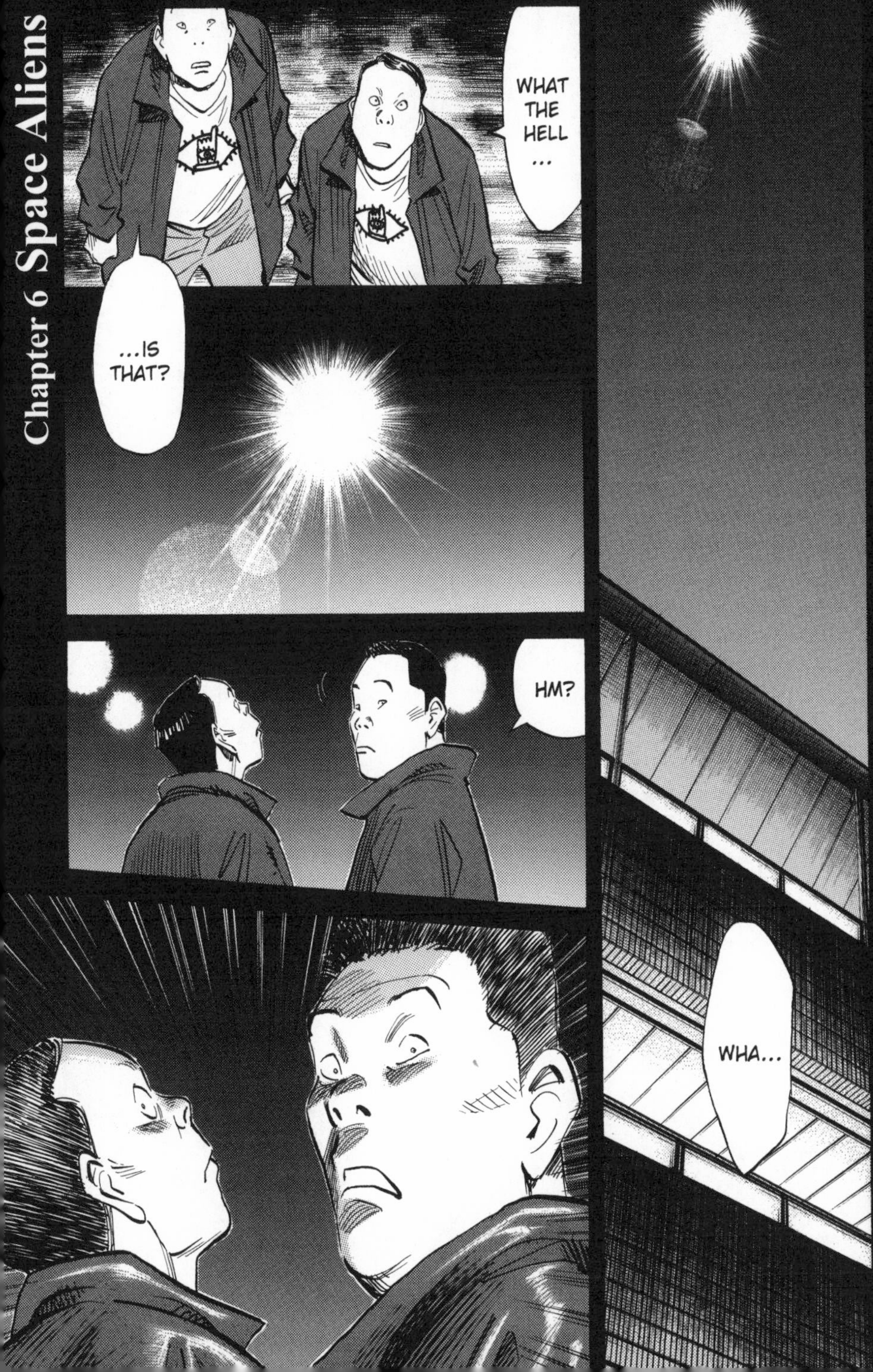
WHA...
WHAT THE HELL ...
...IS THAT?
HM?

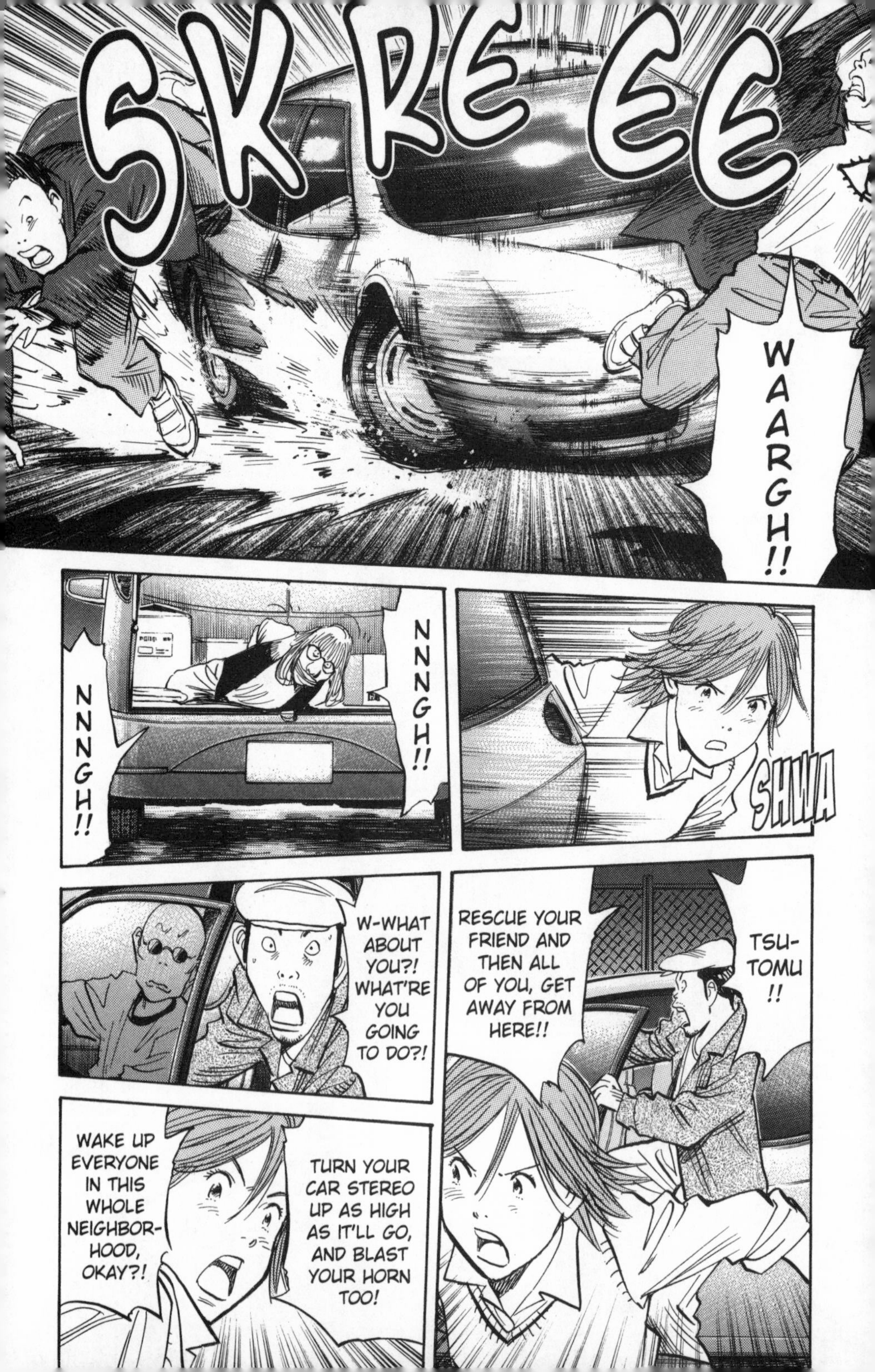
SKREEE
WAARGH!!
SHWA
NNNGH!!
NNNGH!!
TSU-TOMU!!
RESCUE YOUR FRIEND AND THEN ALL OF YOU, GET AWAY FROM HERE!!
W-WHAT ABOUT YOU?! WHAT'RE YOU GOING TO DO?!
TURN YOUR CAR STEREO UP AS HIGH AS IT'LL GO, AND BLAST YOUR HORN TOO!
WAKE UP EVERYONE IN THIS WHOLE NEIGHBOR-HOOD, OKAY?!

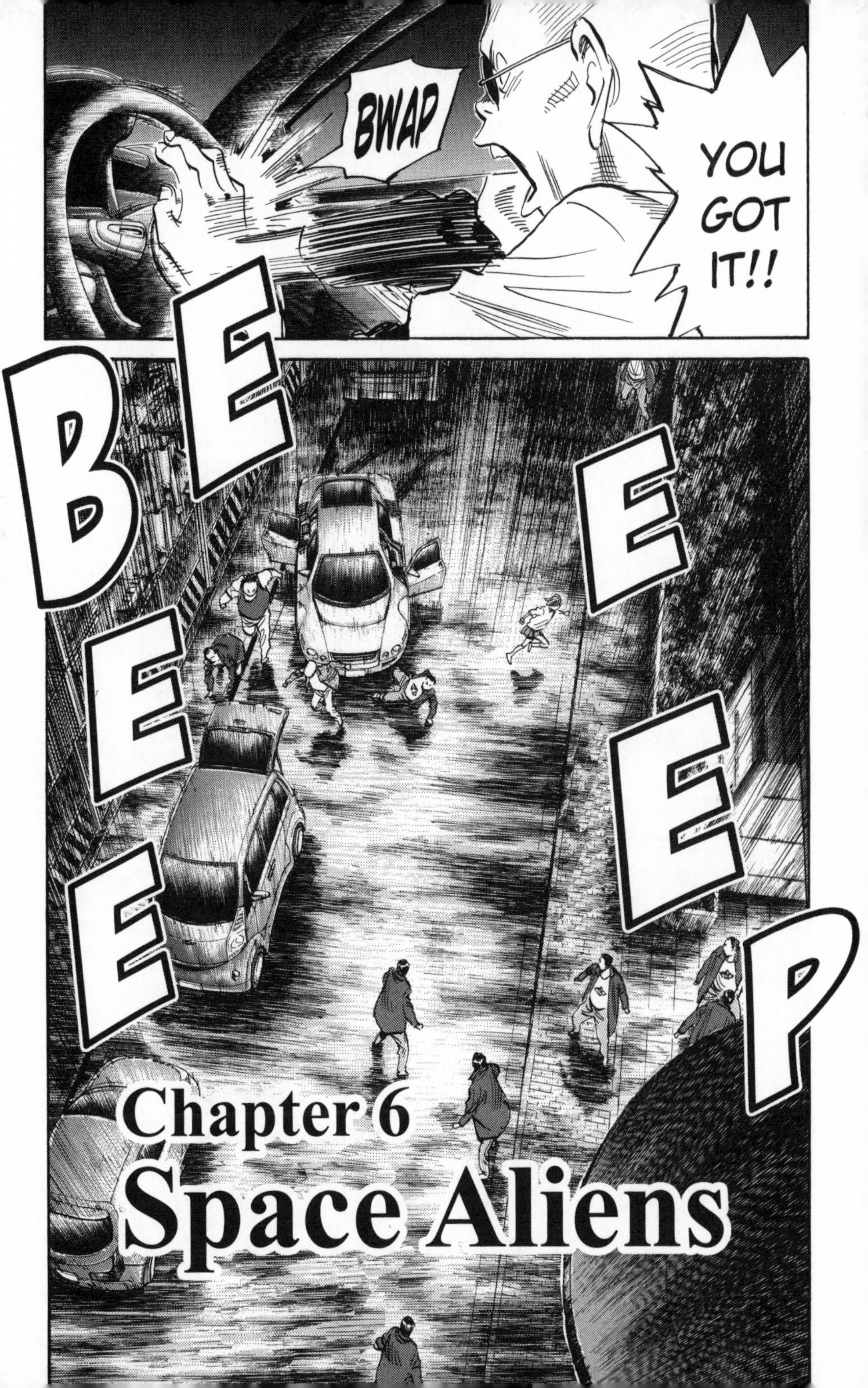
YOU GOT IT!!
BWAP
BEEEEEP

Chapter 6
Space Aliens

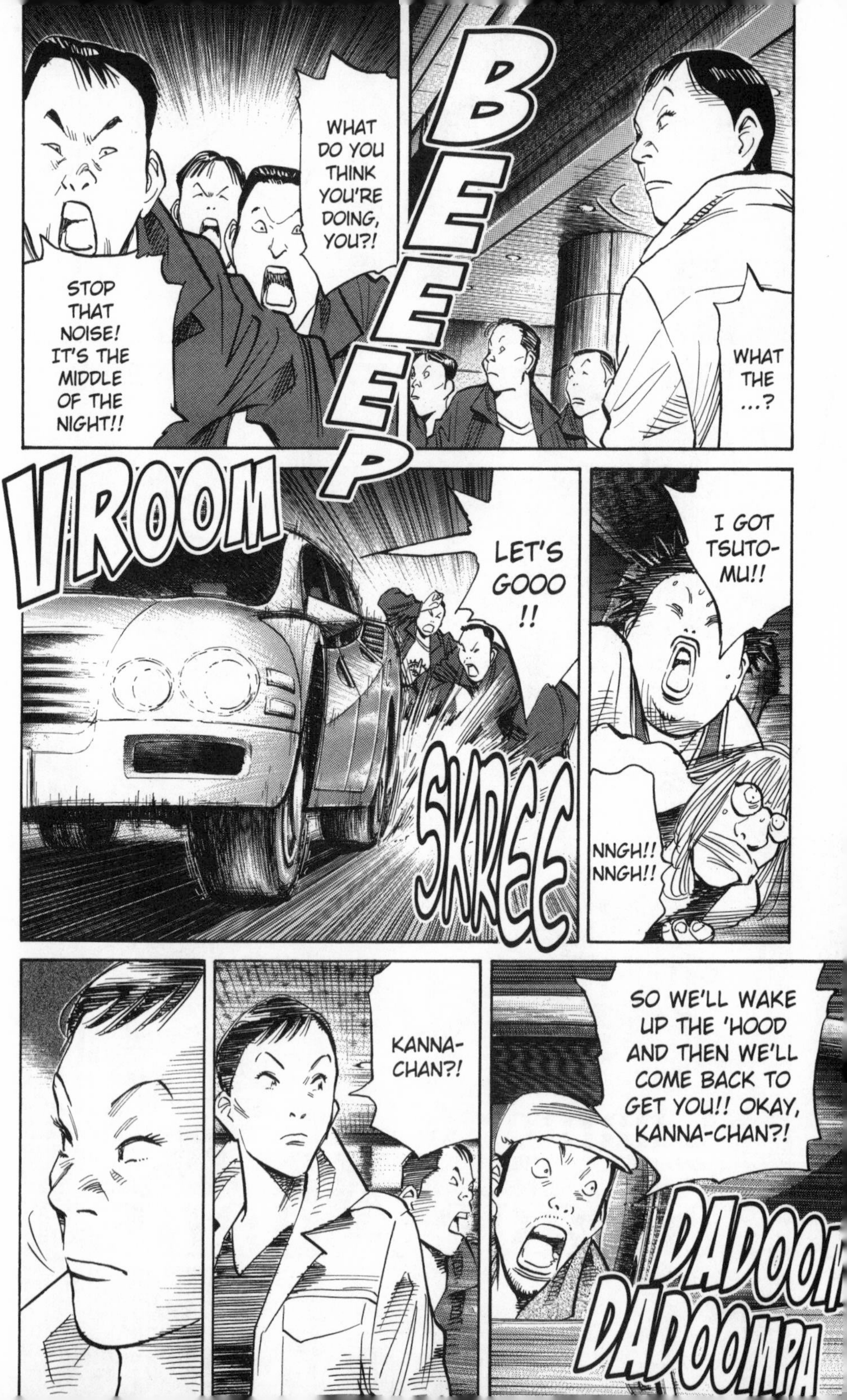
WHAT THE ...?
BEEEEEP
WHAT DO YOU THINK YOU'RE DOING, YOU?!
STOP THAT NOISE! IT'S THE MIDDLE OF THE NIGHT!!
I GOT TSUTO-MU!!
NNGH!! NNGH!!
VROOM
LET'S GOOO !!
SKREE
SO WE'LL WAKE UP THE 'HOOD AND THEN WE'LL COME BACK TO GET YOU!! OKAY, KANNA-CHAN?!
DADOOM DADOOMPA
KANNA-CHAN?!

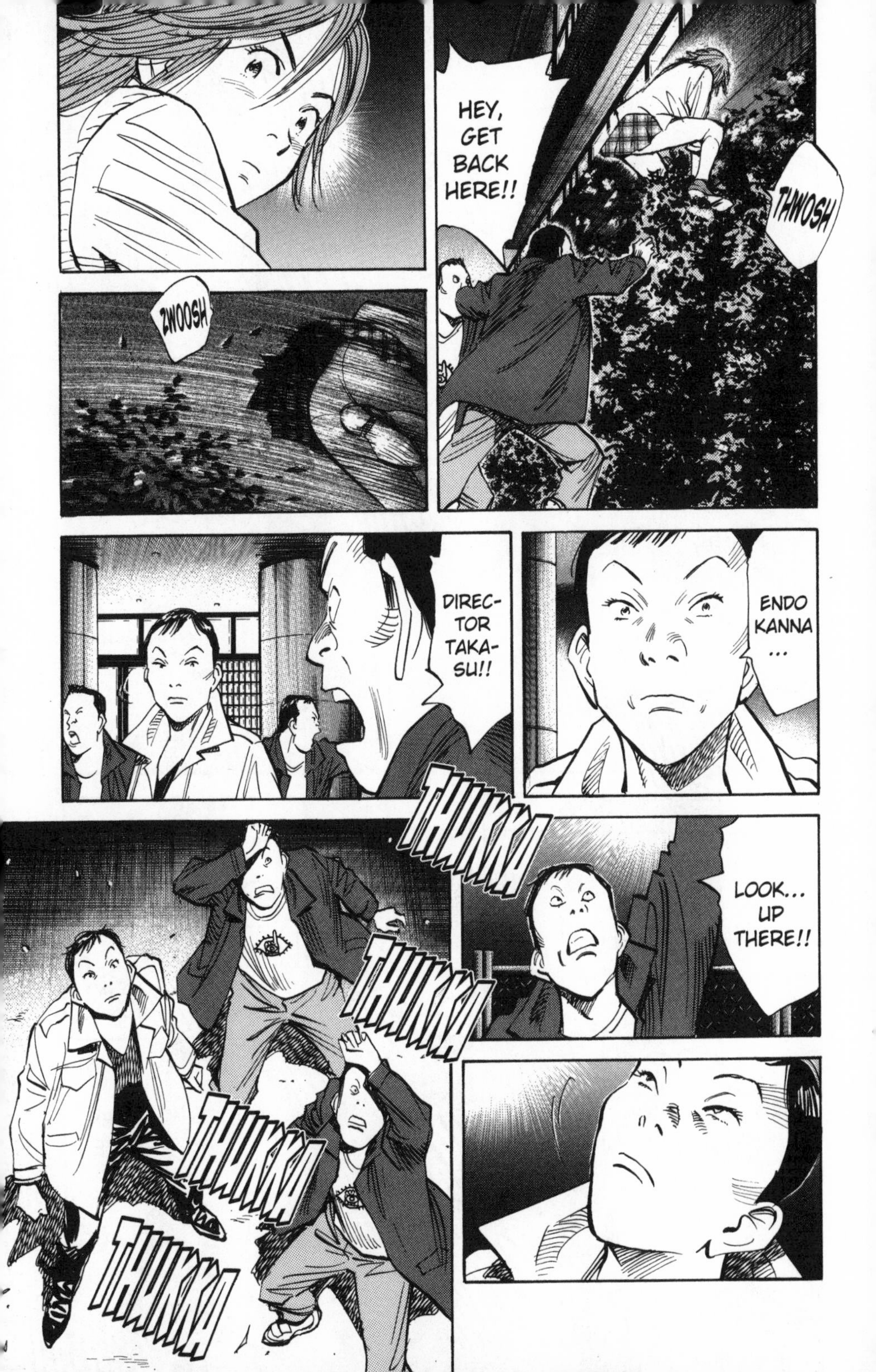
HEY, GET BACK HERE!!
THWOSH
ZWOOSH
ENDO KANNA ...
DIRECTOR TAKASU!!
LOOK... UP THERE!!
THUKKA
THUKKA
THUKKA
THUKKA

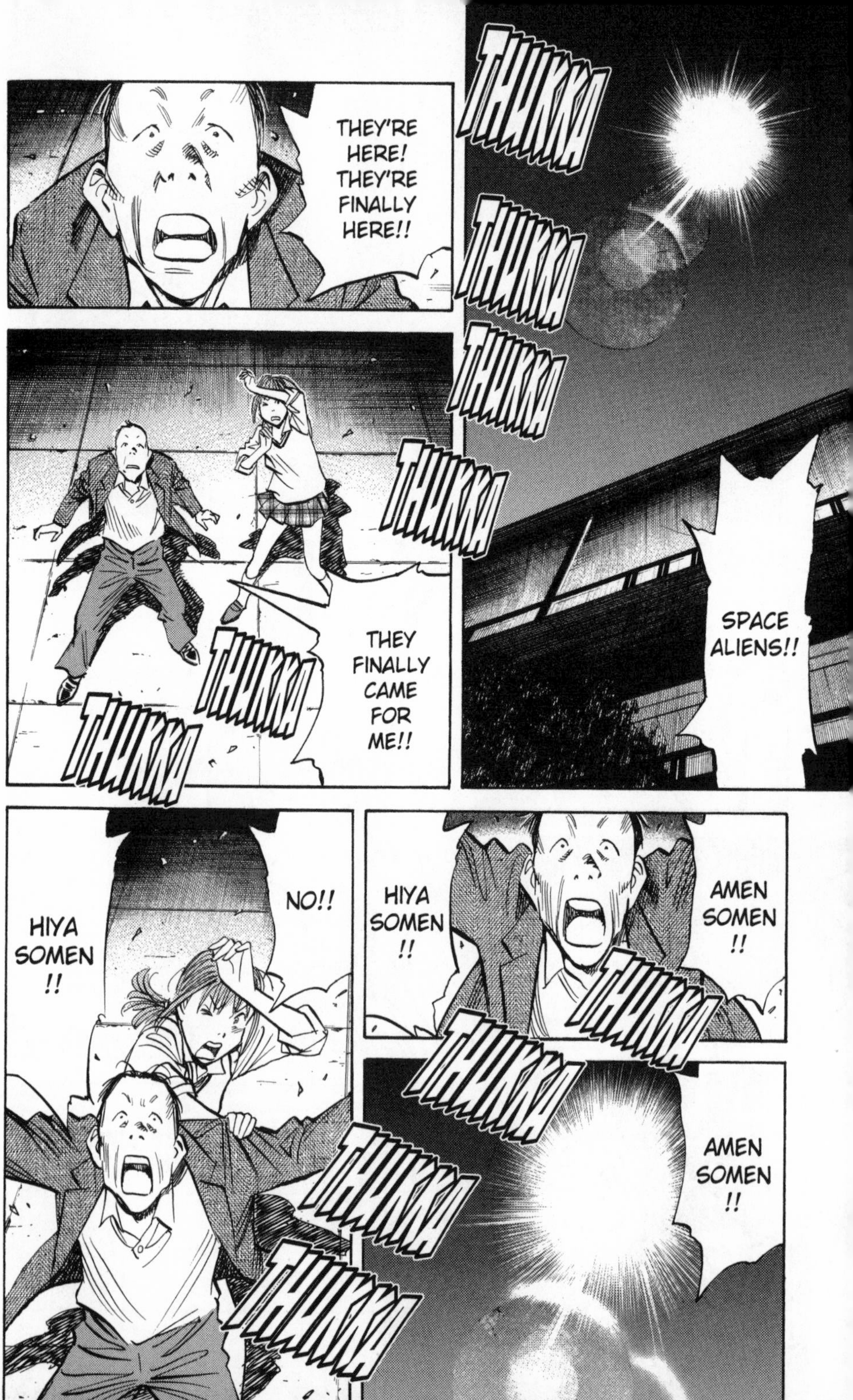
THUKKA
THUKKA
THUKKA
THUKKA
SPACE ALIENS!!
THEY'RE HERE! THEY'RE FINALLY HERE!!
THUKKA
THUKKA
THEY FINALLY CAME FOR ME!!
AMEN SOMEN!!
HIYA SOMEN!!
THUKKA
THUKKA
AMEN SOMEN!!
THUKKA
THUKKA
NO!!
HIYA SOMEN!!

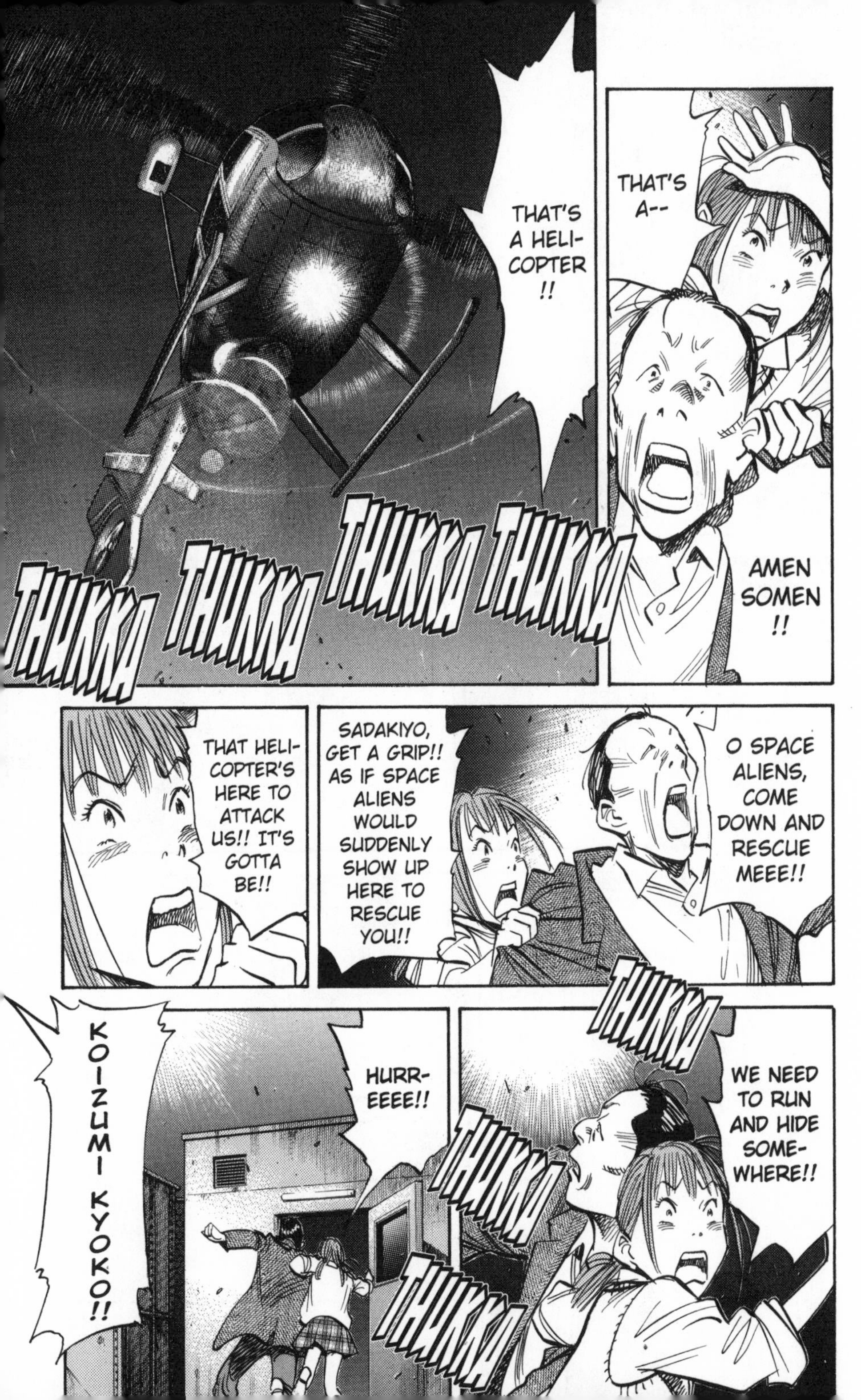
THAT'S A--
AMEN SOMEN!!
THAT'S A HELI-COPTER!!
THUKKA THUKKA THUKKA THUKKA
O SPACE ALIENS, COME DOWN AND RESCUE MEEE!!
SADAKIYO, GET A GRIP!! AS IF SPACE ALIENS WOULD SUDDENLY SHOW UP HERE TO RESCUE YOU!!
THAT HELI-COPTER'S HERE TO ATTACK US!! IT'S GOTTA BE!!
THUKKA
WE NEED TO RUN AND HIDE SOME-WHERE!!
THUKKA
THUKKA
HURR-EEEE!!
KOIZUMI KYOKO!!

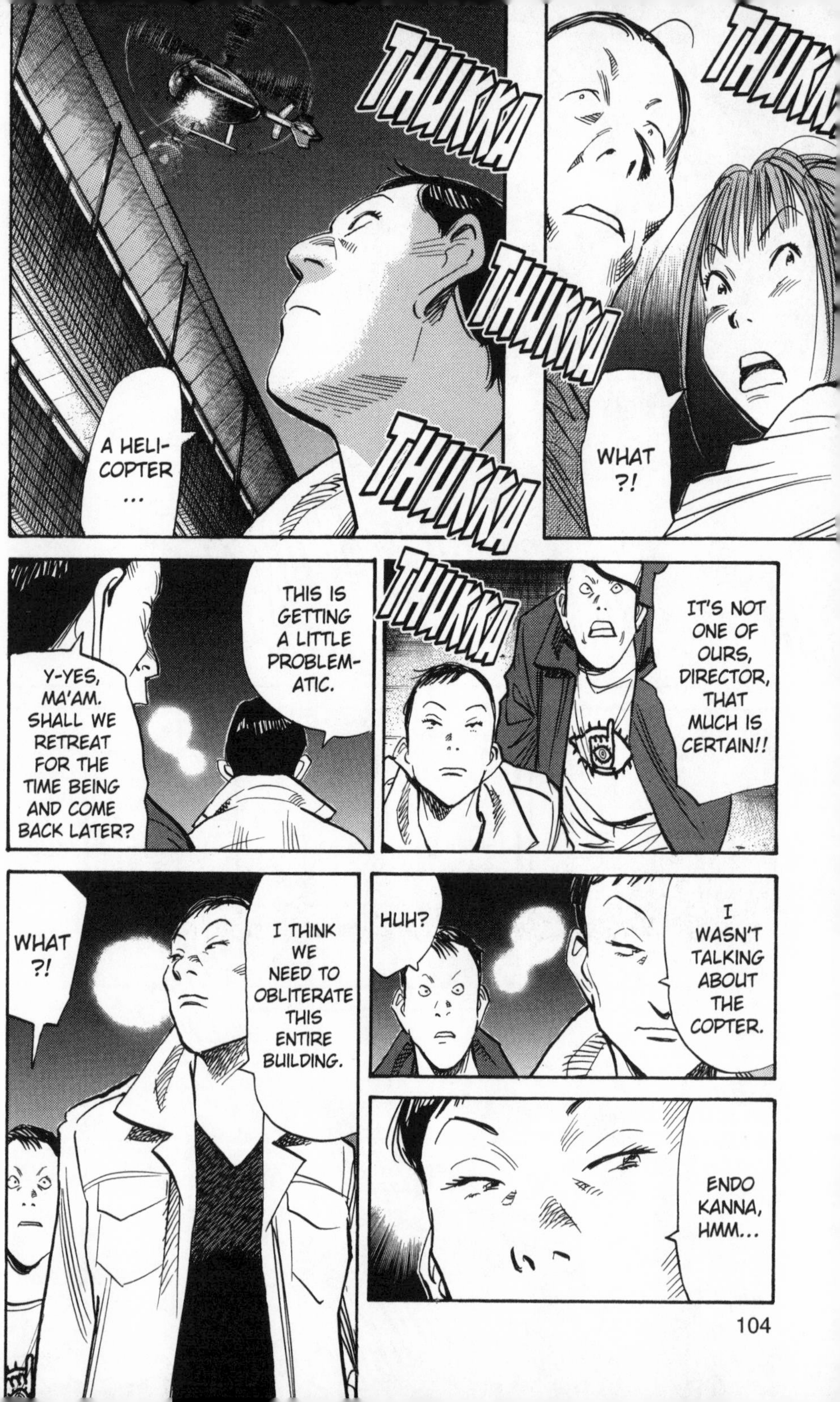
THUKKA
WHAT ?!
THUKKA
THUKKA
THUKKA
A HELI-COPTER ...
THUKKA
IT'S NOT ONE OF OURS, DIRECTOR, THAT MUCH IS CERTAIN!!
THIS IS GETTING A LITTLE PROBLEM-ATIC.
Y-YES, MA'AM. SHALL WE RETREAT FOR THE TIME BEING AND COME BACK LATER?
I WASN'T TALKING ABOUT THE COPTER.
HUH?
ENDO KANNA, HMM...
I THINK WE NEED TO OBLITERATE THIS ENTIRE BUILDING.
WHAT ?!

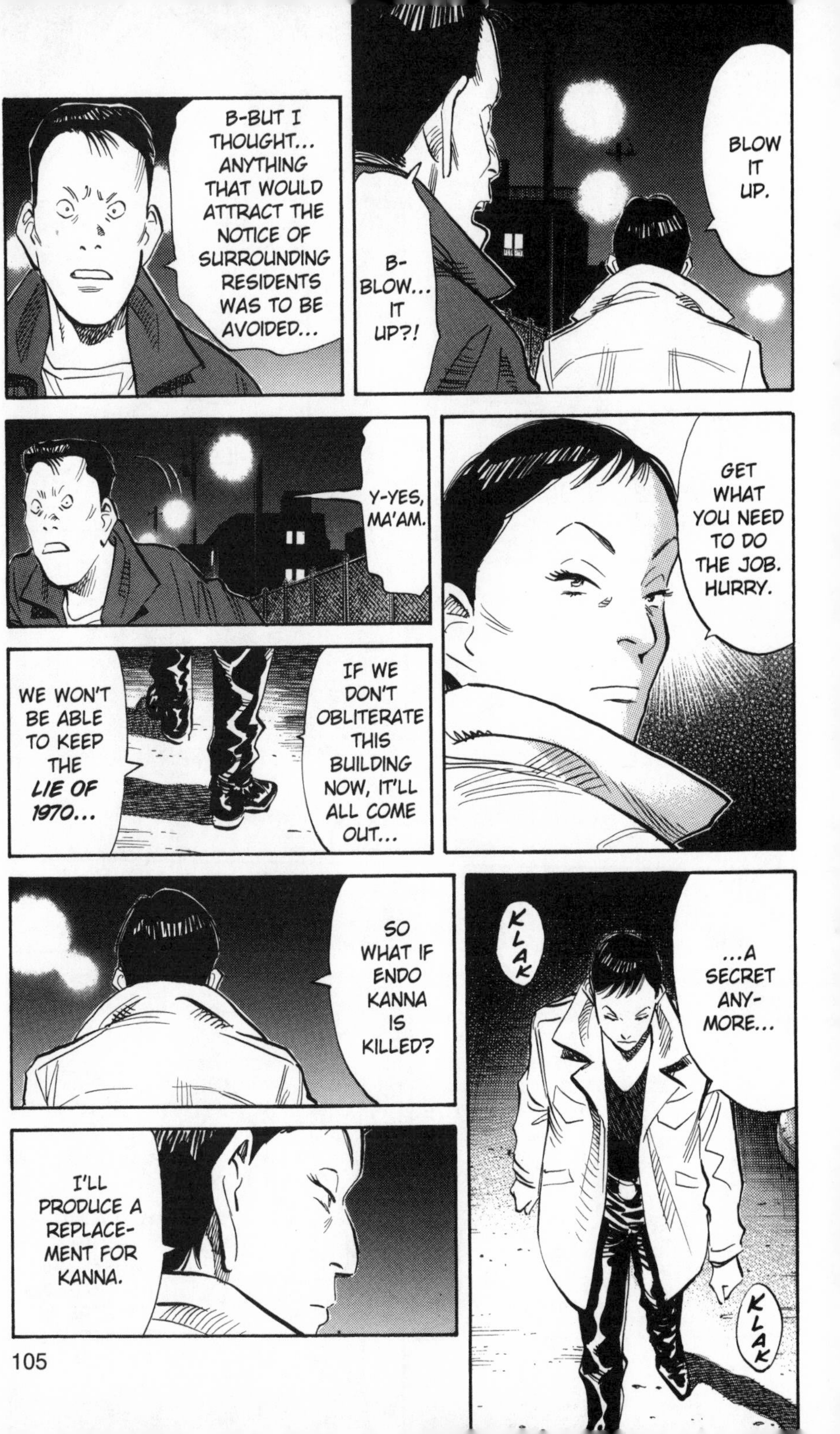
BLOW IT UP.
B-BLOW... IT UP?!
B-BUT I THOUGHT... ANYTHING THAT WOULD ATTRACT THE NOTICE OF SURROUNDING RESIDENTS WAS TO BE AVOIDED...
GET WHAT YOU NEED TO DO THE JOB. HURRY.
Y-YES, MA'AM.
IF WE DON'T OBLITERATE THIS BUILDING NOW, IT'LL ALL COME OUT...
WE WON'T BE ABLE TO KEEP THE *LIE OF 1970*...
KLAK
...A SECRET ANY-MORE...
KLAK
SO WHAT IF ENDO KANNA IS KILLED?
I'LL PRODUCE A REPLACE-MENT FOR KANNA.

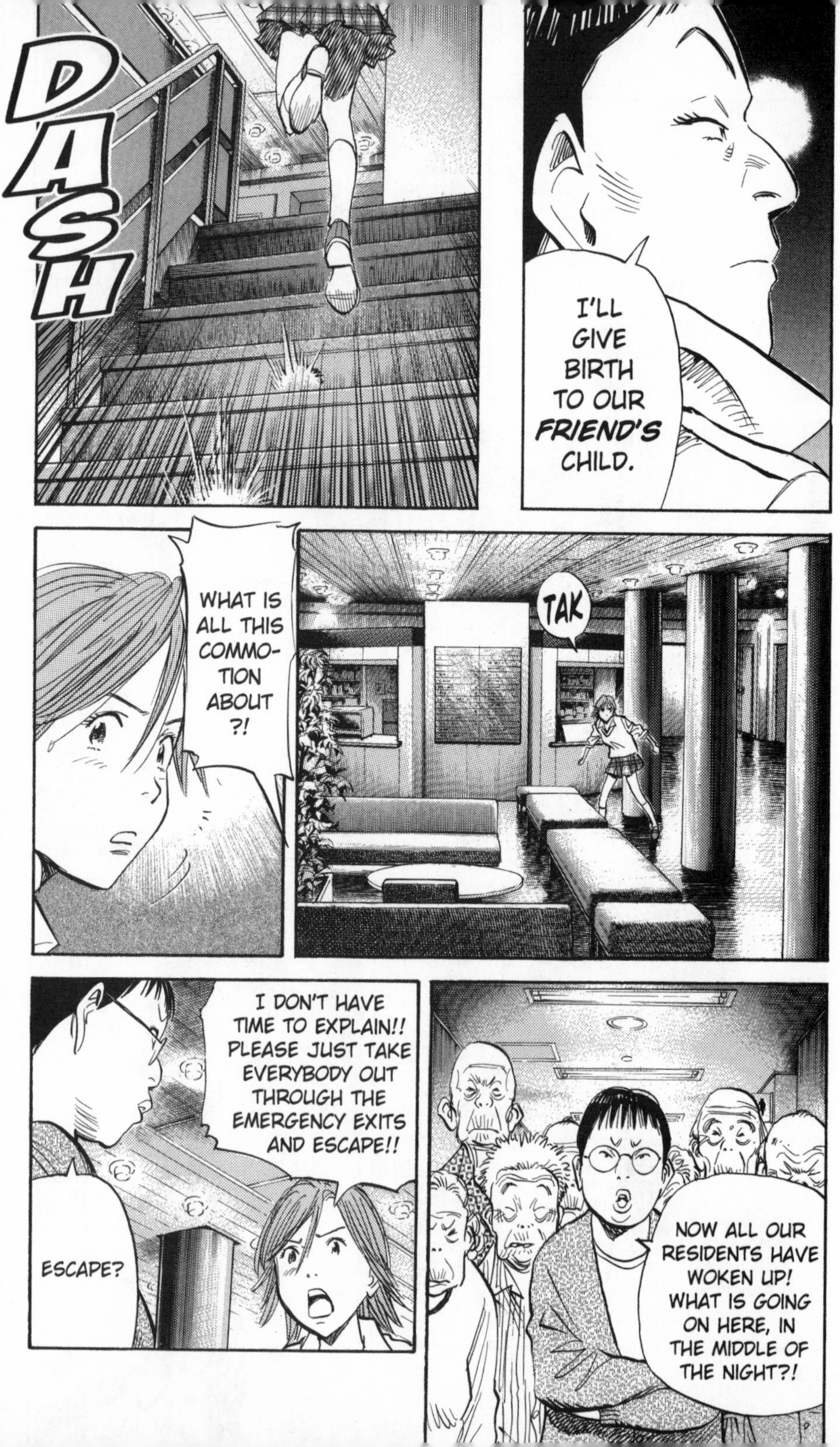
I'LL GIVE BIRTH TO OUR *FRIEND'S* CHILD.
DASH
TAK
WHAT IS ALL THIS COMMO-TION ABOUT ?!
NOW ALL OUR RESIDENTS HAVE WOKEN UP! WHAT IS GOING ON HERE, IN THE MIDDLE OF THE NIGHT?!
I DON'T HAVE TIME TO EXPLAIN!! PLEASE JUST TAKE EVERYBODY OUT THROUGH THE EMERGENCY EXITS AND ESCAPE!!
ESCAPE?

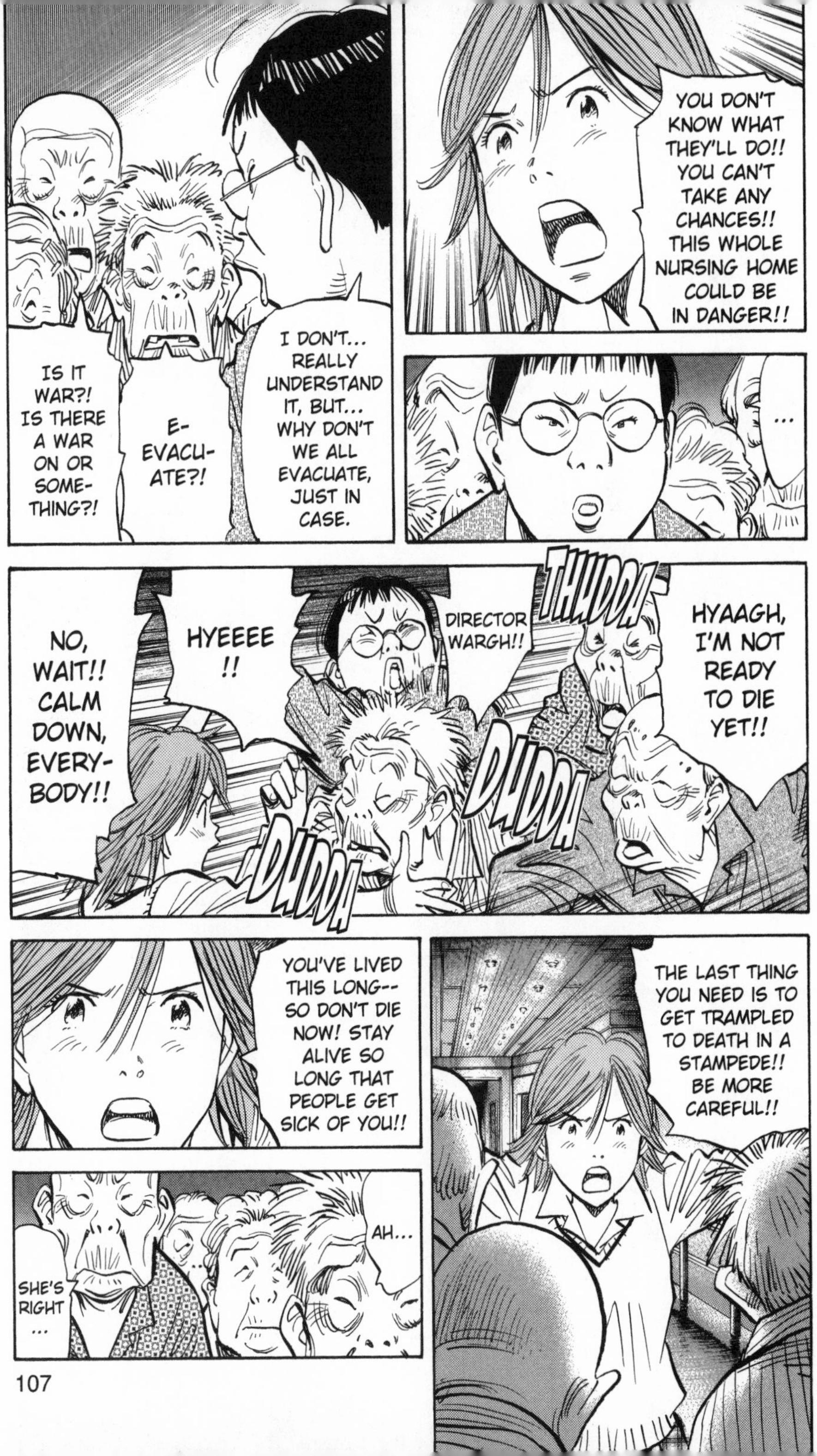
YOU DON'T KNOW WHAT THEY'LL DO!! YOU CAN'T TAKE ANY CHANCES!! THIS WHOLE NURSING HOME COULD BE IN DANGER!!
...
I DON'T... REALLY UNDERSTAND IT, BUT... WHY DON'T WE ALL EVACUATE, JUST IN CASE.
E-EVACUATE?!
IS IT WAR?! IS THERE A WAR ON OR SOMETHING?!
HYAAGH, I'M NOT READY TO DIE YET!!
THUDDA
DIRECTOR WARGH!!
HYEEEE !!
NO, WAIT!! CALM DOWN, EVERYBODY!!
DUDDA
DUDDA
THE LAST THING YOU NEED IS TO GET TRAMPLED TO DEATH IN A STAMPEDE!! BE MORE CAREFUL!!
YOU'VE LIVED THIS LONG-- SO DON'T DIE NOW! STAY ALIVE SO LONG THAT PEOPLE GET SICK OF YOU!!
AH...
...
SHE'S RIGHT ...

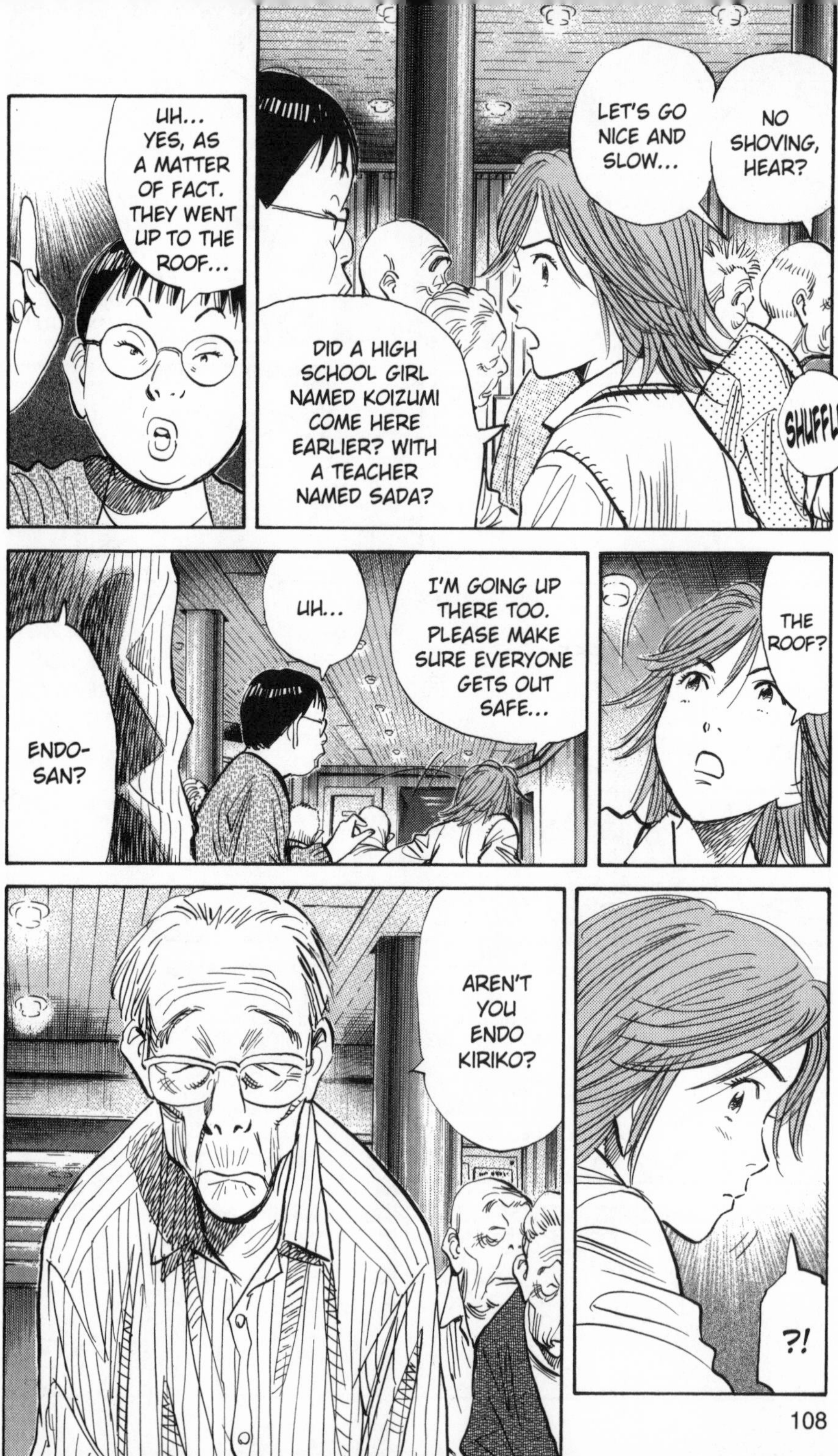
NO SHOVING, HEAR?
LET'S GO NICE AND SLOW...
SHUFFLE
DID A HIGH SCHOOL GIRL NAMED KOIZUMI COME HERE EARLIER? WITH A TEACHER NAMED SADA?
UH... YES, AS A MATTER OF FACT. THEY WENT UP TO THE ROOF...
THE ROOF?
I'M GOING UP THERE TOO. PLEASE MAKE SURE EVERYONE GETS OUT SAFE...
UH...
ENDO-SAN?
?!
AREN'T YOU ENDO KIRIKO?

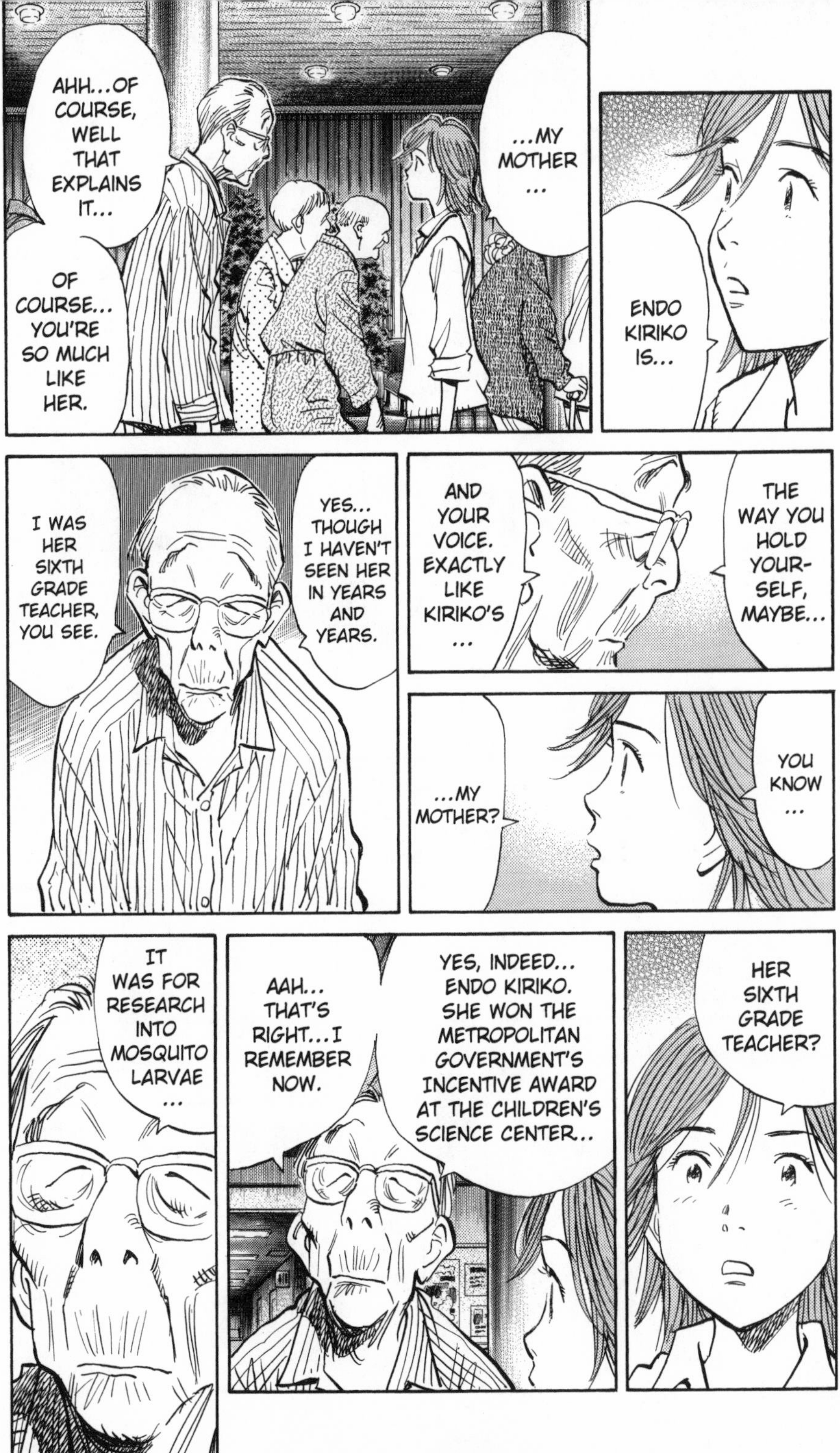
ENDO KIRIKO IS...
...MY MOTHER ...
AHH...OF COURSE, WELL THAT EXPLAINS IT...
OF COURSE... YOU'RE SO MUCH LIKE HER.
THE WAY YOU HOLD YOURSELF, MAYBE...
AND YOUR VOICE. EXACTLY LIKE KIRIKO'S ...
YOU KNOW ...
...MY MOTHER?
YES... THOUGH I HAVEN'T SEEN HER IN YEARS AND YEARS.
I WAS HER SIXTH GRADE TEACHER, YOU SEE.
HER SIXTH GRADE TEACHER?
YES, INDEED... ENDO KIRIKO. SHE WON THE METROPOLITAN GOVERNMENT'S INCENTIVE AWARD AT THE CHILDREN'S SCIENCE CENTER...
AAH... THAT'S RIGHT...I REMEMBER NOW.
IT WAS FOR RESEARCH INTO MOSQUITO LARVAE ...

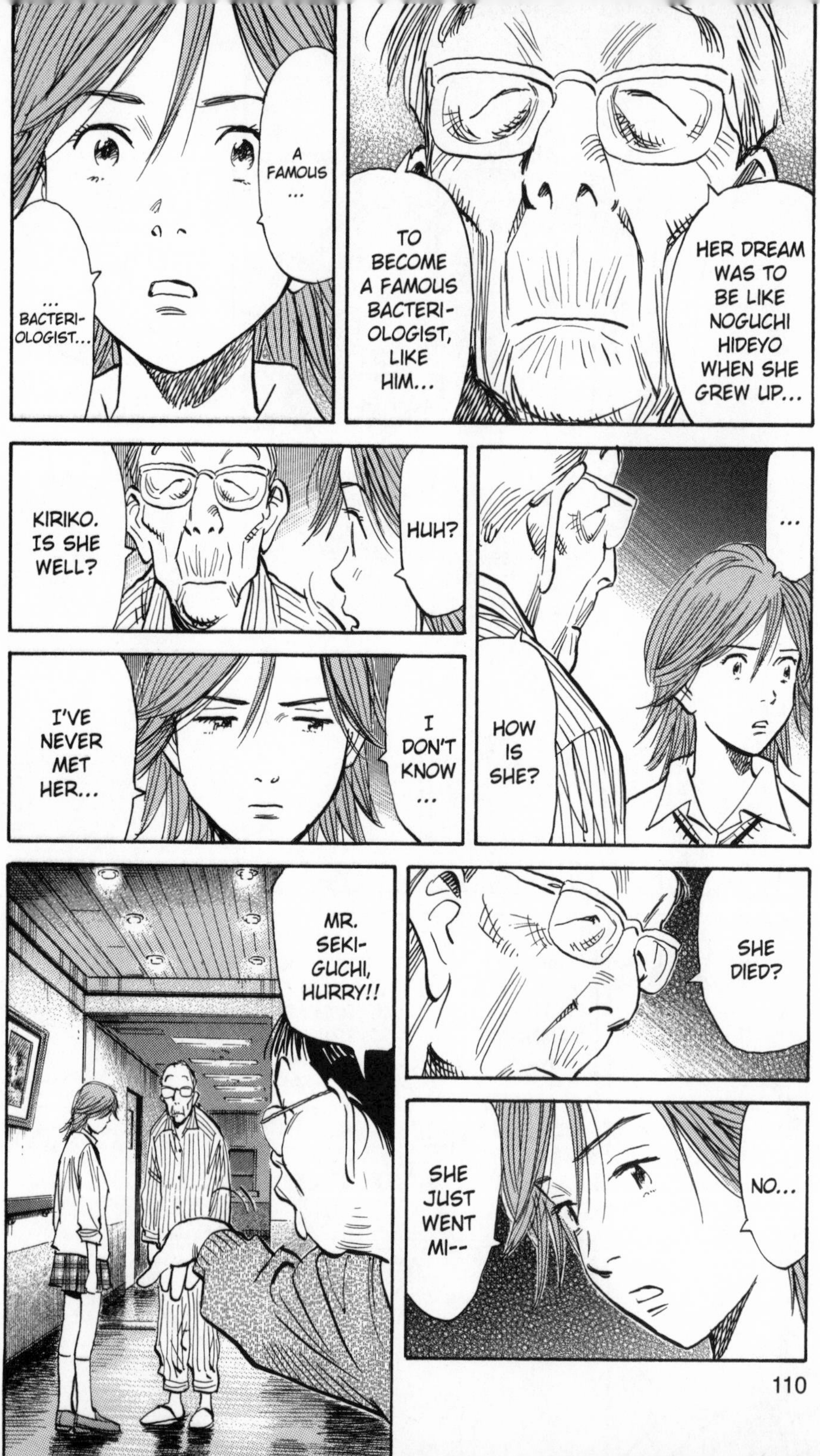
HER DREAM WAS TO BE LIKE NOGUCHI HIDEYO WHEN SHE GREW UP...
TO BECOME A FAMOUS BACTERIOLOGIST, LIKE HIM...
A FAMOUS ...
... BACTERIOLOGIST...
...
HOW IS SHE?
HUH?
KIRIKO. IS SHE WELL?
I DON'T KNOW ...
I'VE NEVER MET HER...
SHE DIED?
NO...
SHE JUST WENT MI--
MR. SEKIGUCHI, HURRY!!

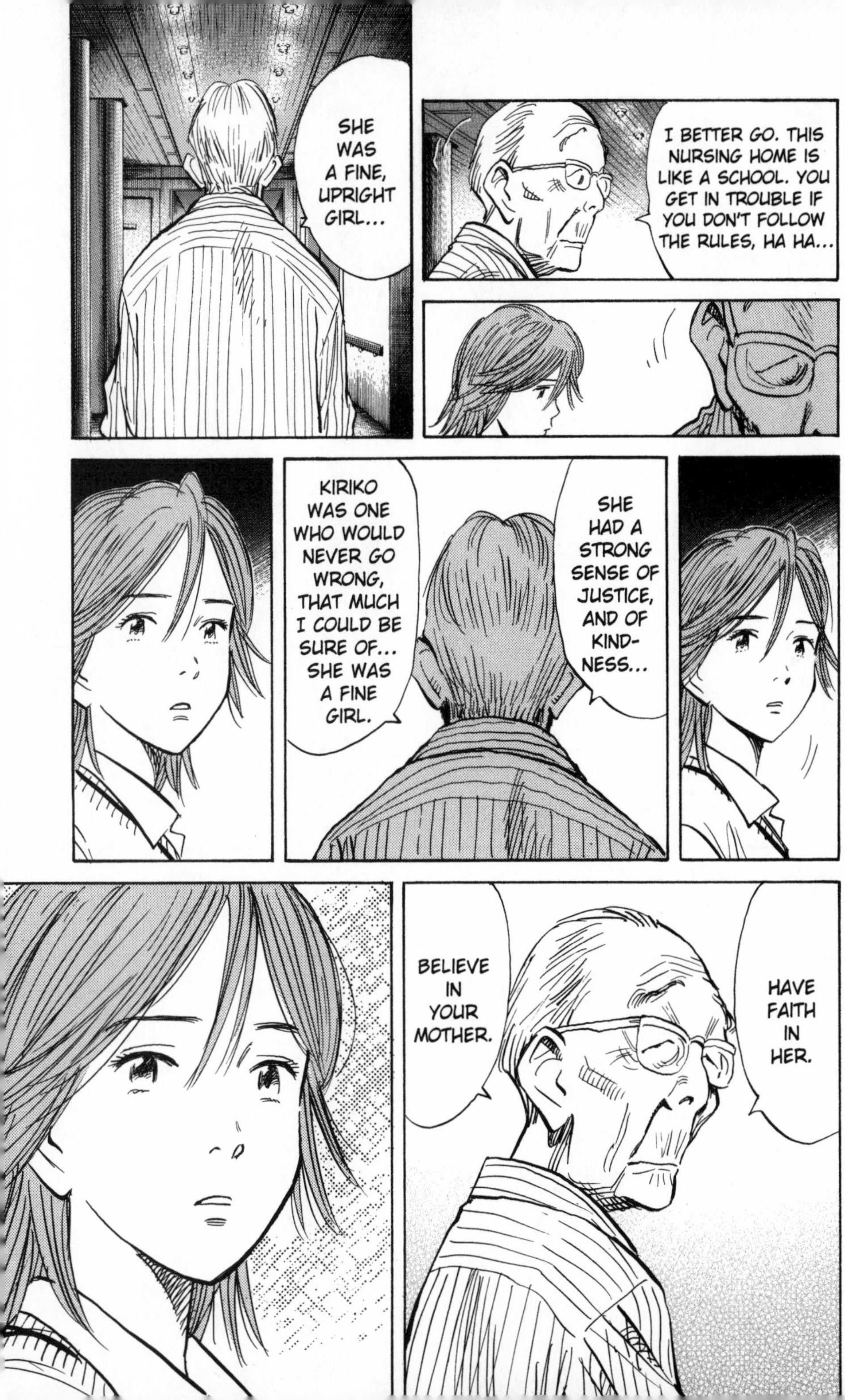
I BETTER GO. THIS NURSING HOME IS LIKE A SCHOOL. YOU GET IN TROUBLE IF YOU DON'T FOLLOW THE RULES, HA HA...
SHE WAS A FINE, UPRIGHT GIRL...
SHE HAD A STRONG SENSE OF JUSTICE, AND OF KIND-NESS...
KIRIKO WAS ONE WHO WOULD NEVER GO WRONG, THAT MUCH I COULD BE SURE OF... SHE WAS A FINE GIRL.
HAVE FAITH IN HER.
BELIEVE IN YOUR MOTHER.

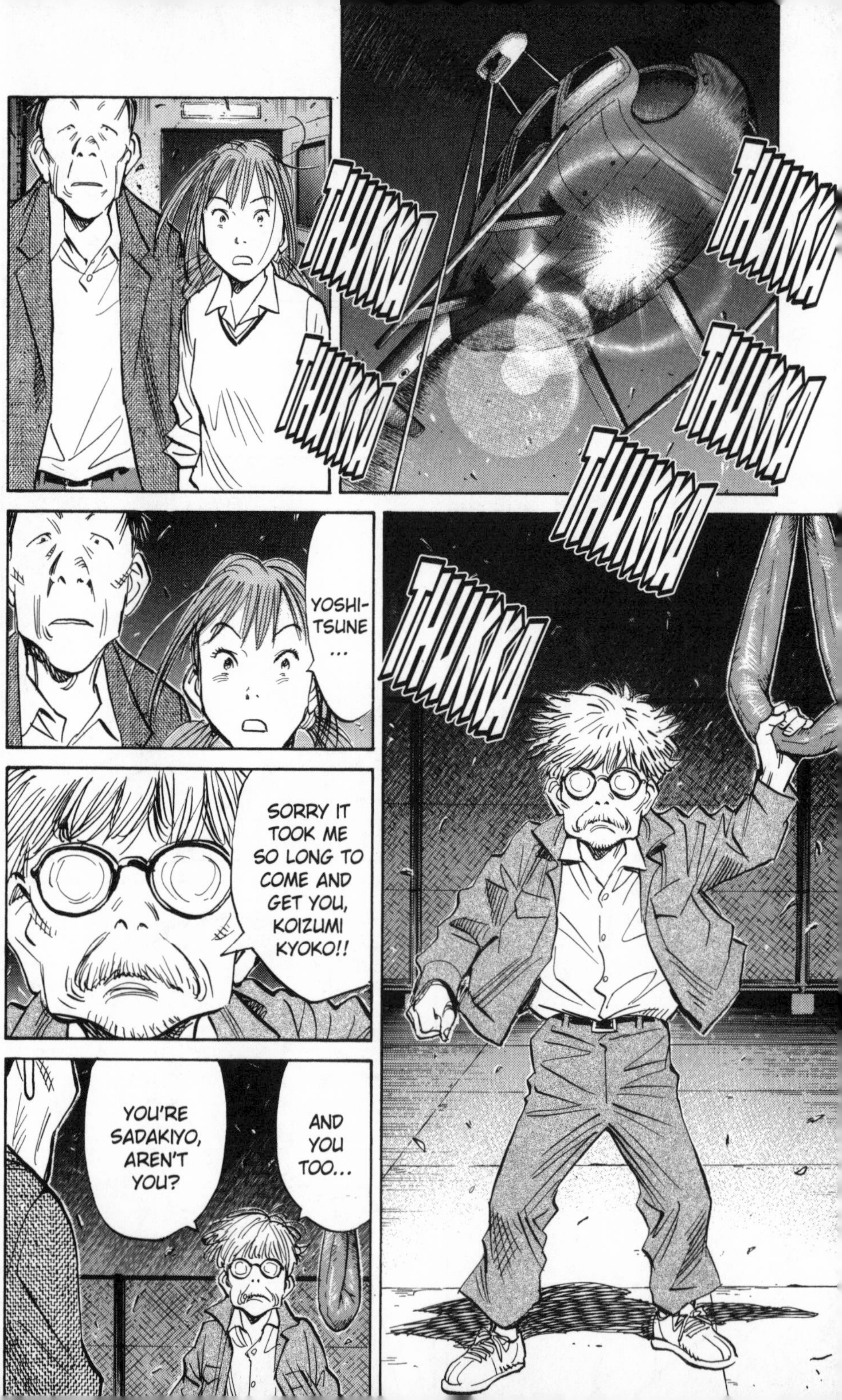
THUKKA
THUKKA
THUKKA
THUKKA
THUKKA
THUKKA
THUKKA
YOSHI-TSUNE...
SORRY IT TOOK ME SO LONG TO COME AND GET YOU, KOIZUMI KYOKO!!
AND YOU TOO...
YOU'RE SADAKIYO, AREN'T YOU?

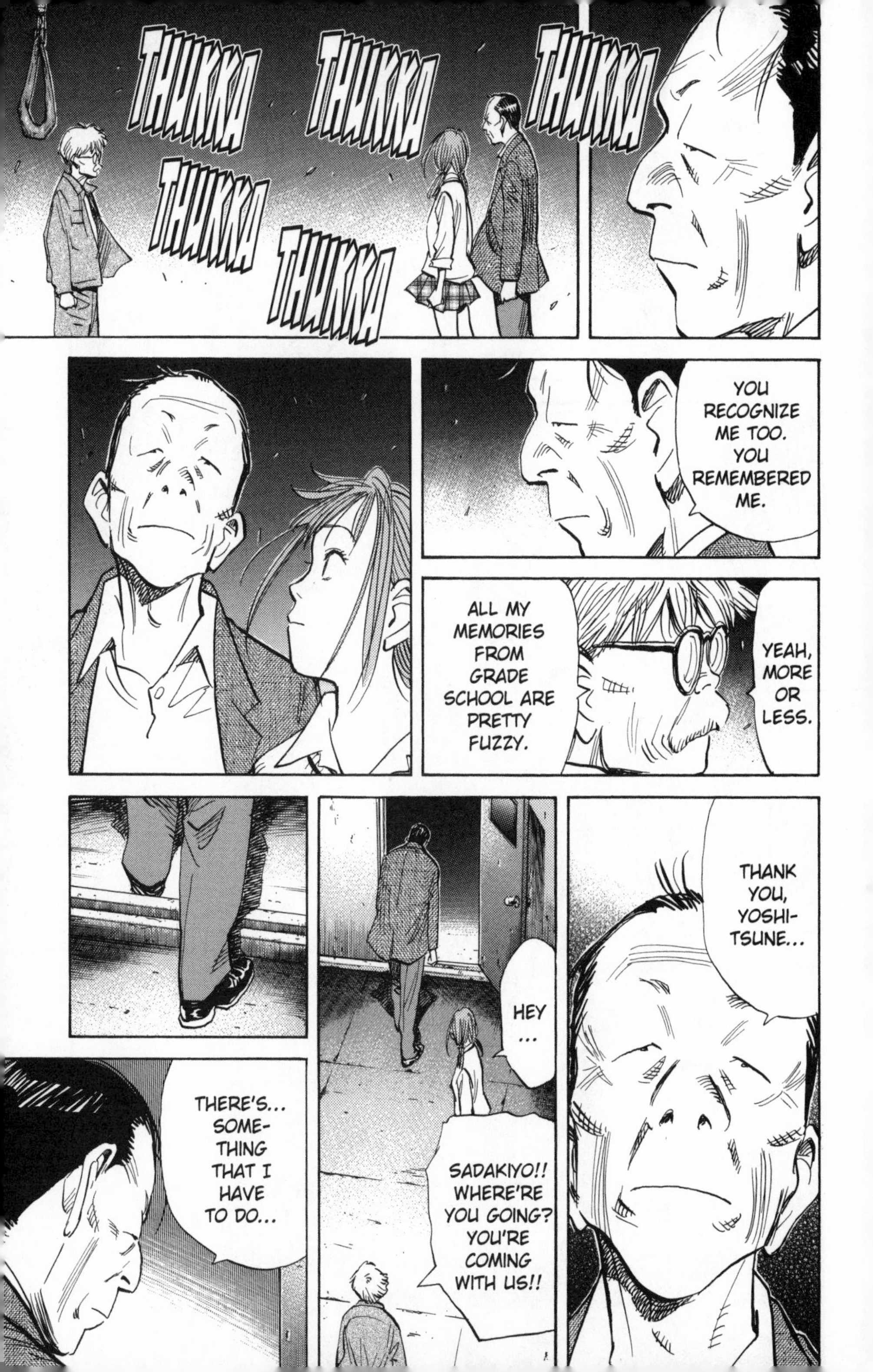
THUKKA
THUKKA
THUKKA
THUKKA
THUKKA
YOU RECOGNIZE ME TOO. YOU REMEMBERED ME.
YEAH, MORE OR LESS.
ALL MY MEMORIES FROM GRADE SCHOOL ARE PRETTY FUZZY.
THANK YOU, YOSHI-TSUNE...
HEY ...
SADAKIYO!! WHERE'RE YOU GOING? YOU'RE COMING WITH US!!
THERE'S... SOME-THING THAT I HAVE TO DO...

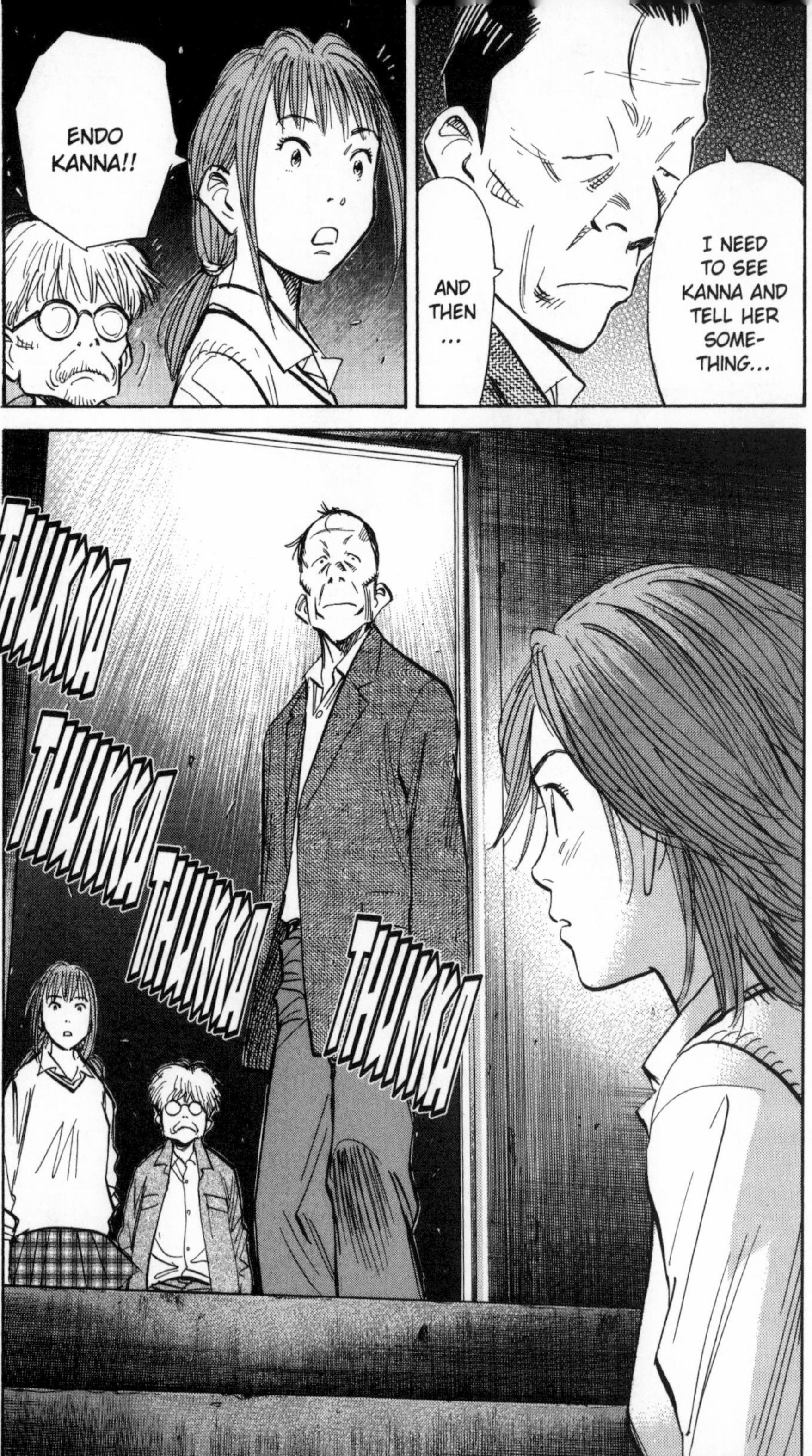
I NEED TO SEE KANNA AND TELL HER SOME-THING...
AND THEN...
ENDO KANNA!!
THUKKA
THUKKA
THUKKA
THUKKA

Chapter 7 Sadakiyo's Decision

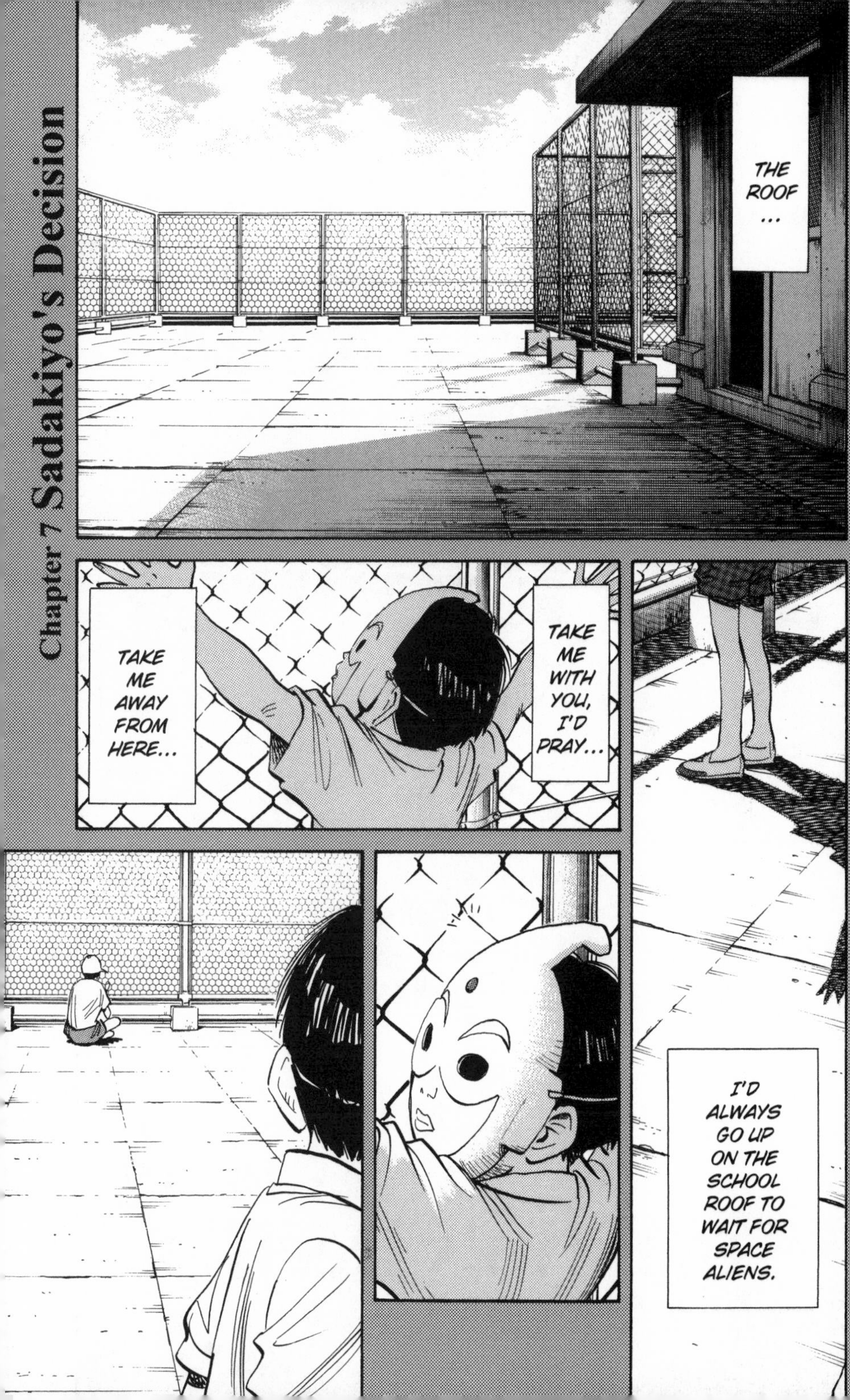
THE ROOF ...
I'D ALWAYS GO UP ON THE SCHOOL ROOF TO WAIT FOR SPACE ALIENS.
TAKE ME WITH YOU, I'D PRAY...
TAKE ME AWAY FROM HERE...

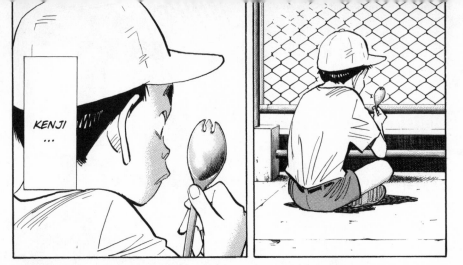

KENJI ...

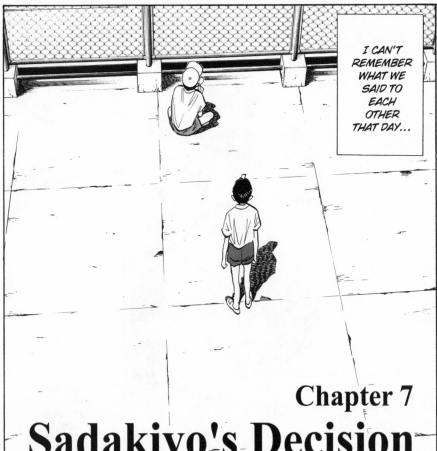

I CAN'T REMEMBER WHAT WE SAID TO EACH OTHER THAT DAY...

Chapter 7
Sadakiyo's Decision

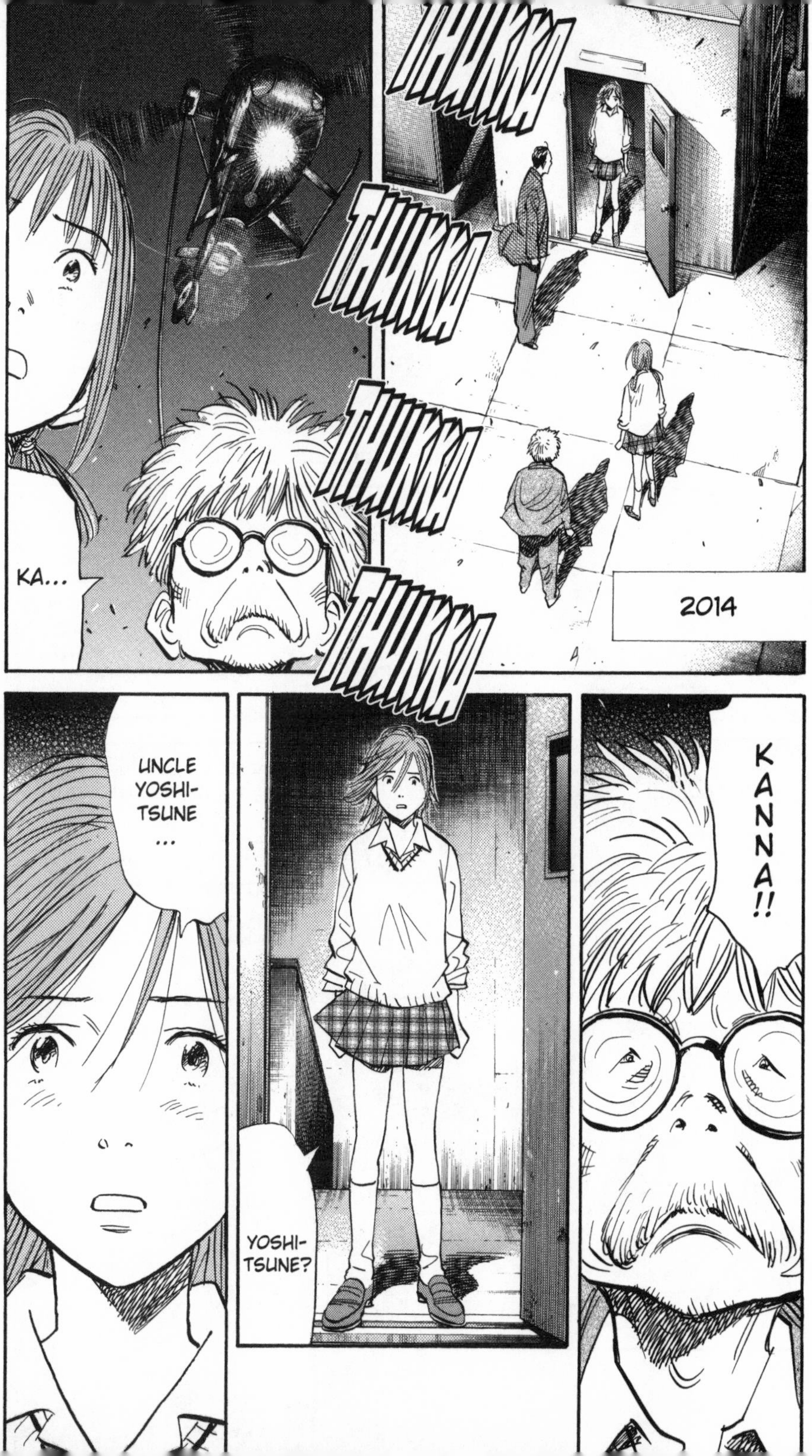
THUKKA
THUKKA
THUKKA
THUKKA
2014
KA...
KANNA!!
YOSHI-TSUNE?
UNCLE YOSHI-TSUNE ...

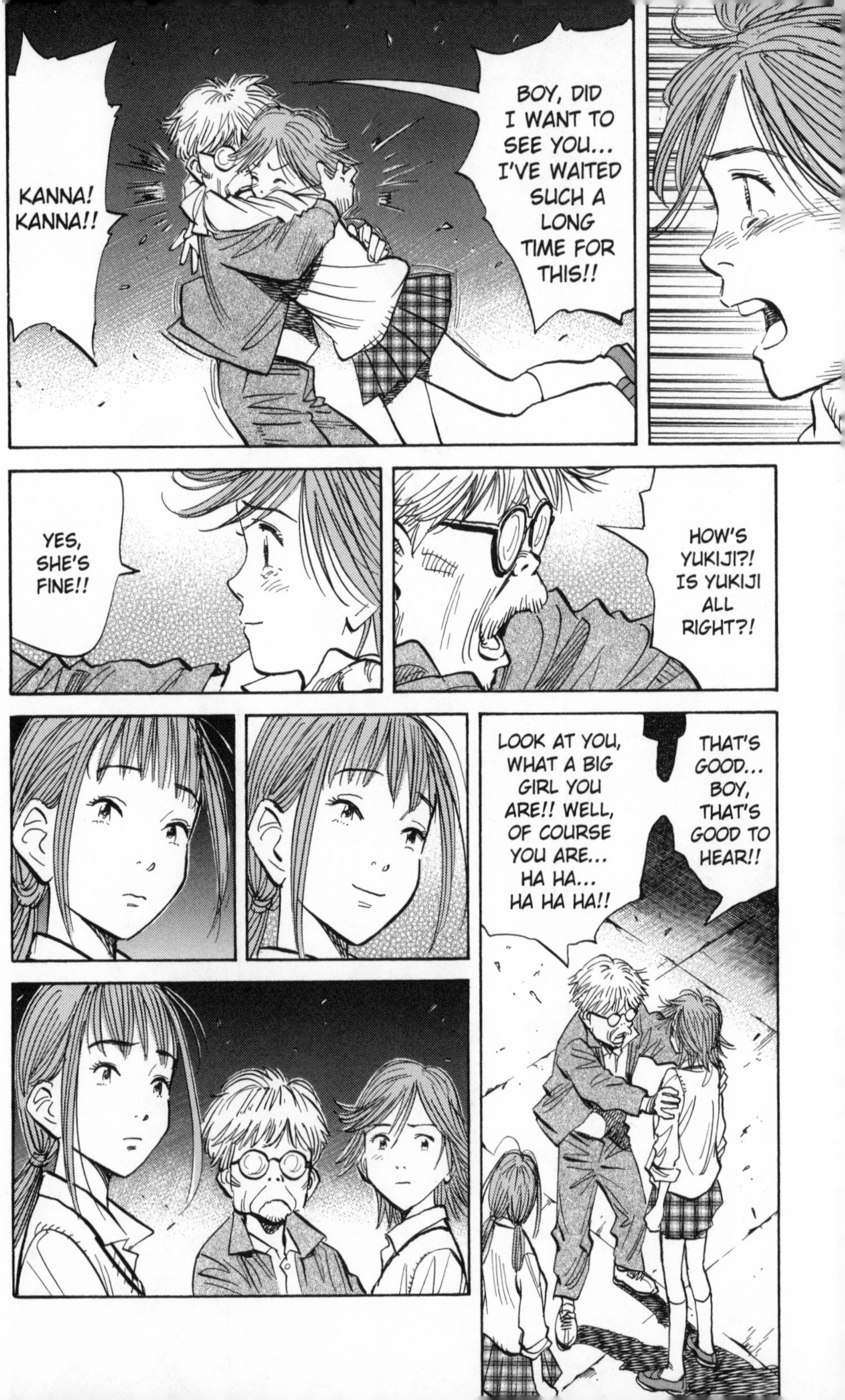
BOY, DID I WANT TO SEE YOU... I'VE WAITED SUCH A LONG TIME FOR THIS!!
KANNA! KANNA!!
HOW'S YUKIJI?! IS YUKIJI ALL RIGHT?!
YES, SHE'S FINE!!
THAT'S GOOD... BOY, THAT'S GOOD TO HEAR!!
LOOK AT YOU, WHAT A BIG GIRL YOU ARE!! WELL, OF COURSE YOU ARE... HA HA... HA HA HA!!

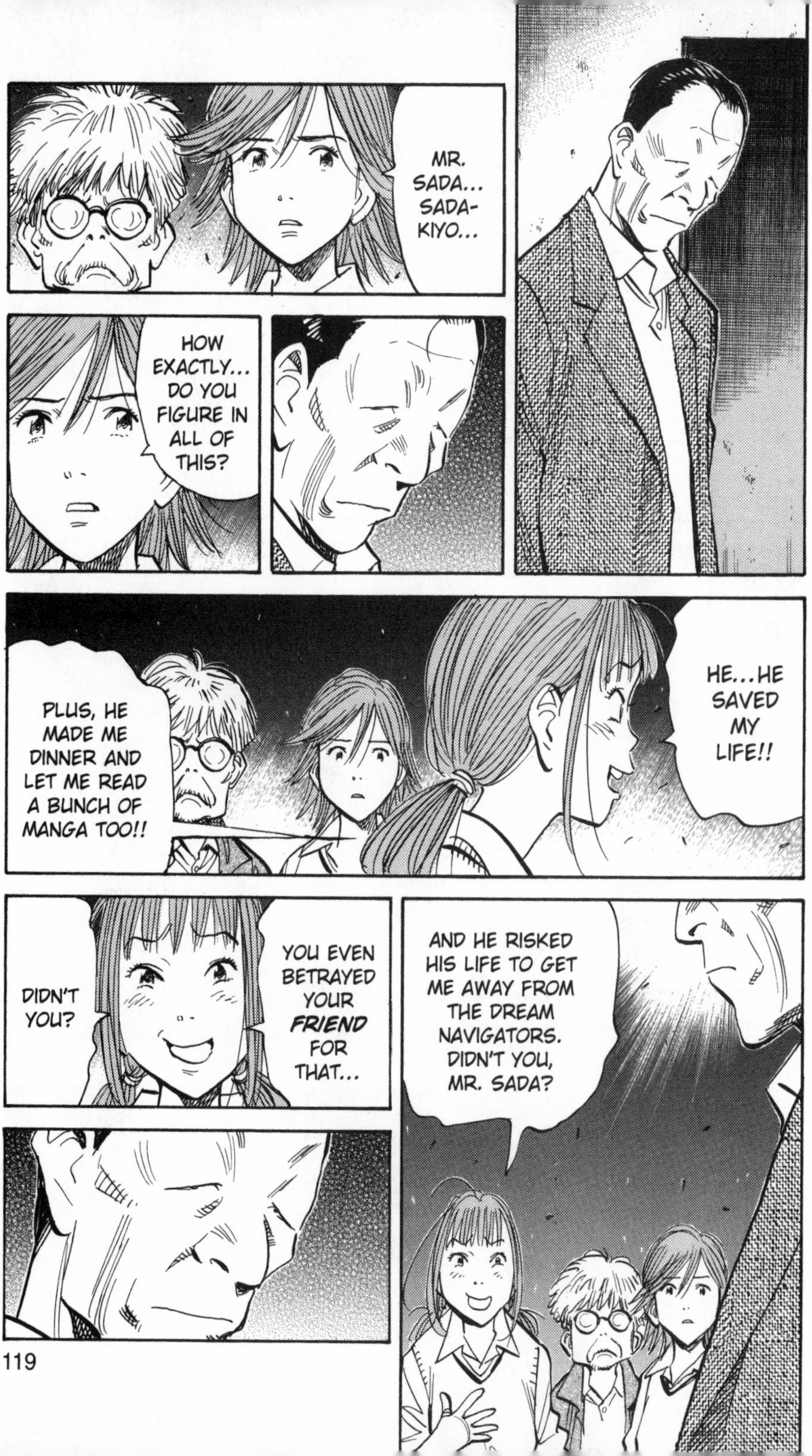
MR. SADA... SADA-KIYO...
HOW EXACTLY... DO YOU FIGURE IN ALL OF THIS?
HE...HE SAVED MY LIFE!!
PLUS, HE MADE ME DINNER AND LET ME READ A BUNCH OF MANGA TOO!!
AND HE RISKED HIS LIFE TO GET ME AWAY FROM THE DREAM NAVIGATORS. DIDN'T YOU, MR. SADA?
YOU EVEN BETRAYED YOUR ***FRIEND*** FOR THAT...
DIDN'T YOU?

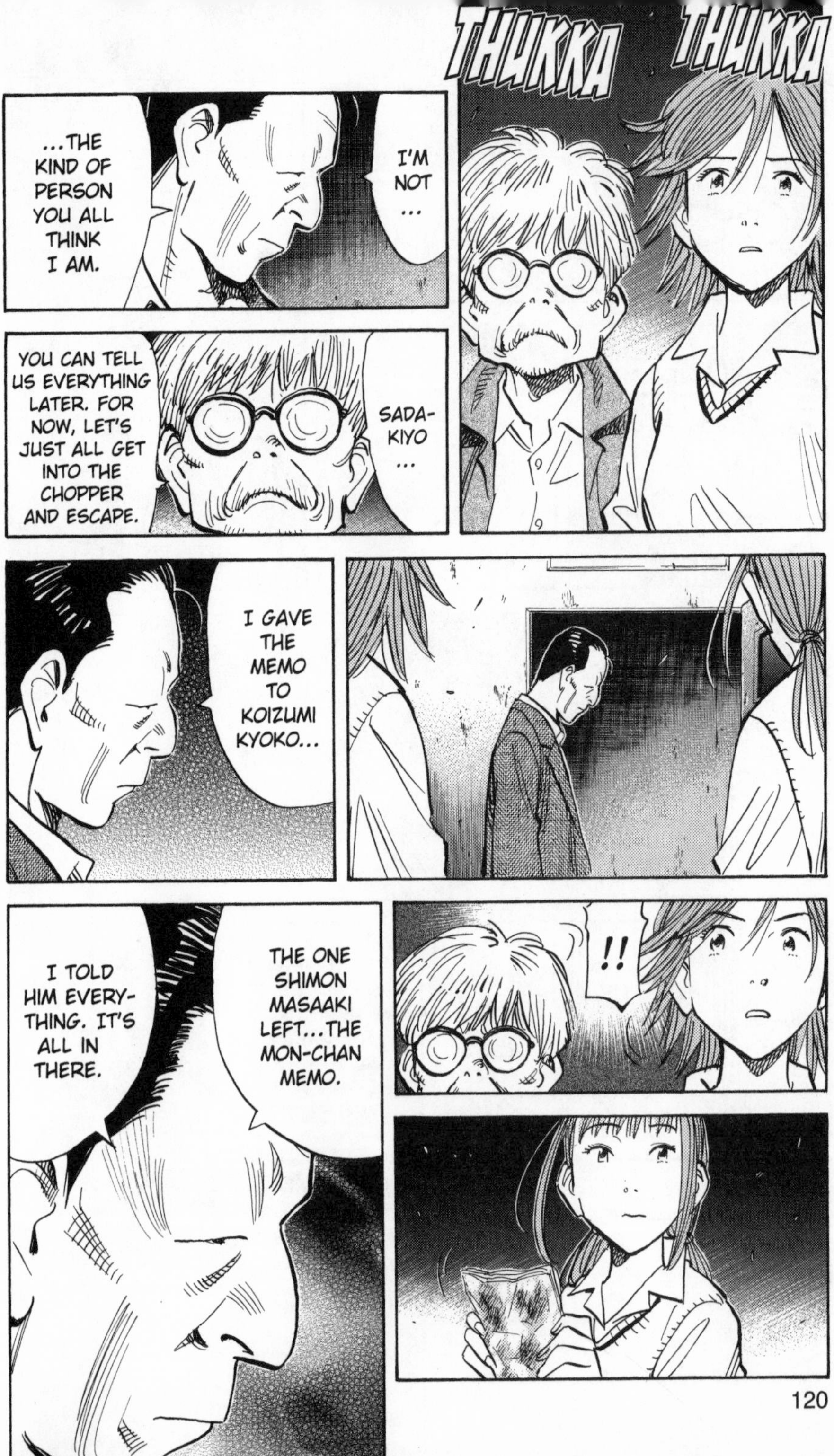
THUKKA THUKKA
I'M NOT ...
...THE KIND OF PERSON YOU ALL THINK I AM.
SADA-KIYO ...
YOU CAN TELL US EVERYTHING LATER. FOR NOW, LET'S JUST ALL GET INTO THE CHOPPER AND ESCAPE.
I GAVE THE MEMO TO KOIZUMI KYOKO...
!!
THE ONE SHIMON MASAAKI LEFT...THE MON-CHAN MEMO.
I TOLD HIM EVERY-THING. IT'S ALL IN THERE.

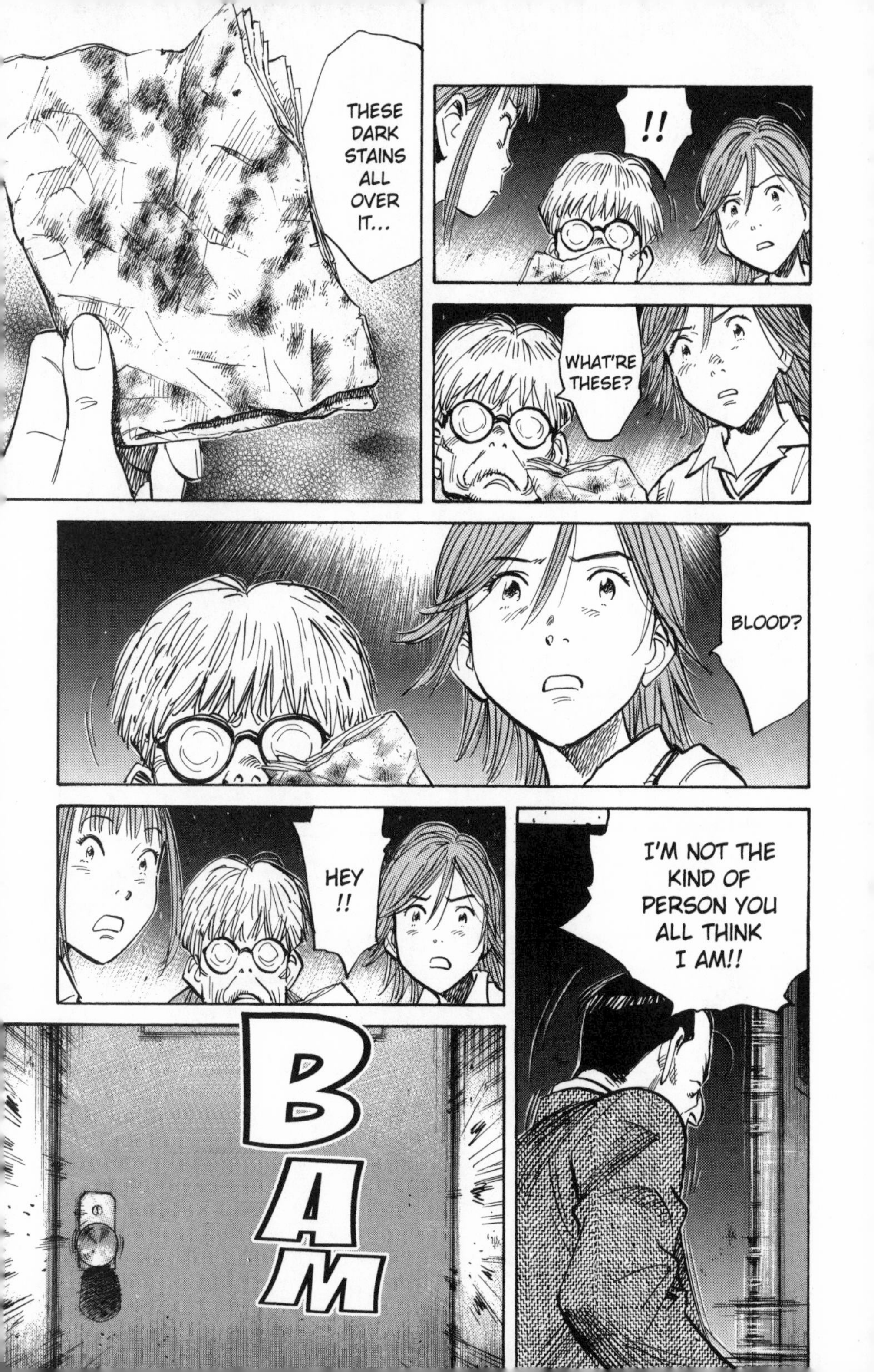
!!
WHAT'RE THESE?
THESE DARK STAINS ALL OVER IT...
BLOOD?
I'M NOT THE KIND OF PERSON YOU ALL THINK I AM!!
HEY !!
BAM

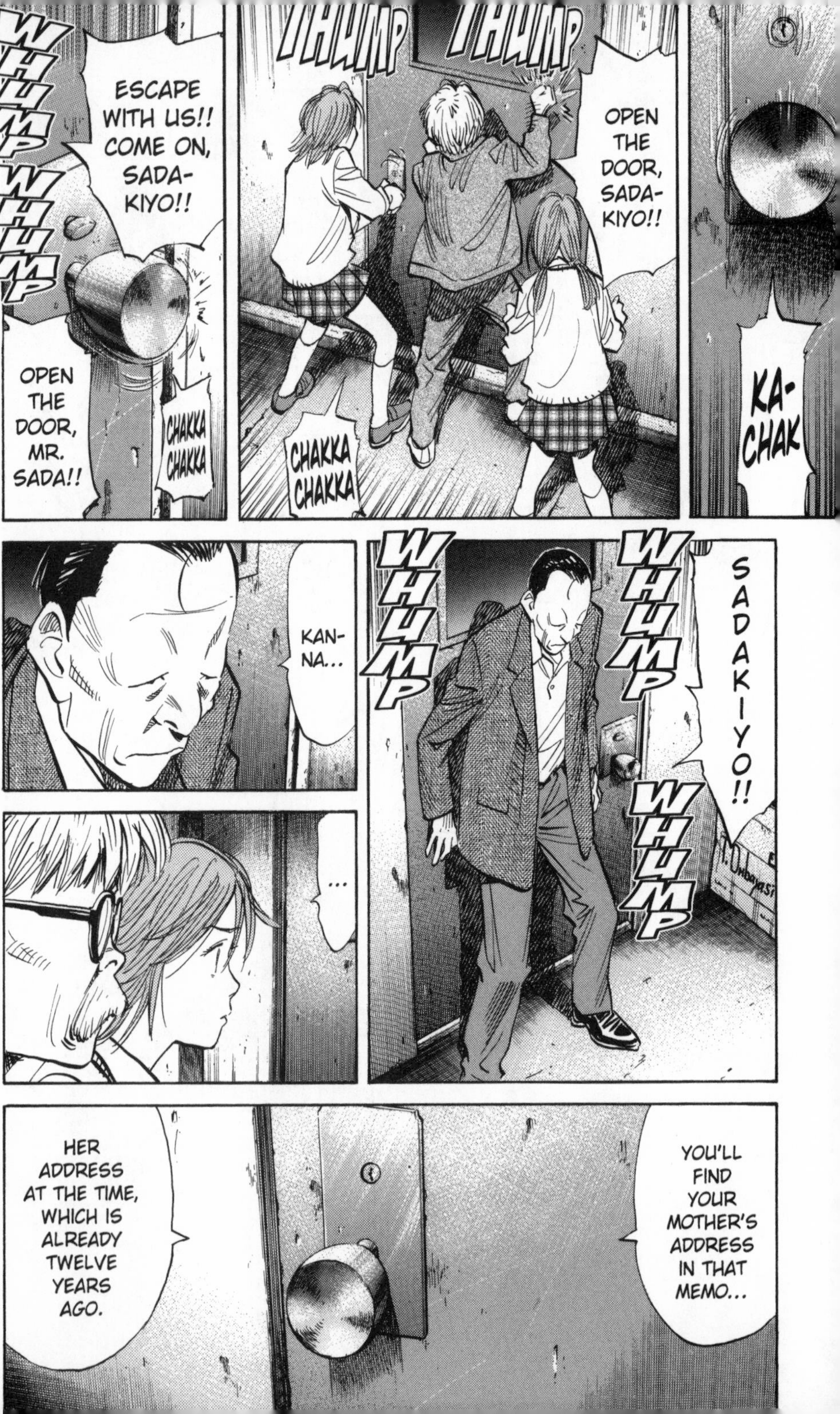
KA-CHAK
THUMP THUMP
OPEN THE DOOR, SADA-KIYO!!
CHAKKA CHAKKA
WHUMP WHUMP
ESCAPE WITH US!! COME ON, SADA-KIYO!!
OPEN THE DOOR, MR. SADA!!
CHAKKA CHAKKA
SADAKIYO!!
WHUMP
WHUMP
WHUMP
KAN-NA...
...
YOU'LL FIND YOUR MOTHER'S ADDRESS IN THAT MEMO...
HER ADDRESS AT THE TIME, WHICH IS ALREADY TWELVE YEARS AGO.

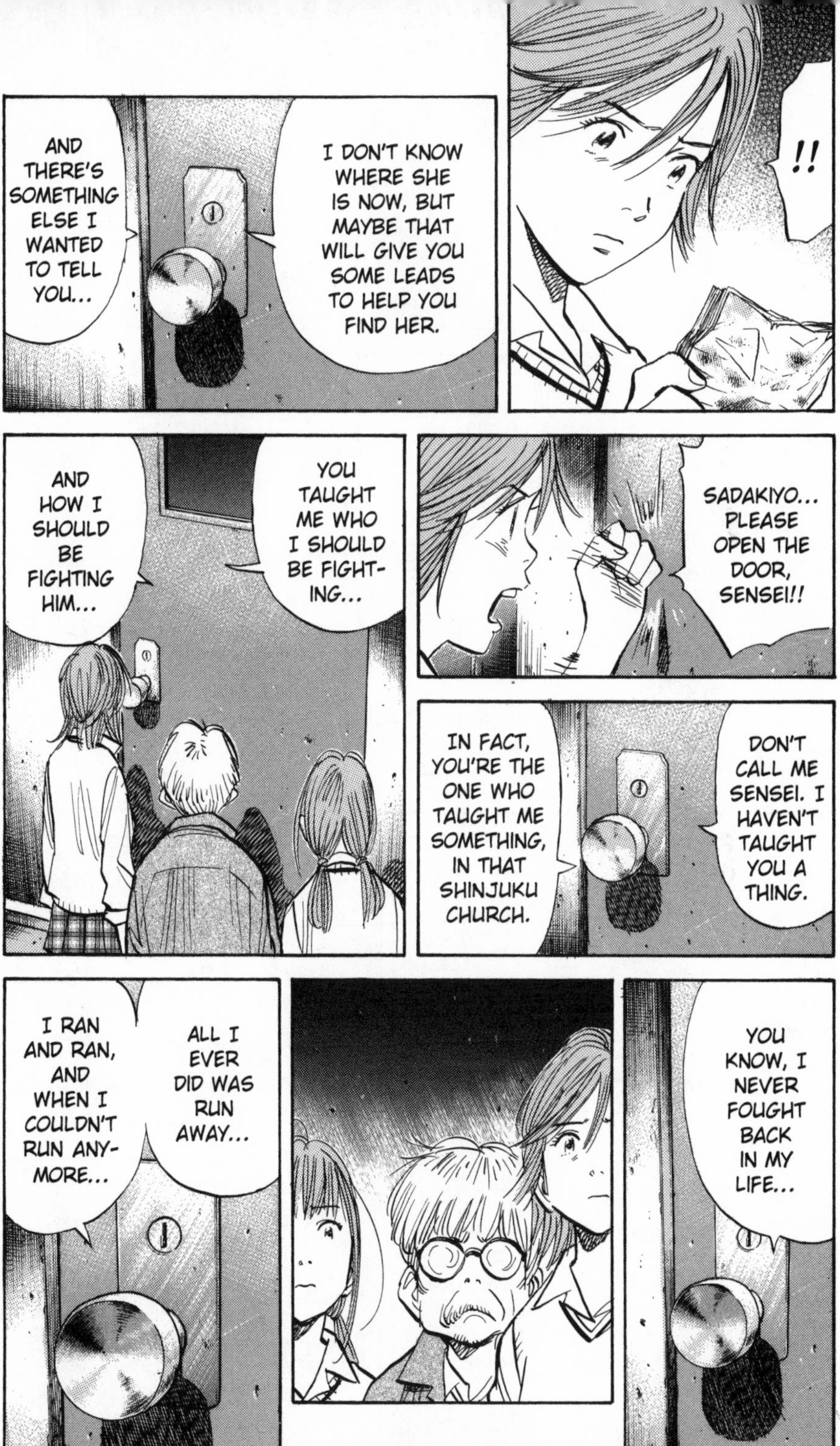

!!
I DON'T KNOW WHERE SHE IS NOW, BUT MAYBE THAT WILL GIVE YOU SOME LEADS TO HELP YOU FIND HER.
AND THERE'S SOMETHING ELSE I WANTED TO TELL YOU...
SADAKIYO... PLEASE OPEN THE DOOR, SENSEI!!
DON'T CALL ME SENSEI. I HAVEN'T TAUGHT YOU A THING.
IN FACT, YOU'RE THE ONE WHO TAUGHT ME SOMETHING, IN THAT SHINJUKU CHURCH.
YOU TAUGHT ME WHO I SHOULD BE FIGHT-ING...
AND HOW I SHOULD BE FIGHTING HIM...
YOU KNOW, I NEVER FOUGHT BACK IN MY LIFE...
ALL I EVER DID WAS RUN AWAY...
I RAN AND RAN, AND WHEN I COULDN'T RUN ANY-MORE...

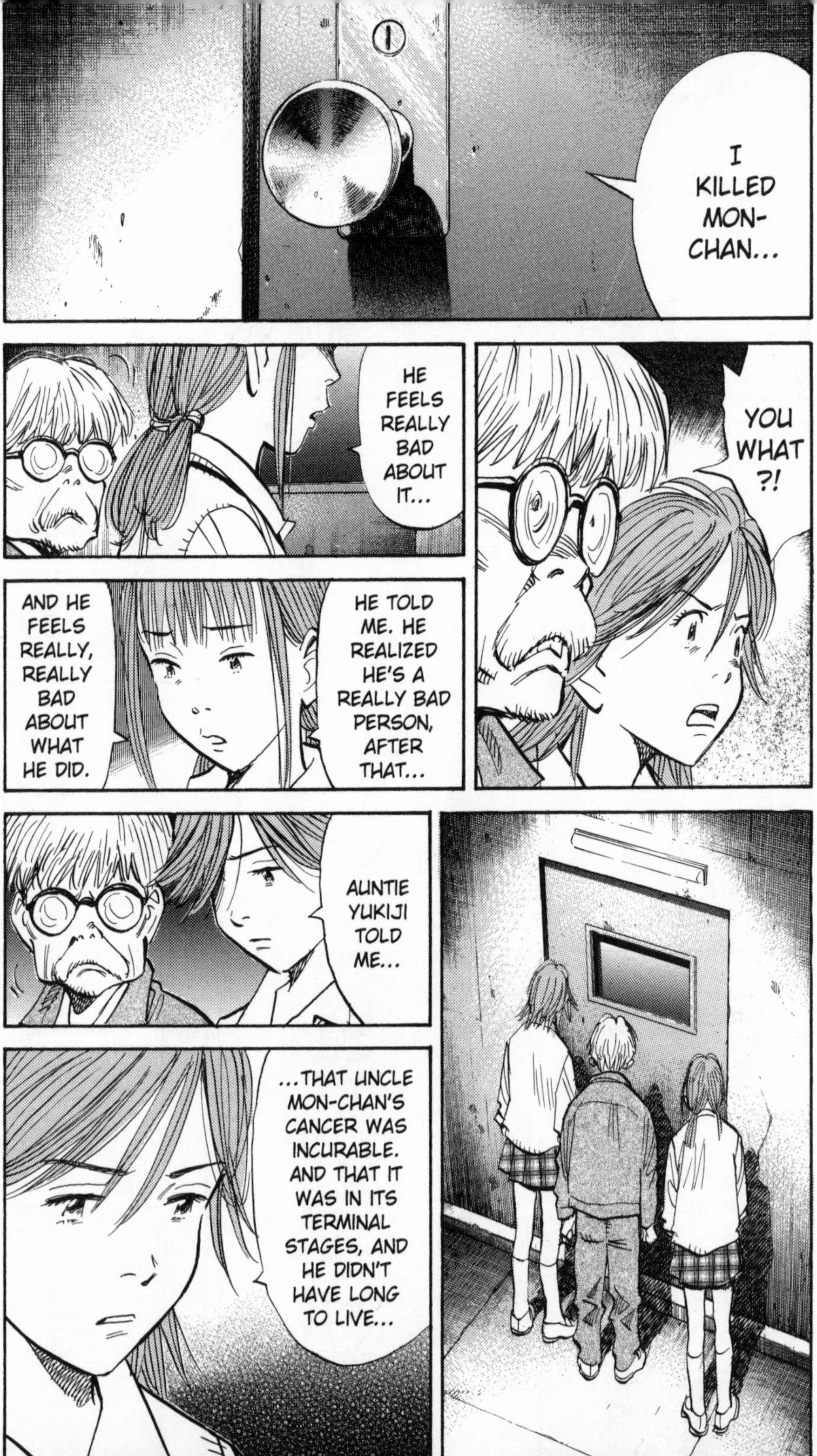
I KILLED MON-CHAN...
YOU WHAT?!
HE FEELS REALLY BAD ABOUT IT...
HE TOLD ME. HE REALIZED HE'S A REALLY BAD PERSON, AFTER THAT...
AND HE FEELS REALLY, REALLY BAD ABOUT WHAT HE DID.
AUNTIE YUKIJI TOLD ME...
...THAT UNCLE MON-CHAN'S CANCER WAS INCURABLE. AND THAT IT WAS IN ITS TERMINAL STAGES, AND HE DIDN'T HAVE LONG TO LIVE...

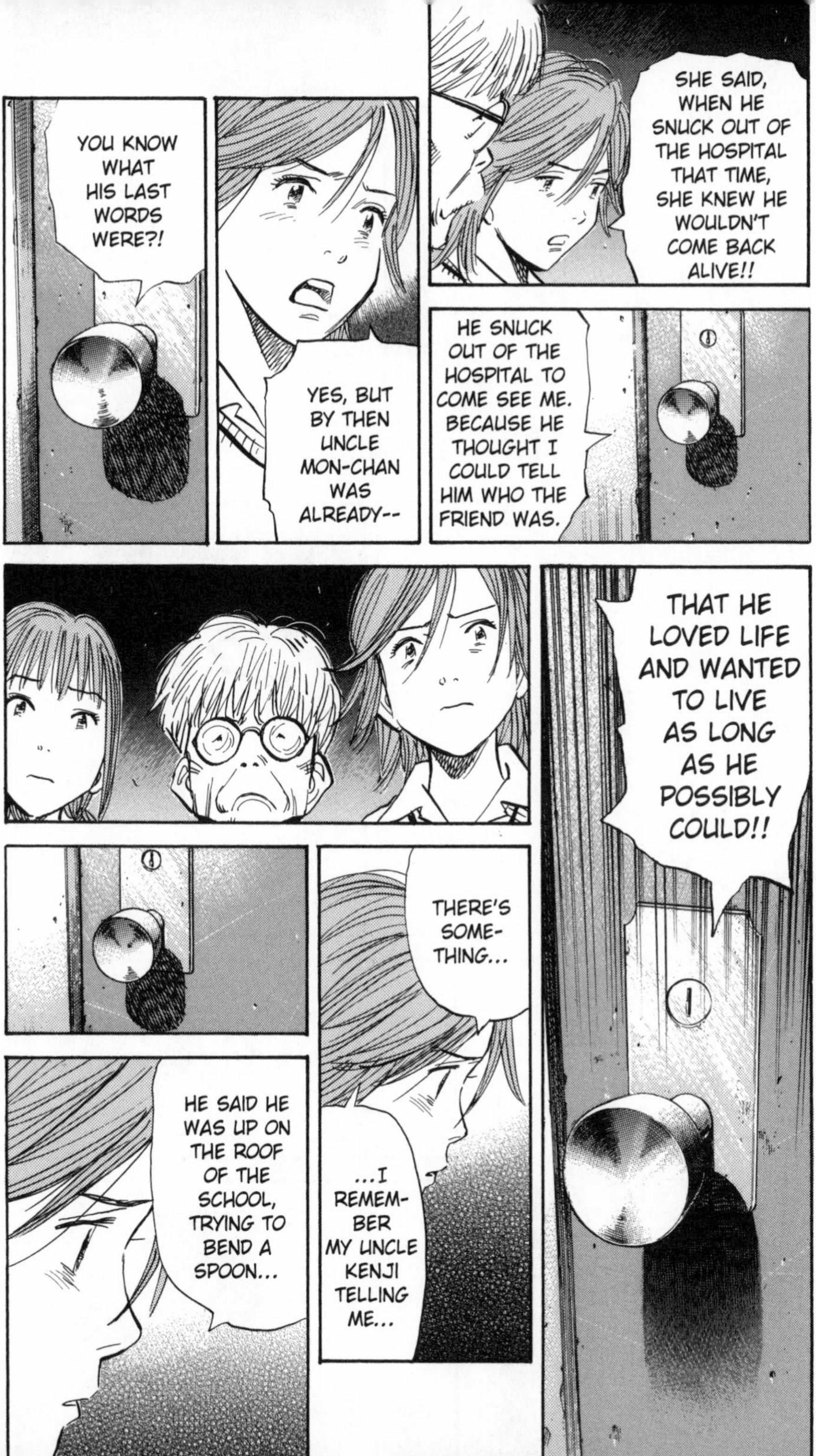
SHE SAID, WHEN HE SNUCK OUT OF THE HOSPITAL THAT TIME, SHE KNEW HE WOULDN'T COME BACK ALIVE!!
HE SNUCK OUT OF THE HOSPITAL TO COME SEE ME. BECAUSE HE THOUGHT I COULD TELL HIM WHO THE FRIEND WAS.
YES, BUT BY THEN UNCLE MON-CHAN WAS ALREADY--
YOU KNOW WHAT HIS LAST WORDS WERE?!
THAT HE LOVED LIFE AND WANTED TO LIVE AS LONG AS HE POSSIBLY COULD!!
THERE'S SOME-THING...
...I REMEM-BER MY UNCLE KENJI TELLING ME...
HE SAID HE WAS UP ON THE ROOF OF THE SCHOOL, TRYING TO BEND A SPOON...

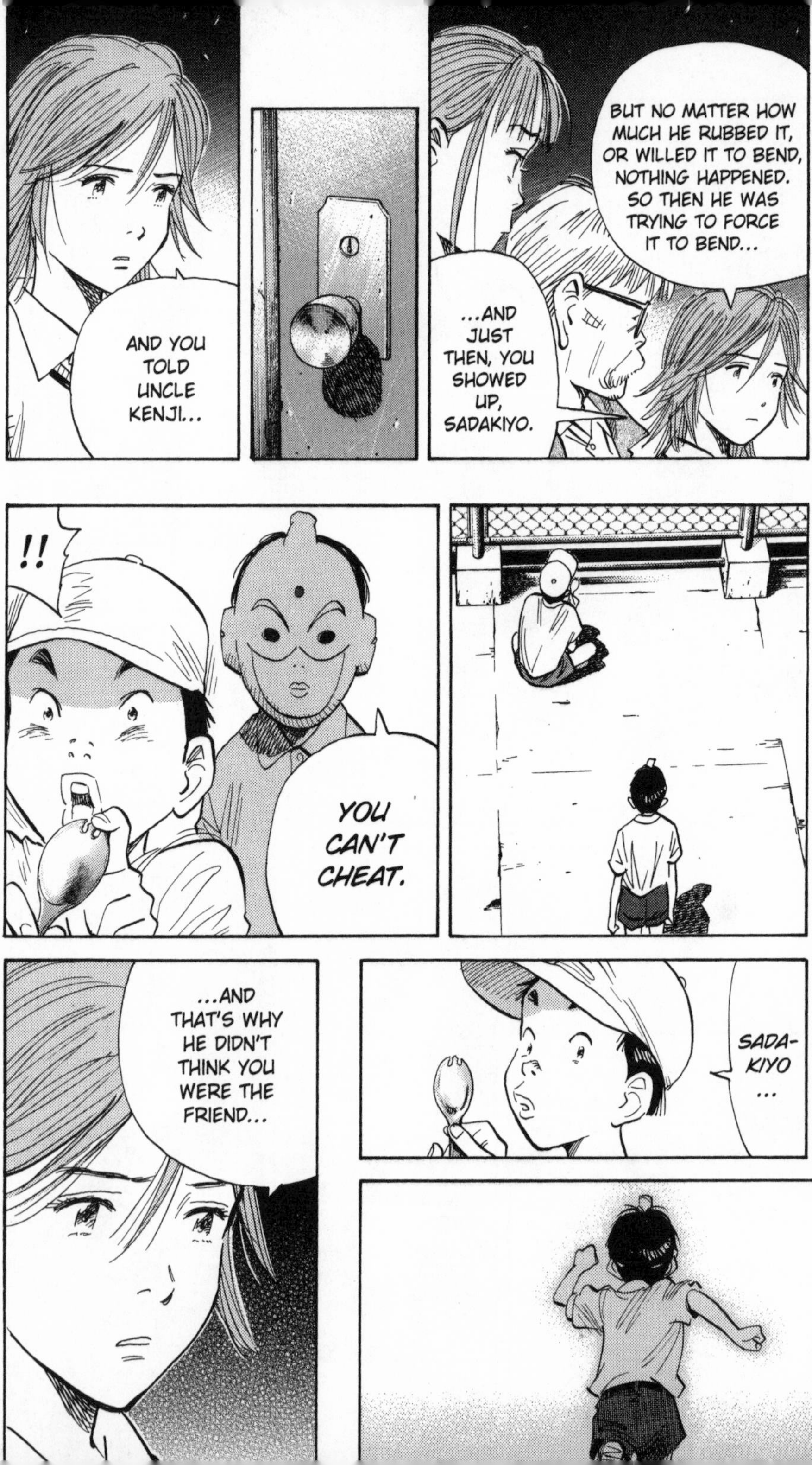
BUT NO MATTER HOW MUCH HE RUBBED IT, OR WILLED IT TO BEND, NOTHING HAPPENED. SO THEN HE WAS TRYING TO FORCE IT TO BEND...
...AND JUST THEN, YOU SHOWED UP, SADAKIYO.
AND YOU TOLD UNCLE KENJI...
!!
YOU CAN'T CHEAT.
SADA-KIYO...
...AND THAT'S WHY HE DIDN'T THINK YOU WERE THE FRIEND...

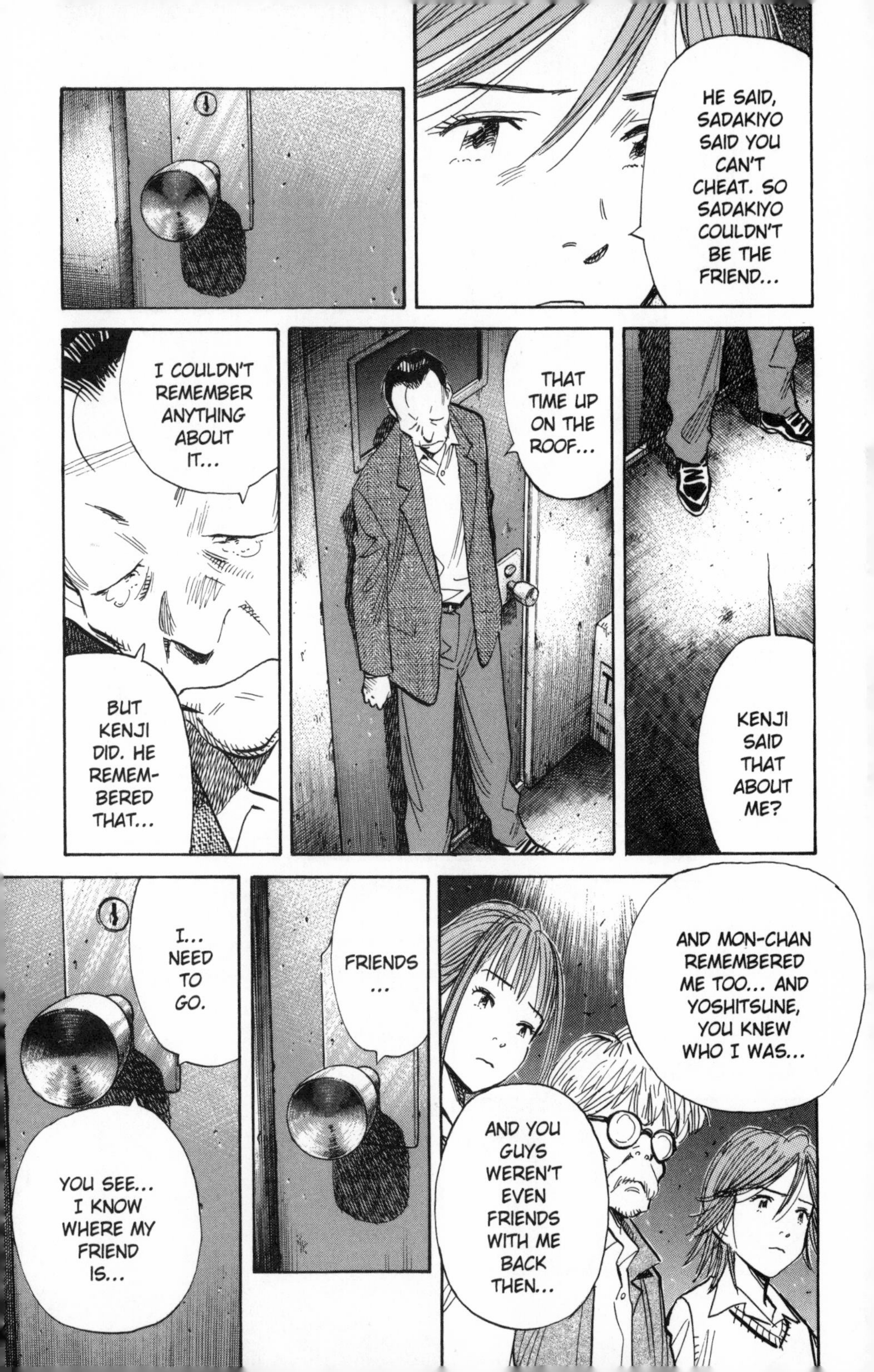
HE SAID, SADAKIYO SAID YOU CAN'T CHEAT. SO SADAKIYO COULDN'T BE THE FRIEND...
KENJI SAID THAT ABOUT ME?
THAT TIME UP ON THE ROOF...
I COULDN'T REMEMBER ANYTHING ABOUT IT...
BUT KENJI DID. HE REMEM-BERED THAT...
AND MON-CHAN REMEMBERED ME TOO... AND YOSHITSUNE, YOU KNEW WHO I WAS...
AND YOU GUYS WEREN'T EVEN FRIENDS WITH ME BACK THEN...
FRIENDS ...
I... NEED TO GO.
YOU SEE... I KNOW WHERE MY FRIEND IS...

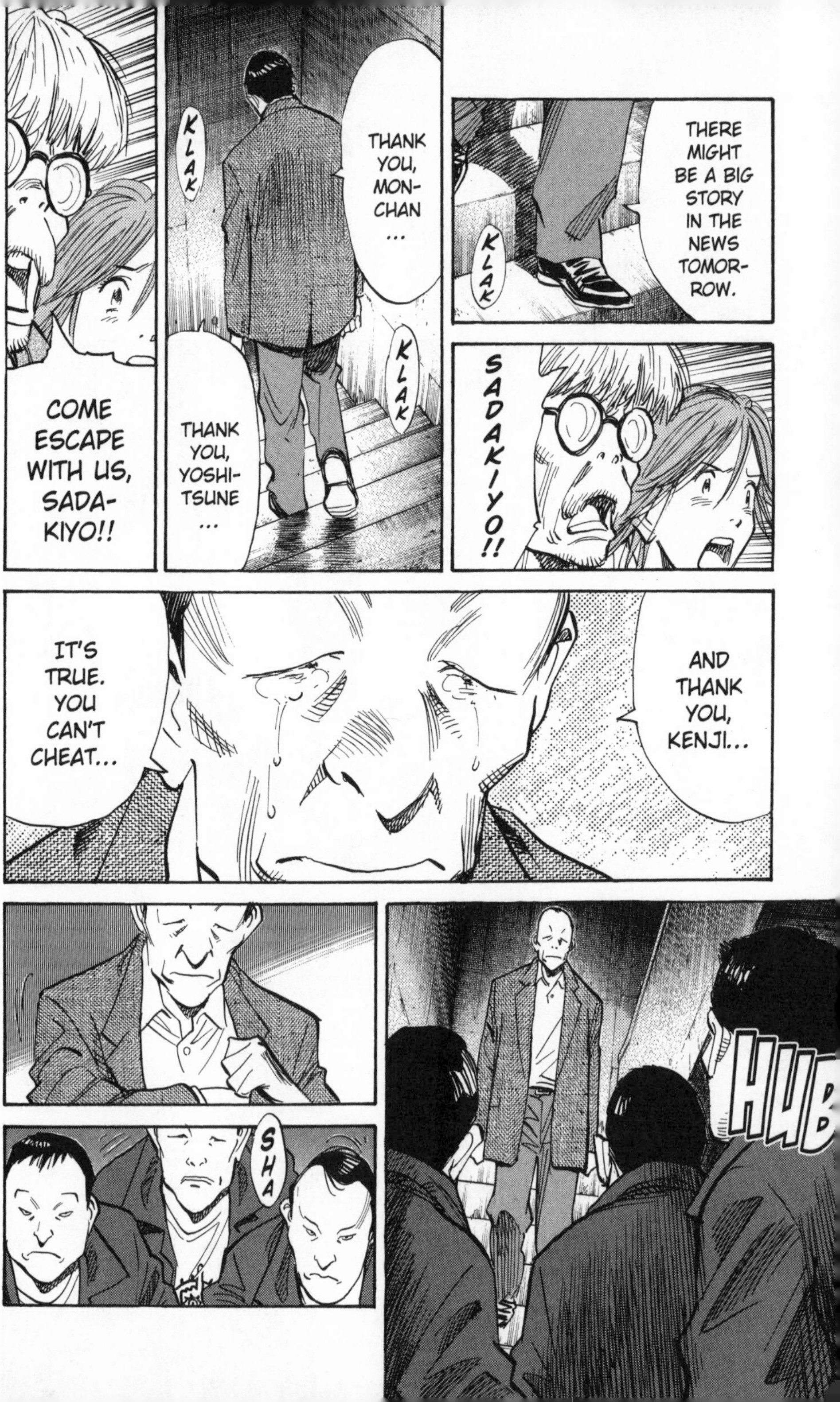
THERE MIGHT BE A BIG STORY IN THE NEWS TOMORROW.
KLAK
SADAKIYO!!
THANK YOU, MON-CHAN...
KLAK
KLAK
THANK YOU, YOSHI-TSUNE...
COME ESCAPE WITH US, SADA-KIYO!!
AND THANK YOU, KENJI...
IT'S TRUE. YOU CAN'T CHEAT...
HUB
SHA

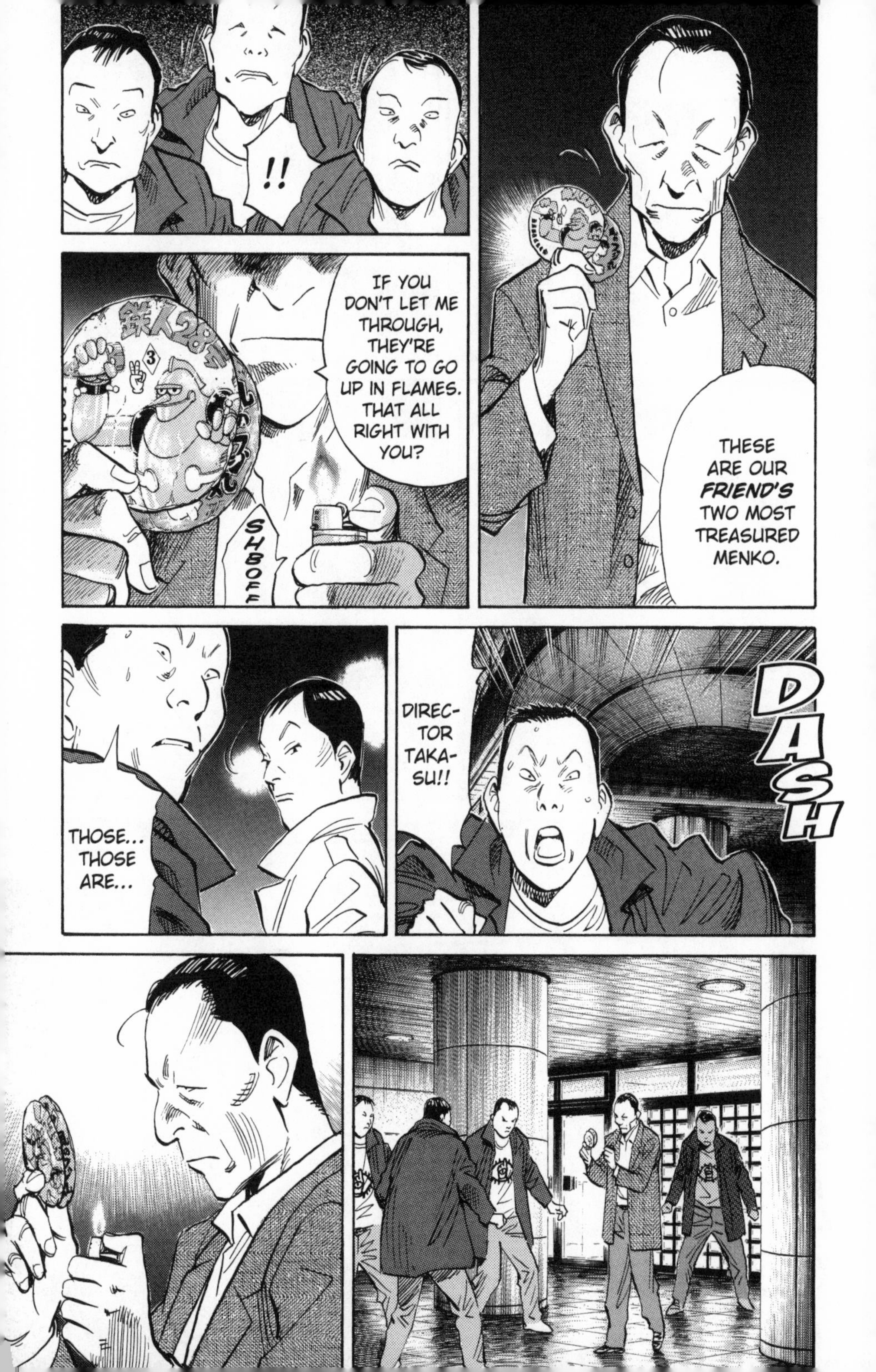
THESE ARE OUR *FRIEND'S* TWO MOST TREASURED MENKO.
!!
IF YOU DON'T LET ME THROUGH, THEY'RE GOING TO GO UP IN FLAMES. THAT ALL RIGHT WITH YOU?
SHBOFF
DASH
DIREC-TOR TAKA-SU!!
THOSE... THOSE ARE...

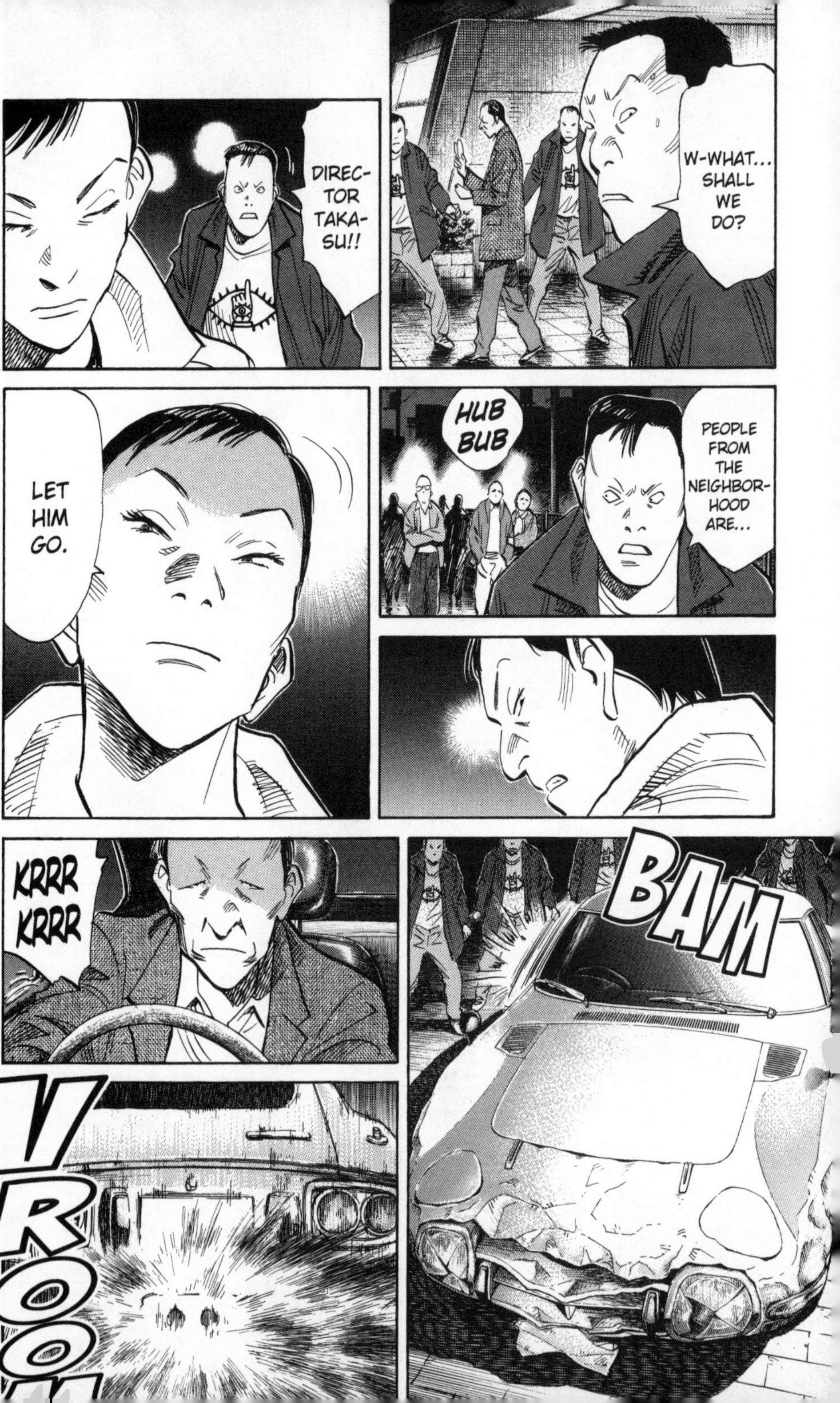
W-WHAT... SHALL WE DO?
DIREC-TOR TAKA-SU!!
PEOPLE FROM THE NEIGHBOR-HOOD ARE...
HUB BUB
LET HIM GO.
BAM
KRRR KRRR
VROOM

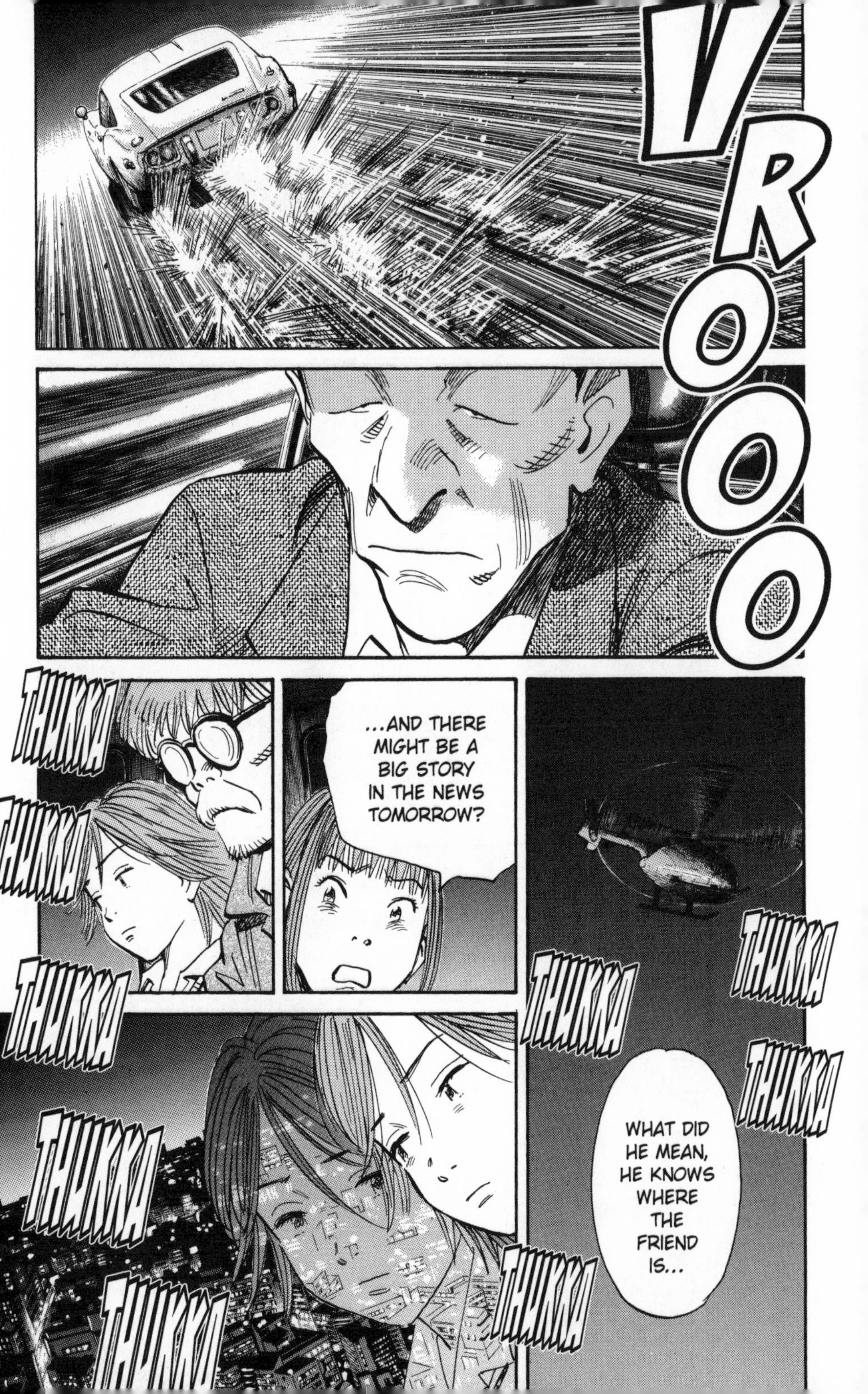
VROOO
THUKKA
THUKKA
...AND THERE MIGHT BE A BIG STORY IN THE NEWS TOMORROW?
THUKKA
THUKKA
THUKKA
THUKKA
WHAT DID HE MEAN, HE KNOWS WHERE THE FRIEND IS...
THUKKA
THUKKA
THUKKA

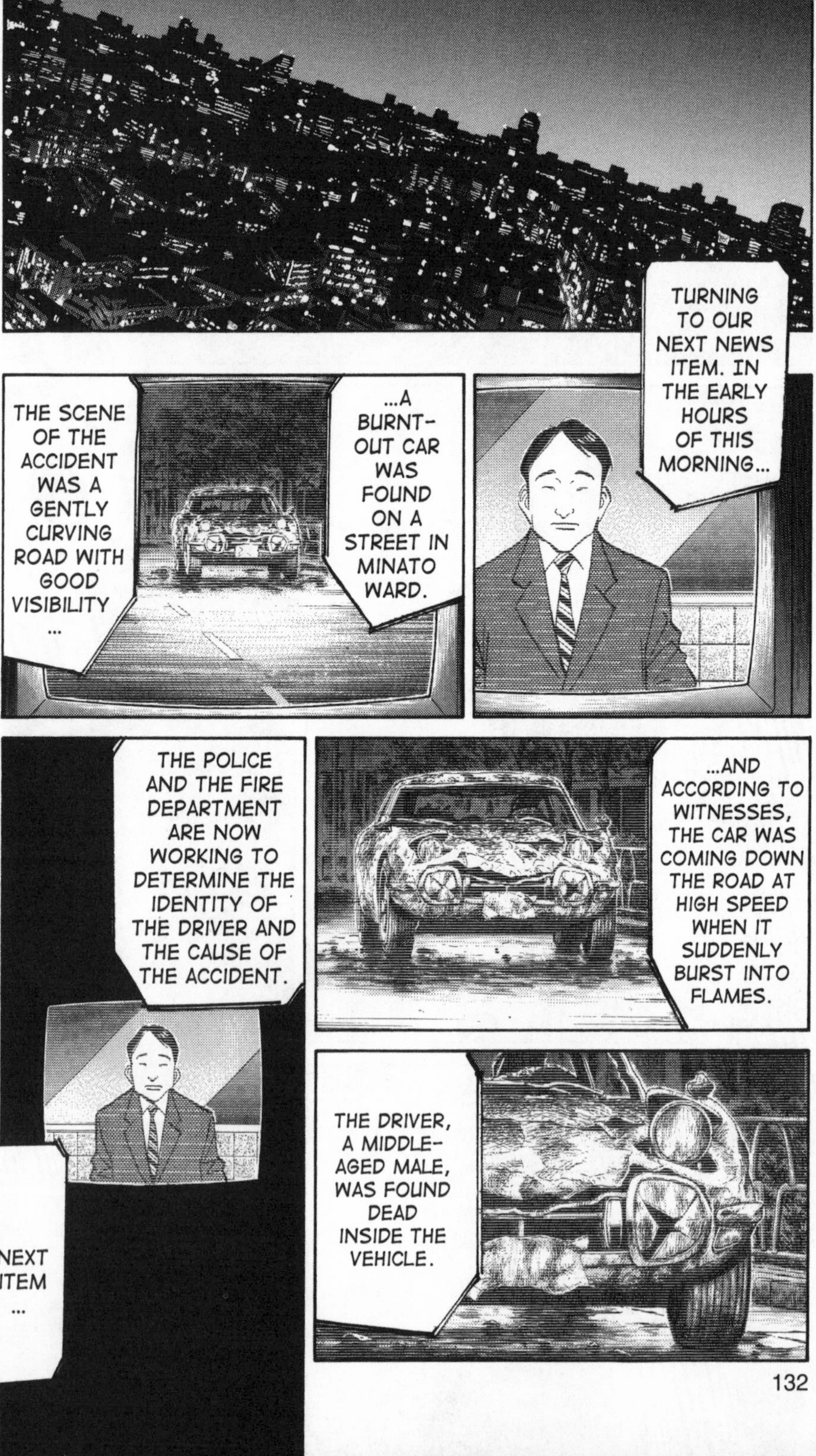
TURNING TO OUR NEXT NEWS ITEM. IN THE EARLY HOURS OF THIS MORNING...
...A BURNT-OUT CAR WAS FOUND ON A STREET IN MINATO WARD.
THE SCENE OF THE ACCIDENT WAS A GENTLY CURVING ROAD WITH GOOD VISIBILITY ...
...AND ACCORDING TO WITNESSES, THE CAR WAS COMING DOWN THE ROAD AT HIGH SPEED WHEN IT SUDDENLY BURST INTO FLAMES.
THE DRIVER, A MIDDLE-AGED MALE, WAS FOUND DEAD INSIDE THE VEHICLE.
THE POLICE AND THE FIRE DEPARTMENT ARE NOW WORKING TO DETERMINE THE IDENTITY OF THE DRIVER AND THE CAUSE OF THE ACCIDENT.
NEXT ITEM ...

Chapter 8 Ruins

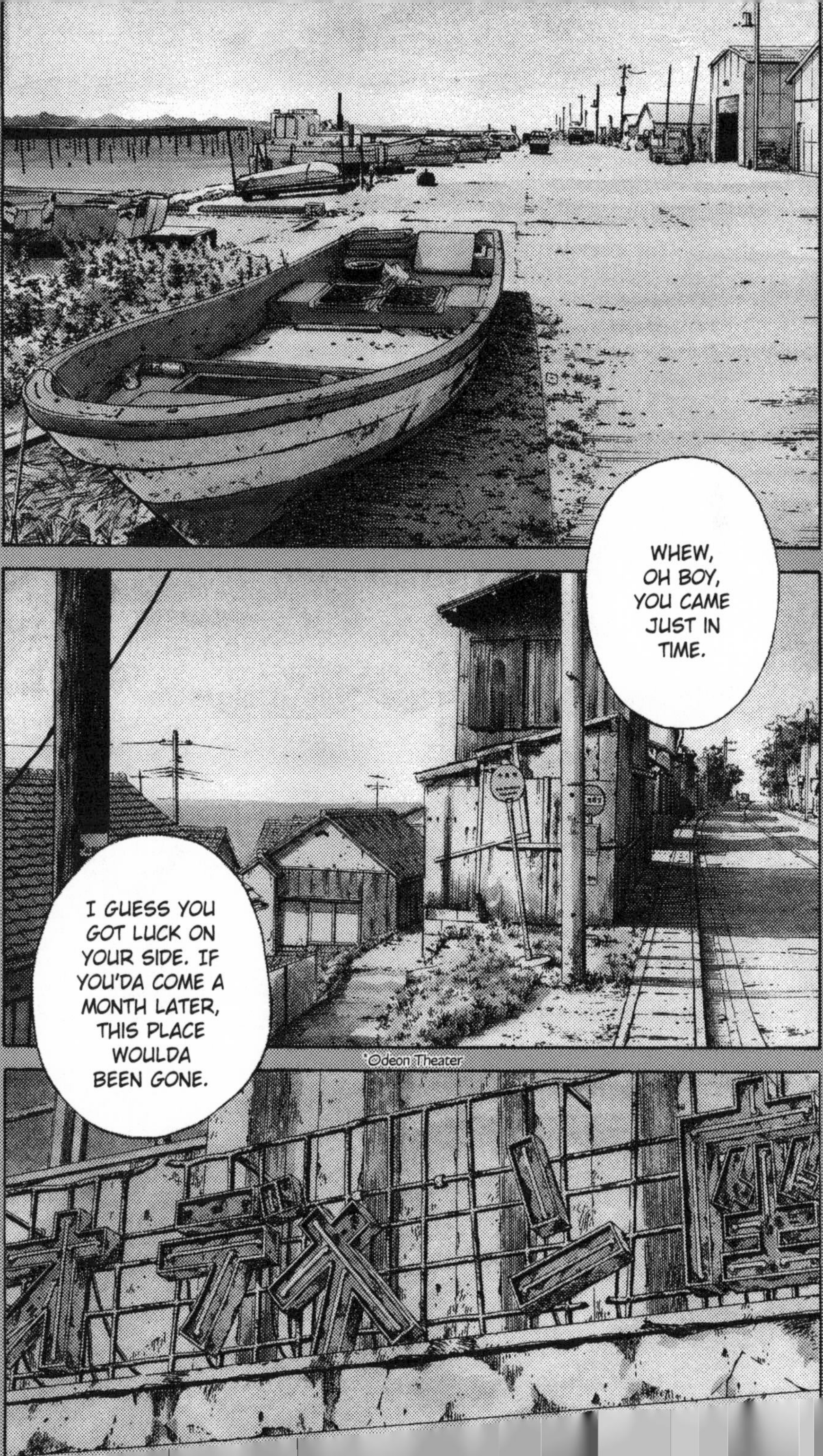
WHEW, OH BOY, YOU CAME JUST IN TIME.
I GUESS YOU GOT LUCK ON YOUR SIDE. IF YOU'DA COME A MONTH LATER, THIS PLACE WOULDA BEEN GONE.
*Odeon Theater

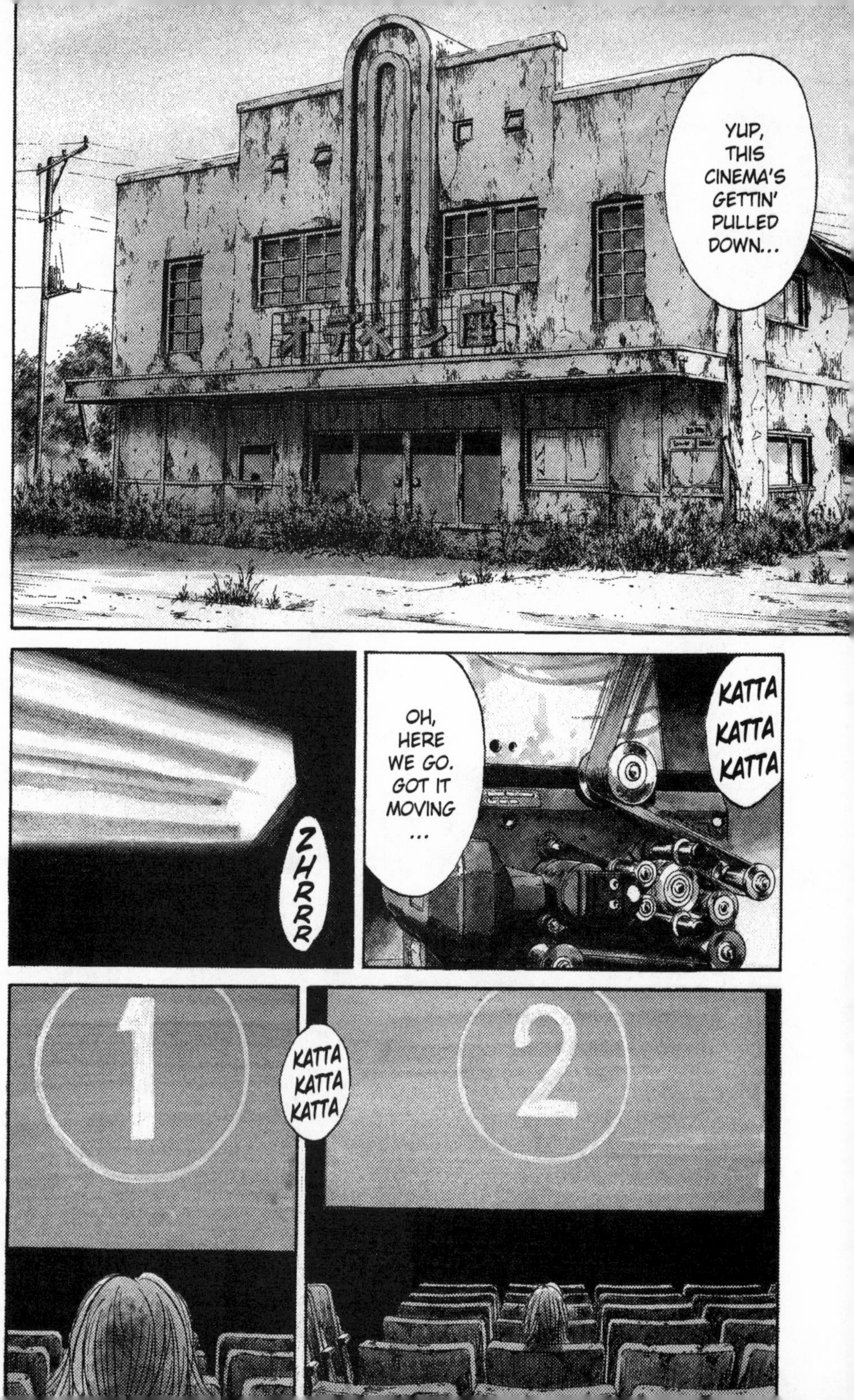
YUP, THIS CINEMA'S GETTIN' PULLED DOWN...
KATTA KATTA KATTA
OH, HERE WE GO. GOT IT MOVING ...
ZHRRR
KATTA KATTA KATTA
2
1

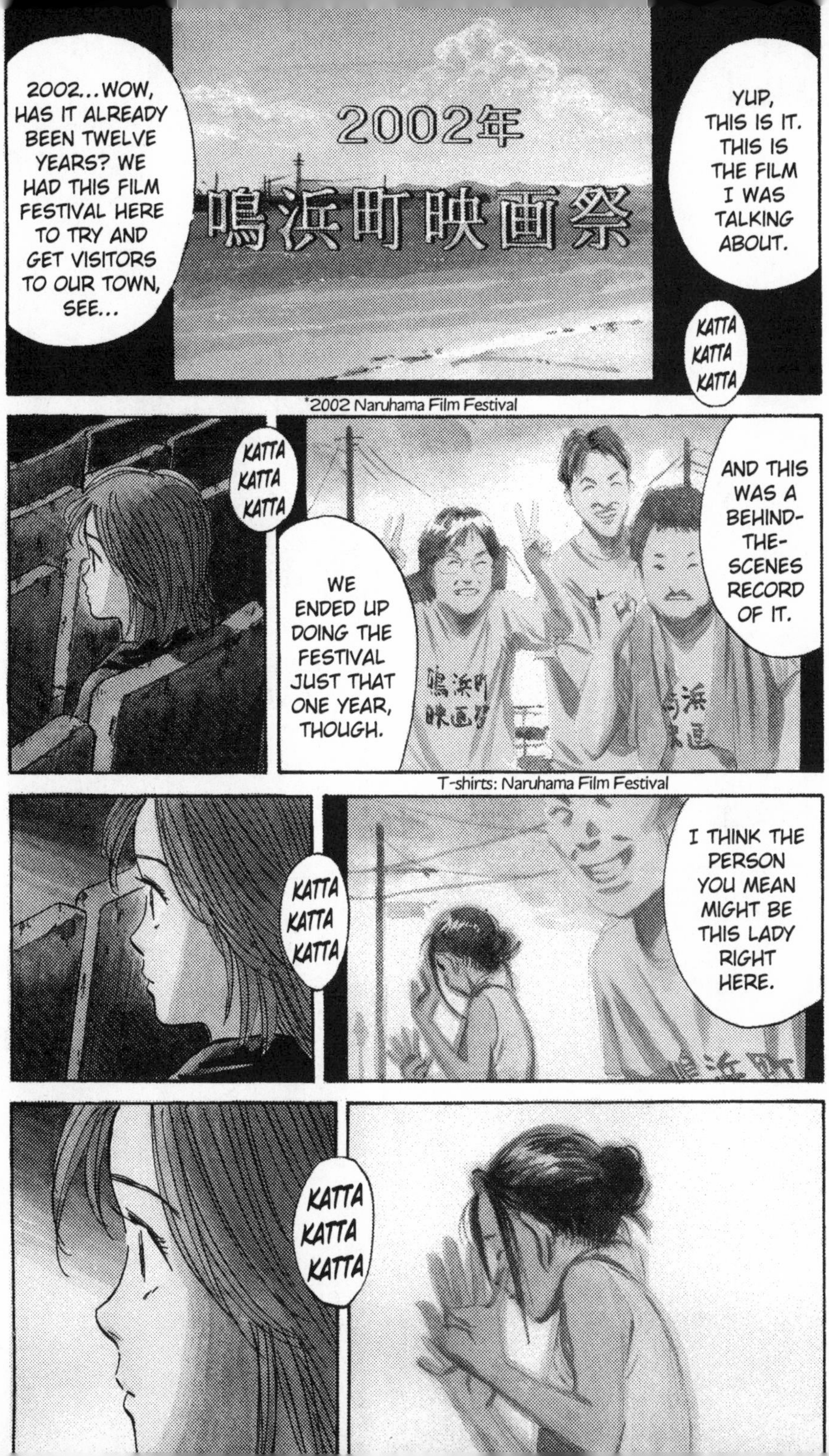
2002年
鳴浜町映画祭
YUP, THIS IS IT. THIS IS THE FILM I WAS TALKING ABOUT.
2002...WOW, HAS IT ALREADY BEEN TWELVE YEARS? WE HAD THIS FILM FESTIVAL HERE TO TRY AND GET VISITORS TO OUR TOWN, SEE...
KATTA KATTA KATTA
*2002 Naruhama Film Festival
AND THIS WAS A BEHIND-THE-SCENES RECORD OF IT.
WE ENDED UP DOING THE FESTIVAL JUST THAT ONE YEAR, THOUGH.
KATTA KATTA KATTA
T-shirts: Naruhama Film Festival
I THINK THE PERSON YOU MEAN MIGHT BE THIS LADY RIGHT HERE.
KATTA KATTA KATTA
KATTA KATTA KATTA

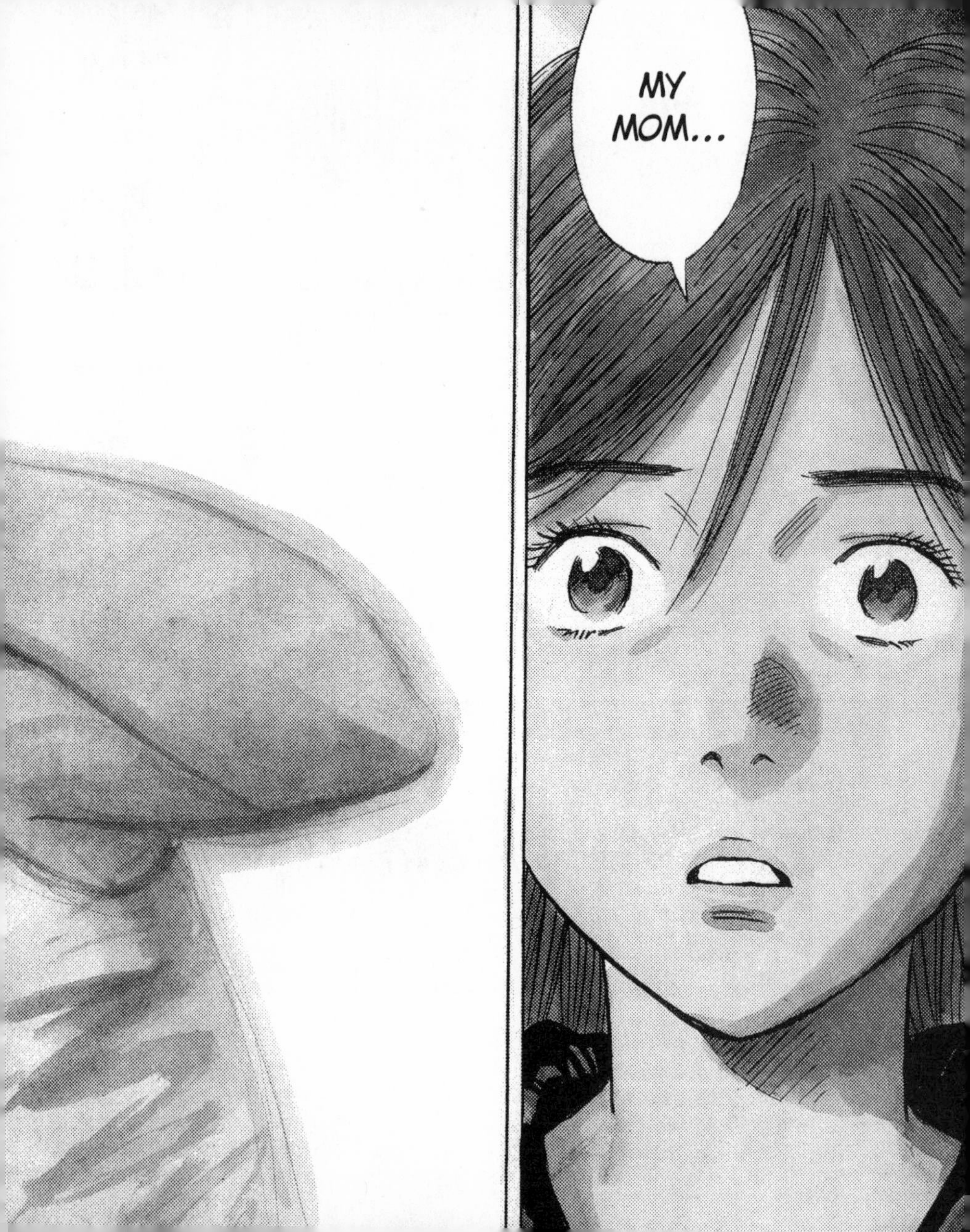
MY MOM...

Chapter 8
Ruins

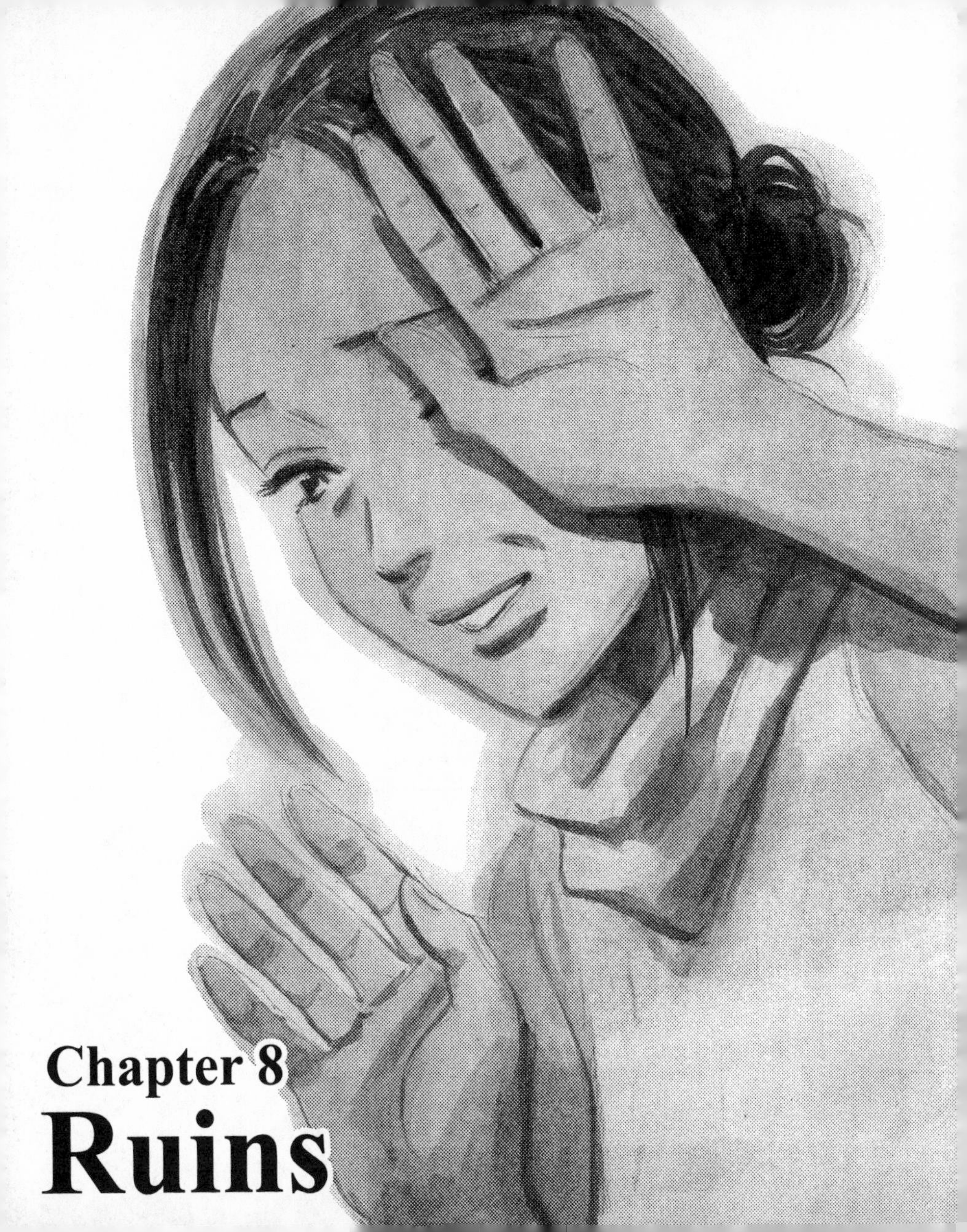

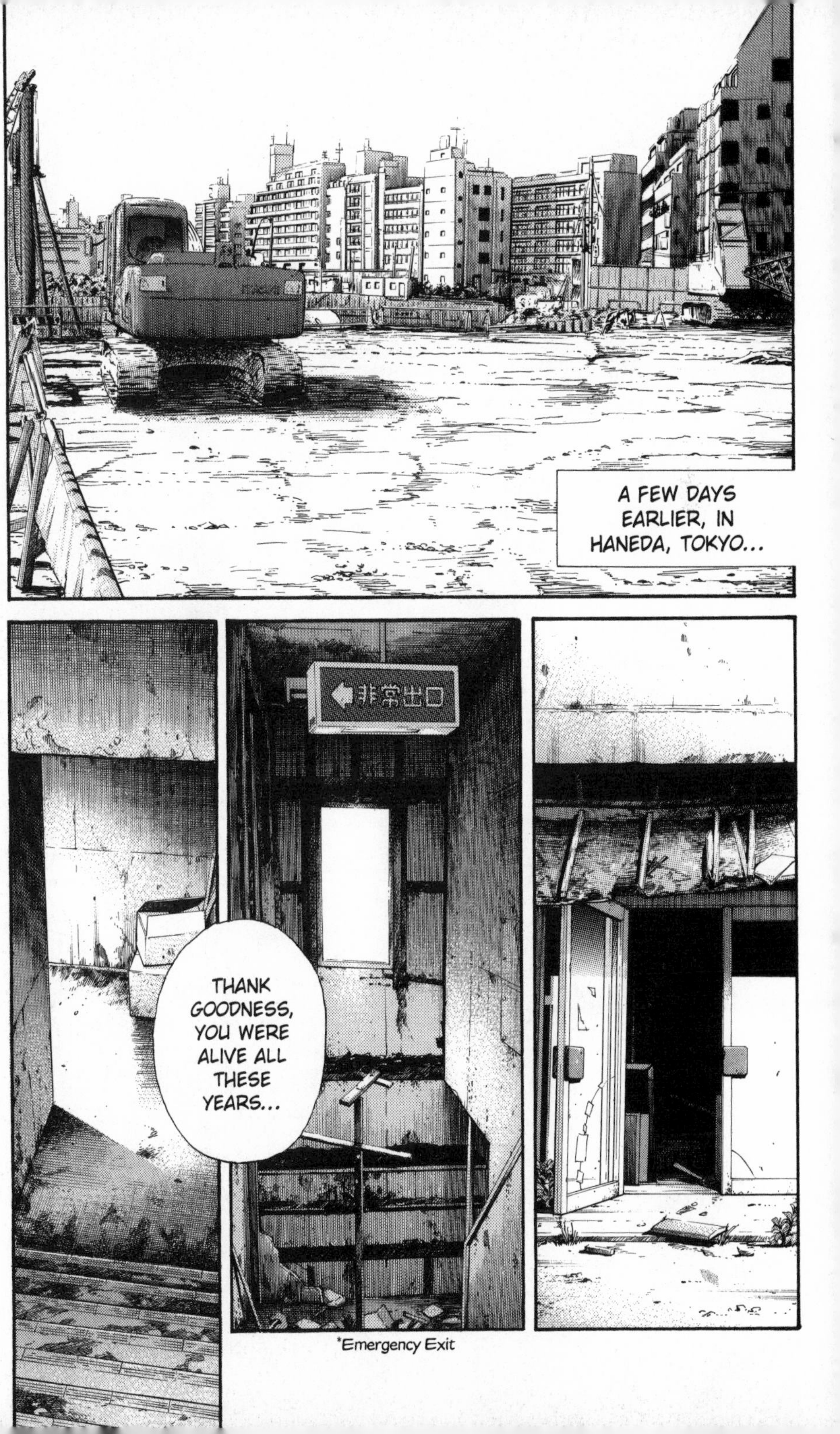
A FEW DAYS EARLIER, IN HANEDA, TOKYO...
非常出口
THANK GOODNESS, YOU WERE ALIVE ALL THESE YEARS...
*Emergency Exit

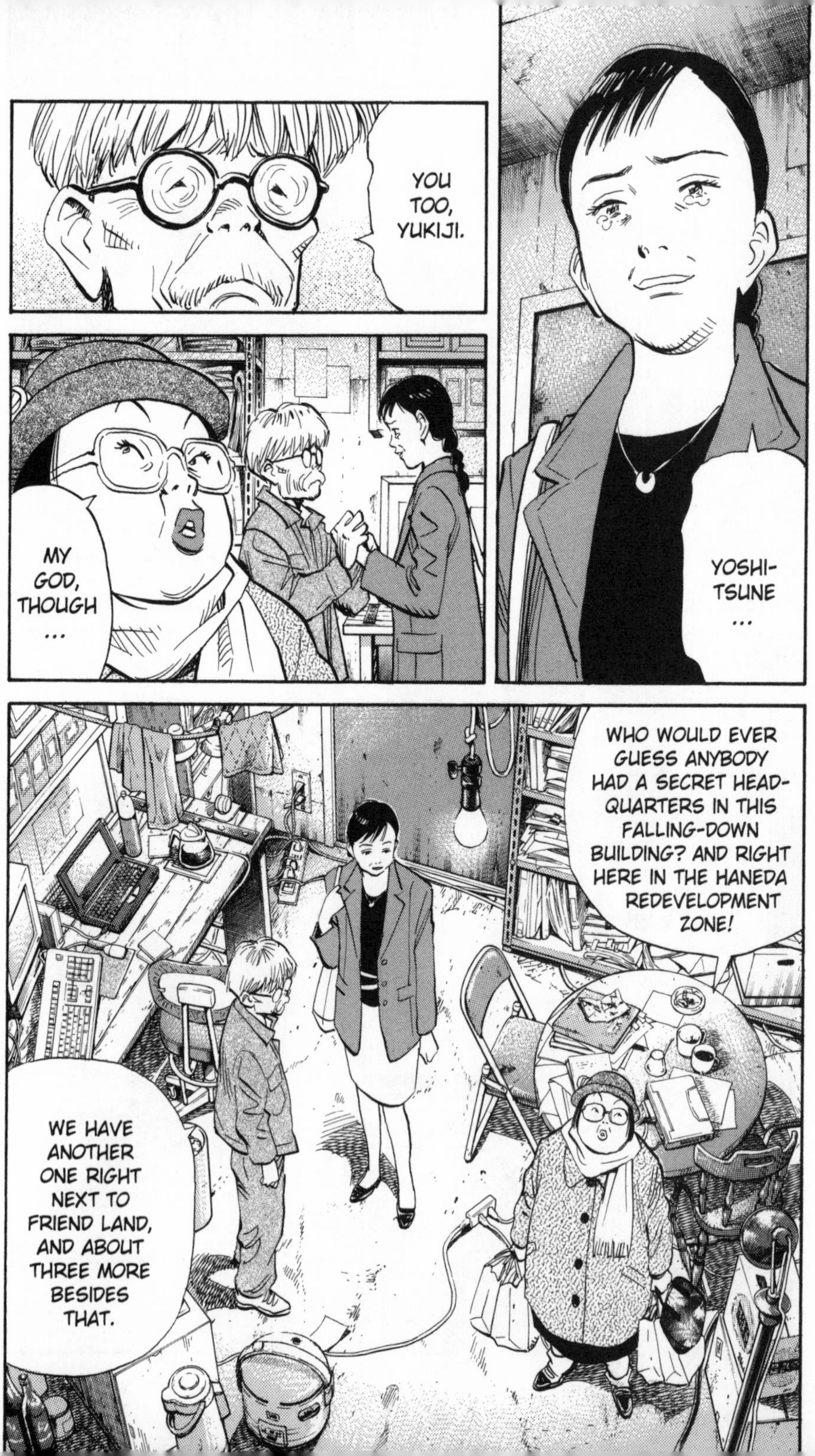
YOSHI-TSUNE ...
YOU TOO, YUKIJI.
MY GOD, THOUGH ...
WHO WOULD EVER GUESS ANYBODY HAD A SECRET HEAD-QUARTERS IN THIS FALLING-DOWN BUILDING? AND RIGHT HERE IN THE HANEDA REDEVELOPMENT ZONE!
WE HAVE ANOTHER ONE RIGHT NEXT TO FRIEND LAND, AND ABOUT THREE MORE BESIDES THAT.

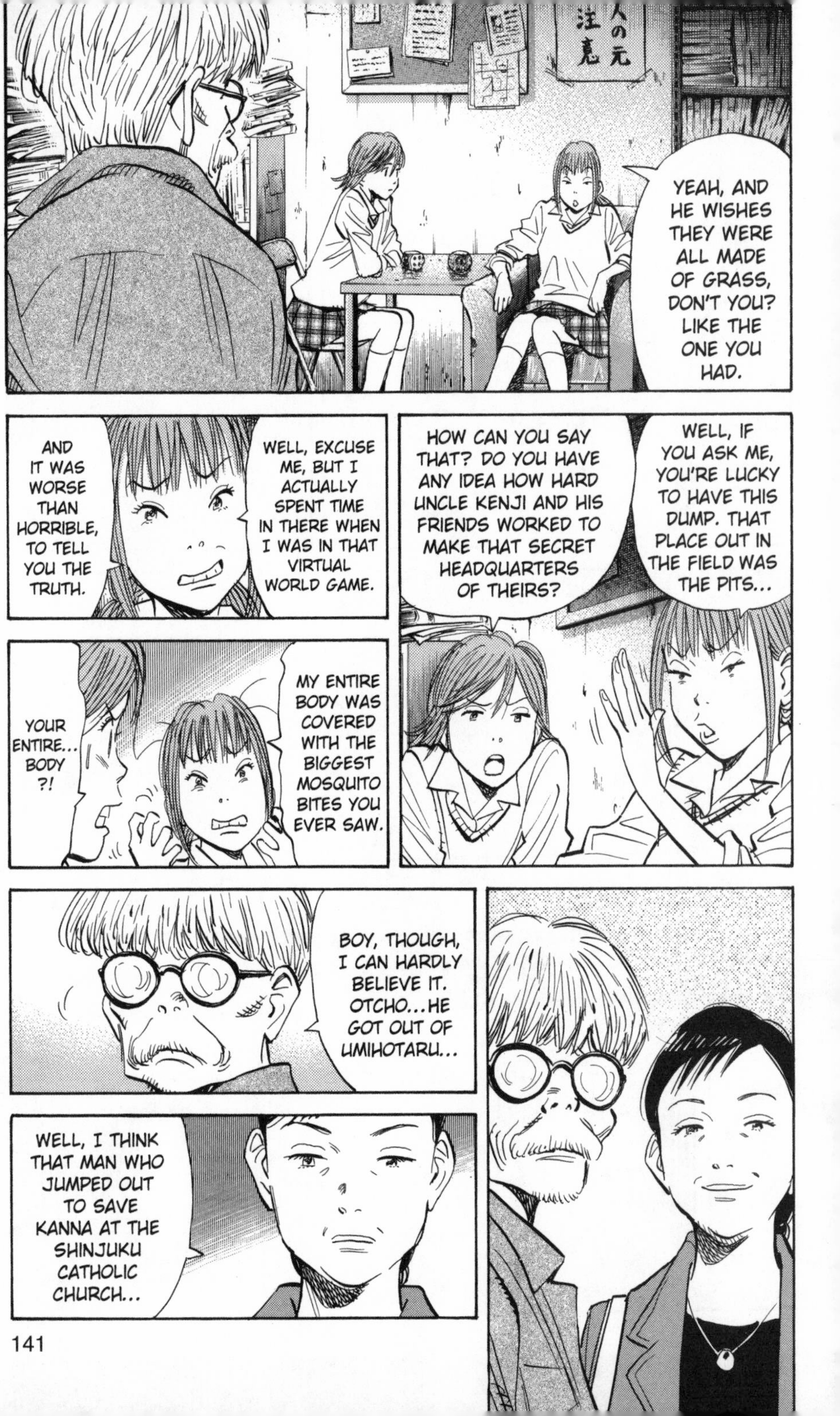
YEAH, AND HE WISHES THEY WERE ALL MADE OF GRASS, DON'T YOU? LIKE THE ONE YOU HAD.
WELL, IF YOU ASK ME, YOU'RE LUCKY TO HAVE THIS DUMP. THAT PLACE OUT IN THE FIELD WAS THE PITS...
HOW CAN YOU SAY THAT? DO YOU HAVE ANY IDEA HOW HARD UNCLE KENJI AND HIS FRIENDS WORKED TO MAKE THAT SECRET HEADQUARTERS OF THEIRS?
WELL, EXCUSE ME, BUT I ACTUALLY SPENT TIME IN THERE WHEN I WAS IN THAT VIRTUAL WORLD GAME.
AND IT WAS WORSE THAN HORRIBLE, TO TELL YOU THE TRUTH.
MY ENTIRE BODY WAS COVERED WITH THE BIGGEST MOSQUITO BITES YOU EVER SAW.
YOUR ENTIRE... BODY ?!
BOY, THOUGH, I CAN HARDLY BELIEVE IT. OTCHO...HE GOT OUT OF UMIHOTARU...
WELL, I THINK THAT MAN WHO JUMPED OUT TO SAVE KANNA AT THE SHINJUKU CATHOLIC CHURCH...

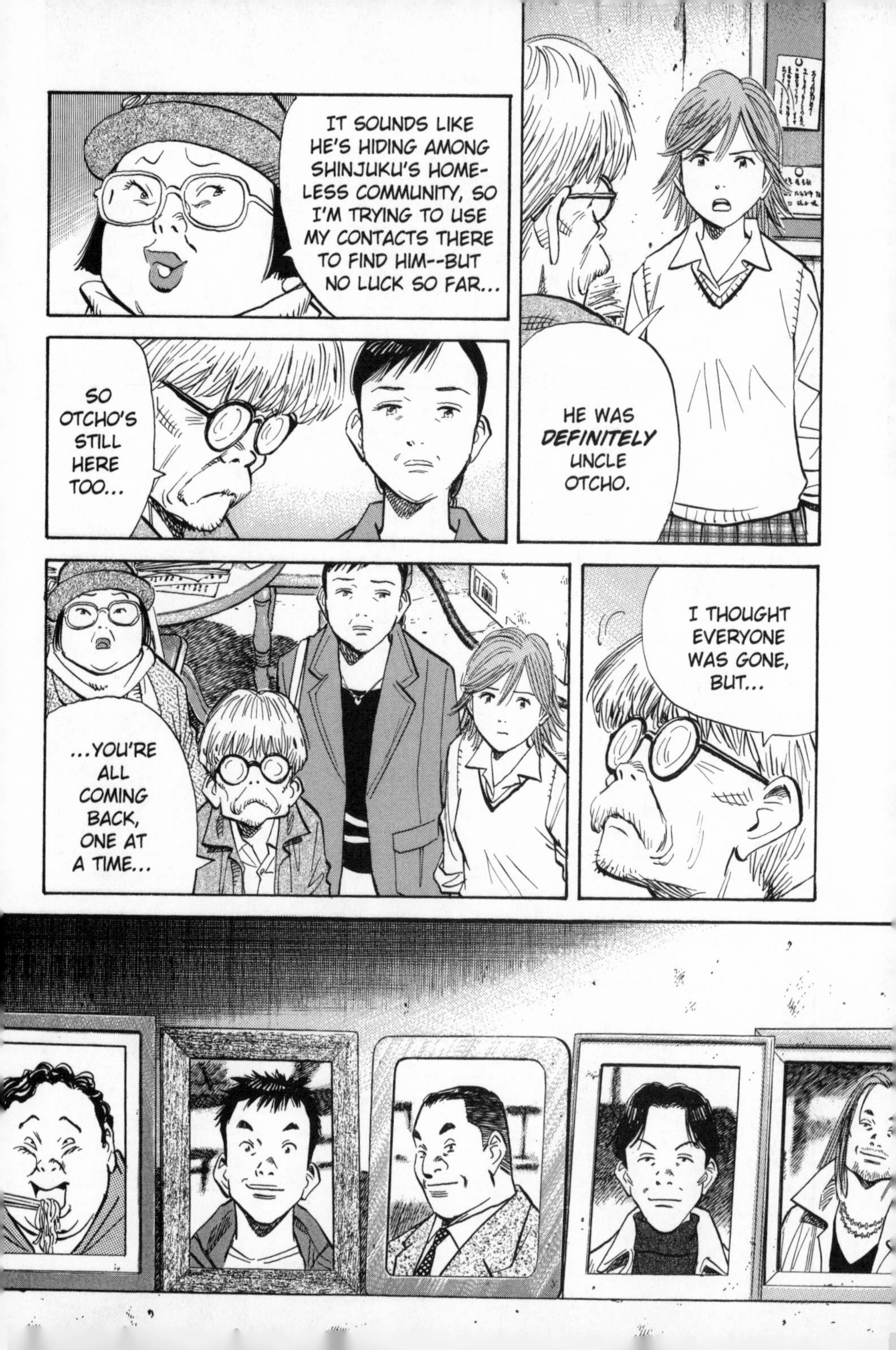

HE WAS *DEFINITELY* UNCLE OTCHO.
IT SOUNDS LIKE HE'S HIDING AMONG SHINJUKU'S HOME-LESS COMMUNITY, SO I'M TRYING TO USE MY CONTACTS THERE TO FIND HIM--BUT NO LUCK SO FAR...
SO OTCHO'S STILL HERE TOO...
I THOUGHT EVERYONE WAS GONE, BUT...
...YOU'RE ALL COMING BACK, ONE AT A TIME...

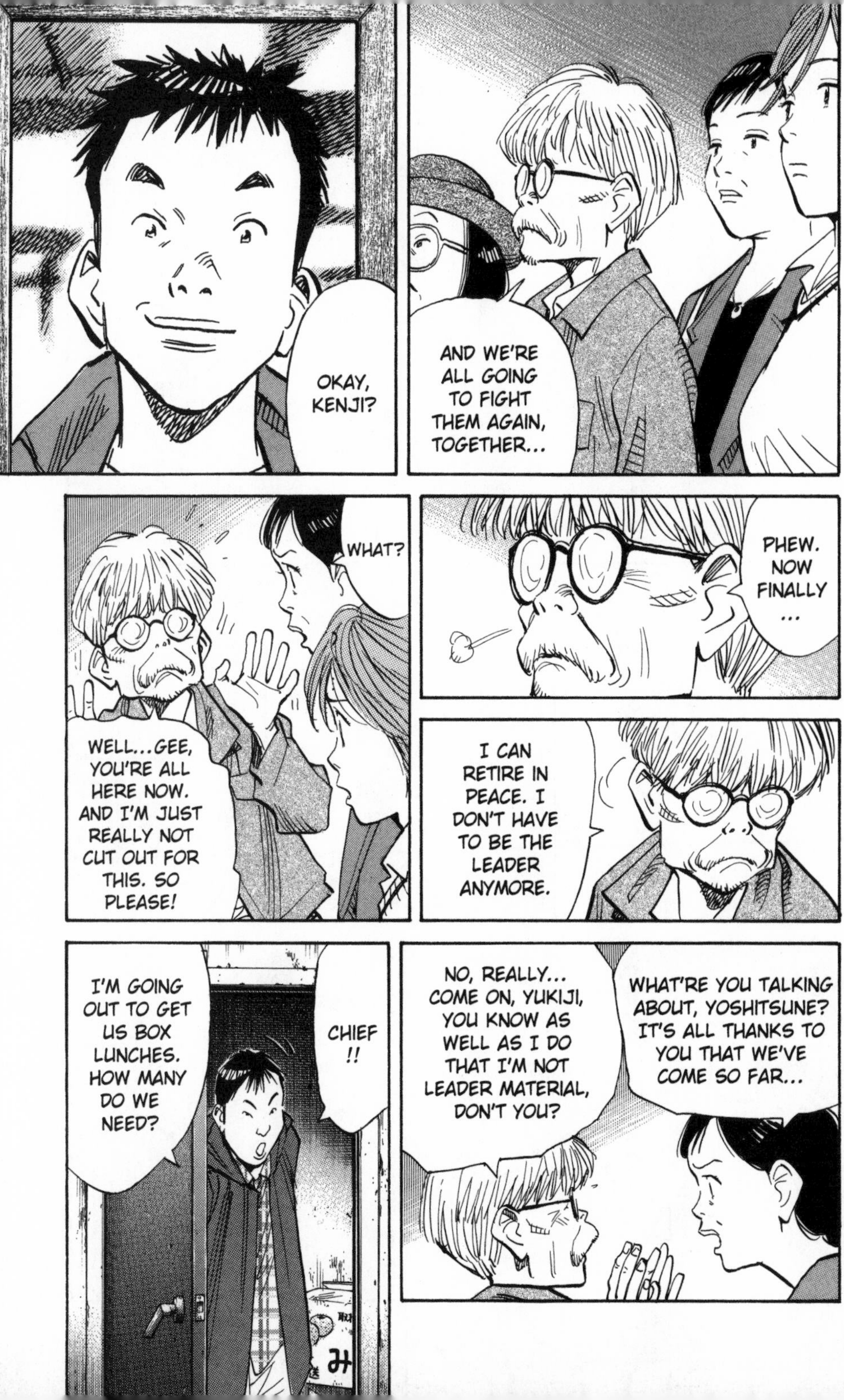
AND WE'RE ALL GOING TO FIGHT THEM AGAIN, TOGETHER...
OKAY, KENJI?
PHEW. NOW FINALLY ...
I CAN RETIRE IN PEACE. I DON'T HAVE TO BE THE LEADER ANYMORE.
WHAT?
WELL...GEE, YOU'RE ALL HERE NOW. AND I'M JUST REALLY NOT CUT OUT FOR THIS. SO PLEASE!
WHAT'RE YOU TALKING ABOUT, YOSHITSUNE? IT'S ALL THANKS TO YOU THAT WE'VE COME SO FAR...
NO, REALLY... COME ON, YUKIJI, YOU KNOW AS WELL AS I DO THAT I'M NOT LEADER MATERIAL, DON'T YOU?
CHIEF !!
I'M GOING OUT TO GET US BOX LUNCHES. HOW MANY DO WE NEED?

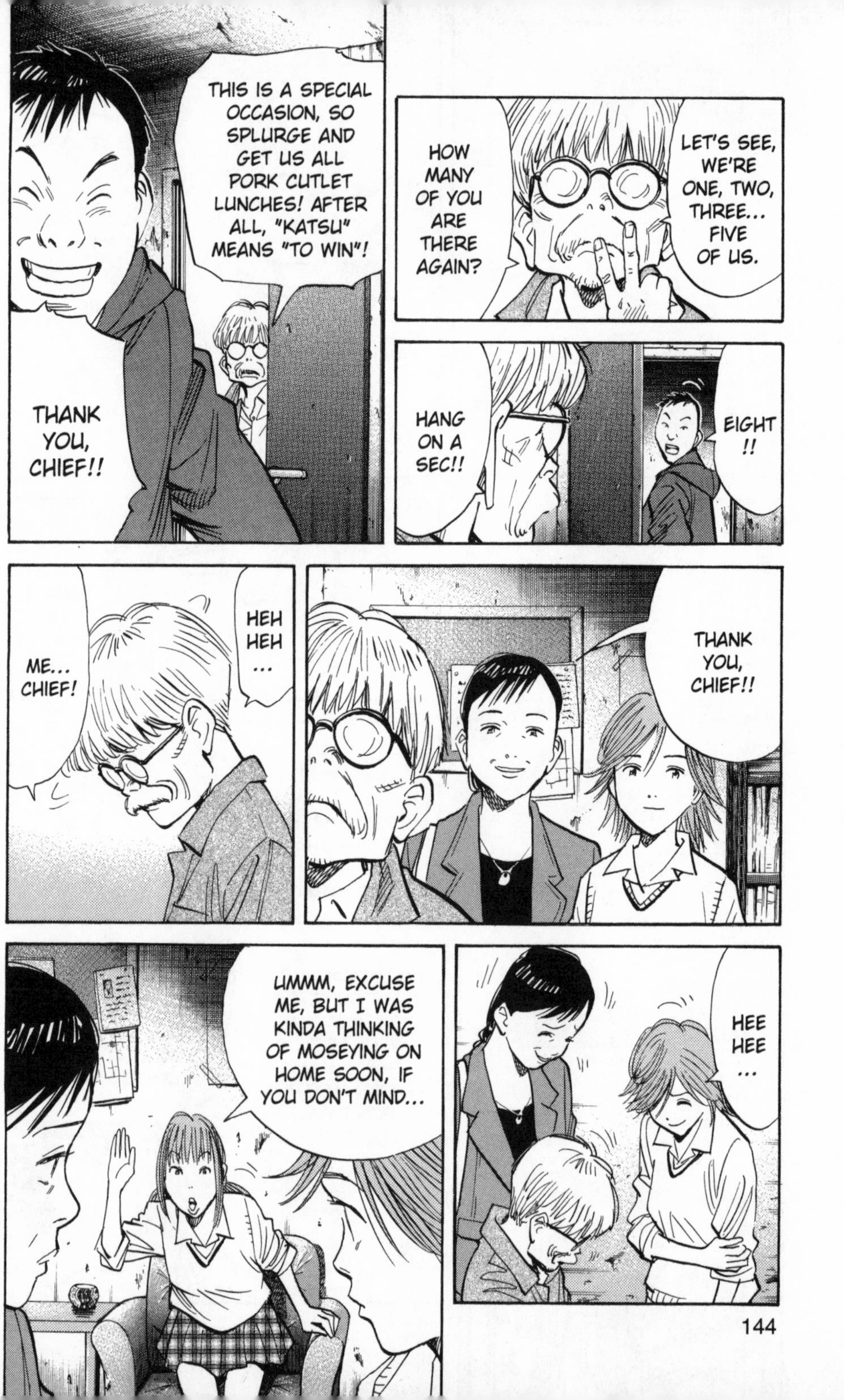
LET'S SEE, WE'RE ONE, TWO, THREE... FIVE OF US.
HOW MANY OF YOU ARE THERE AGAIN?
EIGHT!!
HANG ON A SEC!!
THIS IS A SPECIAL OCCASION, SO SPLURGE AND GET US ALL PORK CUTLET LUNCHES! AFTER ALL, "KATSU" MEANS "TO WIN"!
THANK YOU, CHIEF!!
THANK YOU, CHIEF!!
HEH HEH ...
ME... CHIEF!
HEE HEE ...
UMMM, EXCUSE ME, BUT I WAS KINDA THINKING OF MOSEYING ON HOME SOON, IF YOU DON'T MIND...

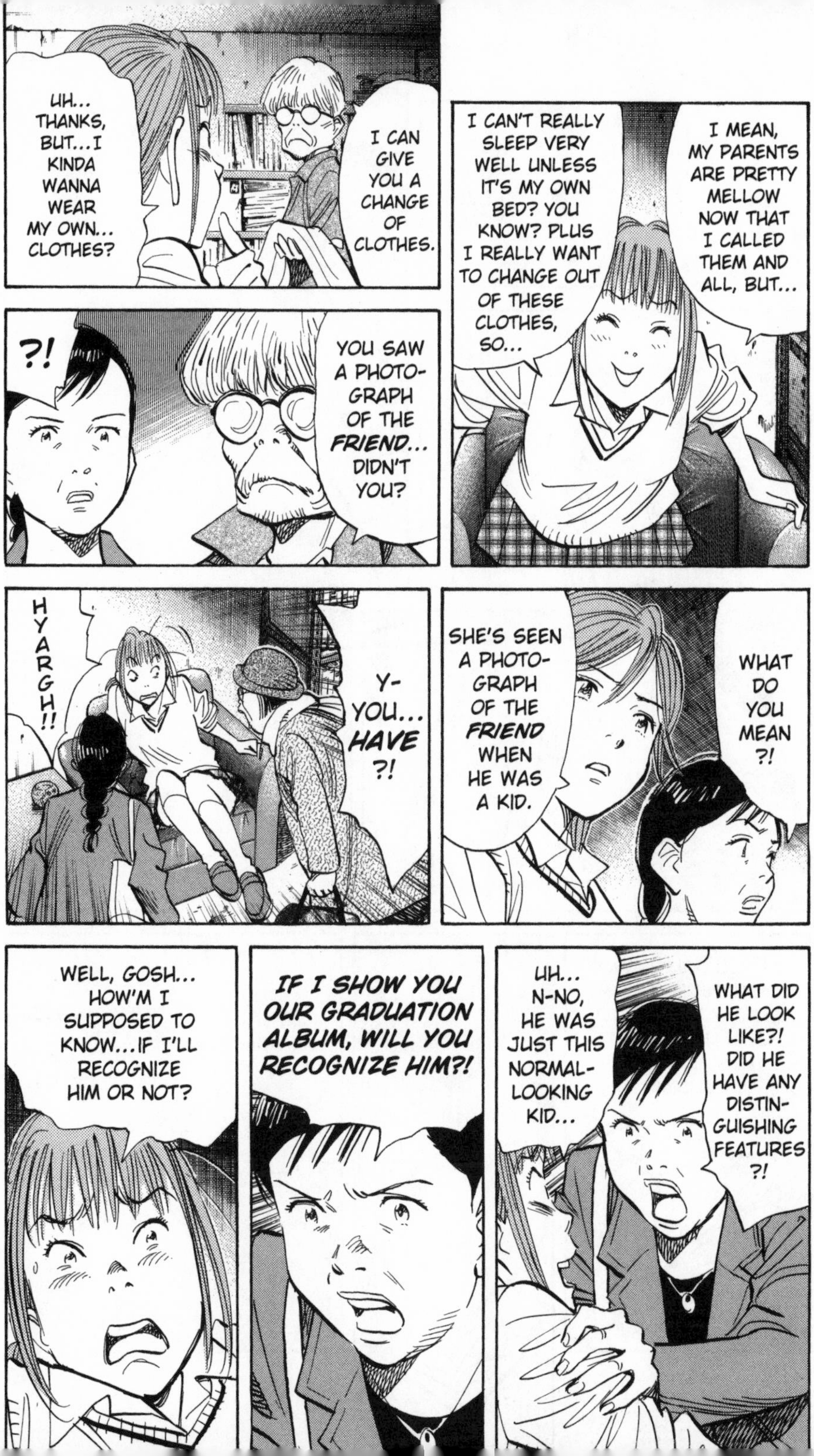
I MEAN, MY PARENTS ARE PRETTY MELLOW NOW THAT I CALLED THEM AND ALL, BUT...
I CAN'T REALLY SLEEP VERY WELL UNLESS IT'S MY OWN BED? YOU KNOW? PLUS I REALLY WANT TO CHANGE OUT OF THESE CLOTHES, SO...
I CAN GIVE YOU A CHANGE OF CLOTHES.
UH... THANKS, BUT...I KINDA WANNA WEAR MY OWN... CLOTHES?
YOU SAW A PHOTOGRAPH OF THE *FRIEND*... DIDN'T YOU?
?!
WHAT DO YOU MEAN?!
SHE'S SEEN A PHOTOGRAPH OF THE *FRIEND* WHEN HE WAS A KID.
Y-YOU... *HAVE*?!
HYARGH!!
WHAT DID HE LOOK LIKE?! DID HE HAVE ANY DISTINGUISHING FEATURES?!
UH... N-NO, HE WAS JUST THIS NORMAL-LOOKING KID...
IF I SHOW YOU OUR GRADUATION ALBUM, WILL YOU RECOGNIZE HIM?!
WELL, GOSH... HOW'M I SUPPOSED TO KNOW...IF I'LL RECOGNIZE HIM OR NOT?

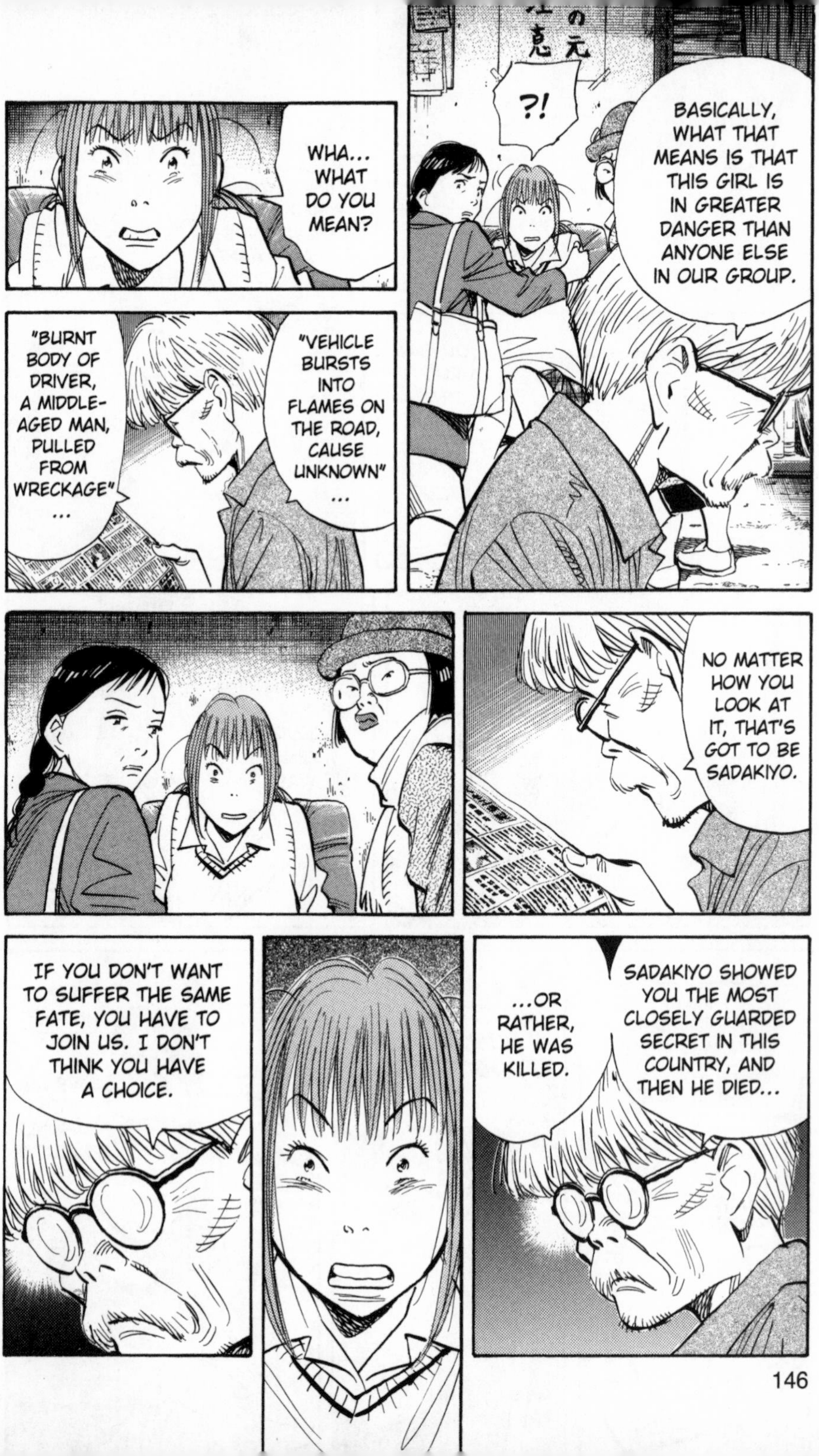
BASICALLY, WHAT THAT MEANS IS THAT THIS GIRL IS IN GREATER DANGER THAN ANYONE ELSE IN OUR GROUP.
?!
WHA... WHAT DO YOU MEAN?
"VEHICLE BURSTS INTO FLAMES ON THE ROAD, CAUSE UNKNOWN" ...
"BURNT BODY OF DRIVER, A MIDDLE-AGED MAN, PULLED FROM WRECKAGE" ...
NO MATTER HOW YOU LOOK AT IT, THAT'S GOT TO BE SADAKIYO.
SADAKIYO SHOWED YOU THE MOST CLOSELY GUARDED SECRET IN THIS COUNTRY, AND THEN HE DIED...
...OR RATHER, HE WAS KILLED.
IF YOU DON'T WANT TO SUFFER THE SAME FATE, YOU HAVE TO JOIN US. I DON'T THINK YOU HAVE A CHOICE.

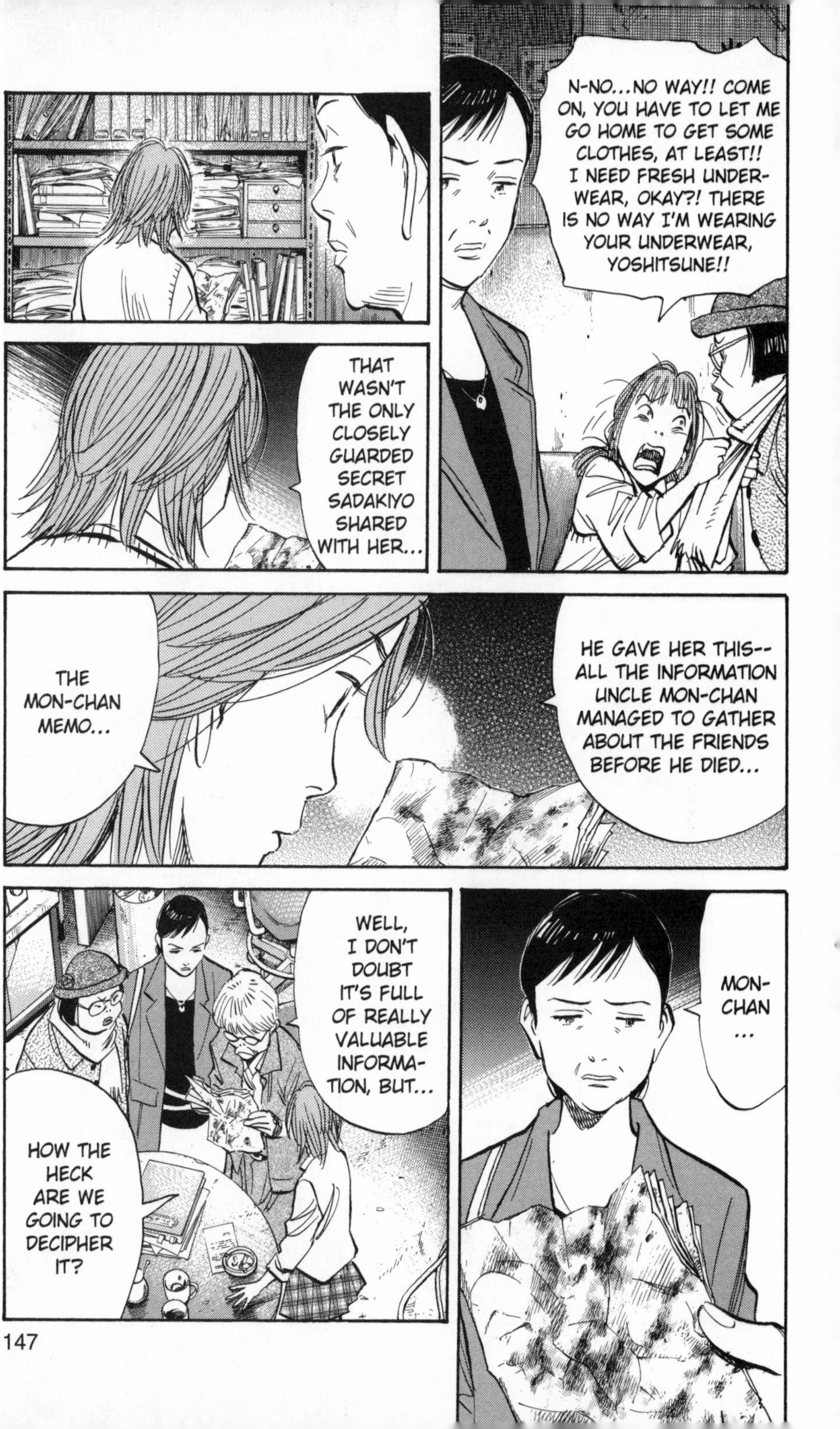
N-NO...NO WAY!! COME ON, YOU HAVE TO LET ME GO HOME TO GET SOME CLOTHES, AT LEAST!! I NEED FRESH UNDER-WEAR, OKAY?! THERE IS NO WAY I'M WEARING YOUR UNDERWEAR, YOSHITSUNE!!
THAT WASN'T THE ONLY CLOSELY GUARDED SECRET SADAKIYO SHARED WITH HER...
HE GAVE HER THIS--ALL THE INFORMATION UNCLE MON-CHAN MANAGED TO GATHER ABOUT THE FRIENDS BEFORE HE DIED...
THE MON-CHAN MEMO...
MON-CHAN...
WELL, I DON'T DOUBT IT'S FULL OF REALLY VALUABLE INFORMA-TION, BUT...
HOW THE HECK ARE WE GOING TO DECIPHER IT?

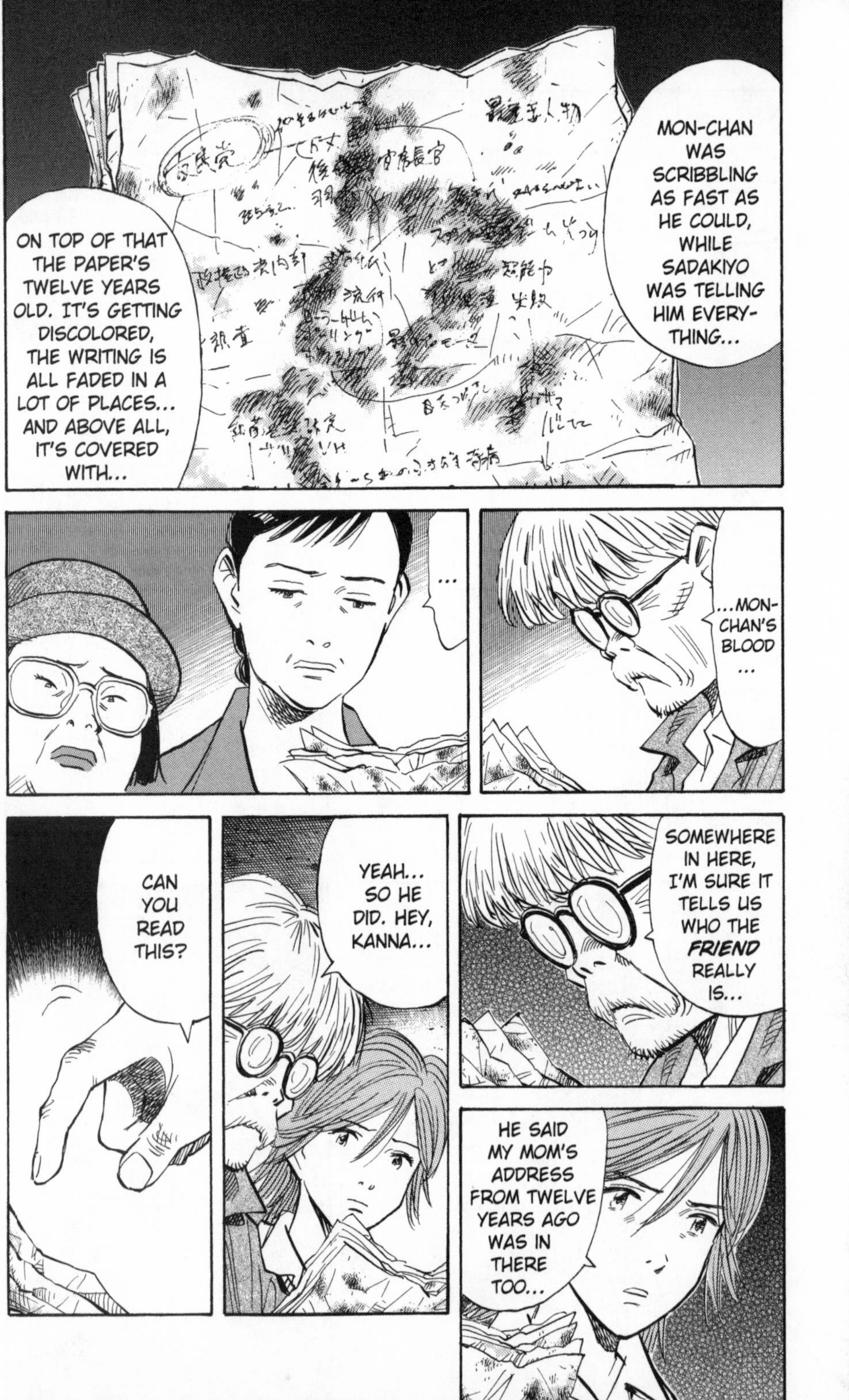
MON-CHAN WAS SCRIBBLING AS FAST AS HE COULD, WHILE SADAKIYO WAS TELLING HIM EVERY-THING...
ON TOP OF THAT THE PAPER'S TWELVE YEARS OLD. IT'S GETTING DISCOLORED, THE WRITING IS ALL FADED IN A LOT OF PLACES... AND ABOVE ALL, IT'S COVERED WITH...
...MON-CHAN'S BLOOD ...
...
SOMEWHERE IN HERE, I'M SURE IT TELLS US WHO THE ***FRIEND*** REALLY IS...
HE SAID MY MOM'S ADDRESS FROM TWELVE YEARS AGO WAS IN THERE TOO...
YEAH... SO HE DID. HEY, KANNA...
CAN YOU READ THIS?

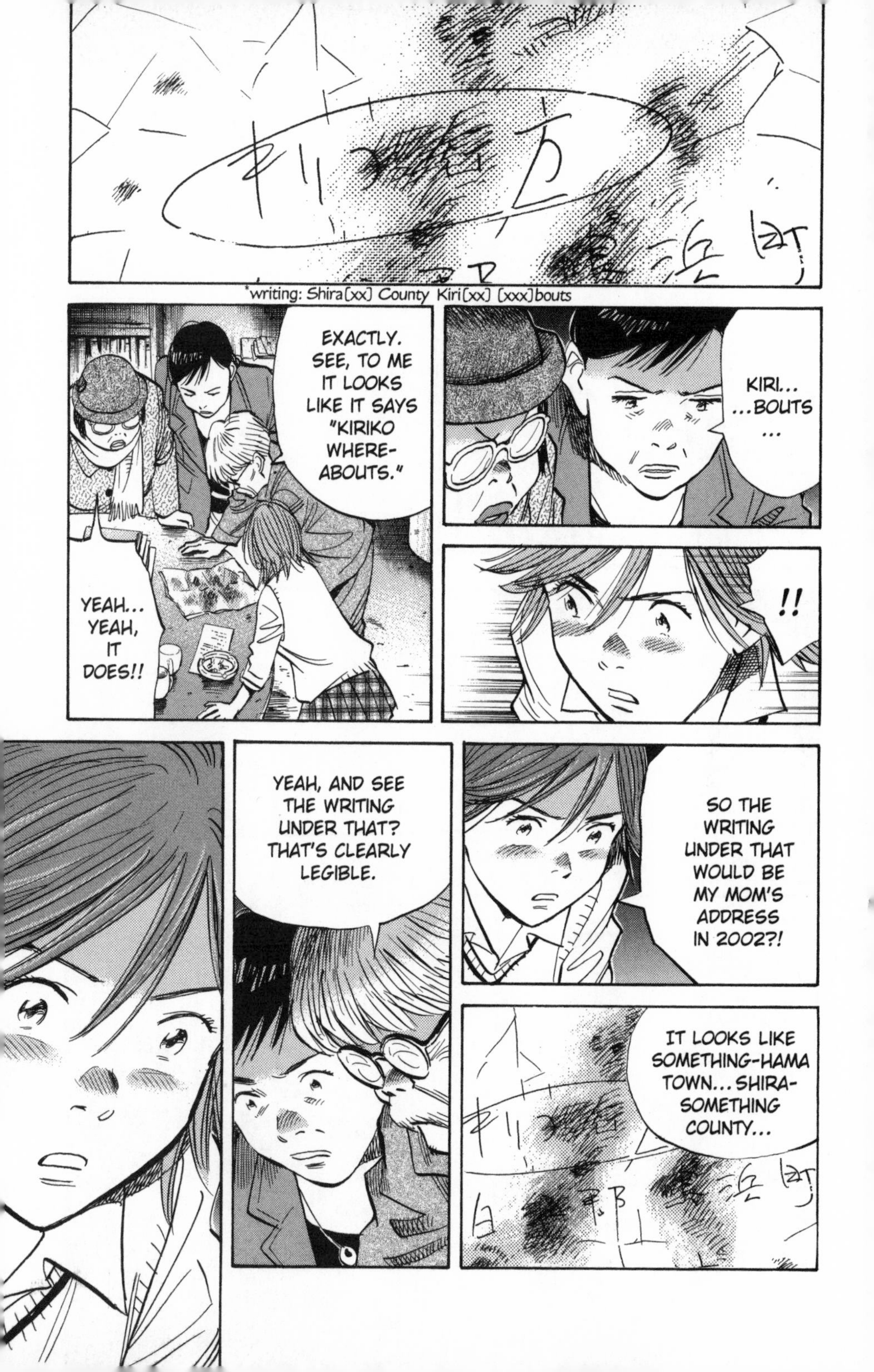
*writing: Shira[xx] County Kiri[xx] [xxx]bouts
KIRI... ...BOUTS ...
!!
EXACTLY. SEE, TO ME IT LOOKS LIKE IT SAYS "KIRIKO WHERE-ABOUTS."
YEAH... YEAH, IT DOES!!
SO THE WRITING UNDER THAT WOULD BE MY MOM'S ADDRESS IN 2002?!
IT LOOKS LIKE SOMETHING-HAMA TOWN... SHIRA-SOMETHING COUNTY...
YEAH, AND SEE THE WRITING UNDER THAT? THAT'S CLEARLY LEGIBLE.

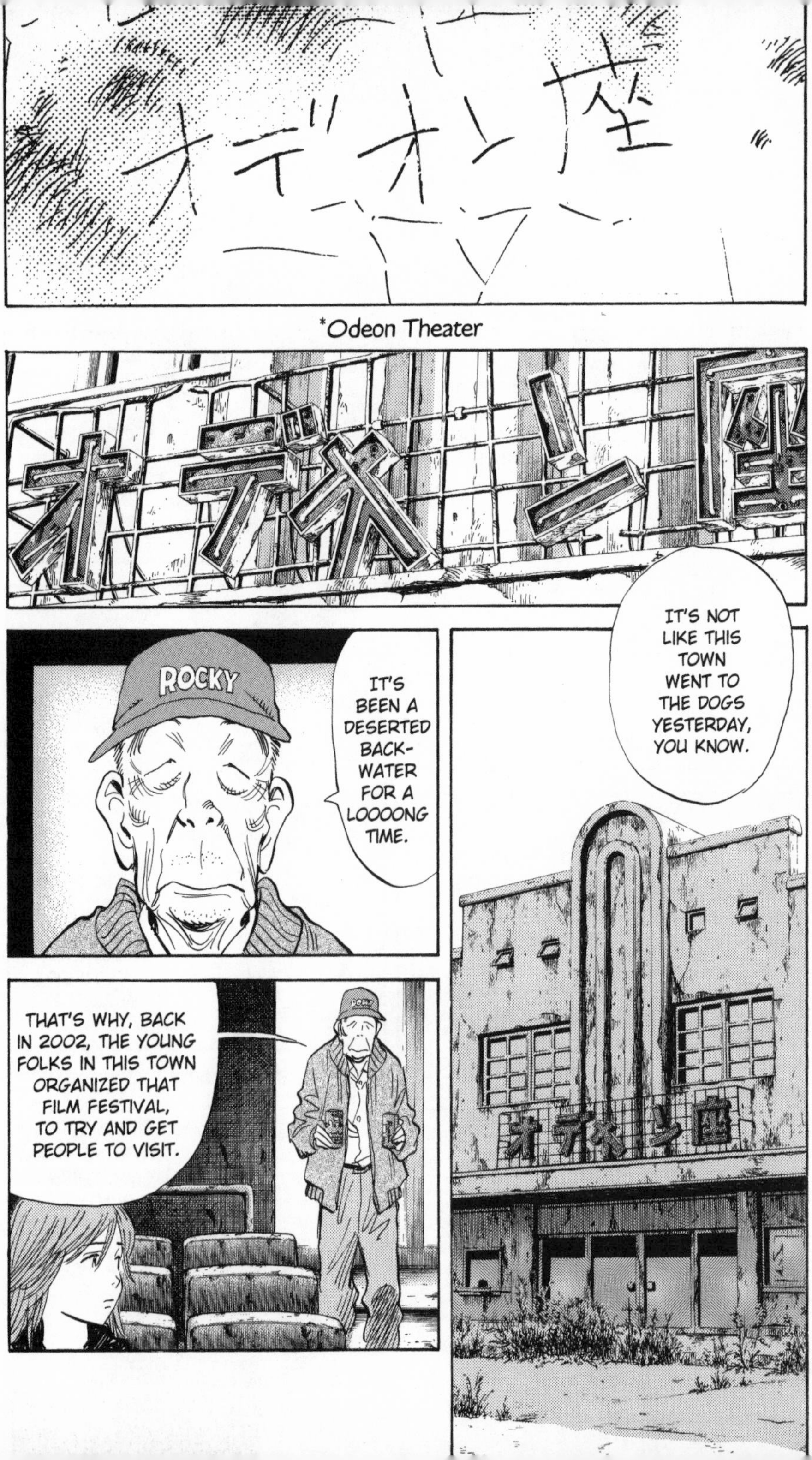
オデオン座
*Odeon Theater
IT'S NOT LIKE THIS TOWN WENT TO THE DOGS YESTERDAY, YOU KNOW.
ROCKY
IT'S BEEN A DESERTED BACK-WATER FOR A LOOOONG TIME.
THAT'S WHY, BACK IN 2002, THE YOUNG FOLKS IN THIS TOWN ORGANIZED THAT FILM FESTIVAL, TO TRY AND GET PEOPLE TO VISIT.

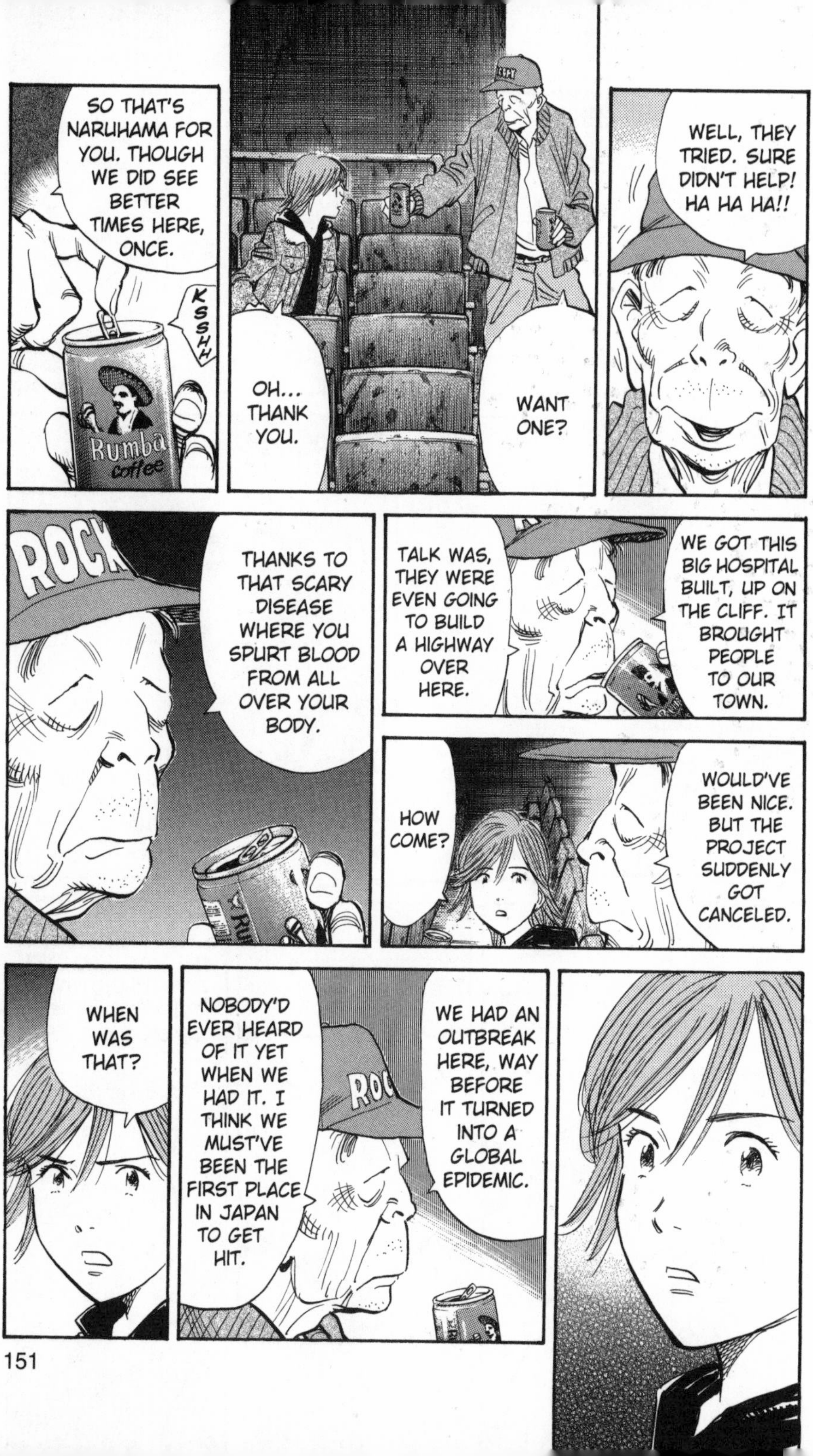
WELL, THEY TRIED. SURE DIDN'T HELP! HA HA HA!!
WANT ONE?
OH... THANK YOU.
SO THAT'S NARUHAMA FOR YOU. THOUGH WE DID SEE BETTER TIMES HERE, ONCE.
KSSHH
Rumba coffee
WE GOT THIS BIG HOSPITAL BUILT, UP ON THE CLIFF. IT BROUGHT PEOPLE TO OUR TOWN.
TALK WAS, THEY WERE EVEN GOING TO BUILD A HIGHWAY OVER HERE.
WOULD'VE BEEN NICE. BUT THE PROJECT SUDDENLY GOT CANCELED.
HOW COME?
ROCK
THANKS TO THAT SCARY DISEASE WHERE YOU SPURT BLOOD FROM ALL OVER YOUR BODY.
WE HAD AN OUTBREAK HERE, WAY BEFORE IT TURNED INTO A GLOBAL EPIDEMIC.
NOBODY'D EVER HEARD OF IT YET WHEN WE HAD IT. I THINK WE MUST'VE BEEN THE FIRST PLACE IN JAPAN TO GET HIT.
WHEN WAS THAT?

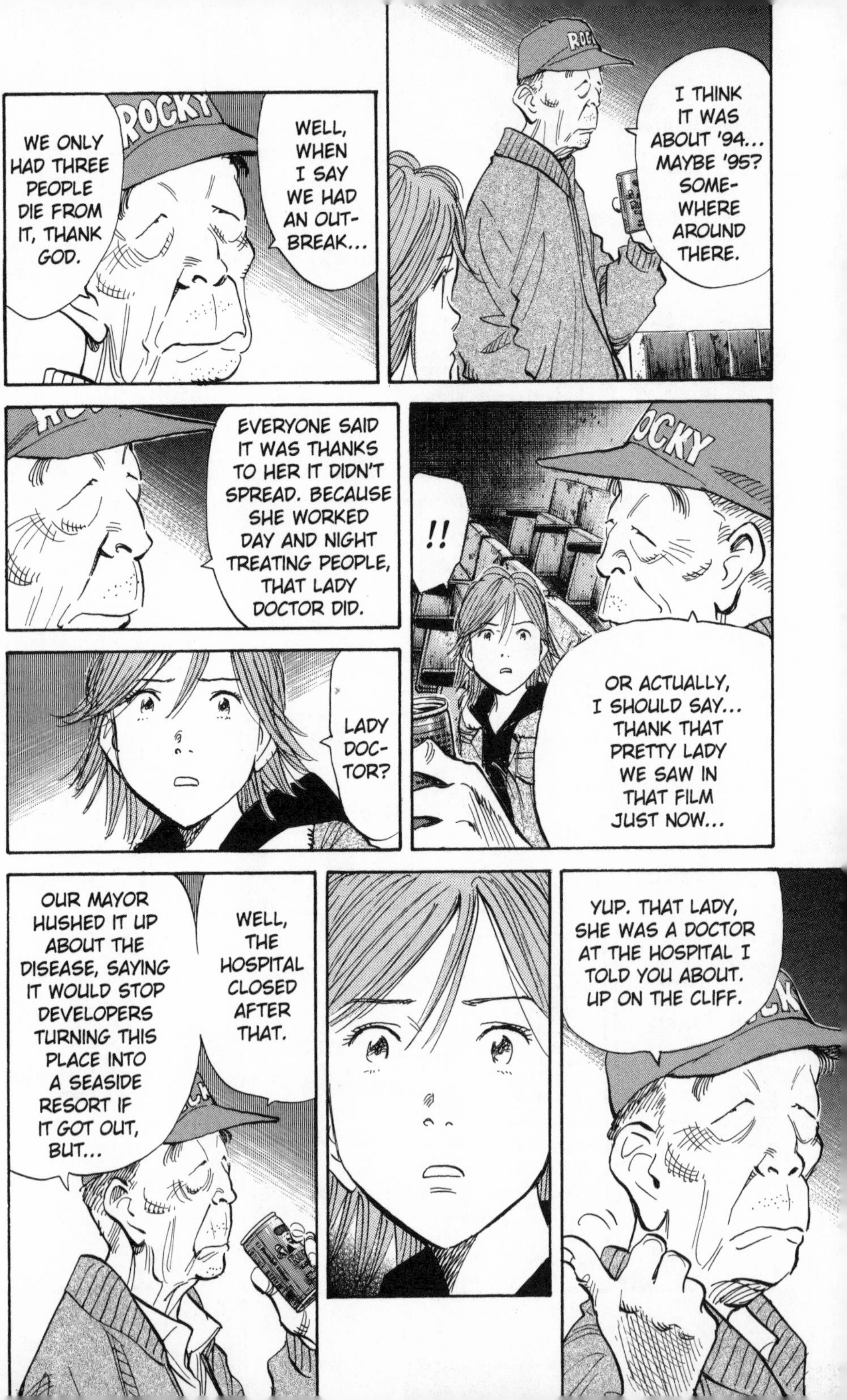
I THINK IT WAS ABOUT '94... MAYBE '95? SOME-WHERE AROUND THERE.
WELL, WHEN I SAY WE HAD AN OUT-BREAK...
WE ONLY HAD THREE PEOPLE DIE FROM IT, THANK GOD.
ROCKY
!!
OR ACTUALLY, I SHOULD SAY... THANK THAT PRETTY LADY WE SAW IN THAT FILM JUST NOW...
EVERYONE SAID IT WAS THANKS TO HER IT DIDN'T SPREAD. BECAUSE SHE WORKED DAY AND NIGHT TREATING PEOPLE, THAT LADY DOCTOR DID.
LADY DOC-TOR?
YUP. THAT LADY, SHE WAS A DOCTOR AT THE HOSPITAL I TOLD YOU ABOUT. UP ON THE CLIFF.
WELL, THE HOSPITAL CLOSED AFTER THAT.
OUR MAYOR HUSHED IT UP ABOUT THE DISEASE, SAYING IT WOULD STOP DEVELOPERS TURNING THIS PLACE INTO A SEASIDE RESORT IF IT GOT OUT, BUT...

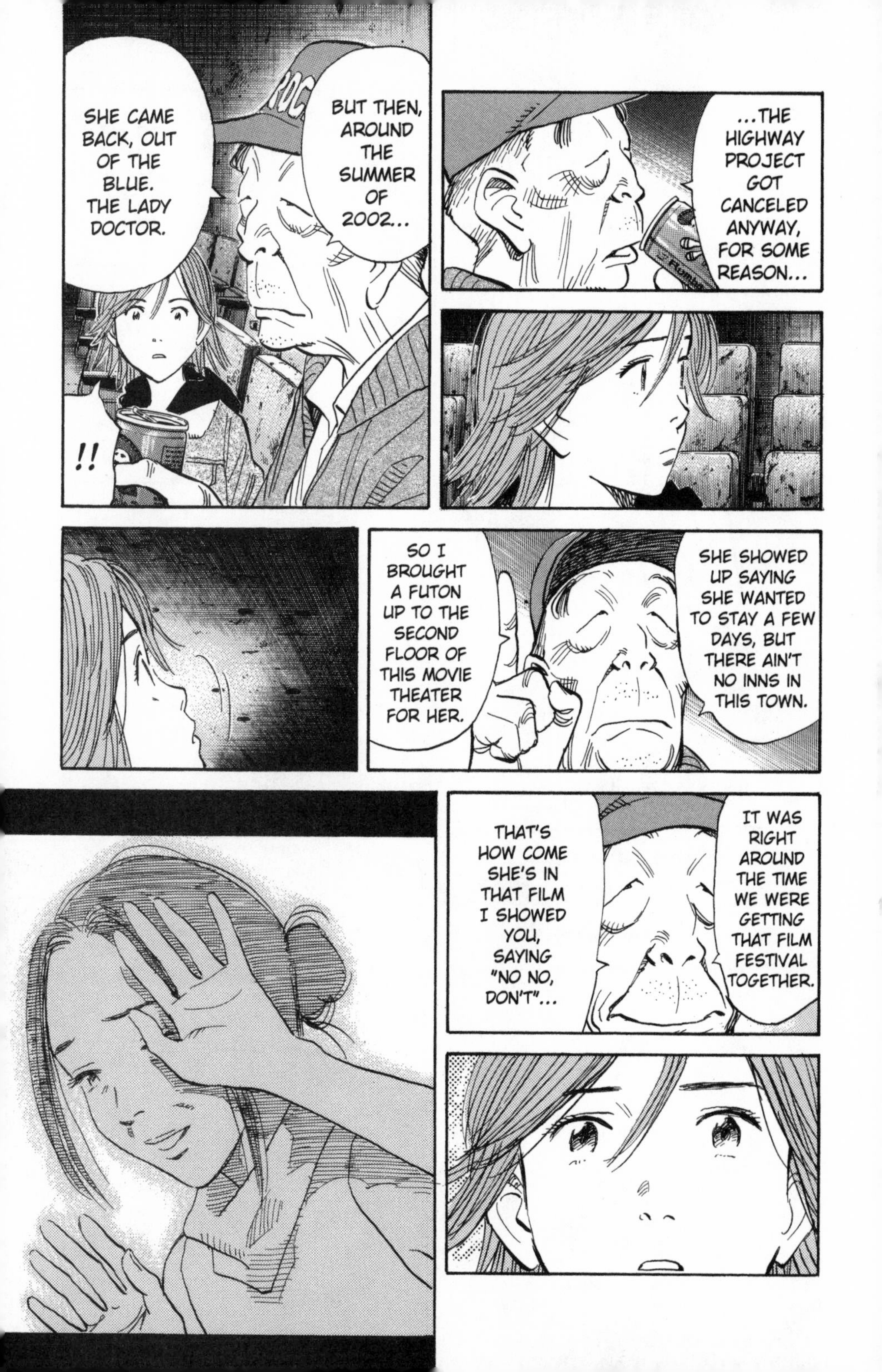
...THE HIGHWAY PROJECT GOT CANCELED ANYWAY, FOR SOME REASON...
BUT THEN, AROUND THE SUMMER OF 2002...
SHE CAME BACK, OUT OF THE BLUE. THE LADY DOCTOR.
!!
SHE SHOWED UP SAYING SHE WANTED TO STAY A FEW DAYS, BUT THERE AIN'T NO INNS IN THIS TOWN.
SO I BROUGHT A FUTON UP TO THE SECOND FLOOR OF THIS MOVIE THEATER FOR HER.
IT WAS RIGHT AROUND THE TIME WE WERE GETTING THAT FILM FESTIVAL TOGETHER.
THAT'S HOW COME SHE'S IN THAT FILM I SHOWED YOU, SAYING "NO NO, DON'T"...

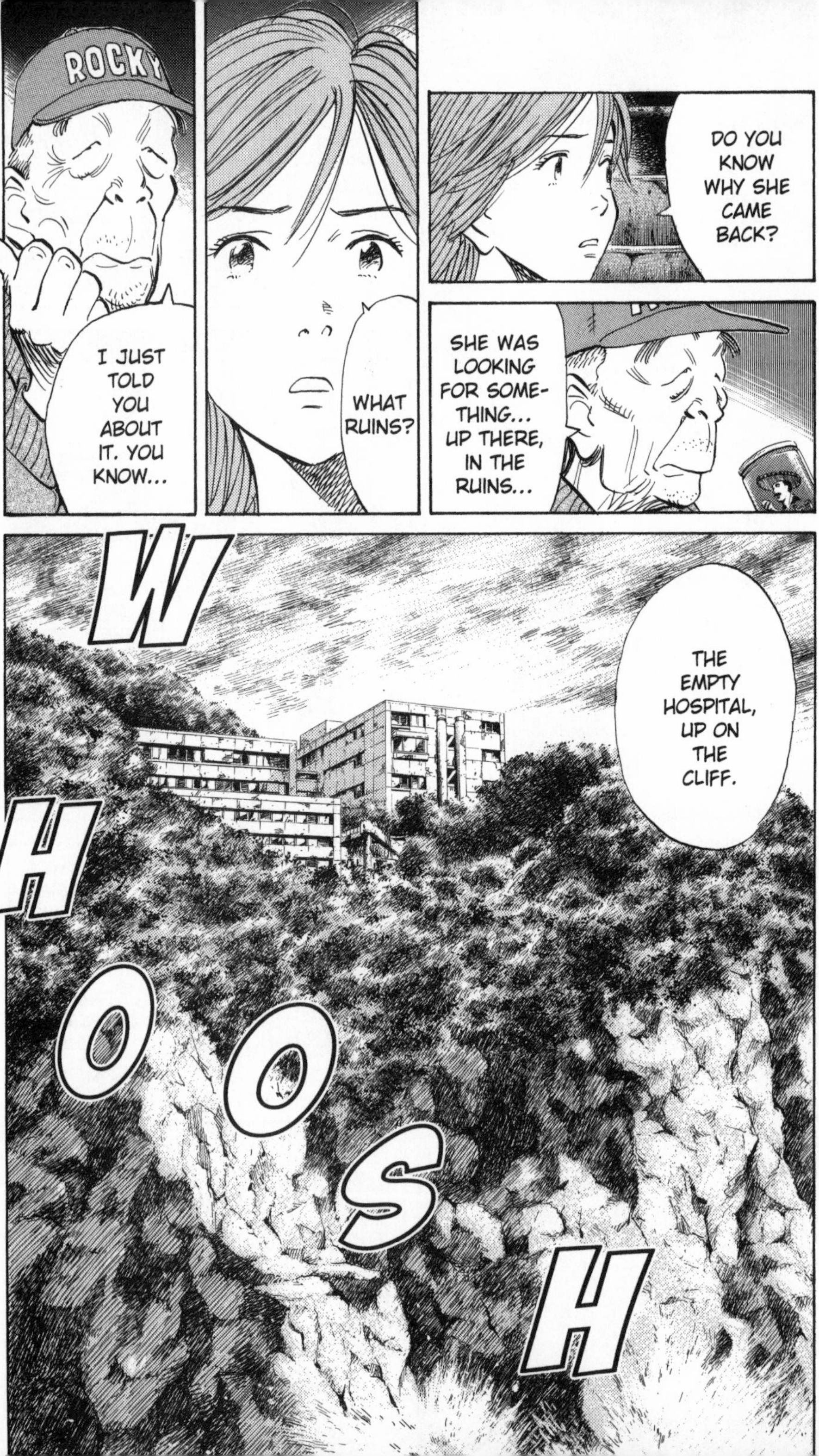
DO YOU KNOW WHY SHE CAME BACK?
SHE WAS LOOKING FOR SOME-THING... UP THERE, IN THE RUINS...
WHAT RUINS?
ROCKY
I JUST TOLD YOU ABOUT IT. YOU KNOW...
THE EMPTY HOSPITAL, UP ON THE CLIFF.
WHOOSH

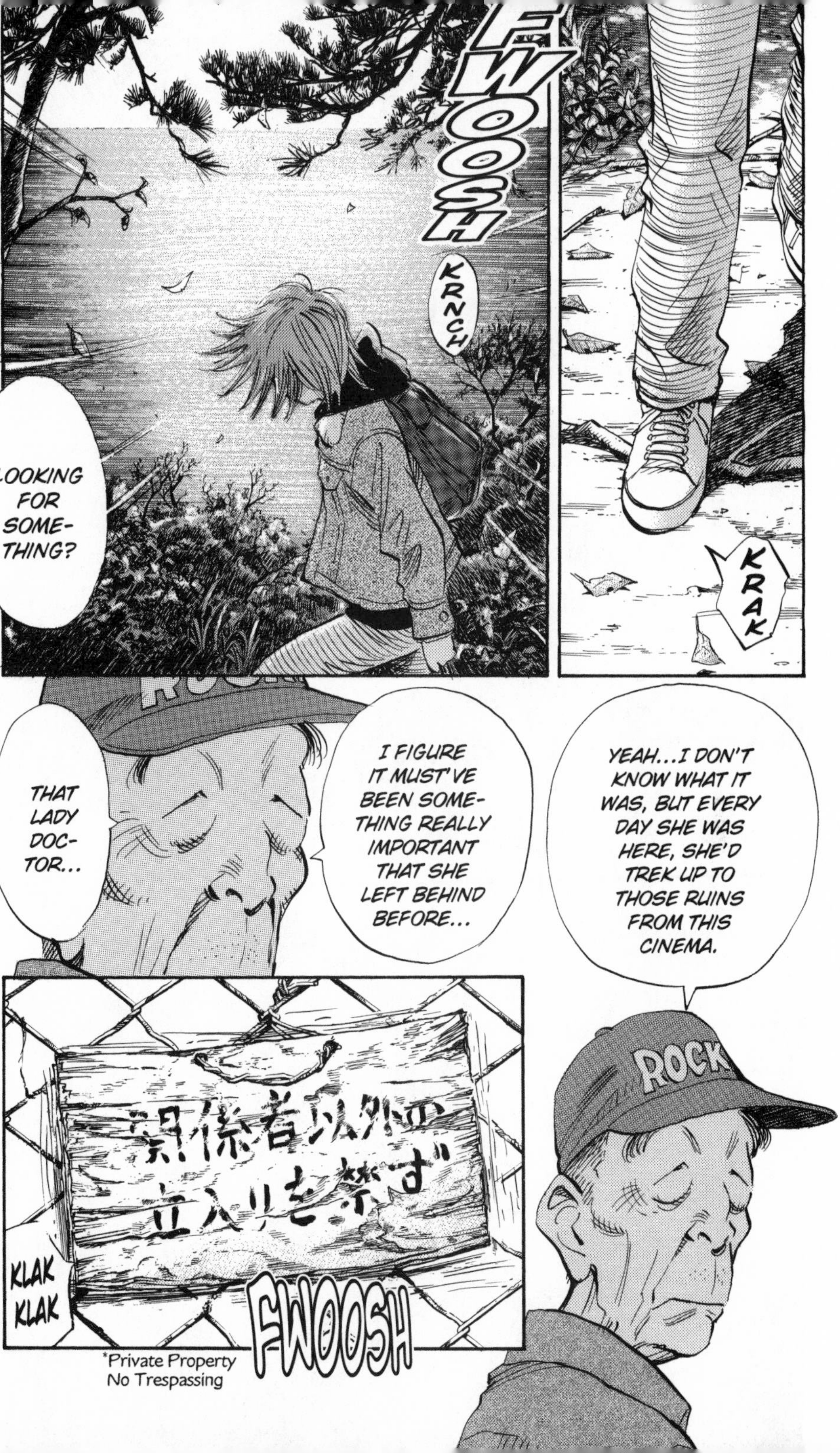
KRAK
FWOOSH
KRNCH
LOOKING FOR SOME-THING?
YEAH...I DON'T KNOW WHAT IT WAS, BUT EVERY DAY SHE WAS HERE, SHE'D TREK UP TO THOSE RUINS FROM THIS CINEMA.
I FIGURE IT MUST'VE BEEN SOME-THING REALLY IMPORTANT THAT SHE LEFT BEHIND BEFORE...
THAT LADY DOC-TOR...
ROCK
関係者以外の立入りを禁ず
FWOOSH
KLAK KLAK
*Private Property No Trespassing

Chapter 9 Godzilla

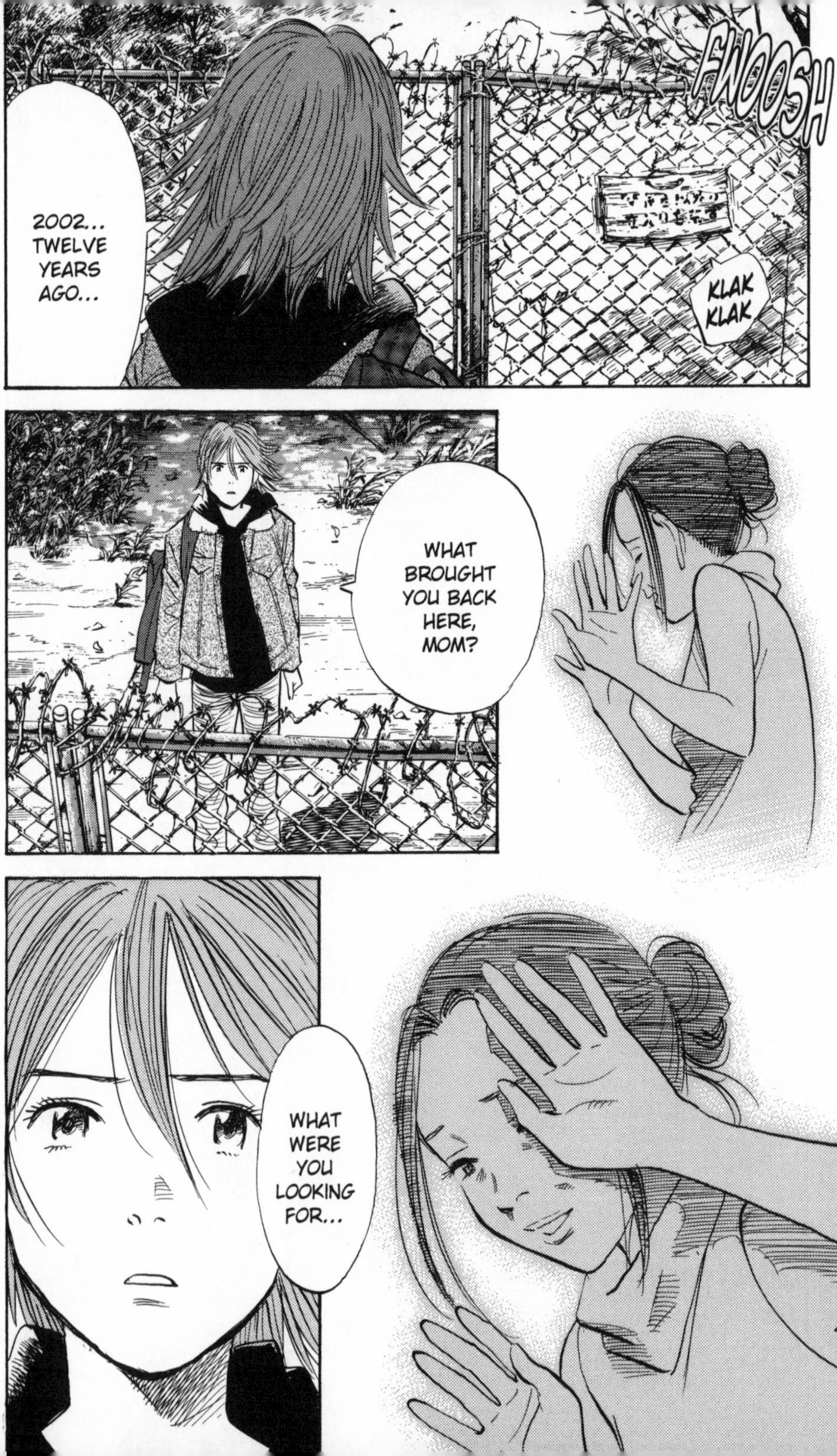
FWOOSH
KLAK KLAK
2002... TWELVE YEARS AGO...
WHAT BROUGHT YOU BACK HERE, MOM?
WHAT WERE YOU LOOKING FOR...

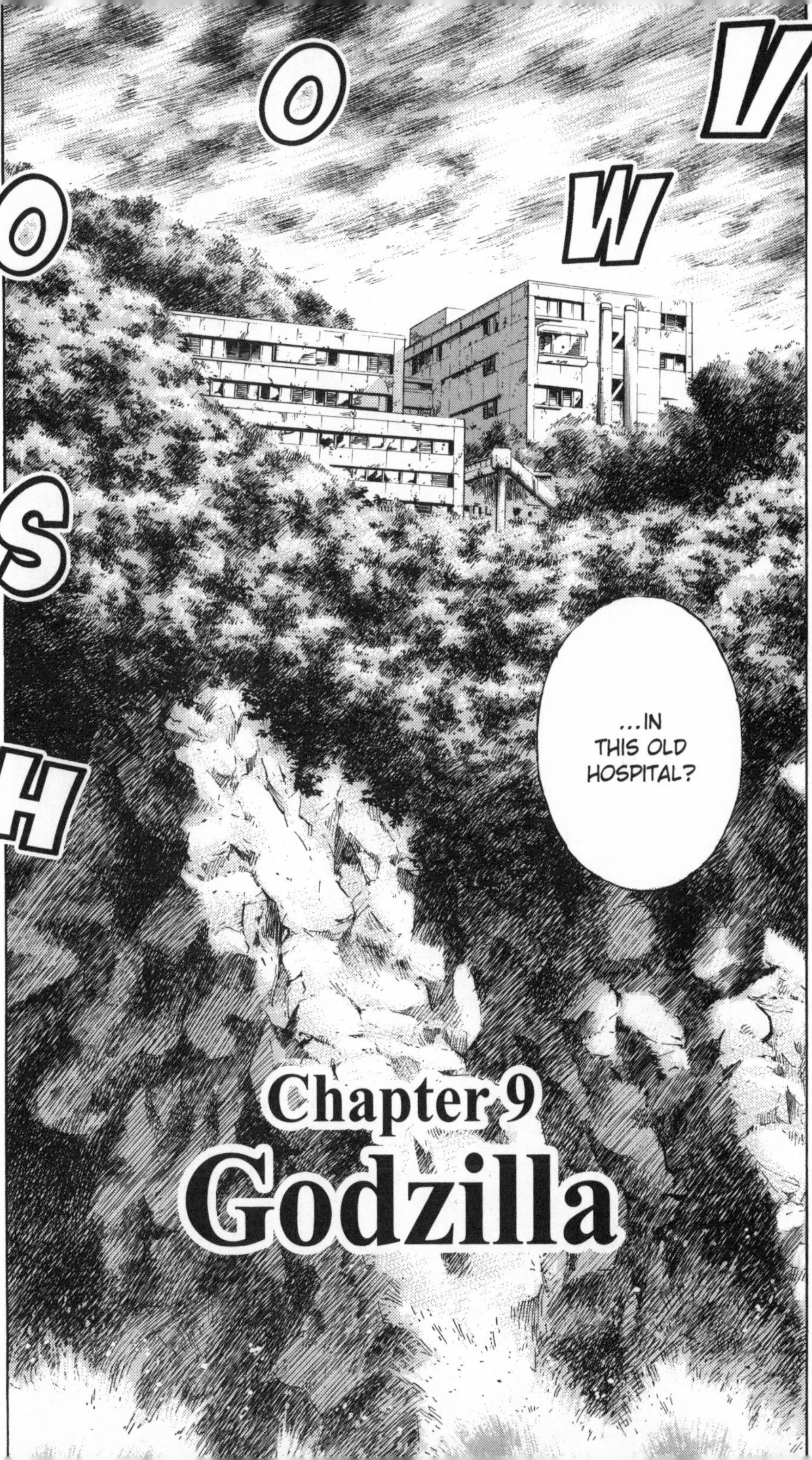
VWOOSH
...IN THIS OLD HOSPITAL?

Chapter 9
Godzilla

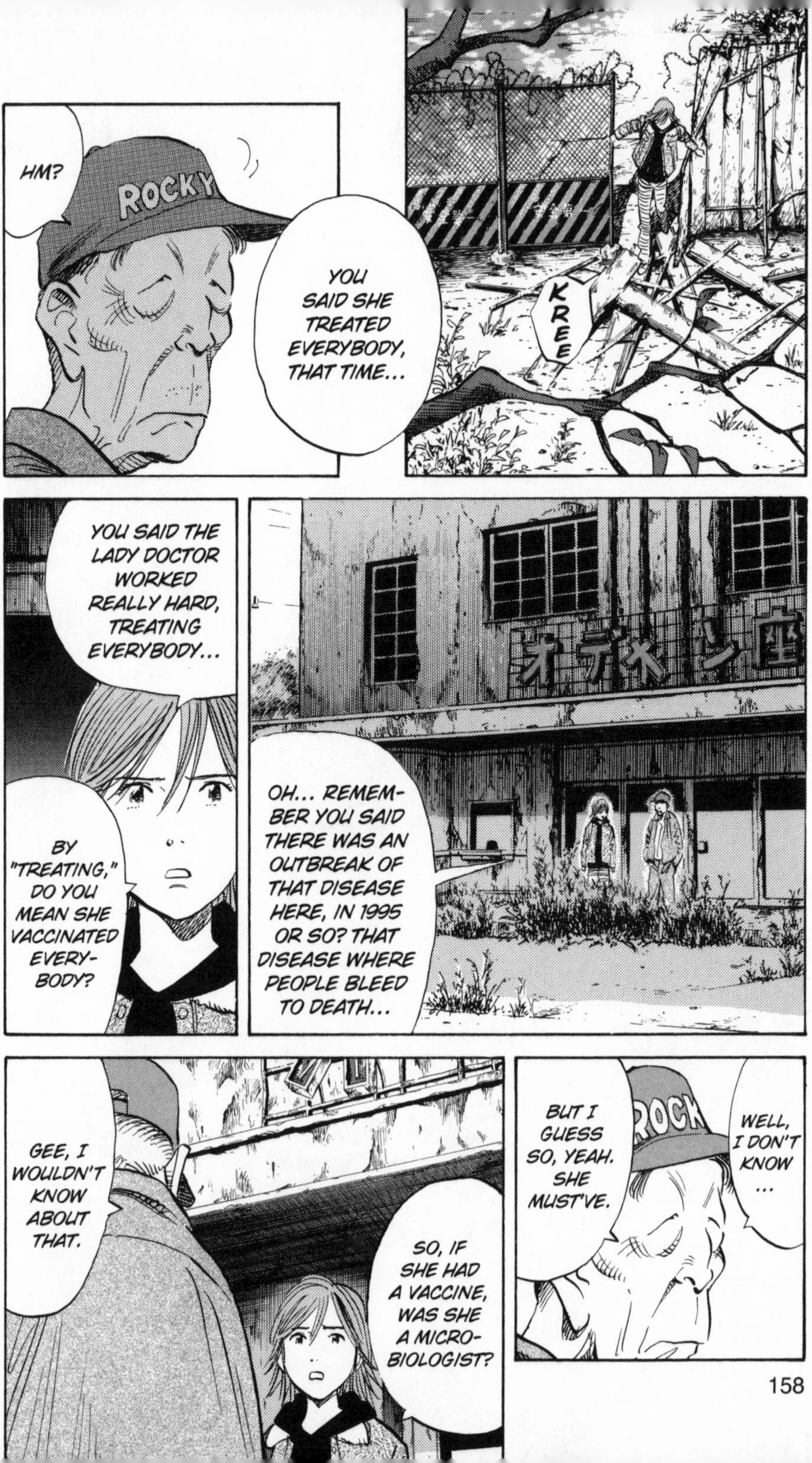
KREE
YOU SAID SHE TREATED EVERYBODY, THAT TIME...
HM?
ROCKY
オデオン座
OH... REMEMBER YOU SAID THERE WAS AN OUTBREAK OF THAT DISEASE HERE, IN 1995 OR SO? THAT DISEASE WHERE PEOPLE BLEED TO DEATH...
YOU SAID THE LADY DOCTOR WORKED REALLY HARD, TREATING EVERYBODY...
BY "TREATING," DO YOU MEAN SHE VACCINATED EVERYBODY?
WELL, I DON'T KNOW...
BUT I GUESS SO, YEAH. SHE MUST'VE.
SO, IF SHE HAD A VACCINE, WAS SHE A MICROBIOLOGIST?
GEE, I WOULDN'T KNOW ABOUT THAT.

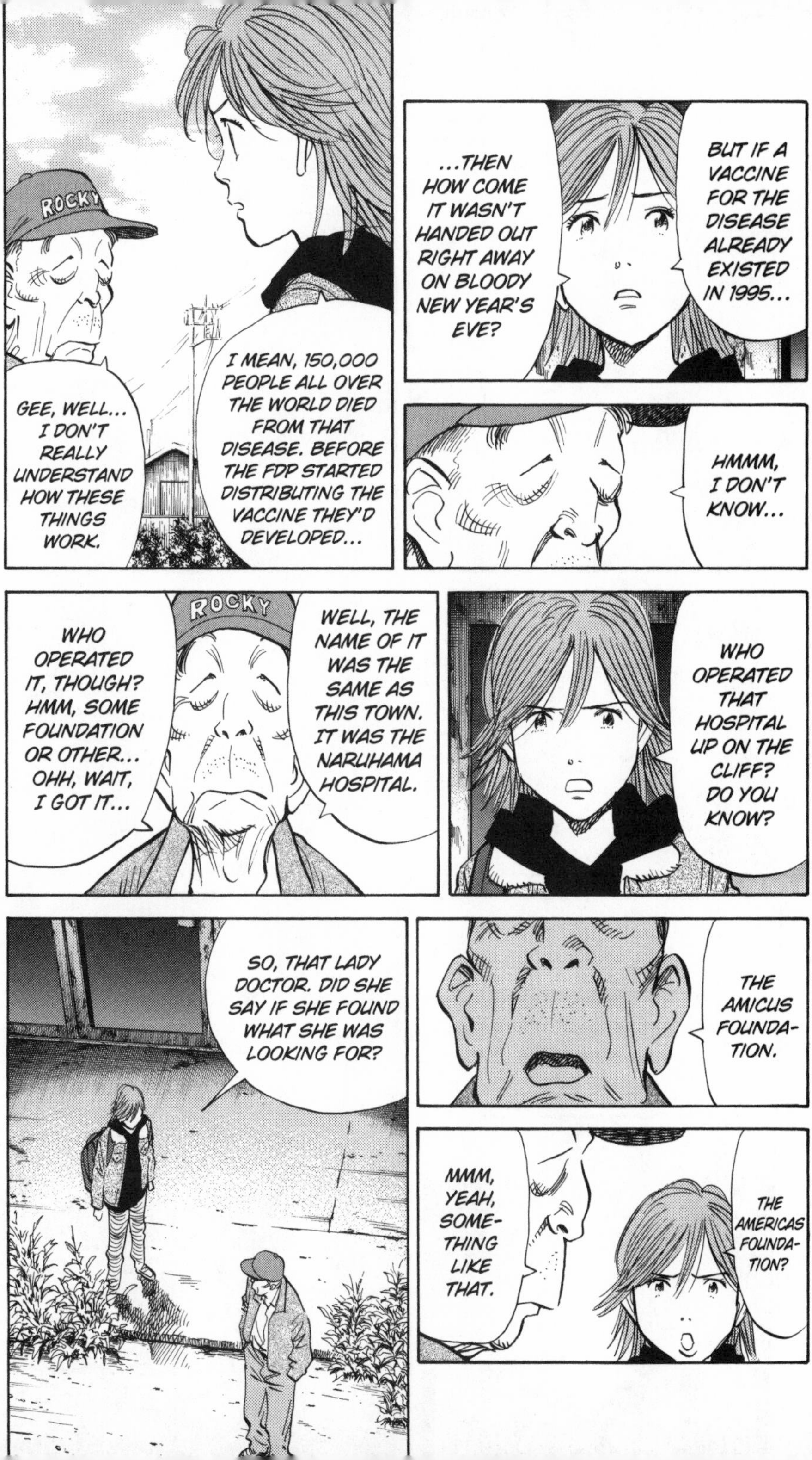

BUT IF A VACCINE FOR THE DISEASE ALREADY EXISTED IN 1995...
...THEN HOW COME IT WASN'T HANDED OUT RIGHT AWAY ON BLOODY NEW YEAR'S EVE?
HMMM, I DON'T KNOW...
ROCKY
I MEAN, 150,000 PEOPLE ALL OVER THE WORLD DIED FROM THAT DISEASE. BEFORE THE FDP STARTED DISTRIBUTING THE VACCINE THEY'D DEVELOPED...
GEE, WELL... I DON'T REALLY UNDERSTAND HOW THESE THINGS WORK.
WHO OPERATED THAT HOSPITAL UP ON THE CLIFF? DO YOU KNOW?
ROCKY
WELL, THE NAME OF IT WAS THE SAME AS THIS TOWN. IT WAS THE NARUHAMA HOSPITAL.
WHO OPERATED IT, THOUGH? HMM, SOME FOUNDATION OR OTHER... OHH, WAIT, I GOT IT...
THE AMICUS FOUNDATION.
THE AMERICAS FOUNDATION?
MMM, YEAH, SOMETHING LIKE THAT.
SO, THAT LADY DOCTOR. DID SHE SAY IF SHE FOUND WHAT SHE WAS LOOKING FOR?

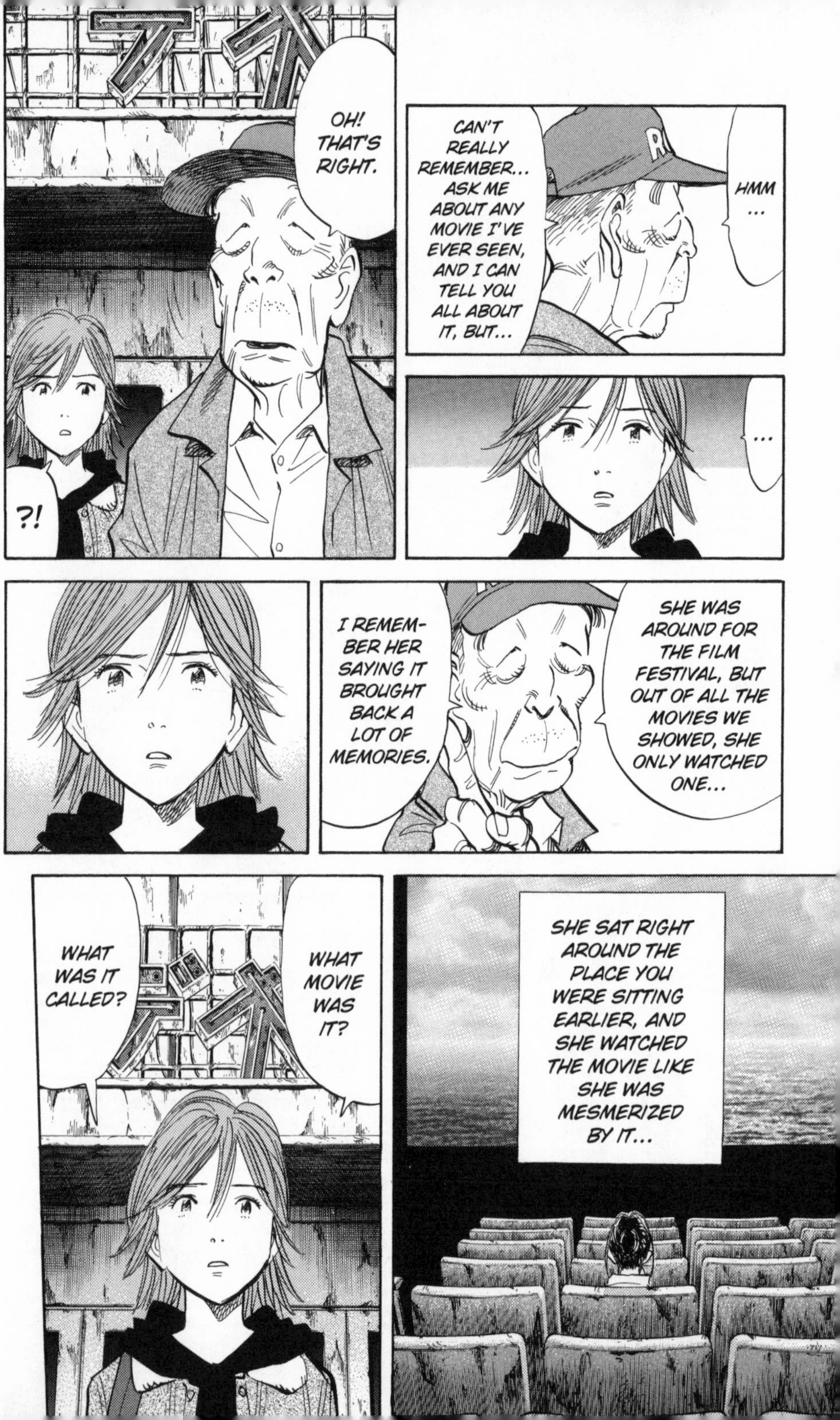
HMM ...
CAN'T REALLY REMEMBER... ASK ME ABOUT ANY MOVIE I'VE EVER SEEN, AND I CAN TELL YOU ALL ABOUT IT, BUT...
...
OH! THAT'S RIGHT.
?!
SHE WAS AROUND FOR THE FILM FESTIVAL, BUT OUT OF ALL THE MOVIES WE SHOWED, SHE ONLY WATCHED ONE...
I REMEMBER HER SAYING IT BROUGHT BACK A LOT OF MEMORIES.
SHE SAT RIGHT AROUND THE PLACE YOU WERE SITTING EARLIER, AND SHE WATCHED THE MOVIE LIKE SHE WAS MESMERIZED BY IT...
WHAT MOVIE WAS IT?
WHAT WAS IT CALLED?

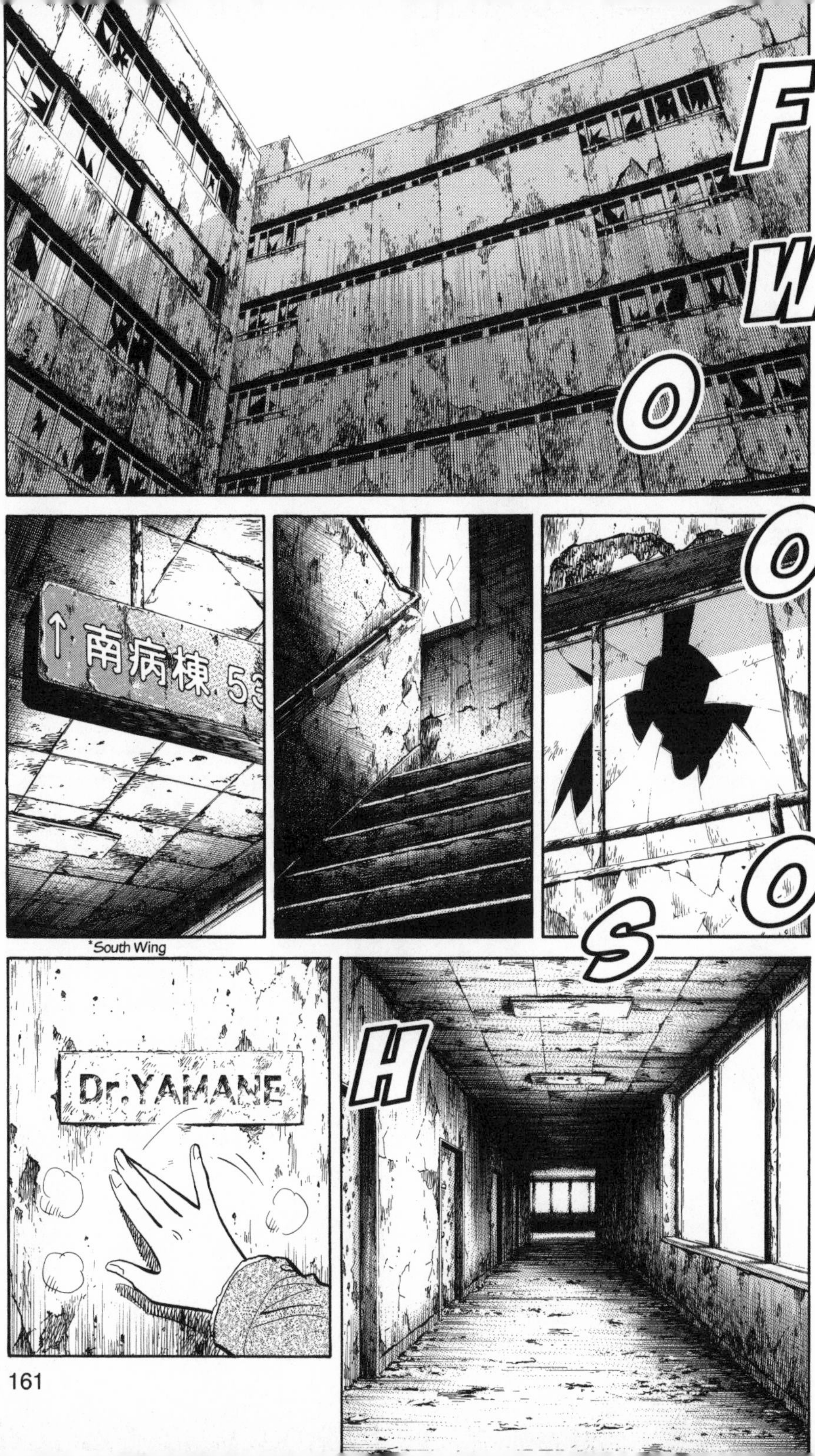
FWOOOOSH
↑南病棟 53
*South Wing
Dr.YAMANE

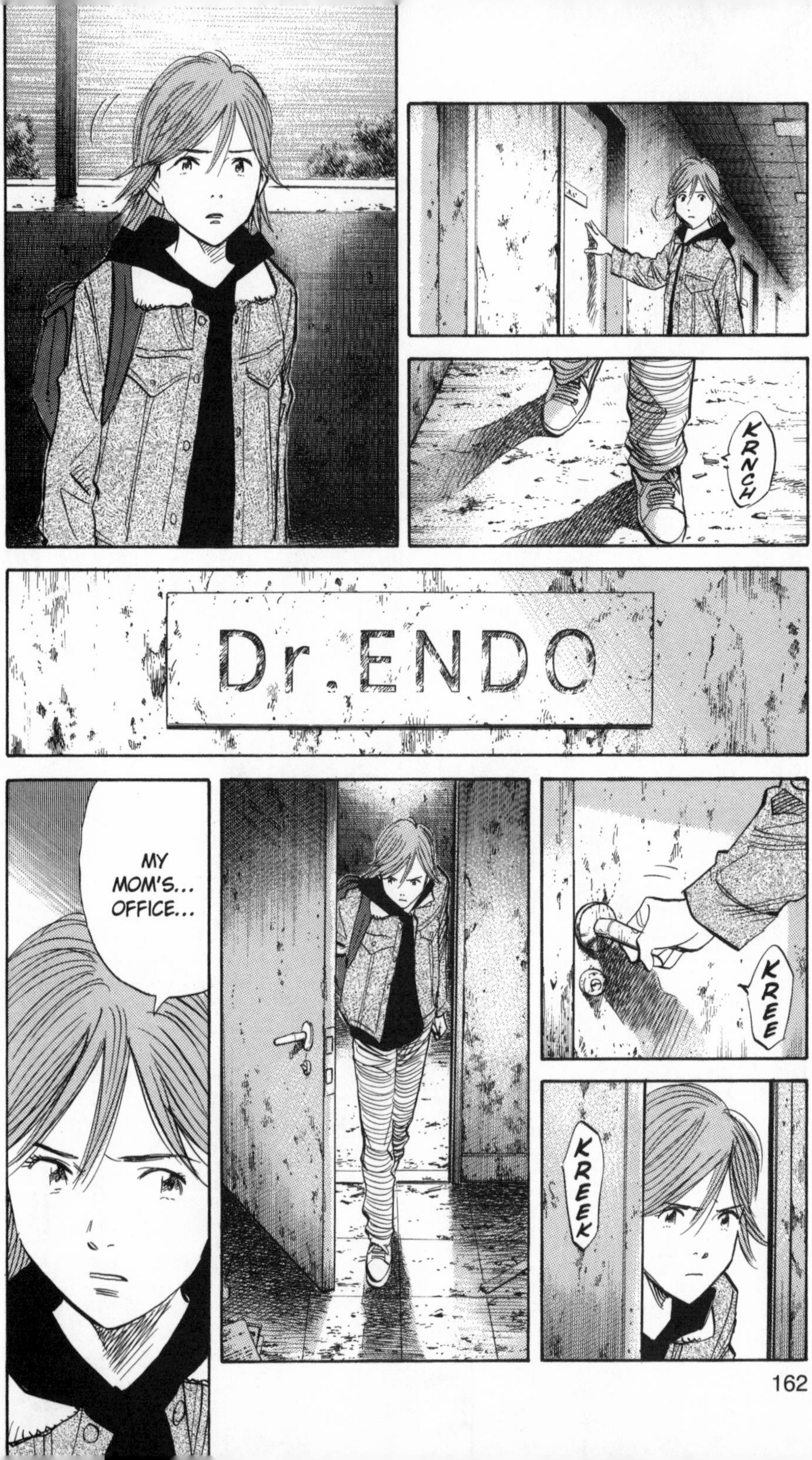
KRNCH
Dr.ENDO
KREE
KREEK
MY MOM'S... OFFICE...

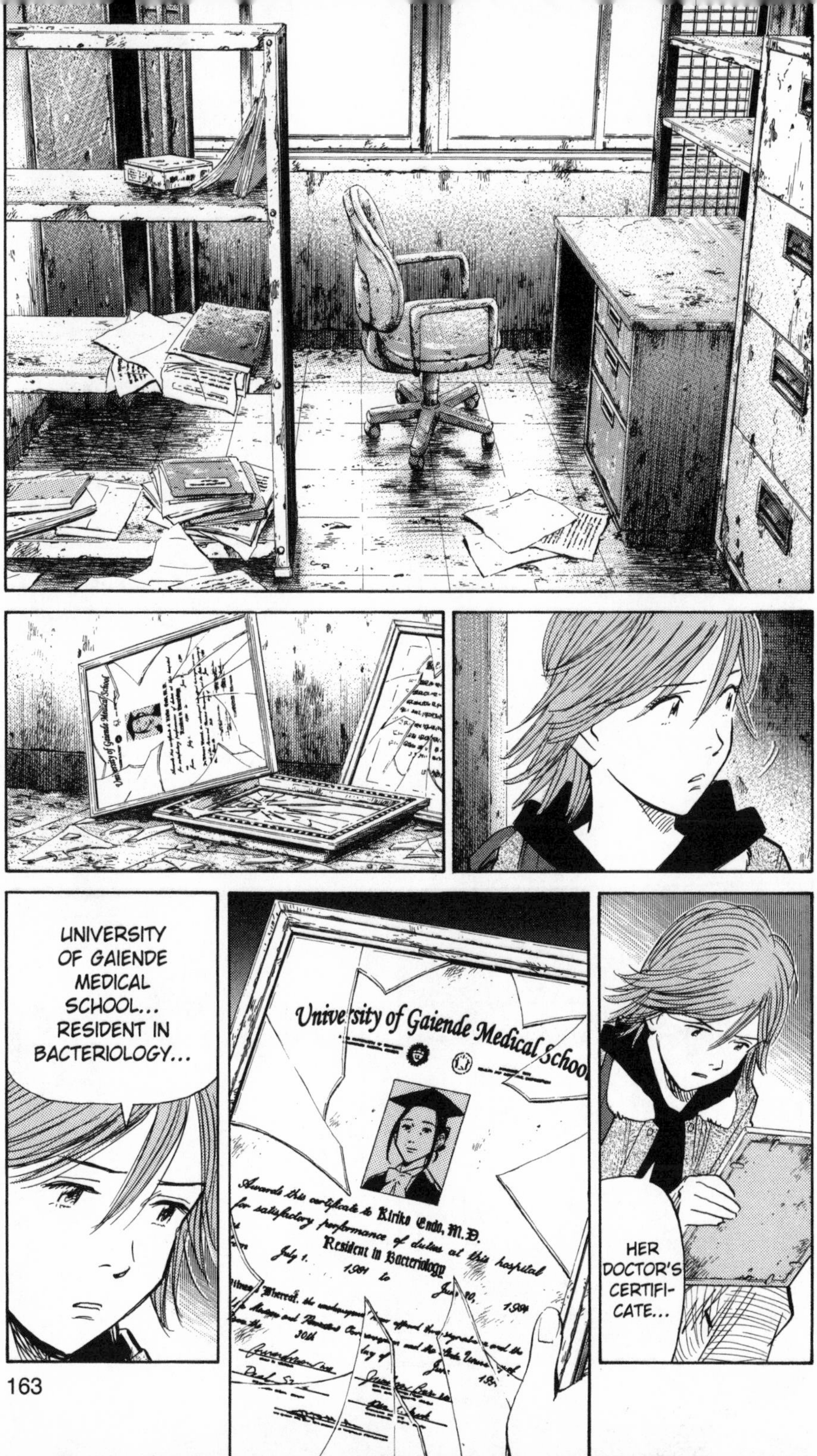
HER DOCTOR'S CERTIFICATE...
University of Gaiende Medical School
Awards this certificate to Kiriko Endo, M.D.
for satisfactory performance of duties at this hospital
Resident in Bacteriology
UNIVERSITY OF GAIENDE MEDICAL SCHOOL... RESIDENT IN BACTERIOLOGY...

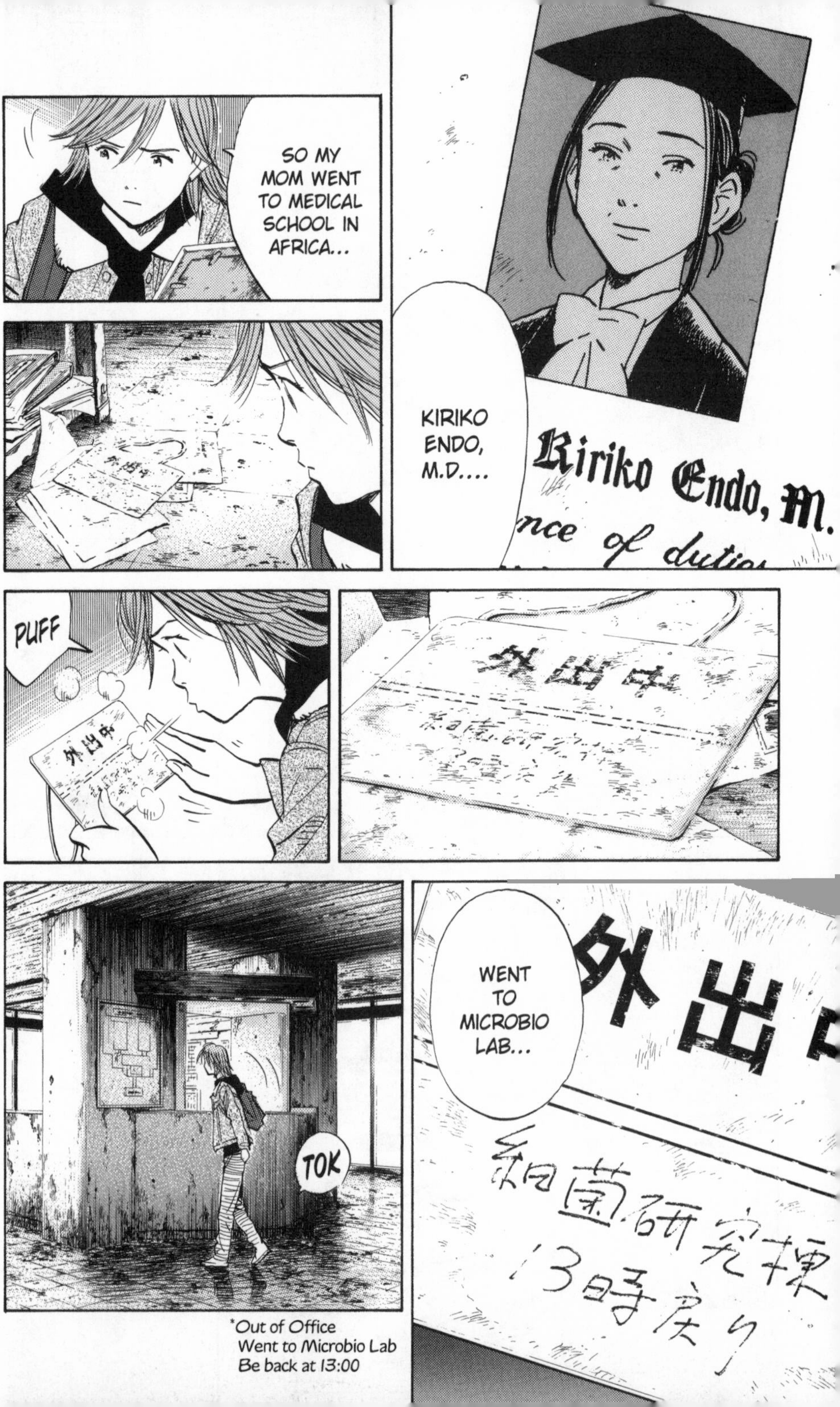
KIRIKO ENDO, M.D....
Kiriko Endo, M.
nce of duties
SO MY MOM WENT TO MEDICAL SCHOOL IN AFRICA...
外出中
PUFF
外出中
WENT TO MICROBIO LAB...
外出中
細菌研究棟
13時戻り
TOK
*Out of Office
Went to Microbio Lab
Be back at 13:00

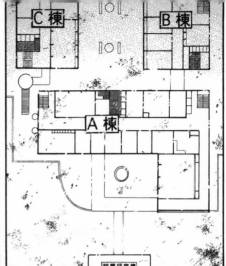

細菌研究棟

*Microbiology Research Center

ZWAASH

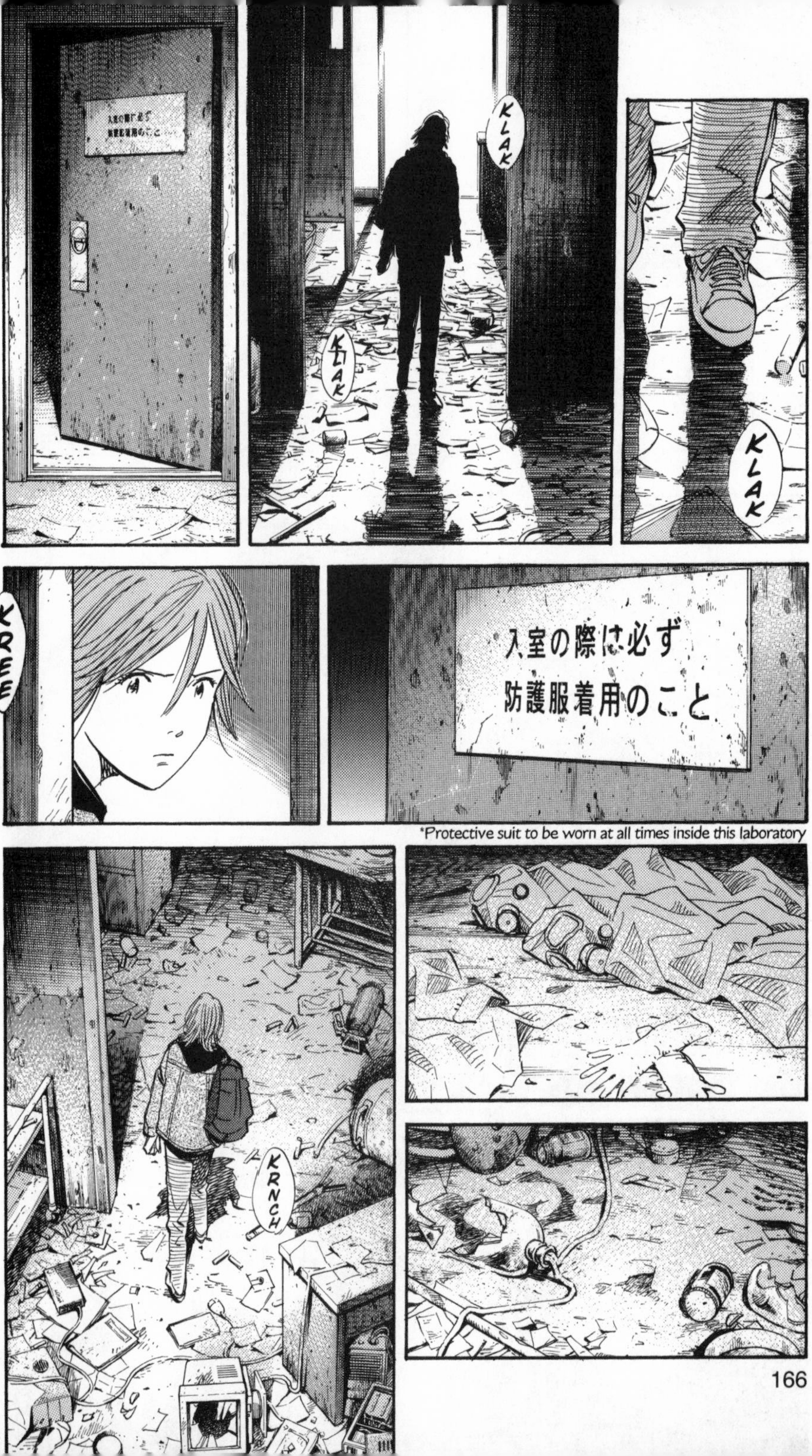
KLAK
KLAK
KLAK
入室の際は必ず
防護服着用のこと
KREE
KRNCH
*Protective suit to be worn at all times inside this laboratory

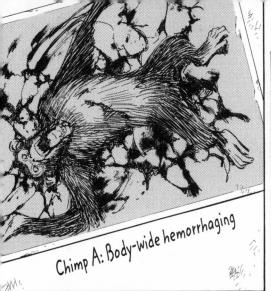

FLAP
FLAP
Chimp A: Body-wide hemorrhaging
Body-wide hemorrhaging
FLAP
FLAP
FLAP
FLAP
!!

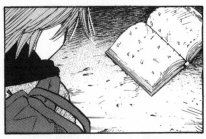

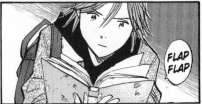

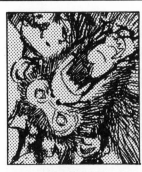

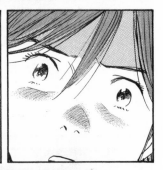

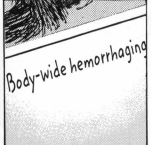

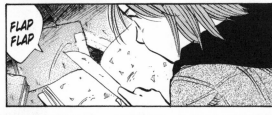

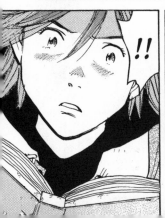

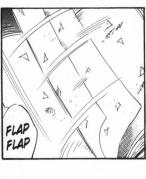

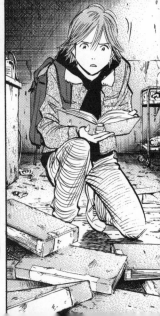

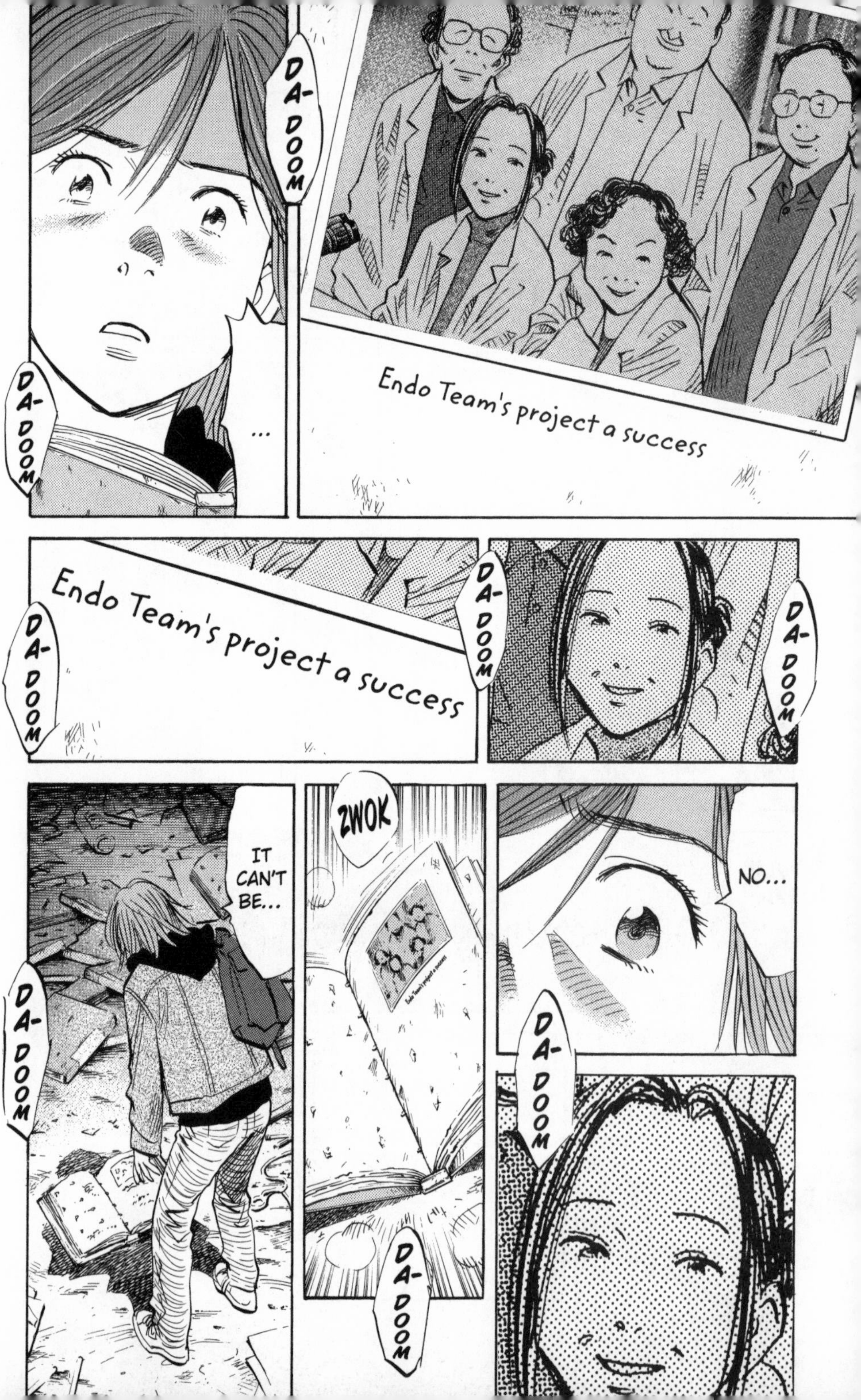
Endo Team's project a success
DA-DOOM
...
DA-DOOM
DA-DOOM
DA-DOOM
Endo Team's project a success
DA-DOOM
NO...
DA-DOOM
ZWOK
DA-DOOM
IT CAN'T BE...
DA-DOOM

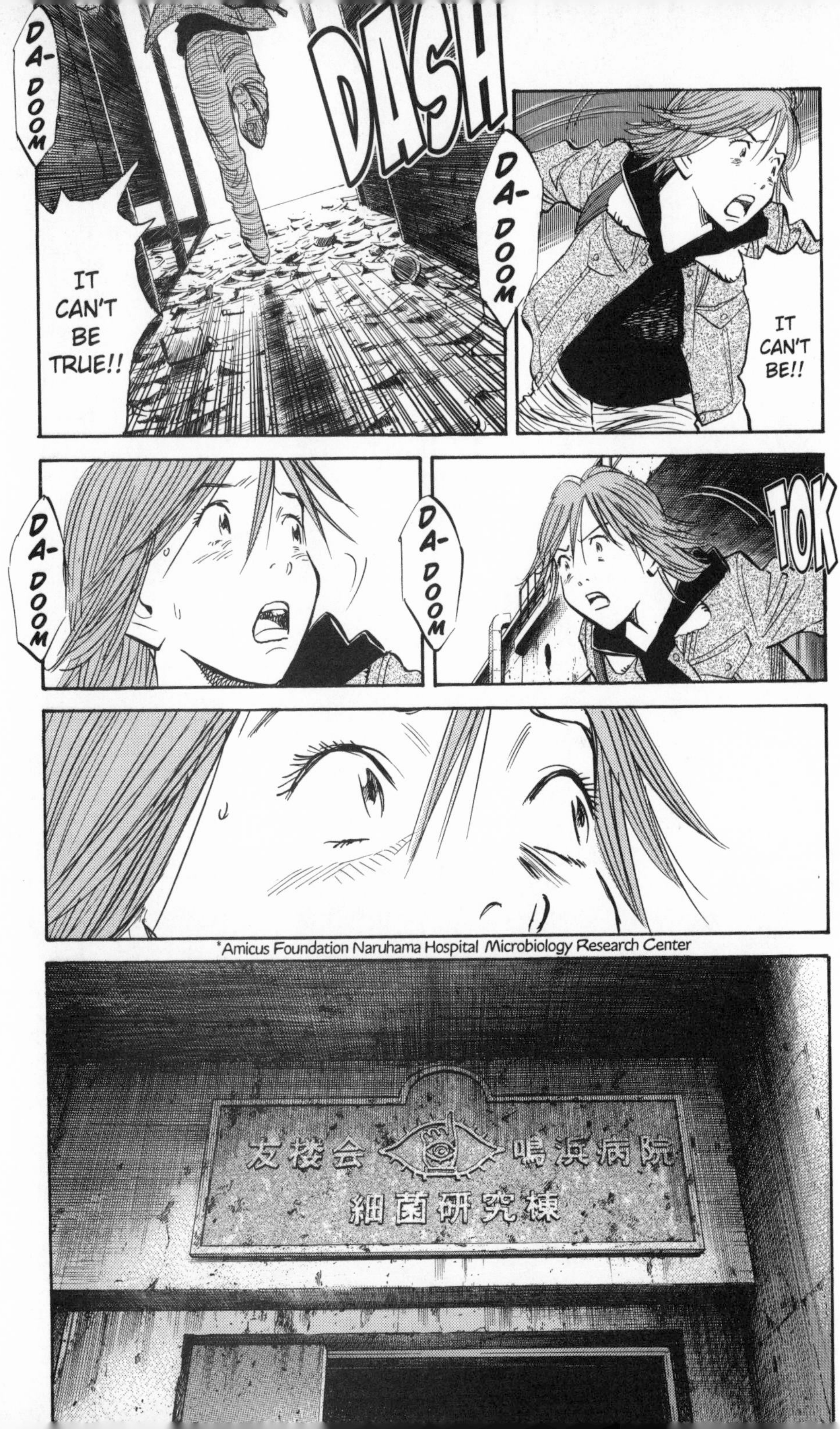
DA-DOOM
IT CAN'T BE!!
DASH
DA-DOOM
IT CAN'T BE TRUE!!
TOK
DA-DOOM
DA-DOOM
*Amicus Foundation Naruhama Hospital Microbiology Research Center
友楼会 鳴浜病院
細菌研究棟

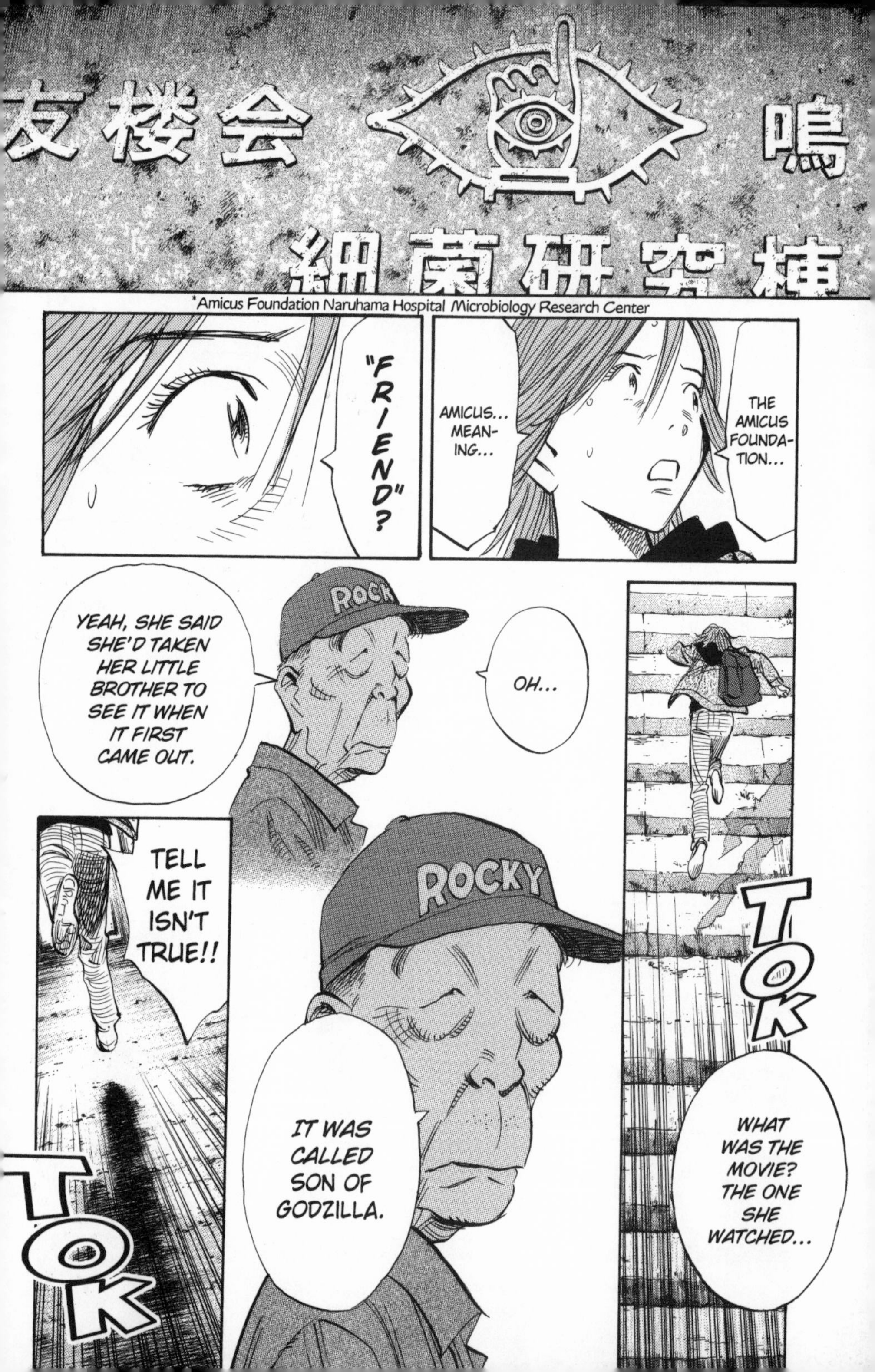
友楼会 鳴
細菌研究棟
*Amicus Foundation Naruhama Hospital Microbiology Research Center
THE AMICUS FOUNDATION...
AMICUS... MEANING...
"FRIEND"?
OH...
YEAH, SHE SAID SHE'D TAKEN HER LITTLE BROTHER TO SEE IT WHEN IT FIRST CAME OUT.
TOK
WHAT WAS THE MOVIE? THE ONE SHE WATCHED...
IT WAS CALLED SON OF GODZILLA.
TELL ME IT ISN'T TRUE!!
TOK

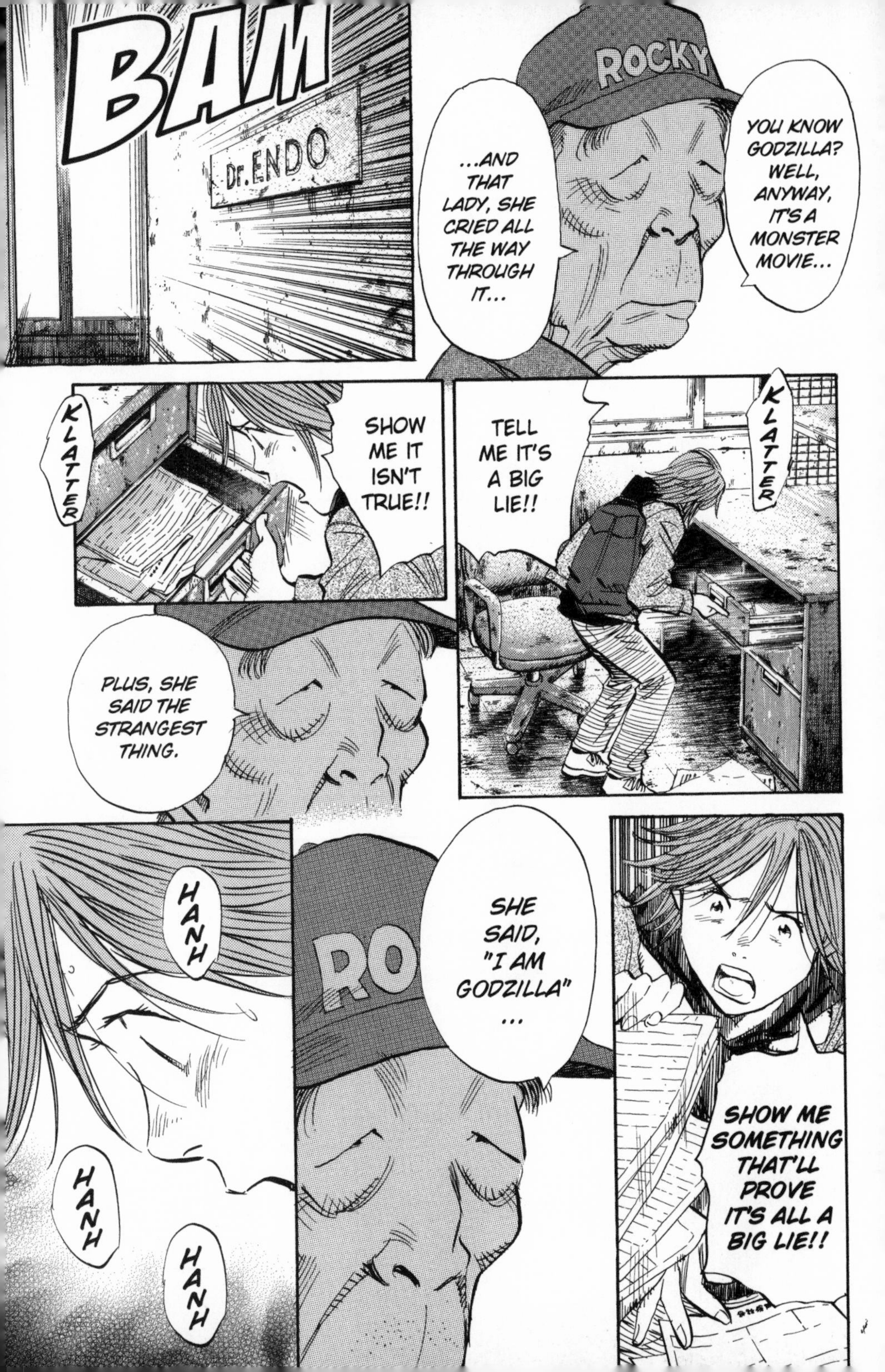

YOU KNOW GODZILLA? WELL, ANYWAY, IT'S A MONSTER MOVIE...
...AND THAT LADY, SHE CRIED ALL THE WAY THROUGH IT...
ROCKY
BAM
Dr. ENDO
KLATTER
TELL ME IT'S A BIG LIE!!
SHOW ME IT ISN'T TRUE!!
KLATTER
PLUS, SHE SAID THE STRANGEST THING.
SHOW ME SOMETHING THAT'LL PROVE IT'S ALL A BIG LIE!!
SHE SAID, "I AM GODZILLA"...
RO
HANH
HANH
HANH

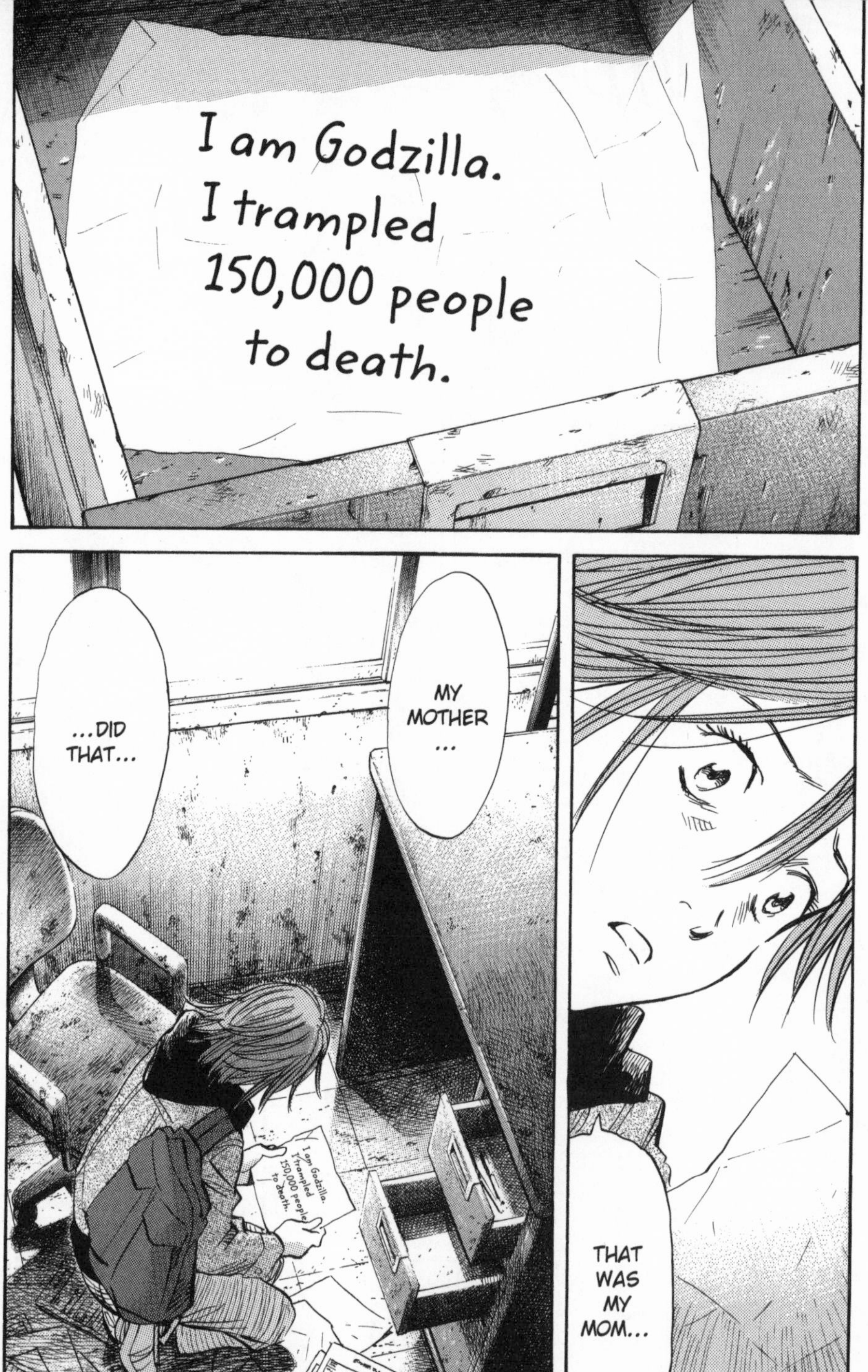
I am Godzilla.
I trampled
150,000 people
to death.
THAT WAS MY MOM...
MY MOTHER ...
...DID THAT...

Chapter 10 Mother's Words

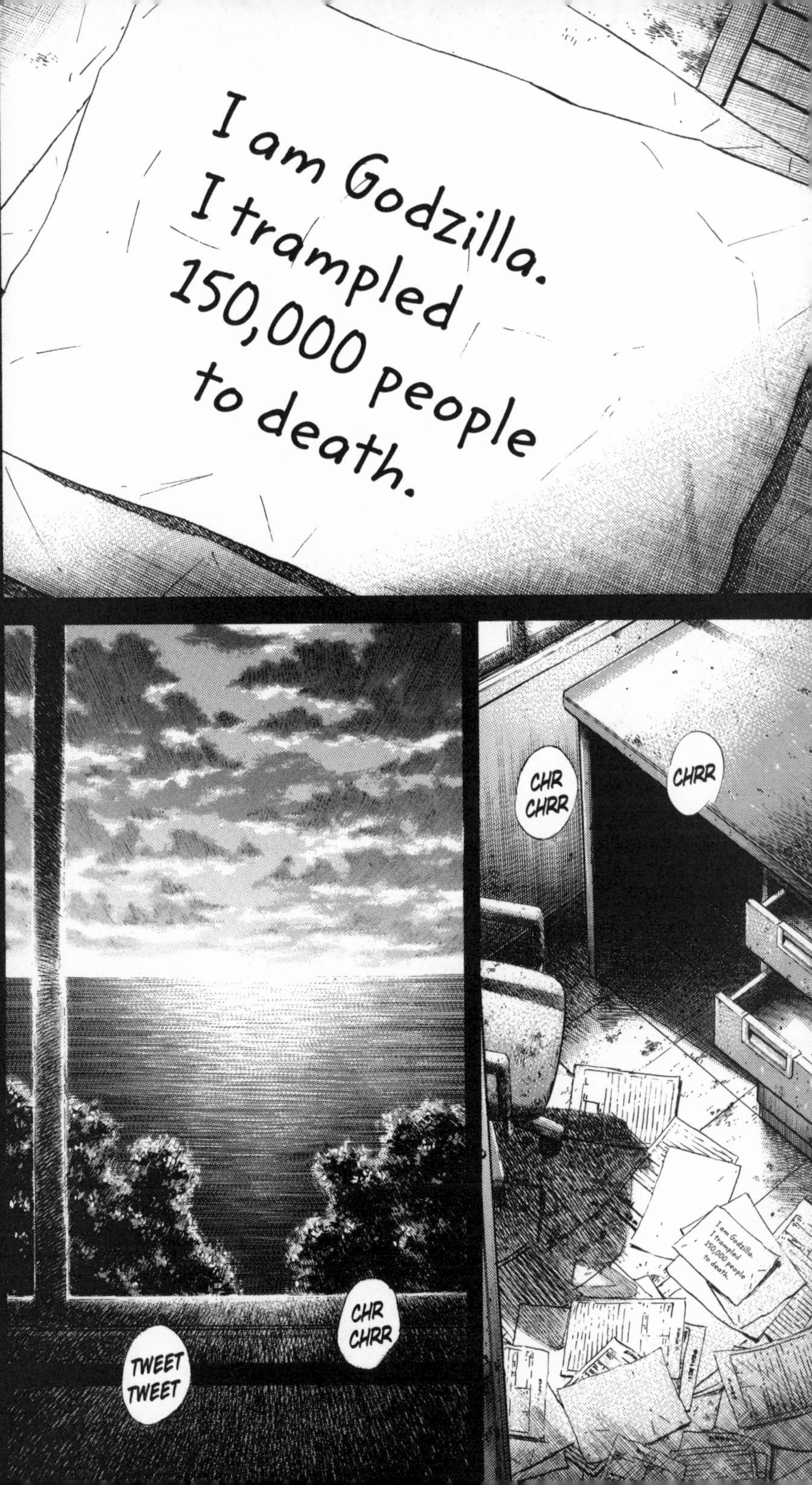
I am Godzilla.
I trampled
150,000 people
to death.
CHRR
CHR CHRR
I am Godzilla. I trampled 150,000 people to death.
CHR CHRR
TWEET TWEET

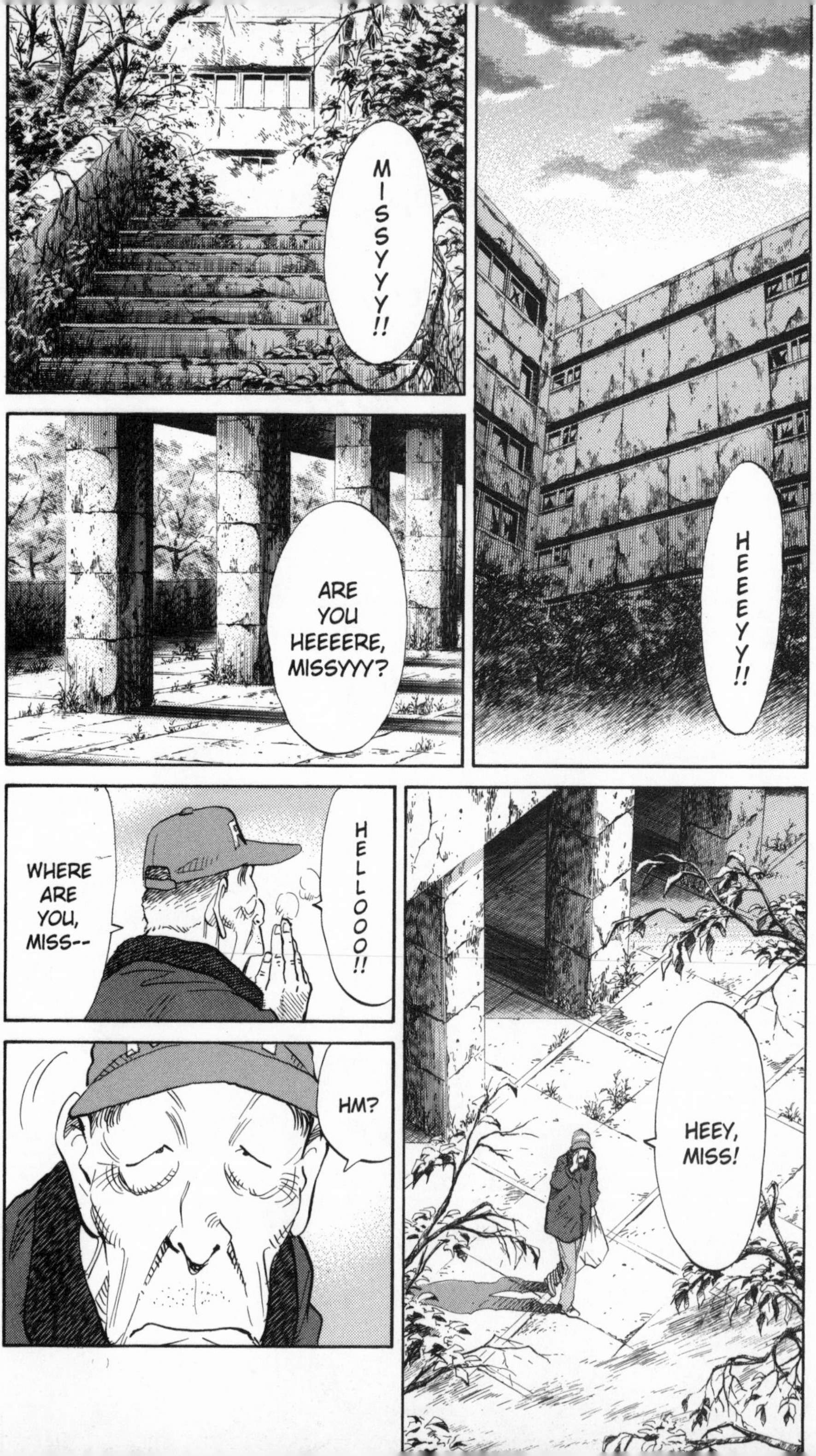
HEEEEYY!!
MISSYYY!!
ARE YOU HEEEERE, MISSYYY?
HEEY, MISS!
HELLOOO!!
WHERE ARE YOU, MISS--
HM?

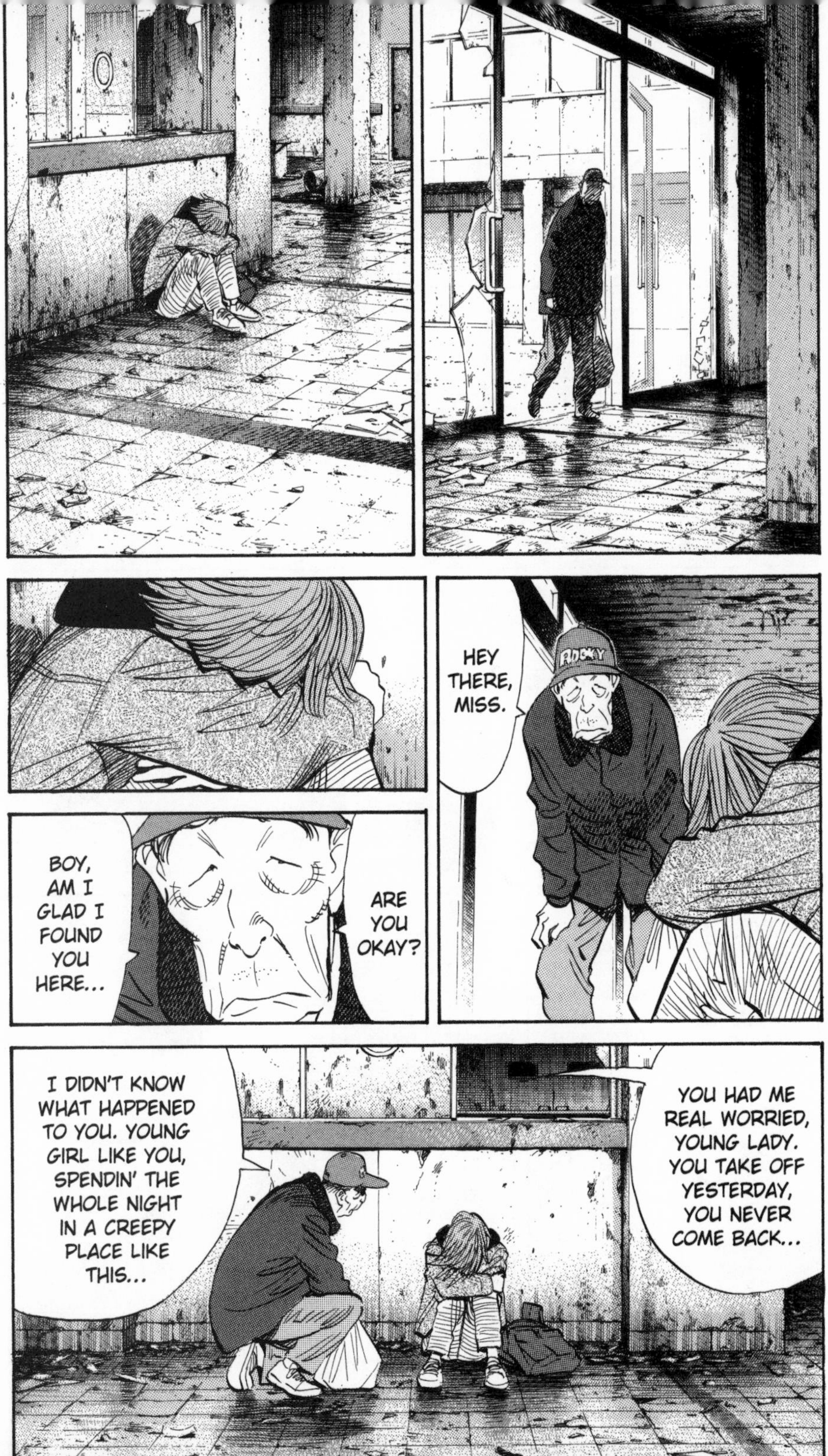
HEY THERE, MISS.
ARE YOU OKAY?
BOY, AM I GLAD I FOUND YOU HERE...
YOU HAD ME REAL WORRIED, YOUNG LADY. YOU TAKE OFF YESTERDAY, YOU NEVER COME BACK...
I DIDN'T KNOW WHAT HAPPENED TO YOU. YOUNG GIRL LIKE YOU, SPENDIN' THE WHOLE NIGHT IN A CREEPY PLACE LIKE THIS...

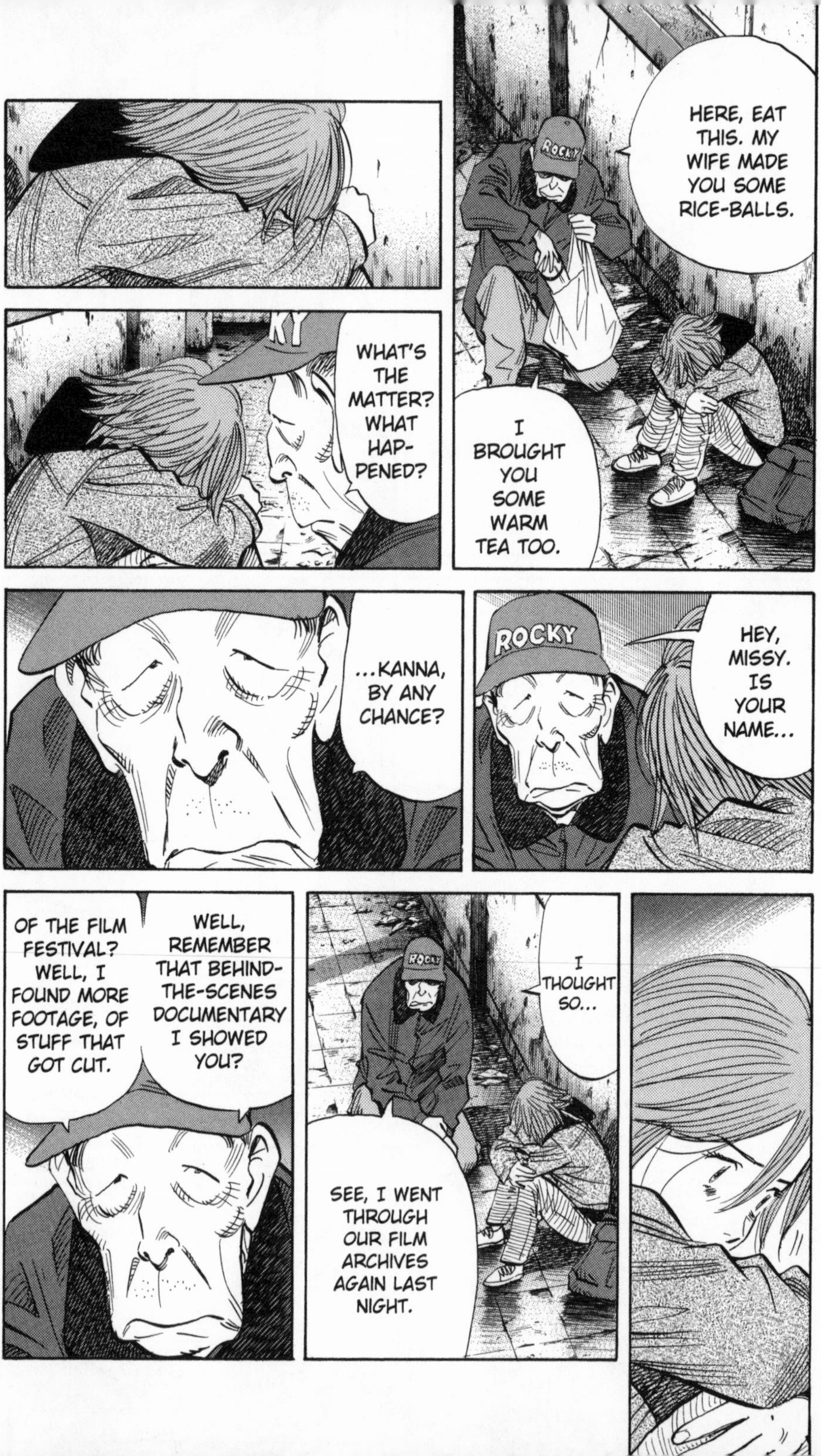
HERE, EAT THIS. MY WIFE MADE YOU SOME RICE-BALLS.
I BROUGHT YOU SOME WARM TEA TOO.
WHAT'S THE MATTER? WHAT HAP-PENED?
HEY, MISSY. IS YOUR NAME...
...KANNA, BY ANY CHANCE?
I THOUGHT SO...
SEE, I WENT THROUGH OUR FILM ARCHIVES AGAIN LAST NIGHT.
WELL, REMEMBER THAT BEHIND-THE-SCENES DOCUMENTARY I SHOWED YOU?
OF THE FILM FESTIVAL? WELL, I FOUND MORE FOOTAGE, OF STUFF THAT GOT CUT.

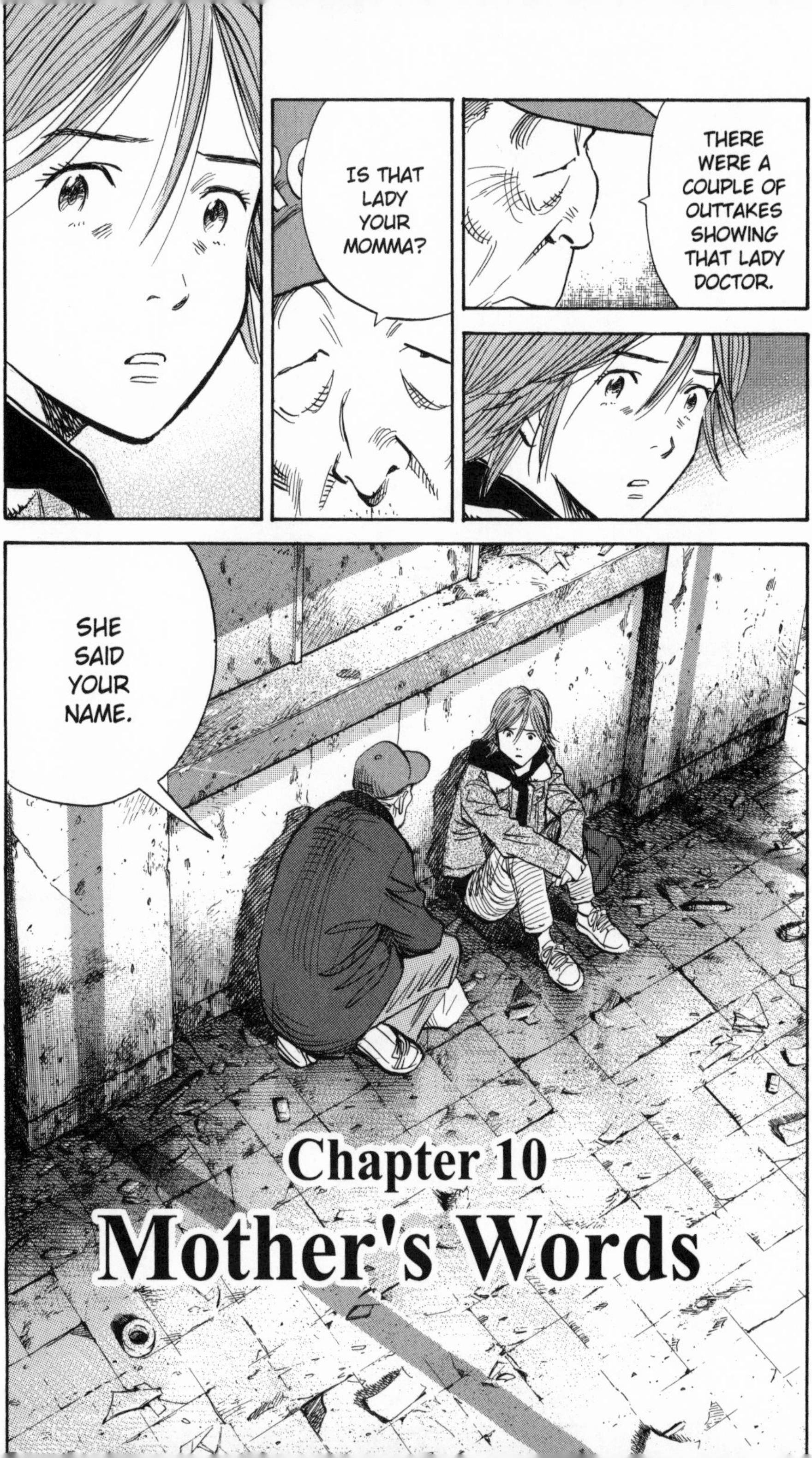
THERE WERE A COUPLE OF OUTTAKES SHOWING THAT LADY DOCTOR.
IS THAT LADY YOUR MOMMA?
SHE SAID YOUR NAME.
Chapter 10
Mother's Words

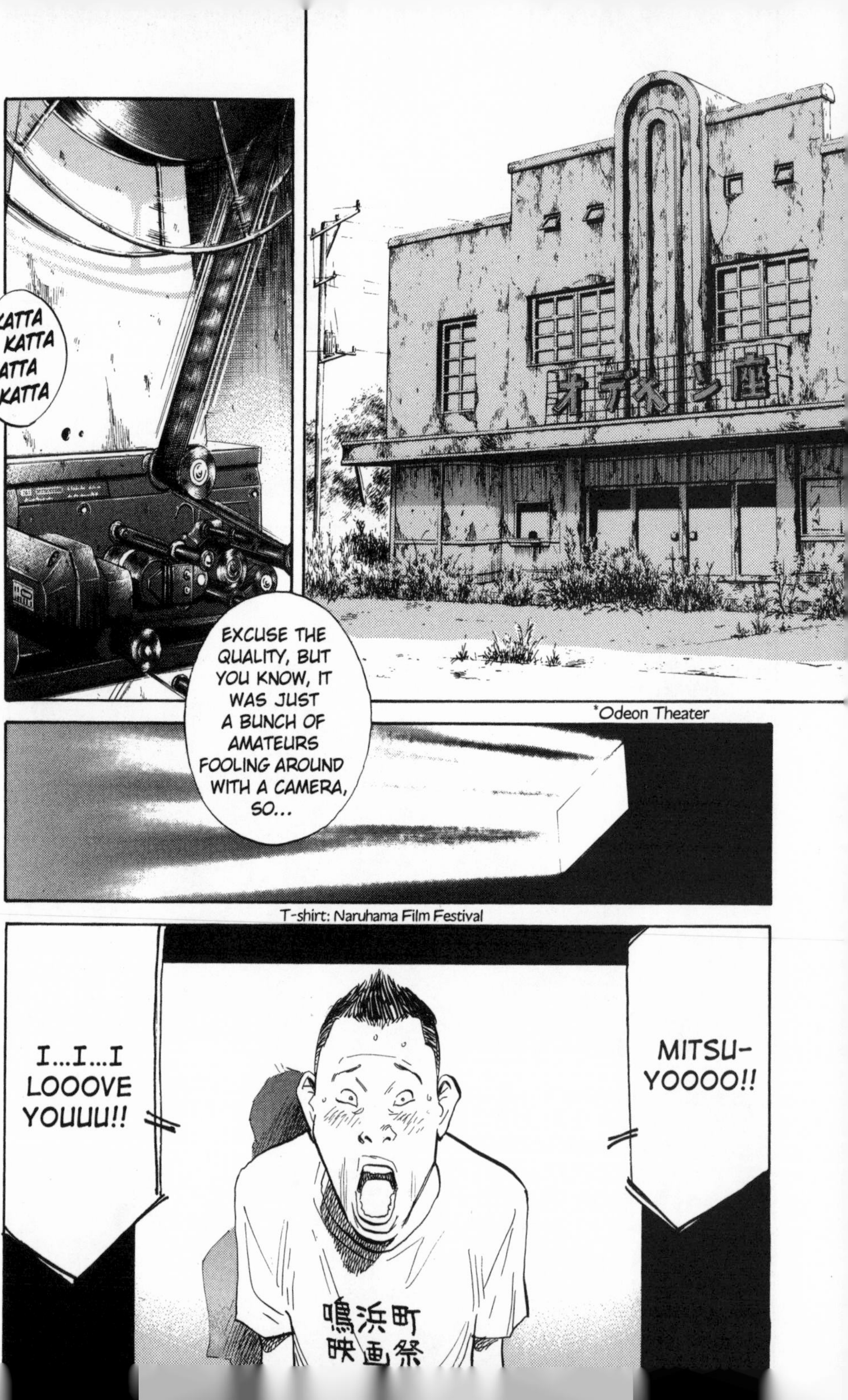
*Odeon Theater
KATTA KATTA KATTA KATTA
EXCUSE THE QUALITY, BUT YOU KNOW, IT WAS JUST A BUNCH OF AMATEURS FOOLING AROUND WITH A CAMERA, SO...
T-shirt: Naruhama Film Festival
MITSU-YOOOO!!
I...I...I LOOOVE YOUUU!!
鳴浜町
映画祭

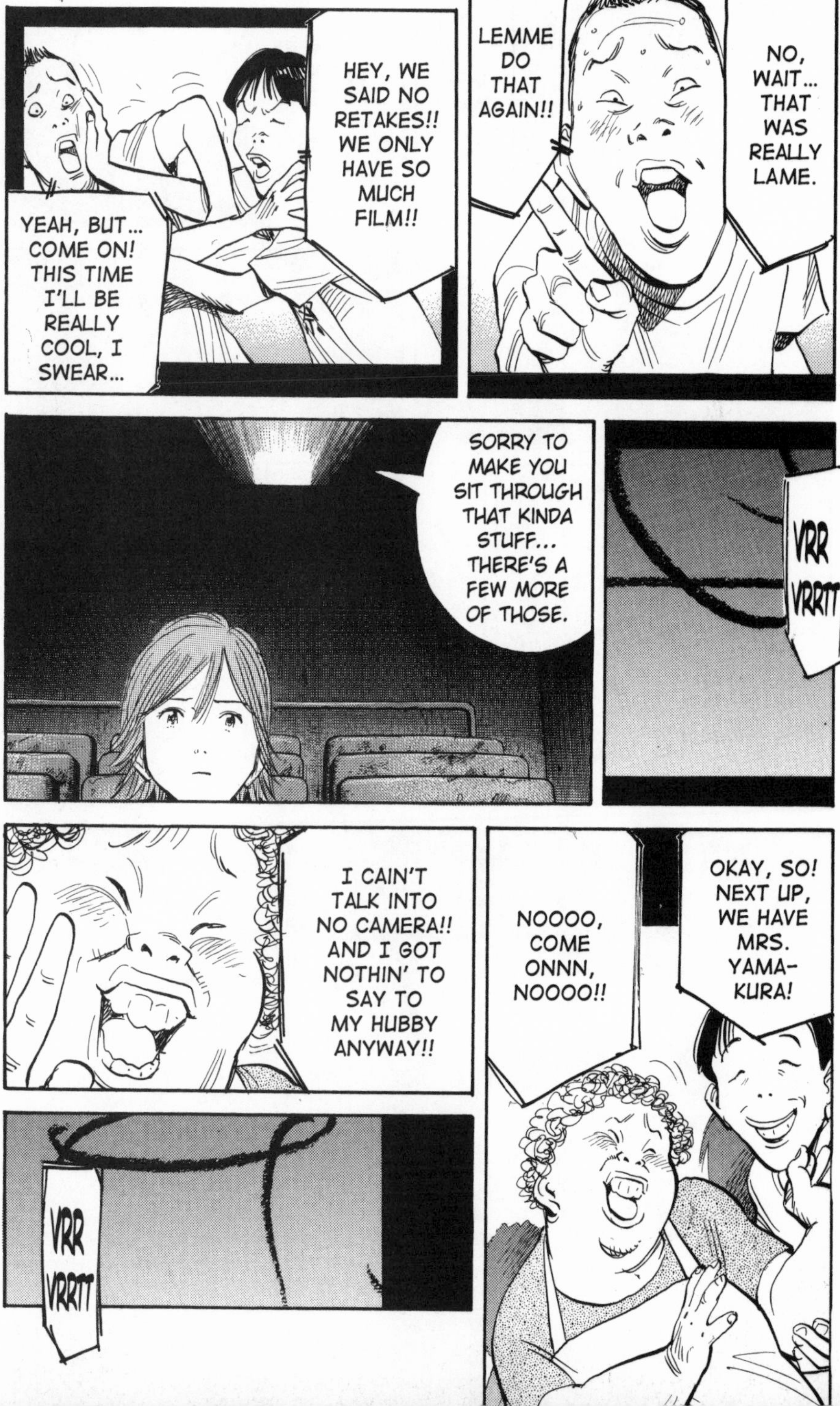
NO, WAIT... THAT WAS REALLY LAME.
LEMME DO THAT AGAIN!!
HEY, WE SAID NO RETAKES!! WE ONLY HAVE SO MUCH FILM!!
YEAH, BUT... COME ON! THIS TIME I'LL BE REALLY COOL, I SWEAR...
VRR VRRTT
SORRY TO MAKE YOU SIT THROUGH THAT KINDA STUFF... THERE'S A FEW MORE OF THOSE.
OKAY, SO! NEXT UP, WE HAVE MRS. YAMA-KURA!
NOOOO, COME ONNN, NOOOO!!
I CAIN'T TALK INTO NO CAMERA!! AND I GOT NOTHIN' TO SAY TO MY HUBBY ANYWAY!!
VRR VRRTT

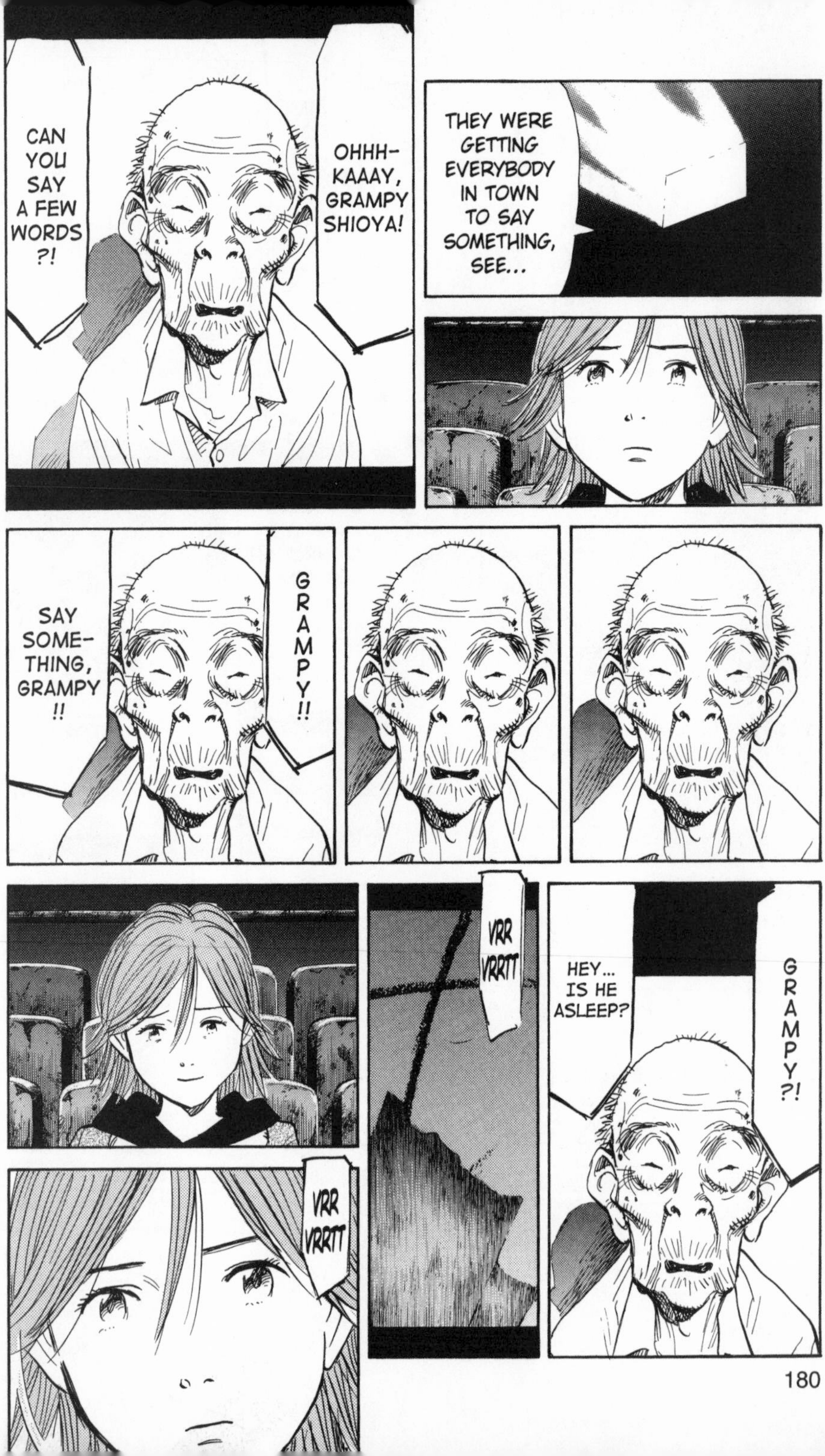
THEY WERE GETTING EVERYBODY IN TOWN TO SAY SOMETHING, SEE...
OHHH-KAAAY, GRAMPY SHIOYA!
CAN YOU SAY A FEW WORDS?!
GRAMPY!!
SAY SOME-THING, GRAMPY!!
GRAMPY?!
HEY... IS HE ASLEEP?
VRR VRRTT
VRR VRRTT

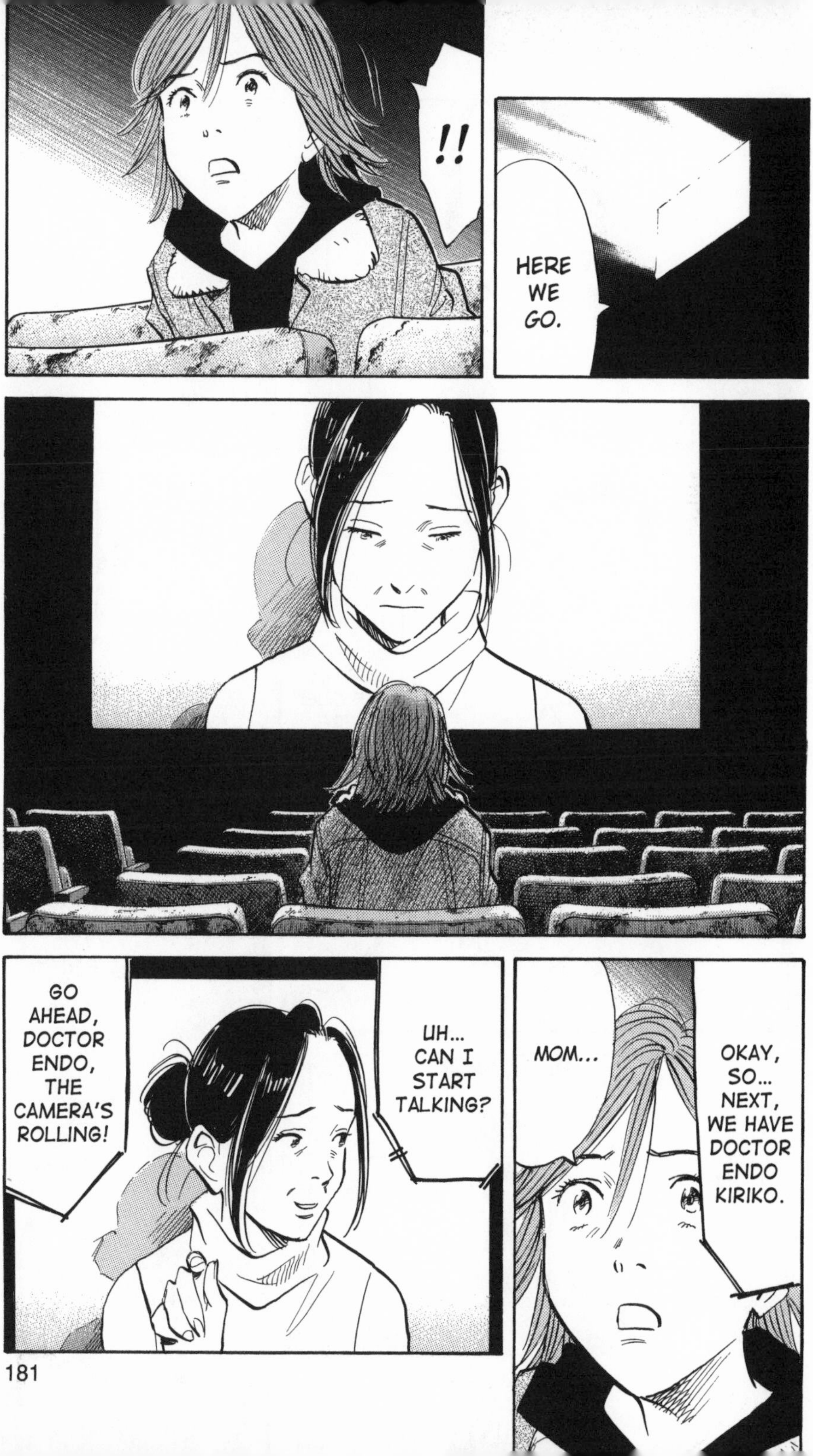
HERE WE GO.
!!
OKAY, SO... NEXT, WE HAVE DOCTOR ENDO KIRIKO.
MOM...
UH... CAN I START TALKING?
GO AHEAD, DOCTOR ENDO, THE CAMERA'S ROLLING!

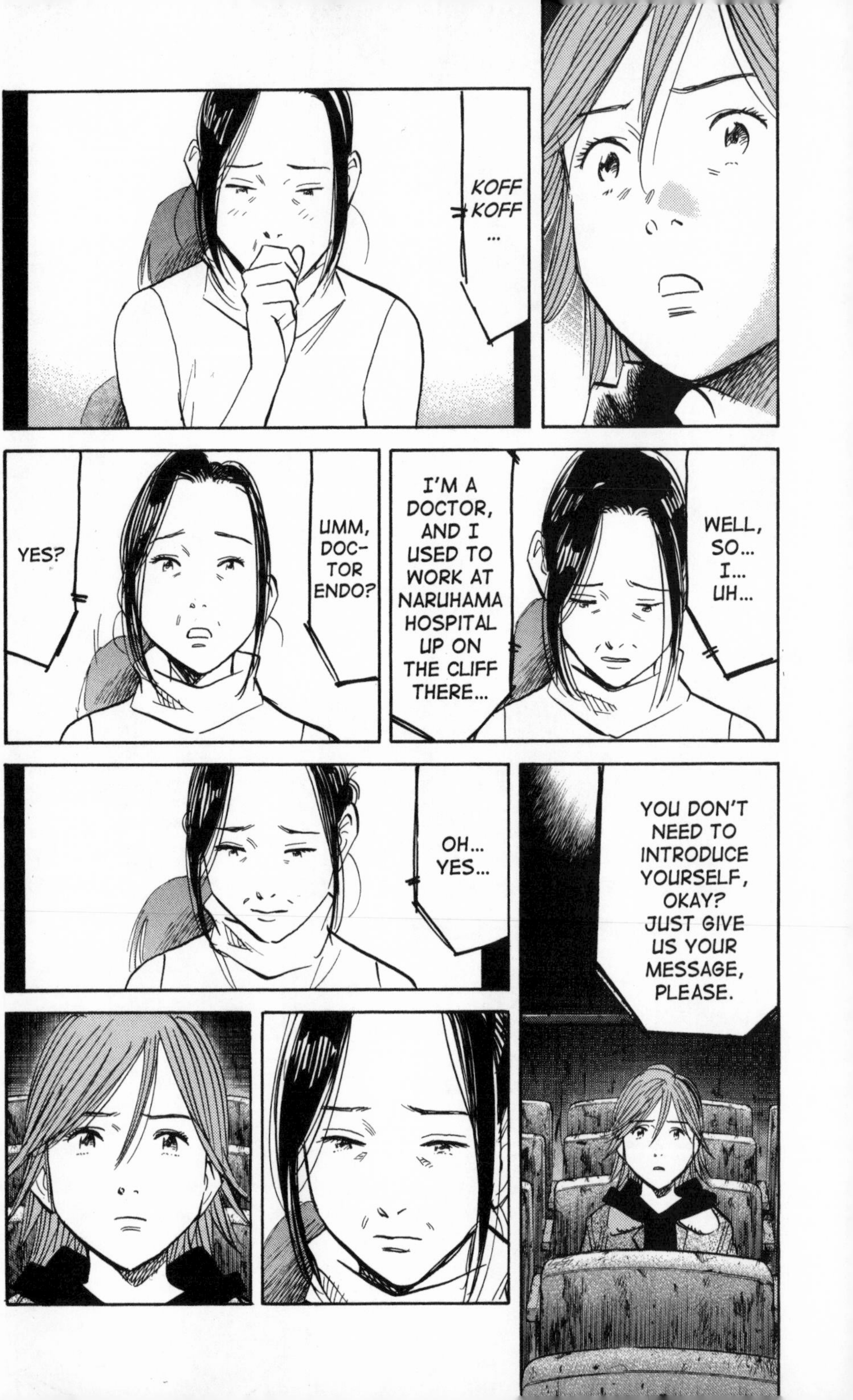
KOFF KOFF ...
WELL, SO... I... UH...
I'M A DOCTOR, AND I USED TO WORK AT NARUHAMA HOSPITAL UP ON THE CLIFF THERE...
UMM, DOC-TOR ENDO?
YES?
YOU DON'T NEED TO INTRODUCE YOURSELF, OKAY? JUST GIVE US YOUR MESSAGE, PLEASE.
OH... YES...

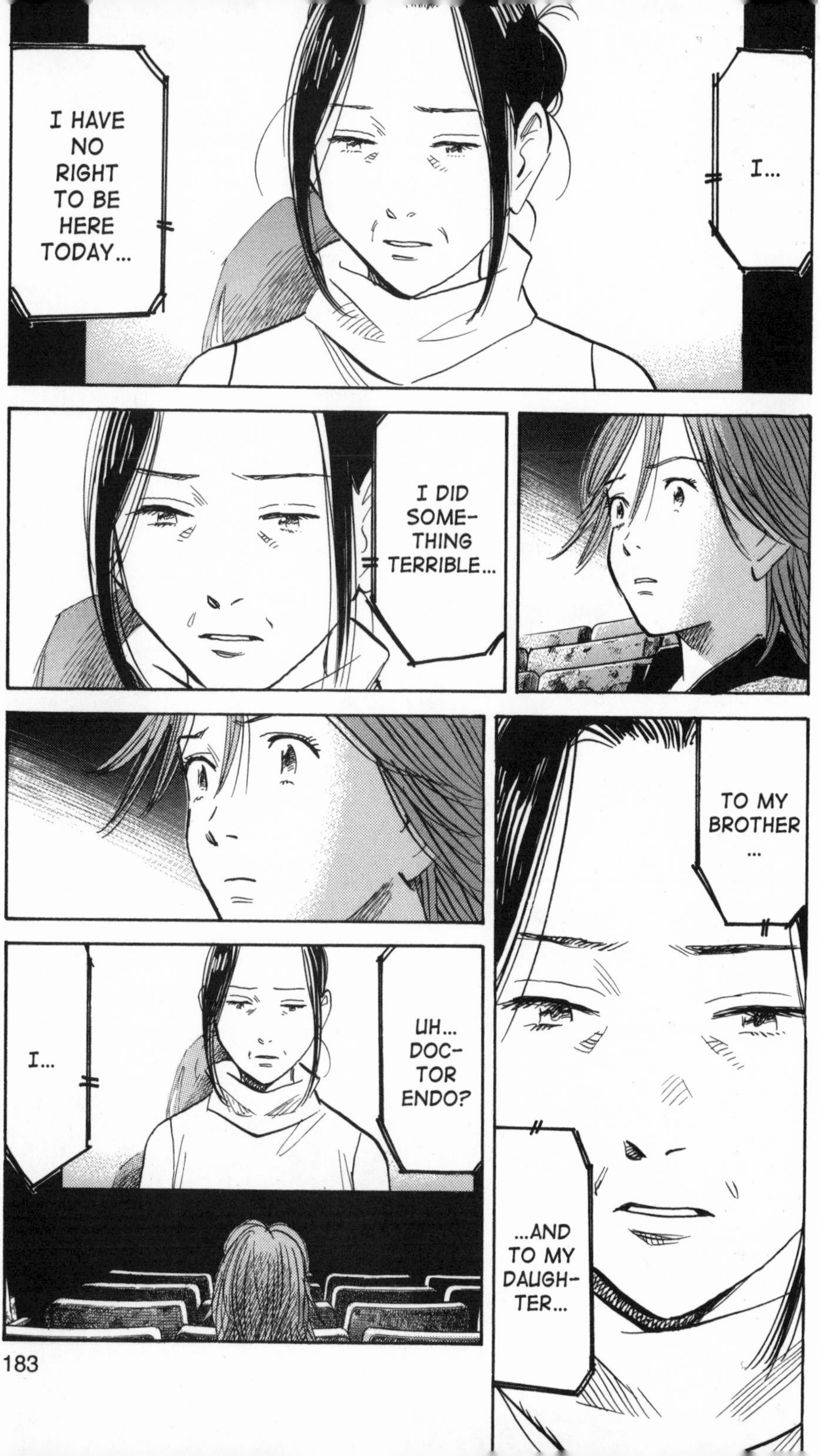
I...
I HAVE NO RIGHT TO BE HERE TODAY...
I DID SOME-THING TERRIBLE...
TO MY BROTHER...
...AND TO MY DAUGHTER...
UH... DOCTOR ENDO?
I...

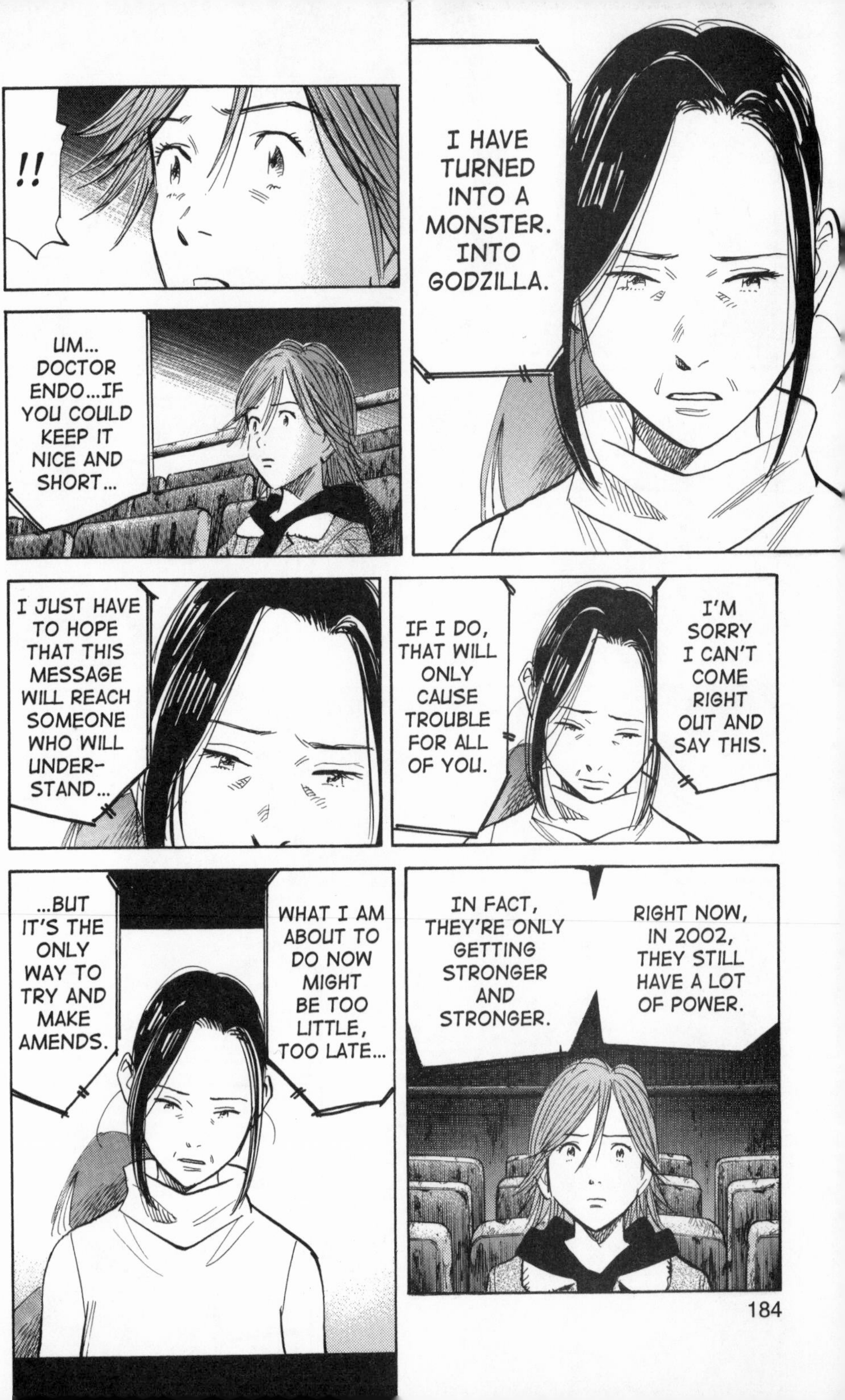
I HAVE TURNED INTO A MONSTER. INTO GODZILLA.
!!
UM... DOCTOR ENDO...IF YOU COULD KEEP IT NICE AND SHORT...
I'M SORRY I CAN'T COME RIGHT OUT AND SAY THIS.
IF I DO, THAT WILL ONLY CAUSE TROUBLE FOR ALL OF YOU.
I JUST HAVE TO HOPE THAT THIS MESSAGE WILL REACH SOMEONE WHO WILL UNDER-STAND...
RIGHT NOW, IN 2002, THEY STILL HAVE A LOT OF POWER.
IN FACT, THEY'RE ONLY GETTING STRONGER AND STRONGER.
WHAT I AM ABOUT TO DO NOW MIGHT BE TOO LITTLE, TOO LATE...
...BUT IT'S THE ONLY WAY TO TRY AND MAKE AMENDS.

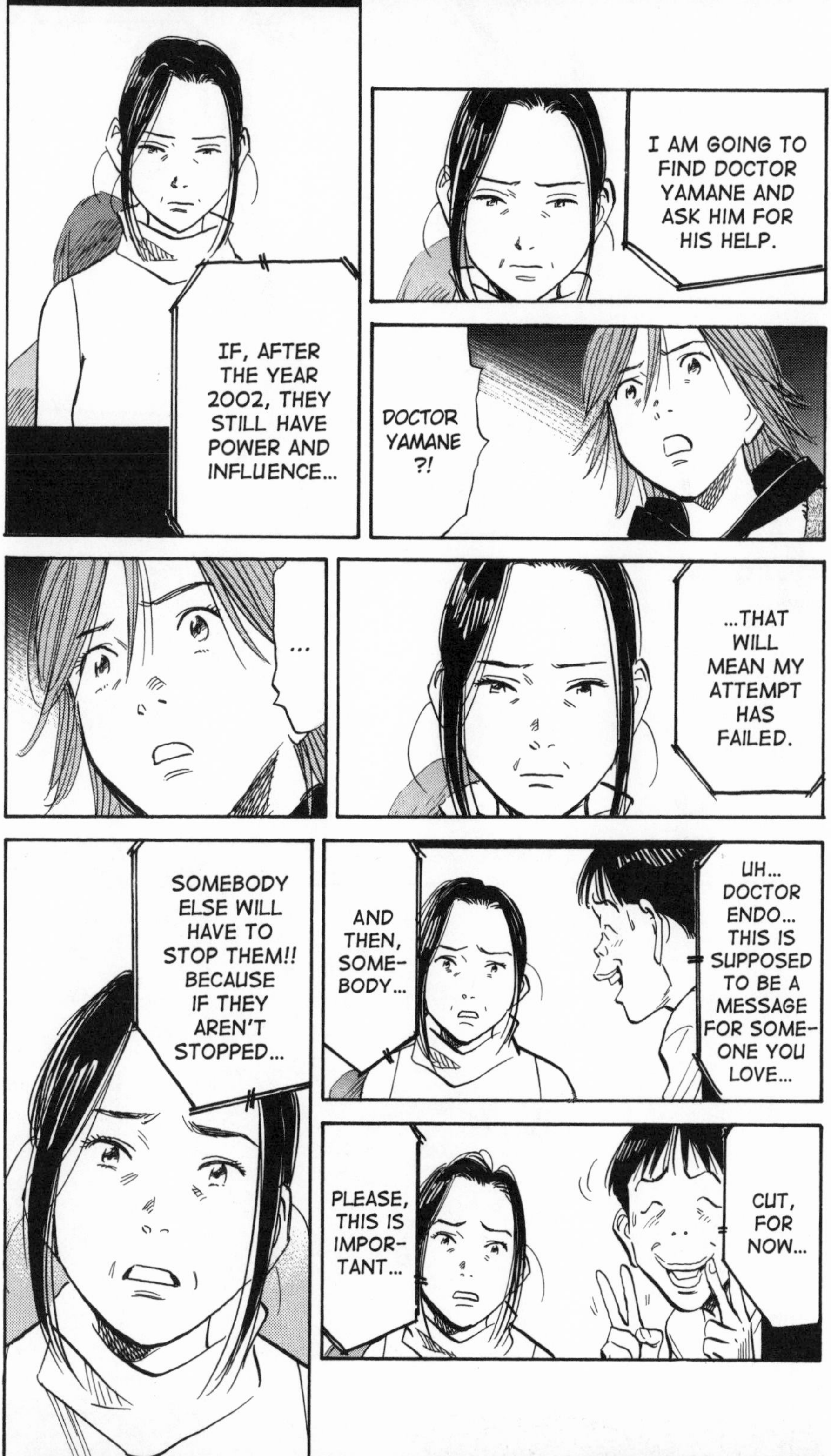
I AM GOING TO FIND DOCTOR YAMANE AND ASK HIM FOR HIS HELP.
DOCTOR YAMANE ?!
IF, AFTER THE YEAR 2002, THEY STILL HAVE POWER AND INFLUENCE...
...THAT WILL MEAN MY ATTEMPT HAS FAILED.
...
UH... DOCTOR ENDO... THIS IS SUPPOSED TO BE A MESSAGE FOR SOME-ONE YOU LOVE...
AND THEN, SOME-BODY...
CUT, FOR NOW...
PLEASE, THIS IS IMPOR-TANT...
SOMEBODY ELSE WILL HAVE TO STOP THEM!! BECAUSE IF THEY AREN'T STOPPED...

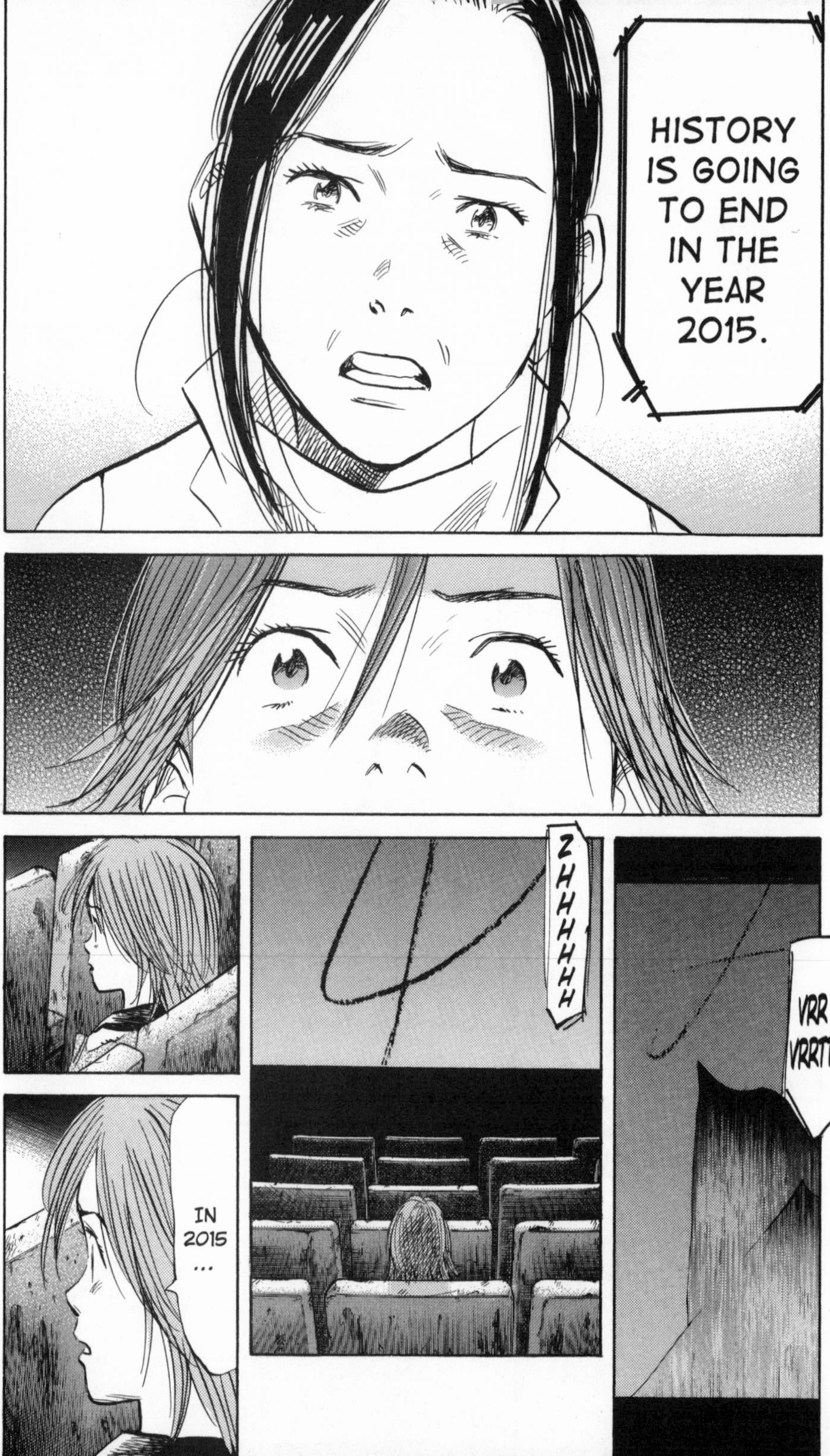
HISTORY IS GOING TO END IN THE YEAR 2015.
VRR VRRTT
ZHHHHHHH
IN 2015 ...

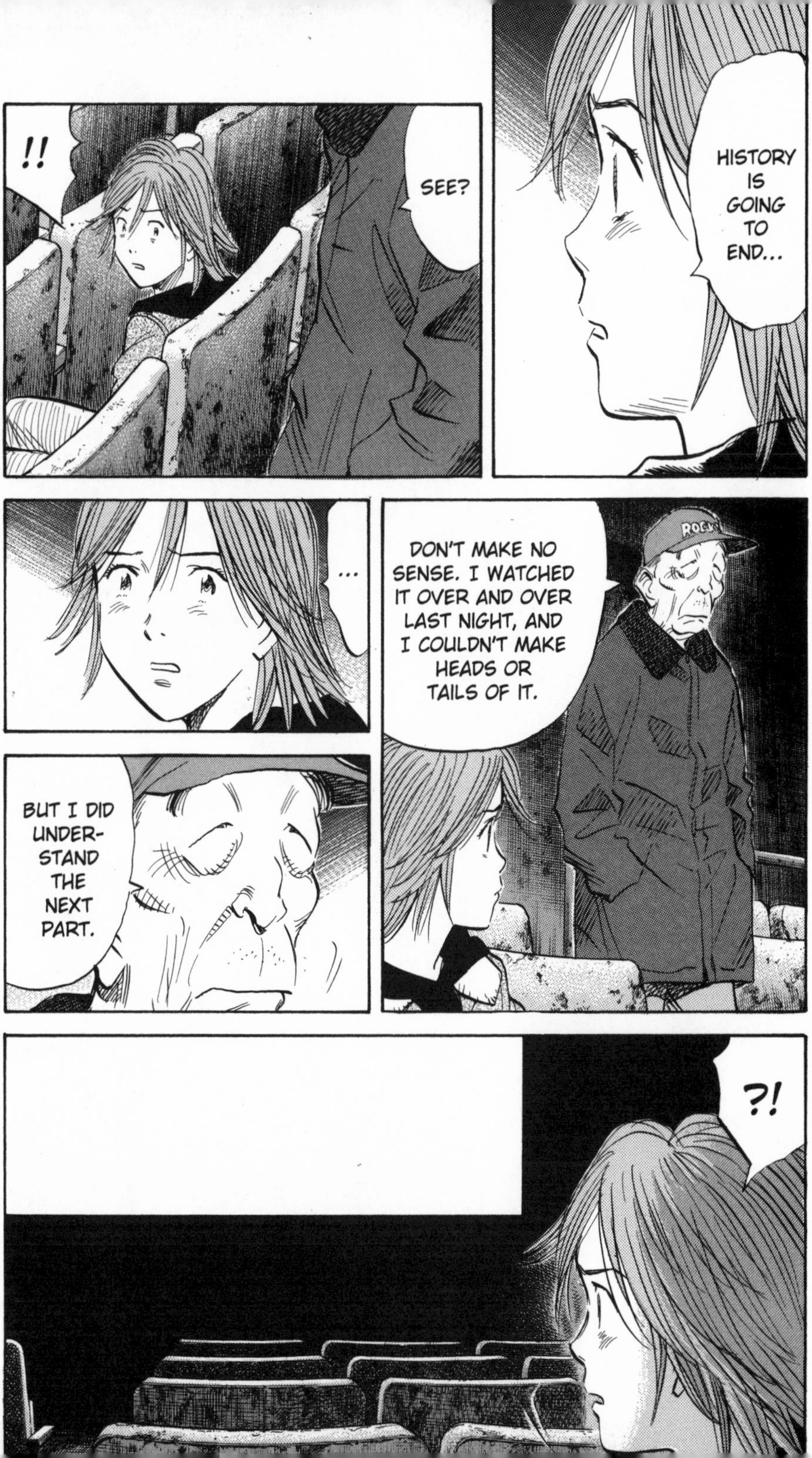
HISTORY IS GOING TO END...
SEE?
!!
DON'T MAKE NO SENSE. I WATCHED IT OVER AND OVER LAST NIGHT, AND I COULDN'T MAKE HEADS OR TAILS OF IT.
...
BUT I DID UNDER-STAND THE NEXT PART.
?!

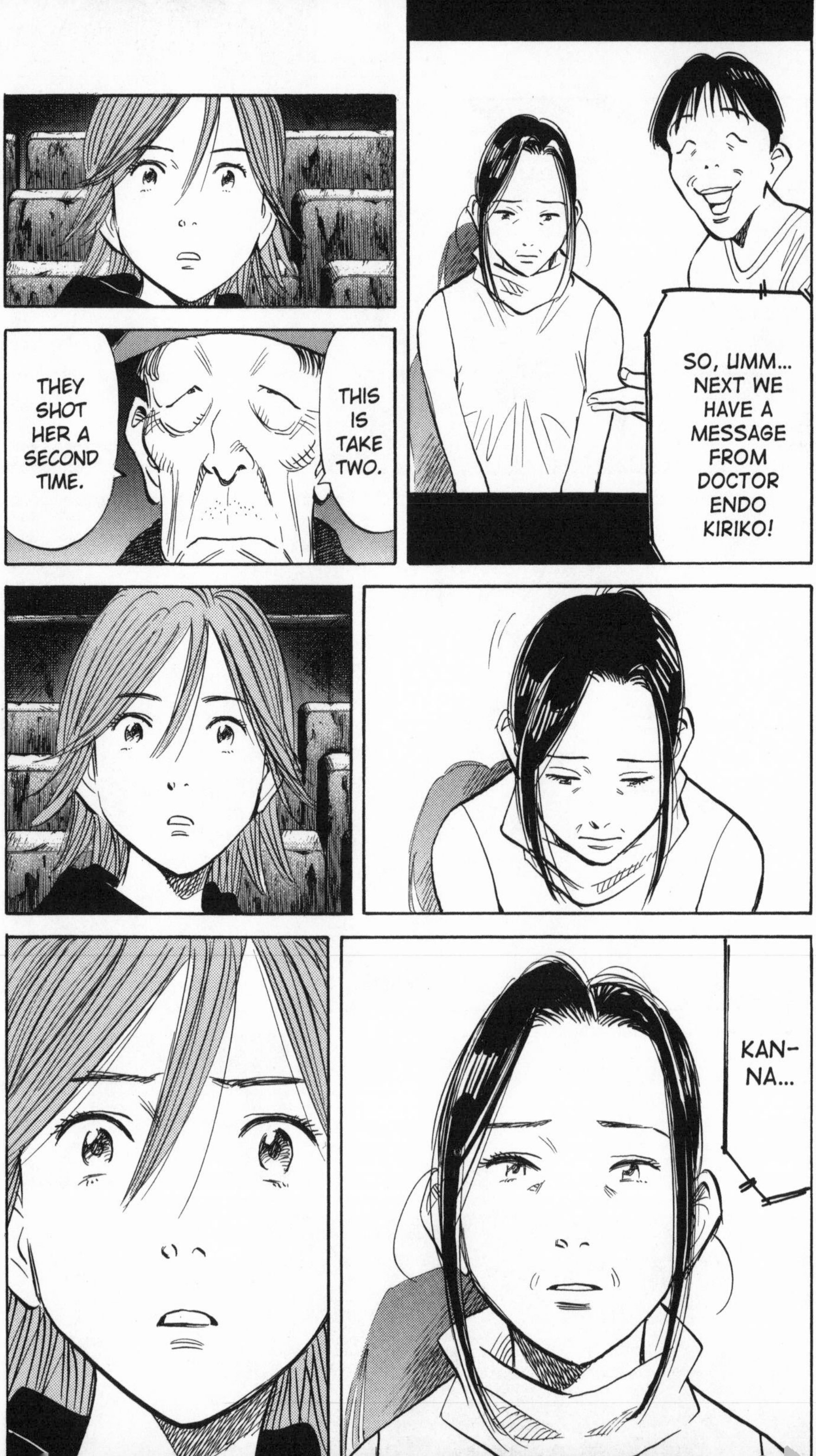
SO, UMM... NEXT WE HAVE A MESSAGE FROM DOCTOR ENDO KIRIKO!
THIS IS TAKE TWO.
THEY SHOT HER A SECOND TIME.
KAN-NA...

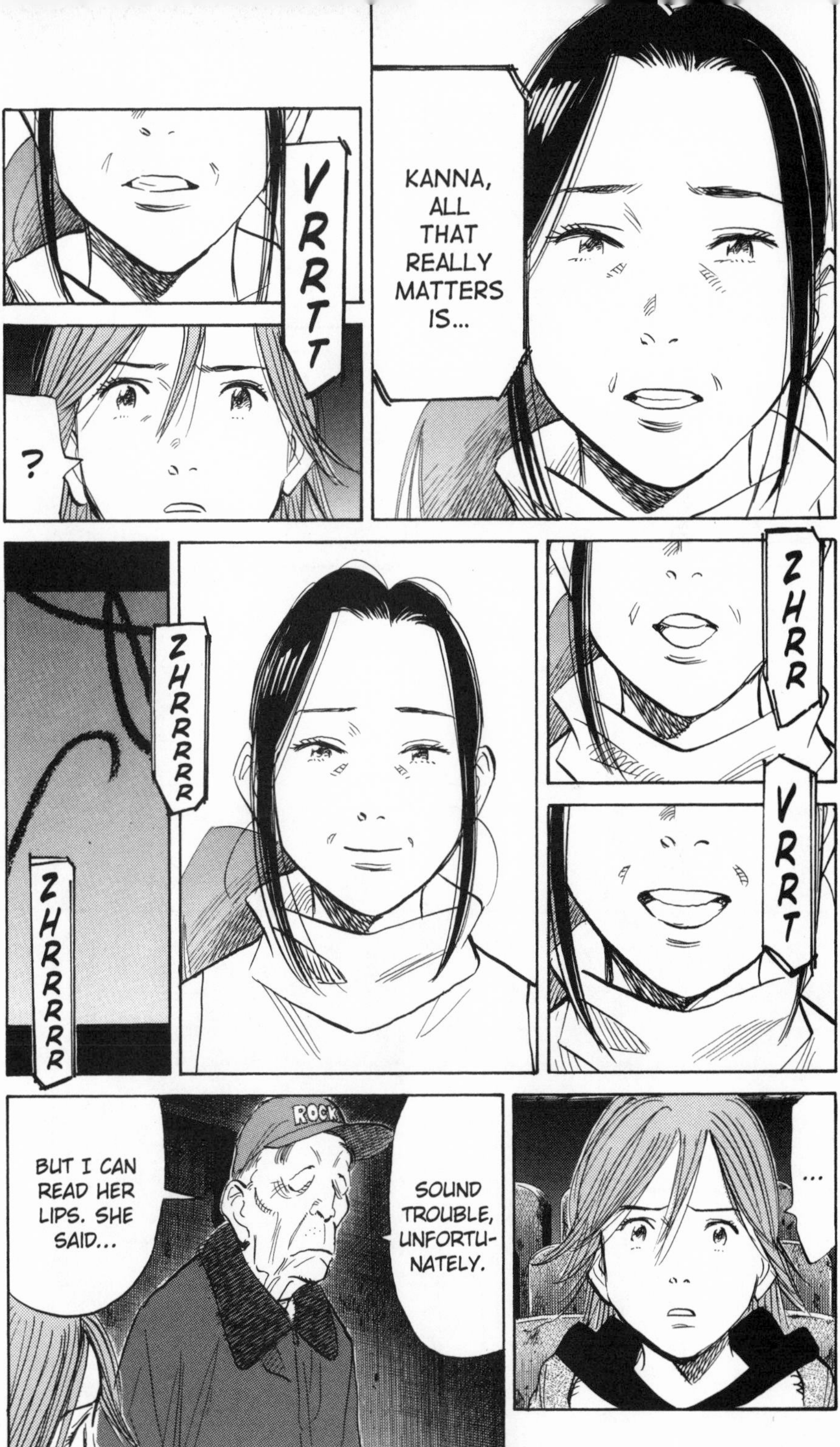
KANNA, ALL THAT REALLY MATTERS IS...
VRRTT
?
ZHRR
VRRT
ZHRRRRR
ZHRRRRRR
...
SOUND TROUBLE, UNFORTU-NATELY.
BUT I CAN READ HER LIPS. SHE SAID...

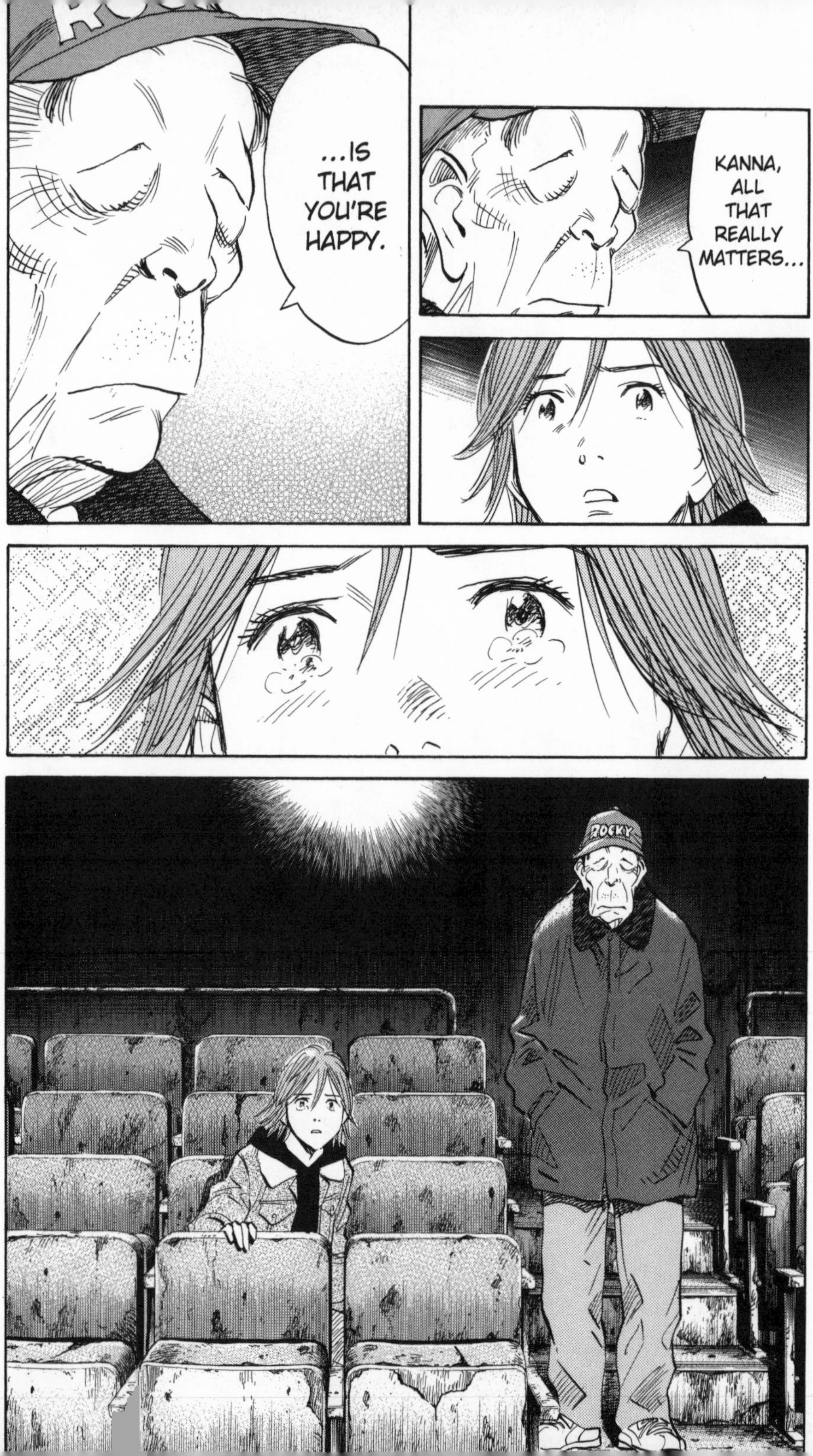
KANNA, ALL THAT REALLY MATTERS...
...IS THAT YOU'RE HAPPY.

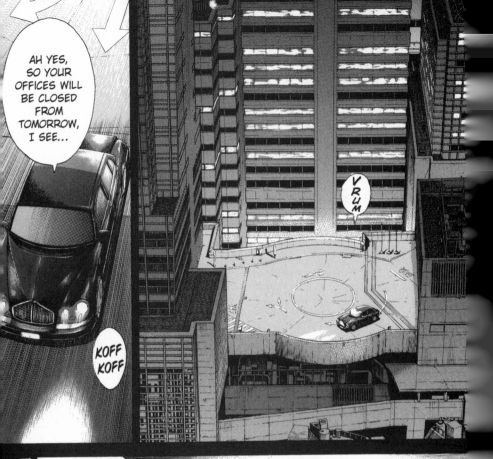

AH YES, SO YOUR OFFICES WILL BE CLOSED FROM TOMORROW, I SEE...

VRUM

KOFF KOFF

OH NO, NO, NOT ME... I WAS NEVER EXPECTING TO HAVE ANY TIME OFF THIS YEAR-END.

大福堂製薬株式会社

DAIFUKU

*Daifukudo Pharmaceutical Company, Limited

KOFF KOF

THOUGH I DOUBT YOU'LL BE GETTING MUCH REST OVER THE NEW YEAR HOLIDAYS YOUR-SELVES, HM? THE FDP NEVER SLEEPS...

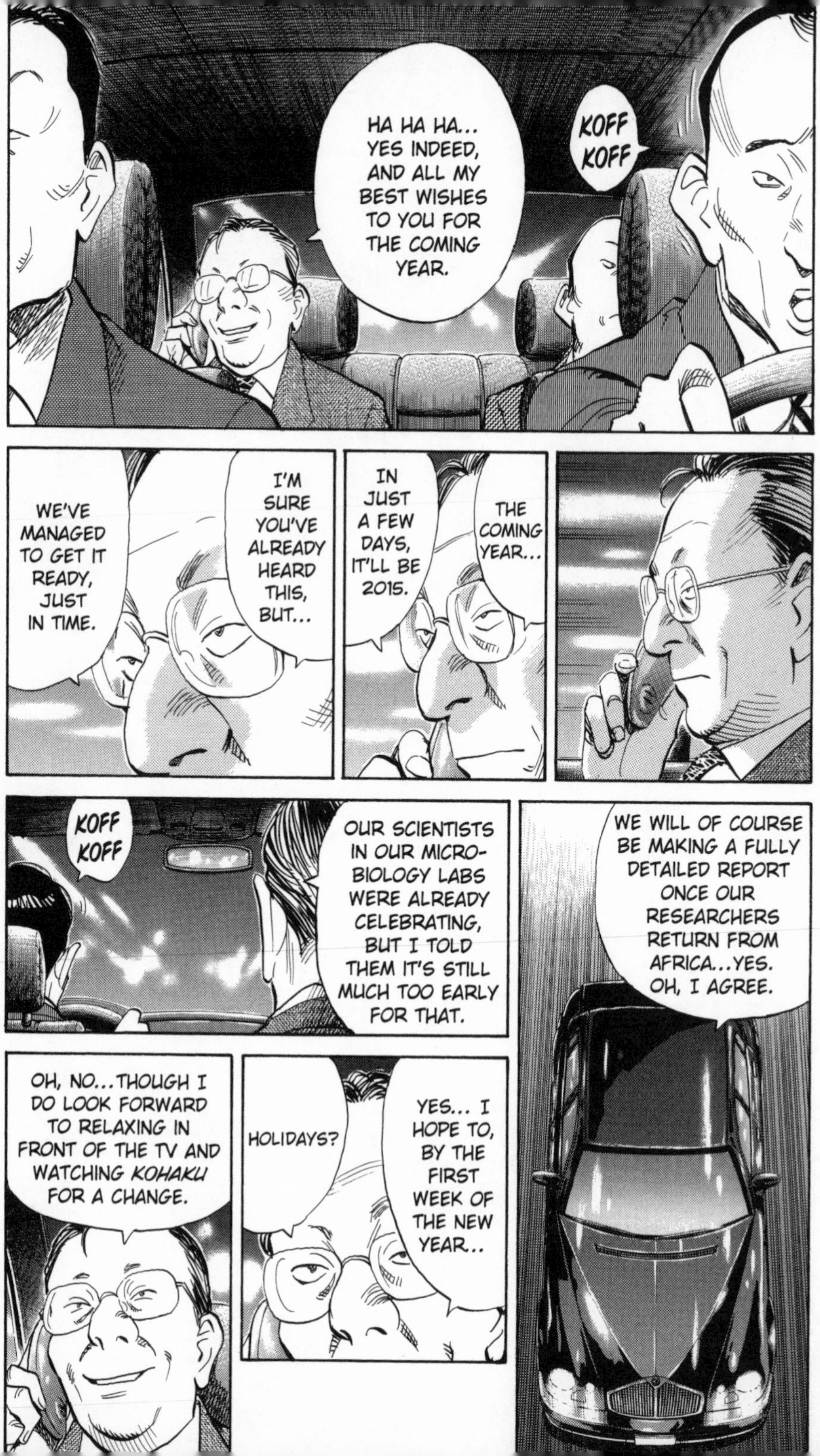
KOFF KOFF
HA HA HA... YES INDEED, AND ALL MY BEST WISHES TO YOU FOR THE COMING YEAR.
THE COMING YEAR...
IN JUST A FEW DAYS, IT'LL BE 2015.
I'M SURE YOU'VE ALREADY HEARD THIS, BUT...
WE'VE MANAGED TO GET IT READY, JUST IN TIME.
WE WILL OF COURSE BE MAKING A FULLY DETAILED REPORT ONCE OUR RESEARCHERS RETURN FROM AFRICA...YES. OH, I AGREE.
OUR SCIENTISTS IN OUR MICRO-BIOLOGY LABS WERE ALREADY CELEBRATING, BUT I TOLD THEM IT'S STILL MUCH TOO EARLY FOR THAT.
KOFF KOFF
HOLIDAYS?
YES... I HOPE TO, BY THE FIRST WEEK OF THE NEW YEAR...
OH, NO...THOUGH I DO LOOK FORWARD TO RELAXING IN FRONT OF THE TV AND WATCHING *KOHAKU* FOR A CHANGE.

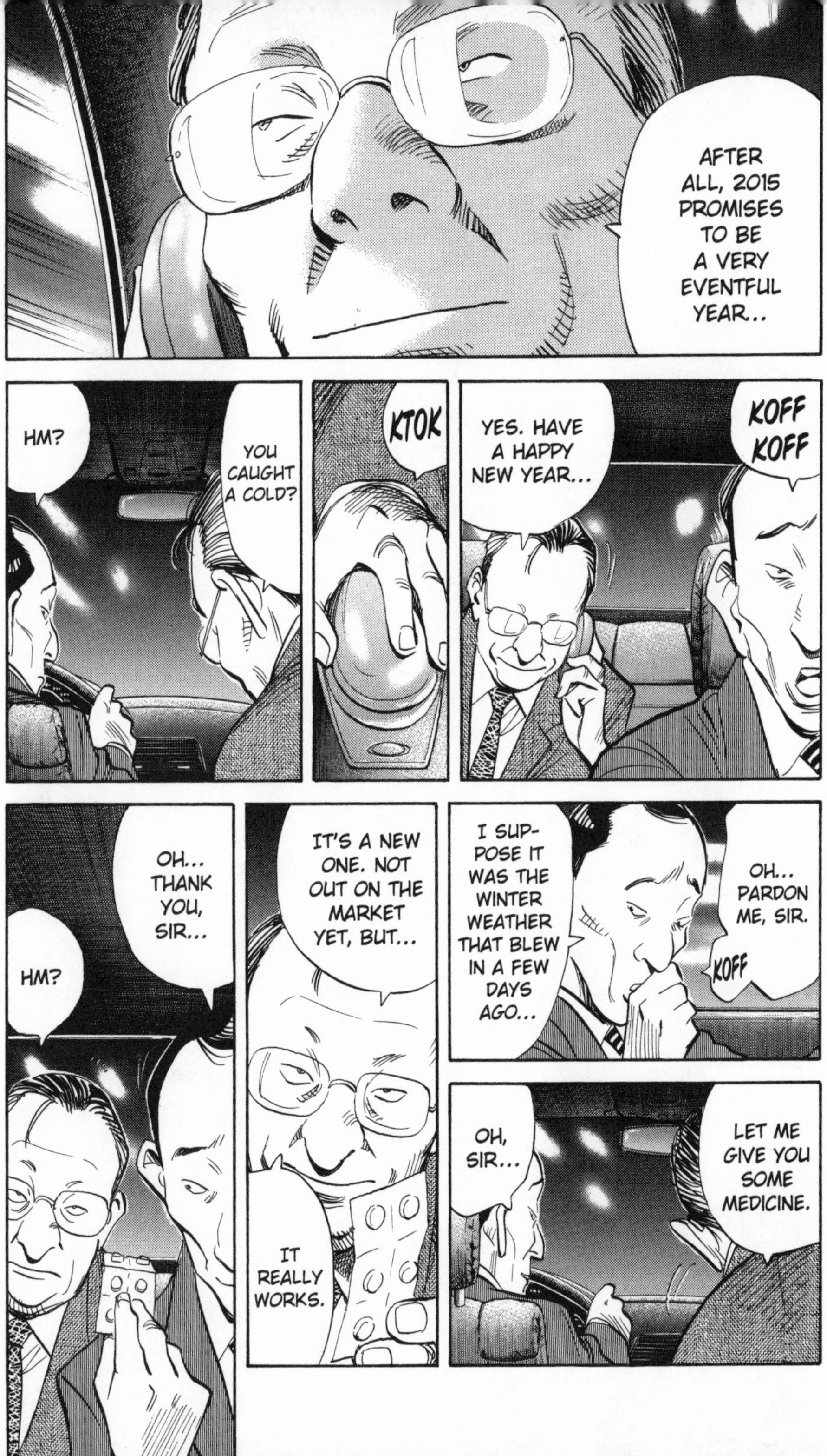
AFTER ALL, 2015 PROMISES TO BE A VERY EVENTFUL YEAR...
KOFF KOFF
YES. HAVE A HAPPY NEW YEAR...
KTOK
YOU CAUGHT A COLD?
HM?
OH... PARDON ME, SIR.
KOFF
I SUP-POSE IT WAS THE WINTER WEATHER THAT BLEW IN A FEW DAYS AGO...
LET ME GIVE YOU SOME MEDICINE.
OH, SIR...
IT'S A NEW ONE. NOT OUT ON THE MARKET YET, BUT...
IT REALLY WORKS.
OH... THANK YOU, SIR...
HM?

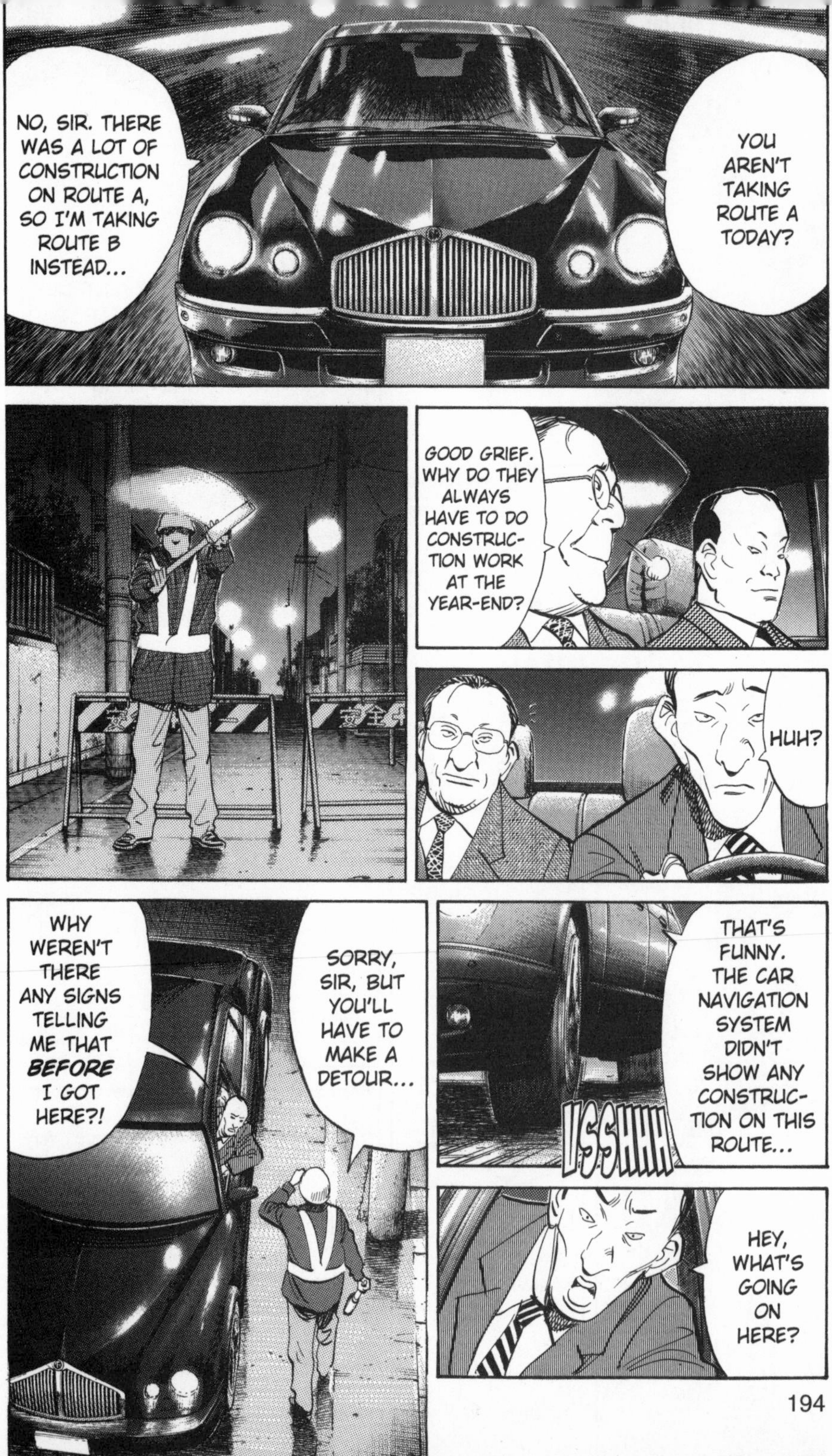
YOU AREN'T TAKING ROUTE A TODAY?
NO, SIR. THERE WAS A LOT OF CONSTRUCTION ON ROUTE A, SO I'M TAKING ROUTE B INSTEAD...
GOOD GRIEF. WHY DO THEY ALWAYS HAVE TO DO CONSTRUCTION WORK AT THE YEAR-END?
HUH?
THAT'S FUNNY. THE CAR NAVIGATION SYSTEM DIDN'T SHOW ANY CONSTRUCTION ON THIS ROUTE...
VSSHHH
HEY, WHAT'S GOING ON HERE?
SORRY, SIR, BUT YOU'LL HAVE TO MAKE A DETOUR...
WHY WEREN'T THERE ANY SIGNS TELLING ME THAT ***BEFORE*** I GOT HERE?!

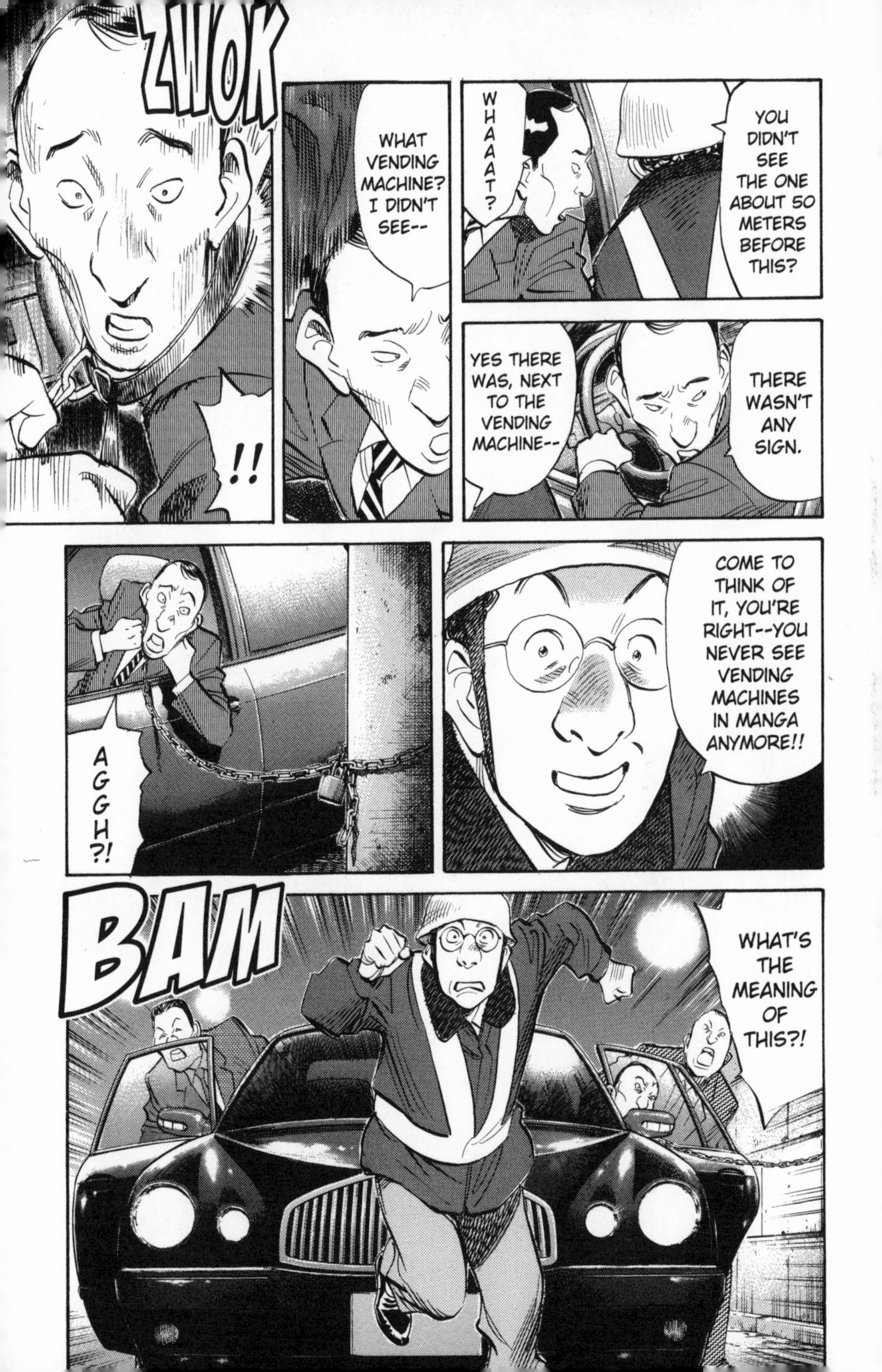
YOU DIDN'T SEE THE ONE ABOUT 50 METERS BEFORE THIS?
WHAAAAT?
THERE WASN'T ANY SIGN.
YES THERE WAS, NEXT TO THE VENDING MACHINE--
WHAT VENDING MACHINE? I DIDN'T SEE--
ZWOK
!!
COME TO THINK OF IT, YOU'RE RIGHT--YOU NEVER SEE VENDING MACHINES IN MANGA ANYMORE!!
AGGH?!
WHAT'S THE MEANING OF THIS?!
BAM

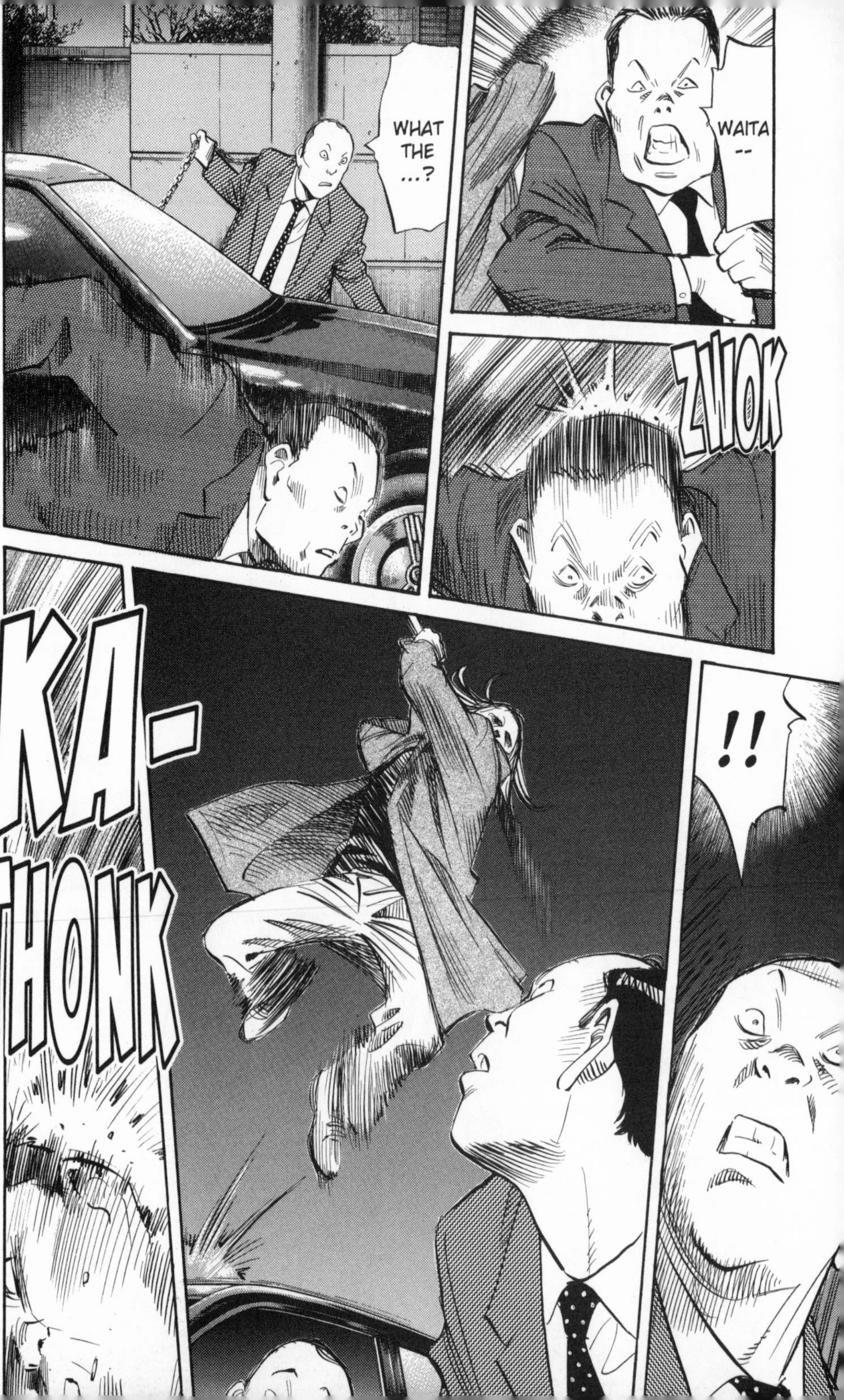
WAITA --
WHAT THE ...?
ZWOK
!!
KA-THONK

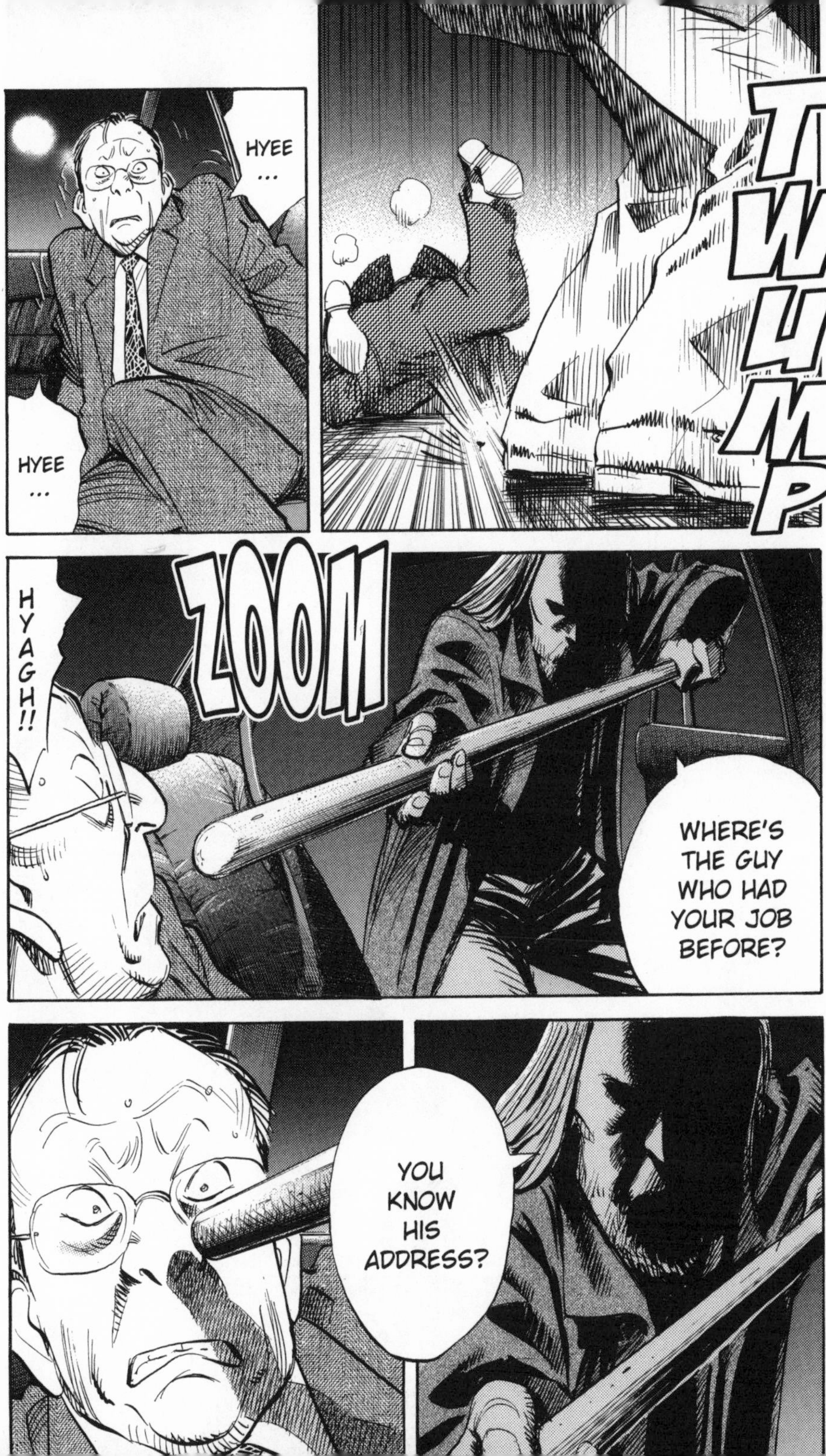
TWUMP
HYEE ...
HYEE ...
ZOOM
HYAGH!!
WHERE'S THE GUY WHO HAD YOUR JOB BEFORE?
YOU KNOW HIS ADDRESS?

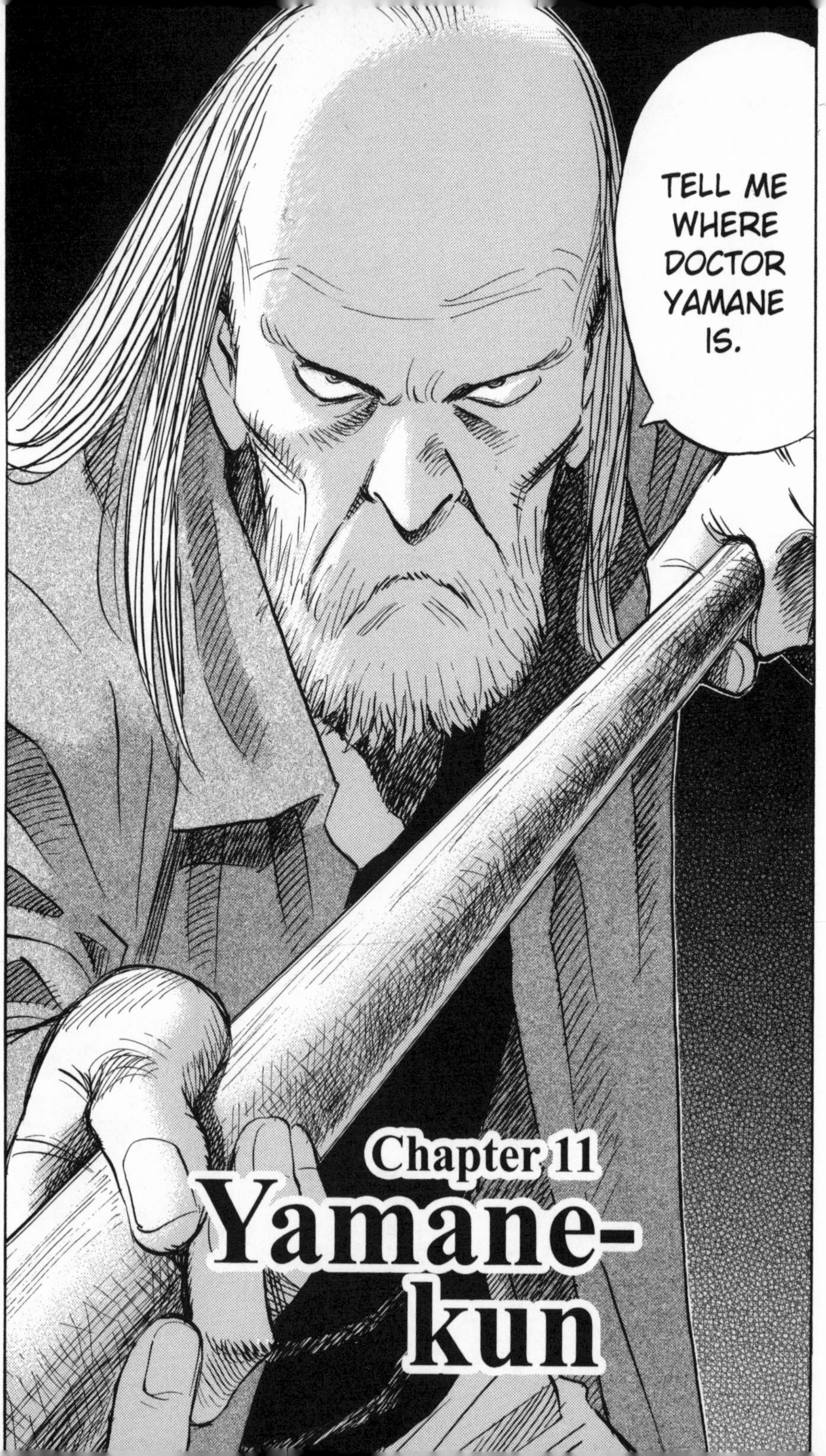
TELL ME WHERE DOCTOR YAMANE IS.
Chapter 11
Yamane-kun

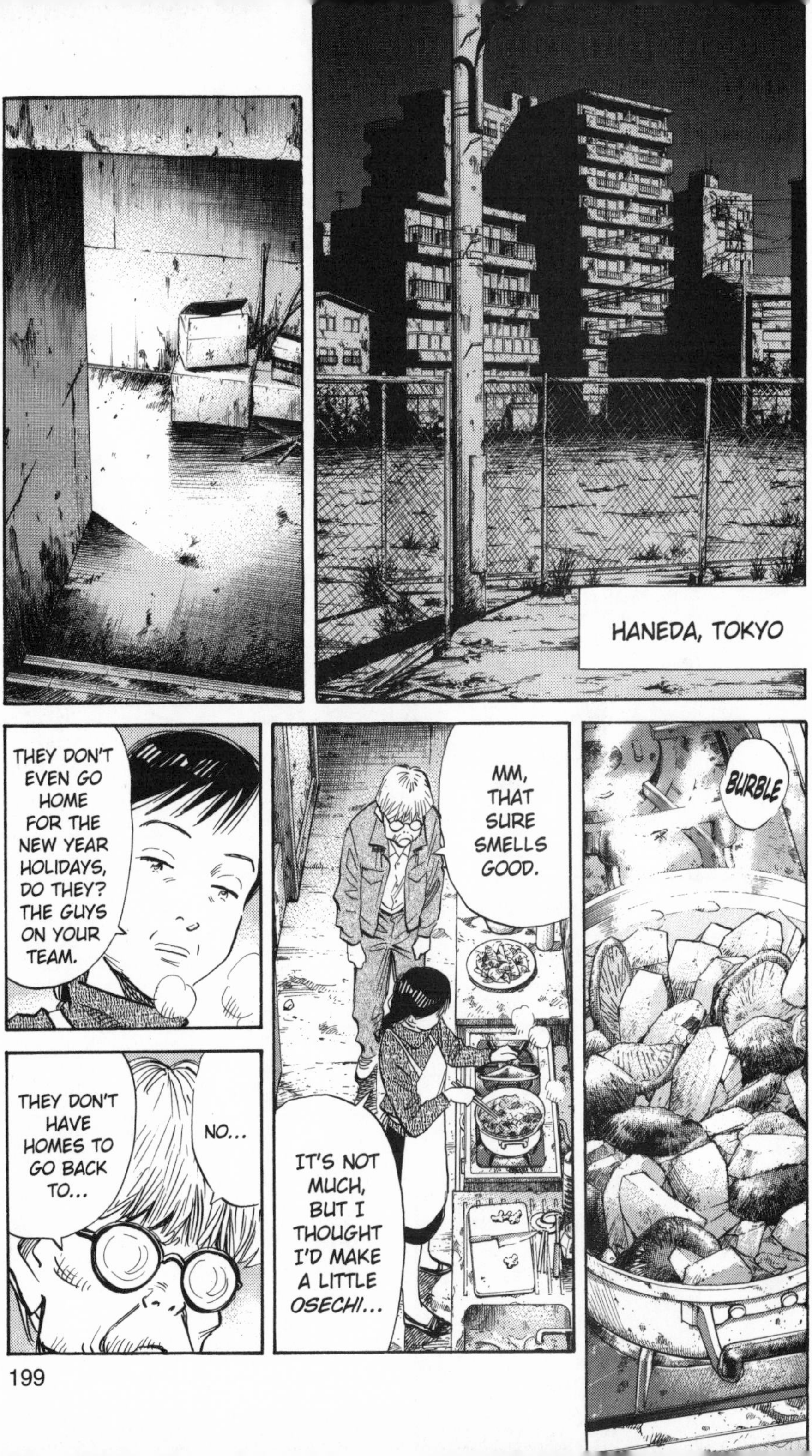
HANEDA, TOKYO
BURBLE
MM, THAT SURE SMELLS GOOD.
IT'S NOT MUCH, BUT I THOUGHT I'D MAKE A LITTLE *OSECHI*...
THEY DON'T EVEN GO HOME FOR THE NEW YEAR HOLIDAYS, DO THEY? THE GUYS ON YOUR TEAM.
NO...
THEY DON'T HAVE HOMES TO GO BACK TO...

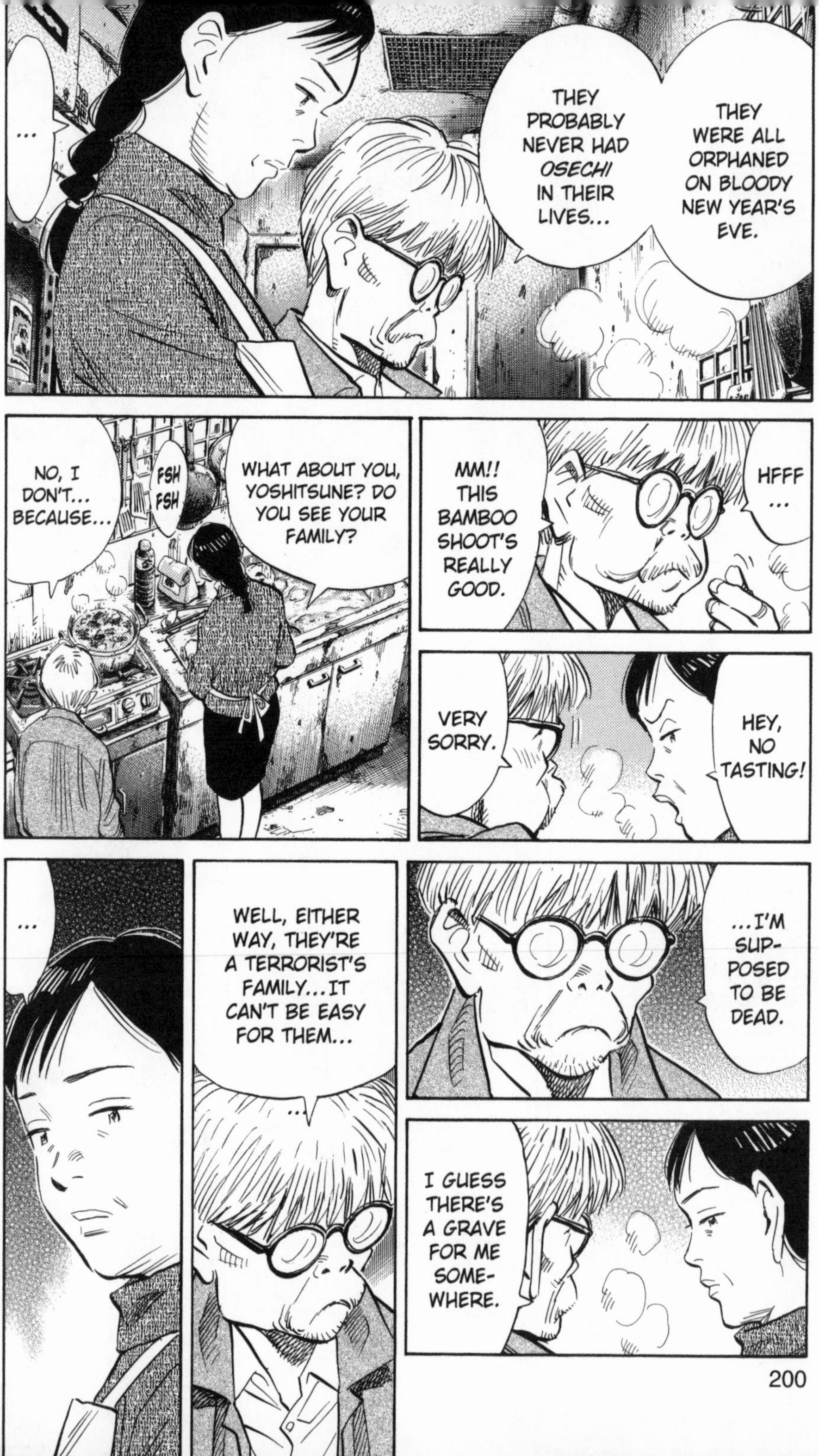
THEY WERE ALL ORPHANED ON BLOODY NEW YEAR'S EVE.
THEY PROBABLY NEVER HAD *OSECHI* IN THEIR LIVES...
...
HFFF ...
MM!! THIS BAMBOO SHOOT'S REALLY GOOD.
HEY, NO TASTING!
VERY SORRY.
WHAT ABOUT YOU, YOSHITSUNE? DO YOU SEE YOUR FAMILY?
FSH FSH
NO, I DON'T... BECAUSE...
...I'M SUP-POSED TO BE DEAD.
I GUESS THERE'S A GRAVE FOR ME SOME-WHERE.
WELL, EITHER WAY, THEY'RE A TERRORIST'S FAMILY...IT CAN'T BE EASY FOR THEM...
...
...

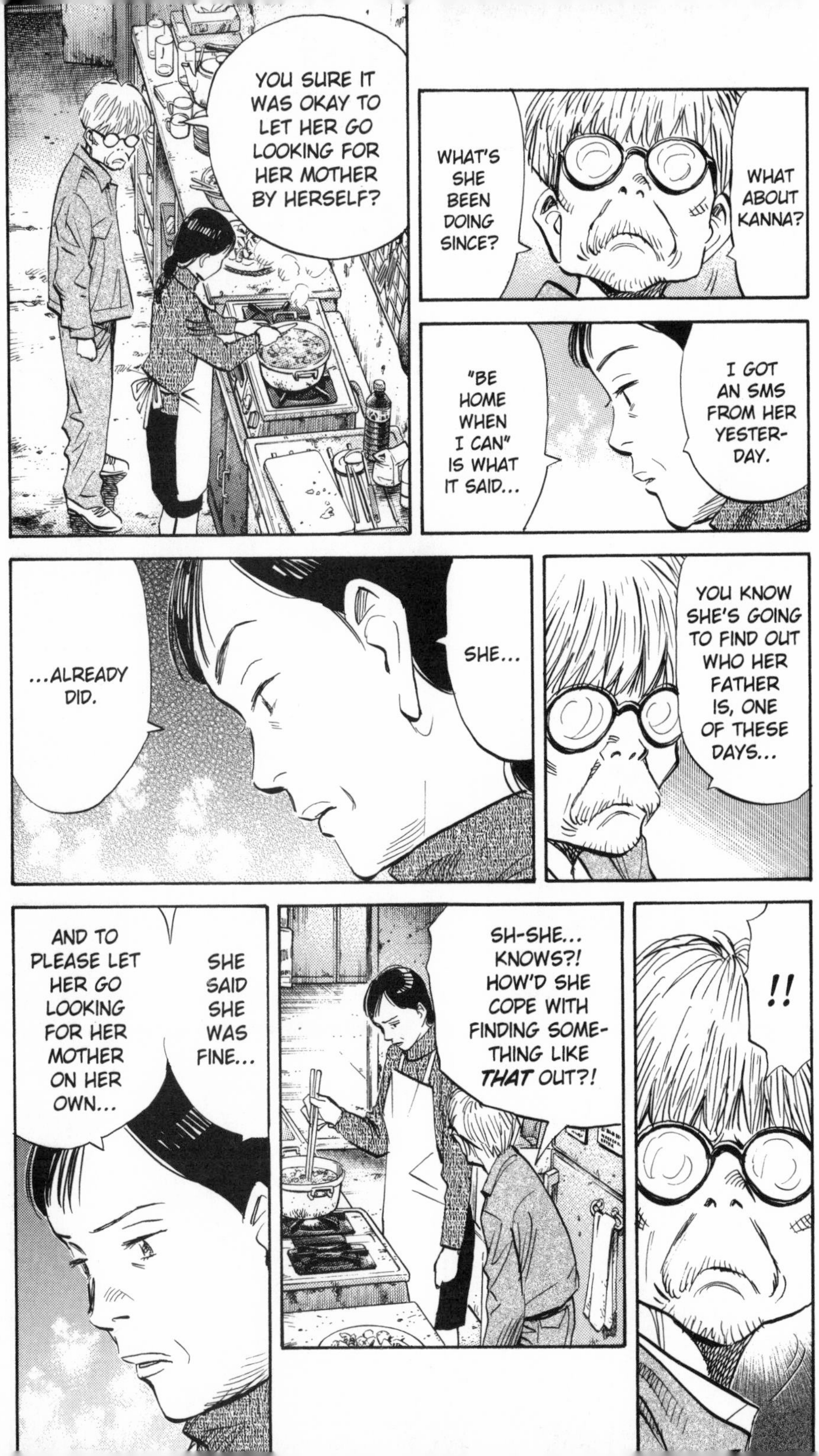
WHAT ABOUT KANNA?
WHAT'S SHE BEEN DOING SINCE?
I GOT AN SMS FROM HER YESTER-DAY.
"BE HOME WHEN I CAN" IS WHAT IT SAID…
YOU SURE IT WAS OKAY TO LET HER GO LOOKING FOR HER MOTHER BY HERSELF?
YOU KNOW SHE'S GOING TO FIND OUT WHO HER FATHER IS, ONE OF THESE DAYS…
SHE…
…ALREADY DID.
!!
SH-SHE… KNOWS?! HOW'D SHE COPE WITH FINDING SOME-THING LIKE *THAT* OUT?!
SHE SAID SHE WAS FINE…
AND TO PLEASE LET HER GO LOOKING FOR HER MOTHER ON HER OWN…

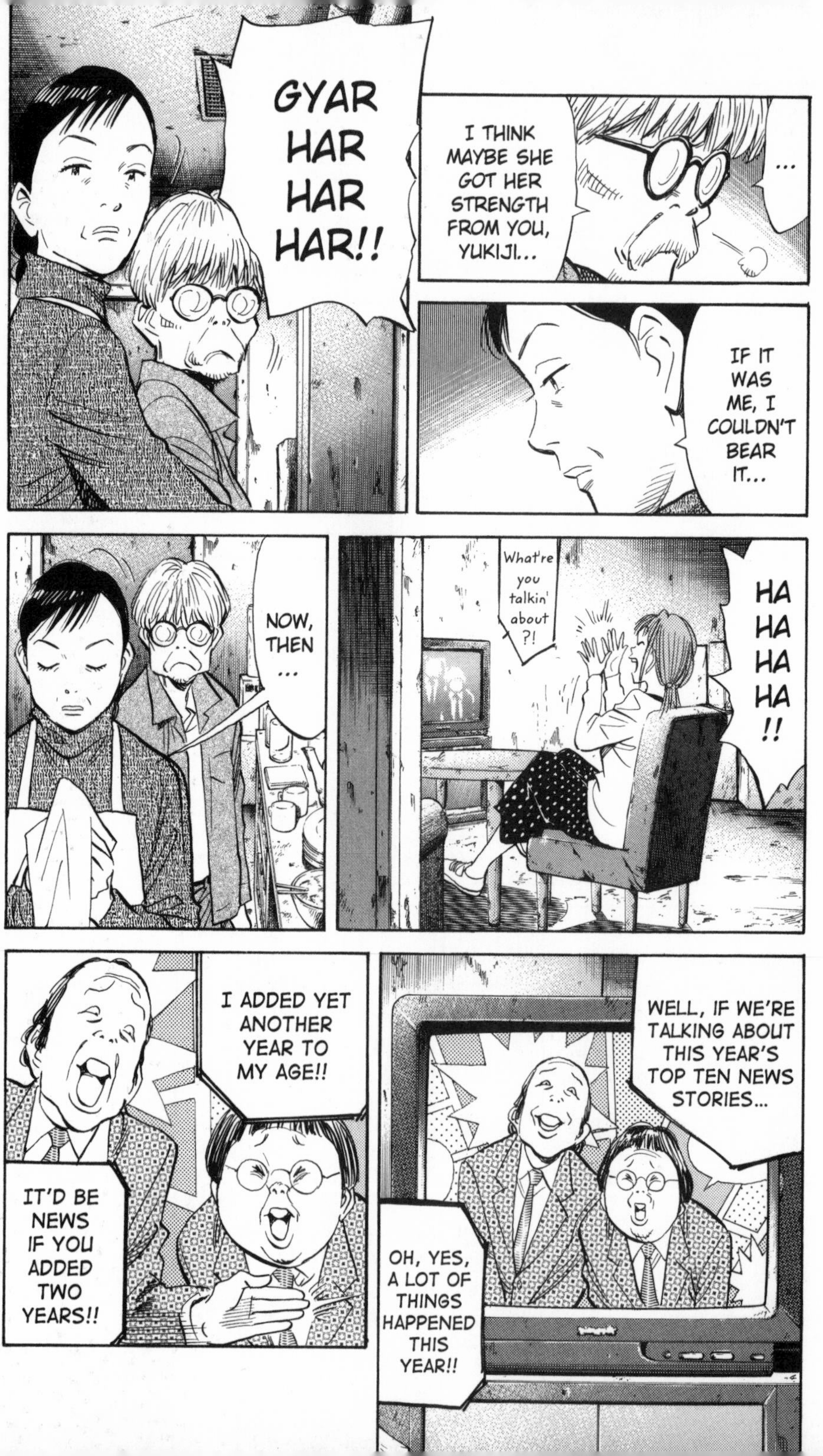
...
I THINK MAYBE SHE GOT HER STRENGTH FROM YOU, YUKIJI...
IF IT WAS ME, I COULDN'T BEAR IT...
GYAR HAR HAR HAR!!
HA HA HA HA!!
What're you talkin' about?!
NOW, THEN...
WELL, IF WE'RE TALKING ABOUT THIS YEAR'S TOP TEN NEWS STORIES...
OH, YES, A LOT OF THINGS HAPPENED THIS YEAR!!
I ADDED YET ANOTHER YEAR TO MY AGE!!
IT'D BE NEWS IF YOU ADDED TWO YEARS!!

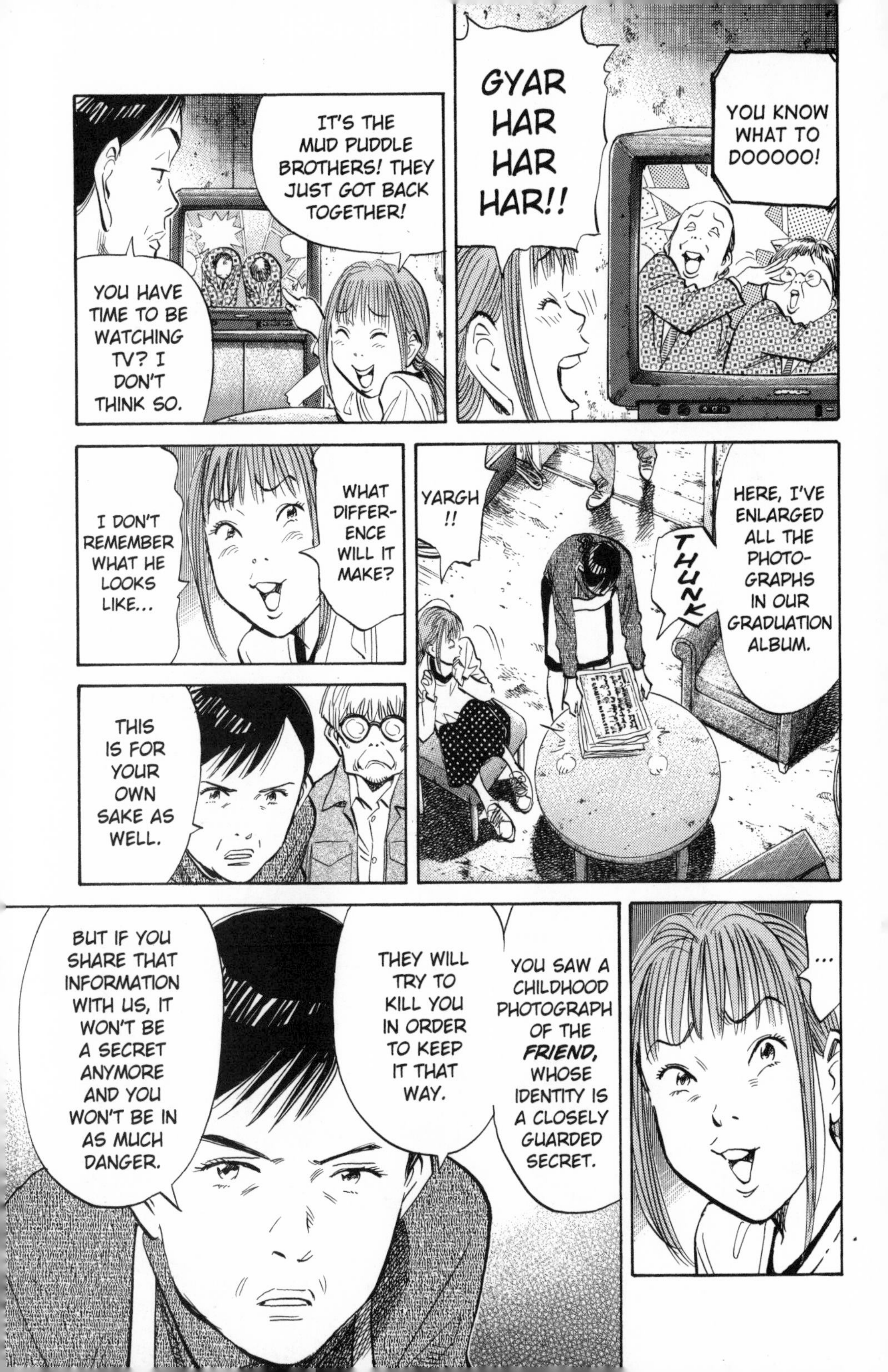
YOU KNOW WHAT TO DOOOOO!
GYAR HAR HAR HAR!!
IT'S THE MUD PUDDLE BROTHERS! THEY JUST GOT BACK TOGETHER!
YOU HAVE TIME TO BE WATCHING TV? I DON'T THINK SO.
HERE, I'VE ENLARGED ALL THE PHOTO-GRAPHS IN OUR GRADUATION ALBUM.
THUNK
YARGH !!
WHAT DIFFER-ENCE WILL IT MAKE?
I DON'T REMEMBER WHAT HE LOOKS LIKE...
THIS IS FOR YOUR OWN SAKE AS WELL.
...
YOU SAW A CHILDHOOD PHOTOGRAPH OF THE *FRIEND,* WHOSE IDENTITY IS A CLOSELY GUARDED SECRET.
THEY WILL TRY TO KILL YOU IN ORDER TO KEEP IT THAT WAY.
BUT IF YOU SHARE THAT INFORMATION WITH US, IT WON'T BE A SECRET ANYMORE AND YOU WON'T BE IN AS MUCH DANGER.

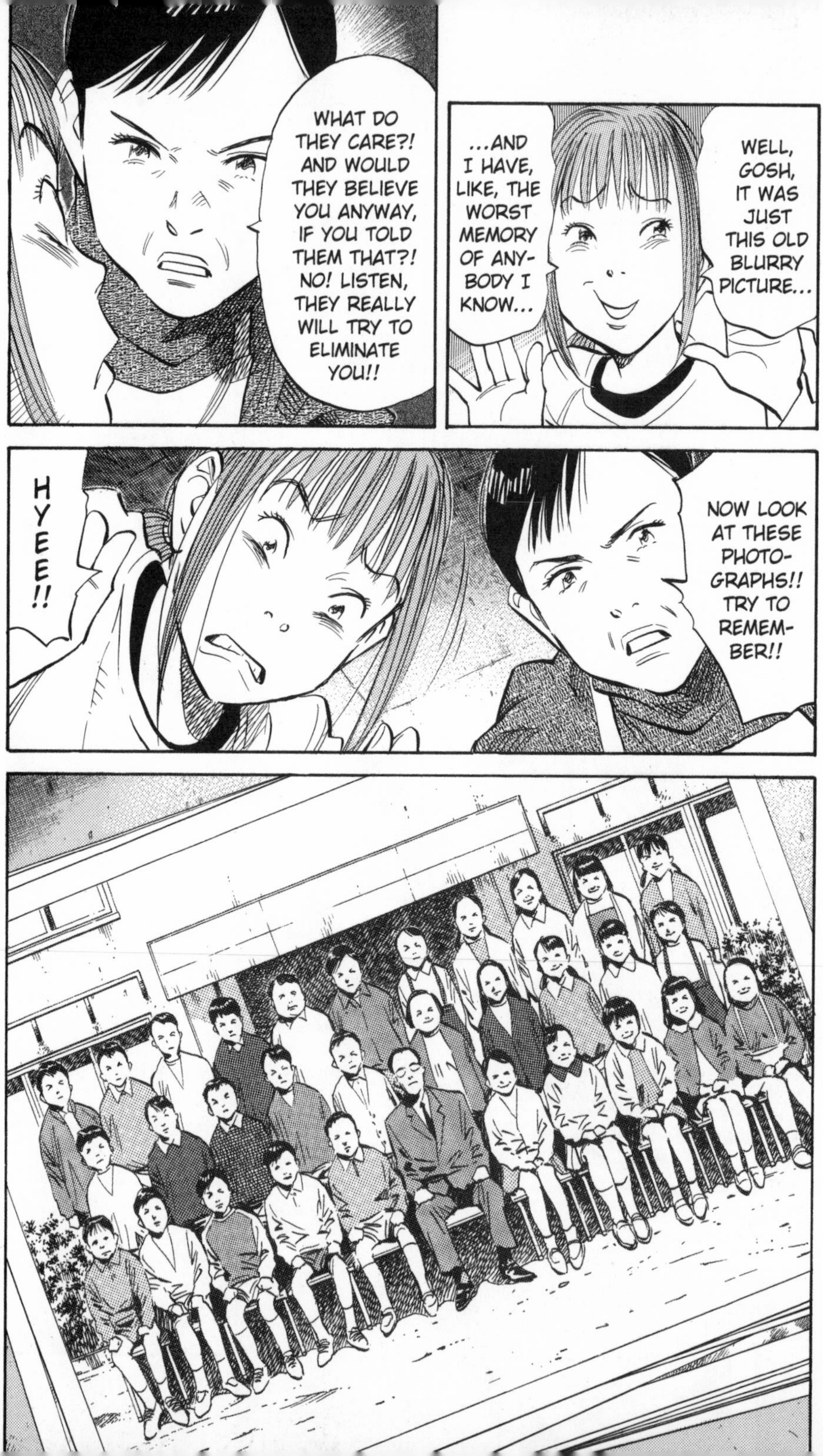
WELL, GOSH, IT WAS JUST THIS OLD BLURRY PICTURE...
...AND I HAVE, LIKE, THE WORST MEMORY OF ANYBODY I KNOW...
WHAT DO THEY CARE?! AND WOULD THEY BELIEVE YOU ANYWAY, IF YOU TOLD THEM THAT?! NO! LISTEN, THEY REALLY WILL TRY TO ELIMINATE YOU!!
NOW LOOK AT THESE PHOTOGRAPHS!! TRY TO REMEMBER!!
HYEEE!!

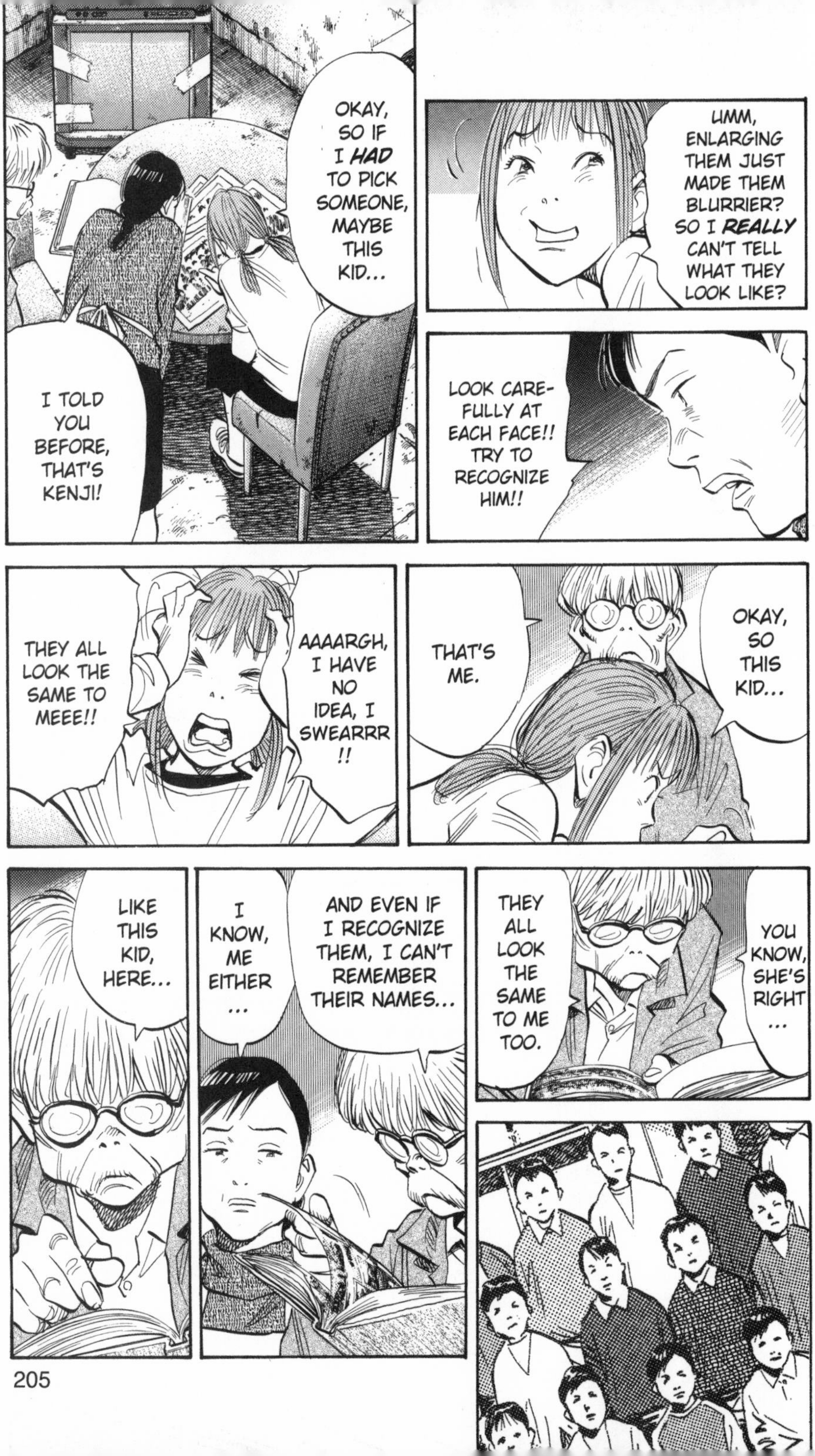
UMM, ENLARGING THEM JUST MADE THEM BLURRIER? SO I *REALLY* CAN'T TELL WHAT THEY LOOK LIKE?
LOOK CARE-FULLY AT EACH FACE!! TRY TO RECOGNIZE HIM!!
OKAY, SO IF I *HAD* TO PICK SOMEONE, MAYBE THIS KID...
I TOLD YOU BEFORE, THAT'S KENJI!
OKAY, SO THIS KID...
THAT'S ME.
AAAARGH, I HAVE NO IDEA, I SWEARRR!!
THEY ALL LOOK THE SAME TO MEEE!!
YOU KNOW, SHE'S RIGHT...
THEY ALL LOOK THE SAME TO ME TOO.
AND EVEN IF I RECOGNIZE THEM, I CAN'T REMEMBER THEIR NAMES...
I KNOW, ME EITHER...
LIKE THIS KID, HERE...

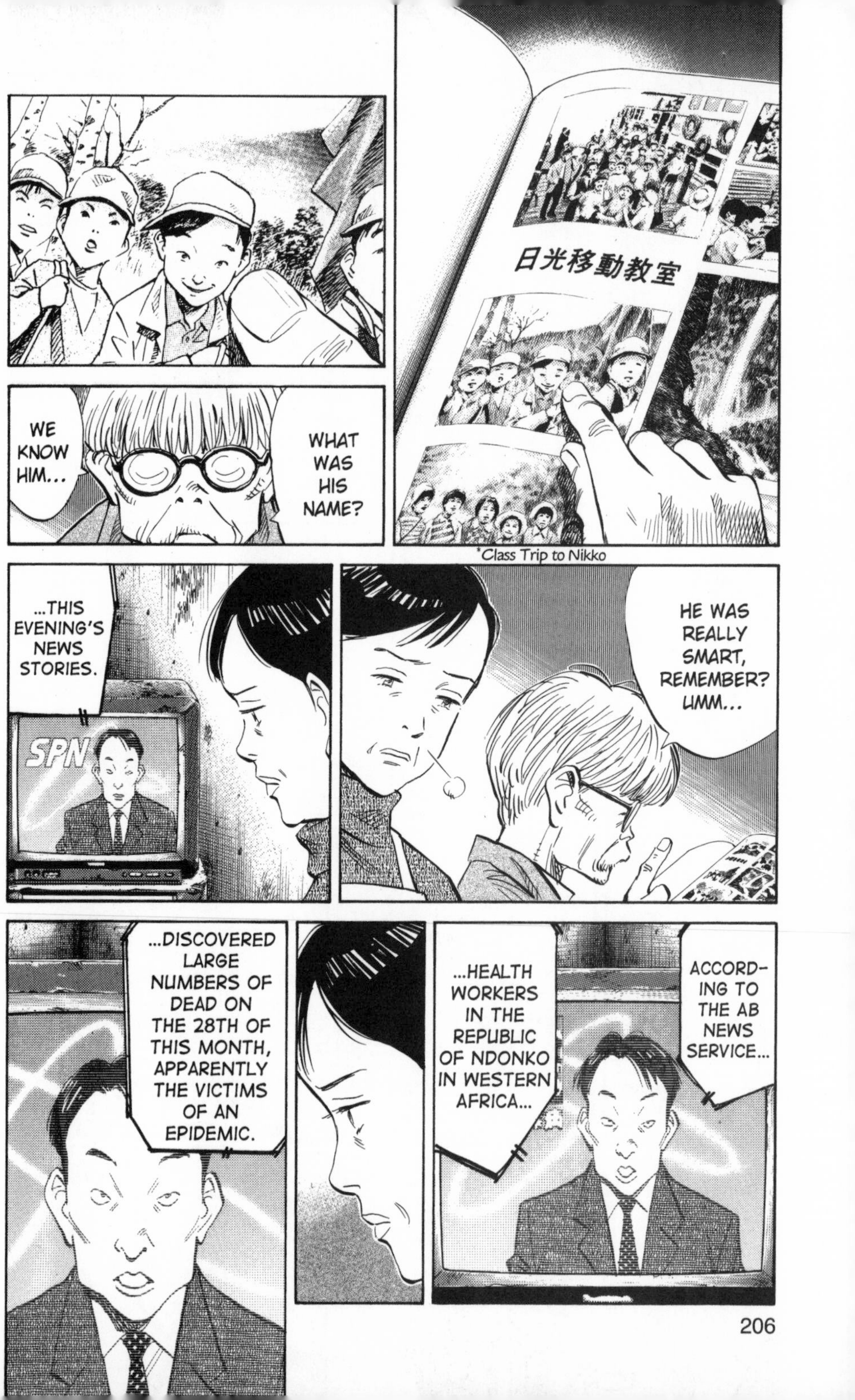
日光移動教室
*Class Trip to Nikko
WHAT WAS HIS NAME?
WE KNOW HIM...
HE WAS REALLY SMART, REMEMBER? UMM...
...THIS EVENING'S NEWS STORIES.
SPN
ACCORD-ING TO THE AB NEWS SERVICE...
...HEALTH WORKERS IN THE REPUBLIC OF NDONKO IN WESTERN AFRICA...
...DISCOVERED LARGE NUMBERS OF DEAD ON THE 28TH OF THIS MONTH, APPARENTLY THE VICTIMS OF AN EPIDEMIC.

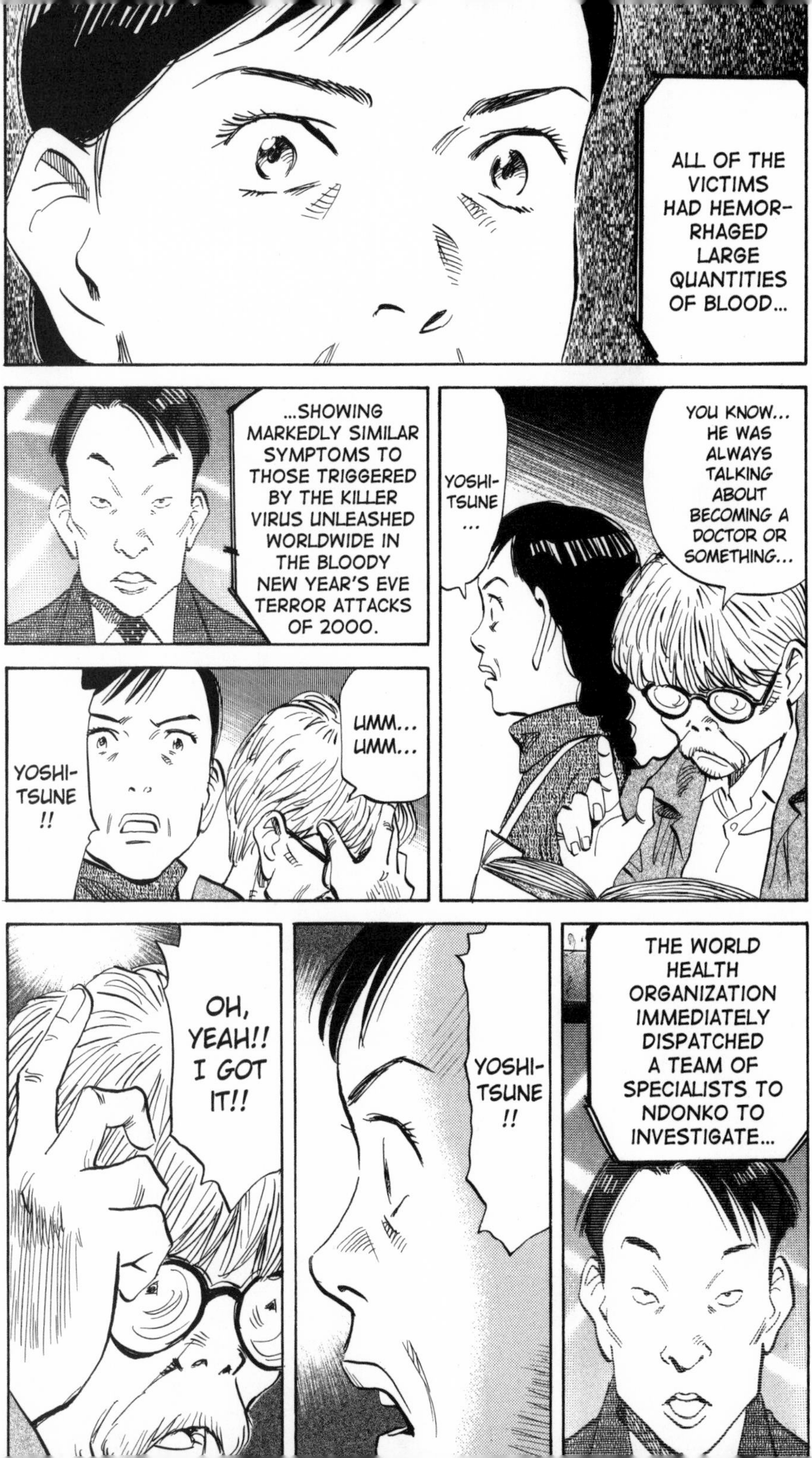
ALL OF THE VICTIMS HAD HEMORRHAGED LARGE QUANTITIES OF BLOOD...
YOU KNOW... HE WAS ALWAYS TALKING ABOUT BECOMING A DOCTOR OR SOMETHING...
YOSHITSUNE...
...SHOWING MARKEDLY SIMILAR SYMPTOMS TO THOSE TRIGGERED BY THE KILLER VIRUS UNLEASHED WORLDWIDE IN THE BLOODY NEW YEAR'S EVE TERROR ATTACKS OF 2000.
UMM... UMM...
YOSHITSUNE!!
THE WORLD HEALTH ORGANIZATION IMMEDIATELY DISPATCHED A TEAM OF SPECIALISTS TO NDONKO TO INVESTIGATE...
YOSHITSUNE!!
OH, YEAH!! I GOT IT!!

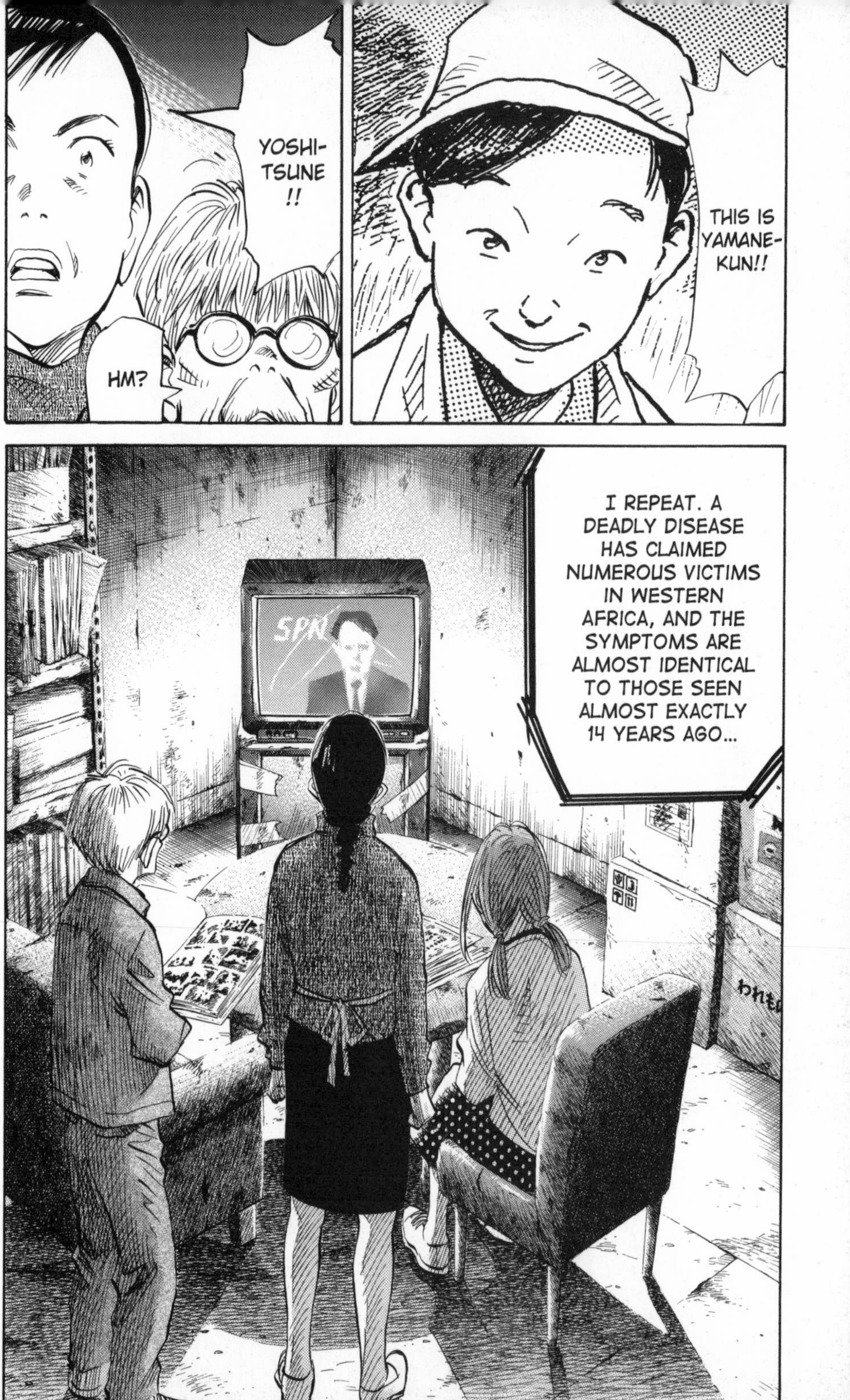
THIS IS YAMANE-KUN!!
YOSHI-TSUNE !!
HM?
I REPEAT. A DEADLY DISEASE HAS CLAIMED NUMEROUS VICTIMS IN WESTERN AFRICA, AND THE SYMPTOMS ARE ALMOST IDENTICAL TO THOSE SEEN ALMOST EXACTLY 14 YEARS AGO...
SPN

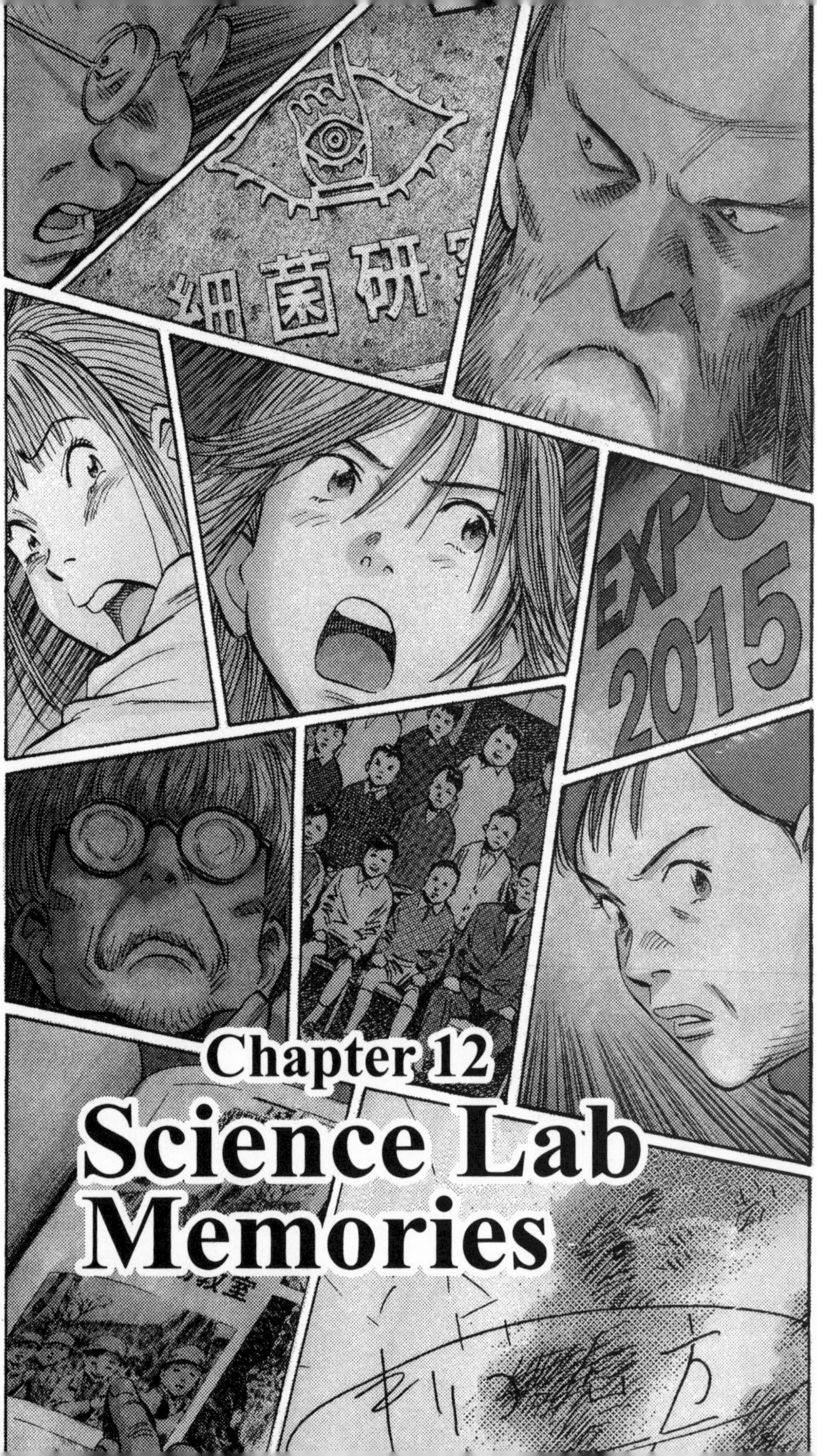
EXPO 2015

Chapter 12
Science Lab Memories

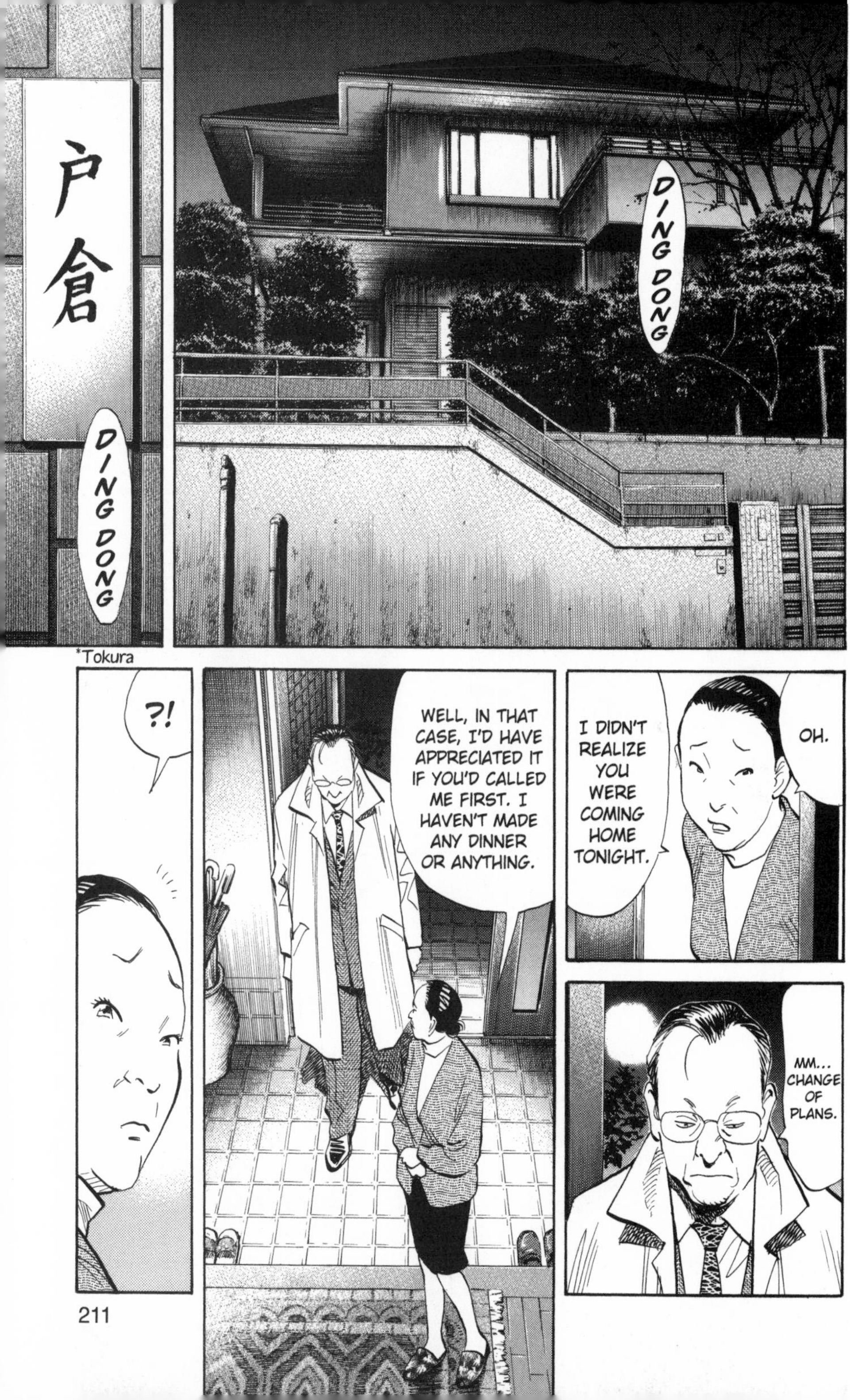
DING DONG
戸倉
DING DONG
OH.
I DIDN'T REALIZE YOU WERE COMING HOME TONIGHT.
MM... CHANGE OF PLANS.
WELL, IN THAT CASE, I'D HAVE APPRECIATED IT IF YOU'D CALLED ME FIRST. I HAVEN'T MADE ANY DINNER OR ANYTHING.
?!

*Tokura

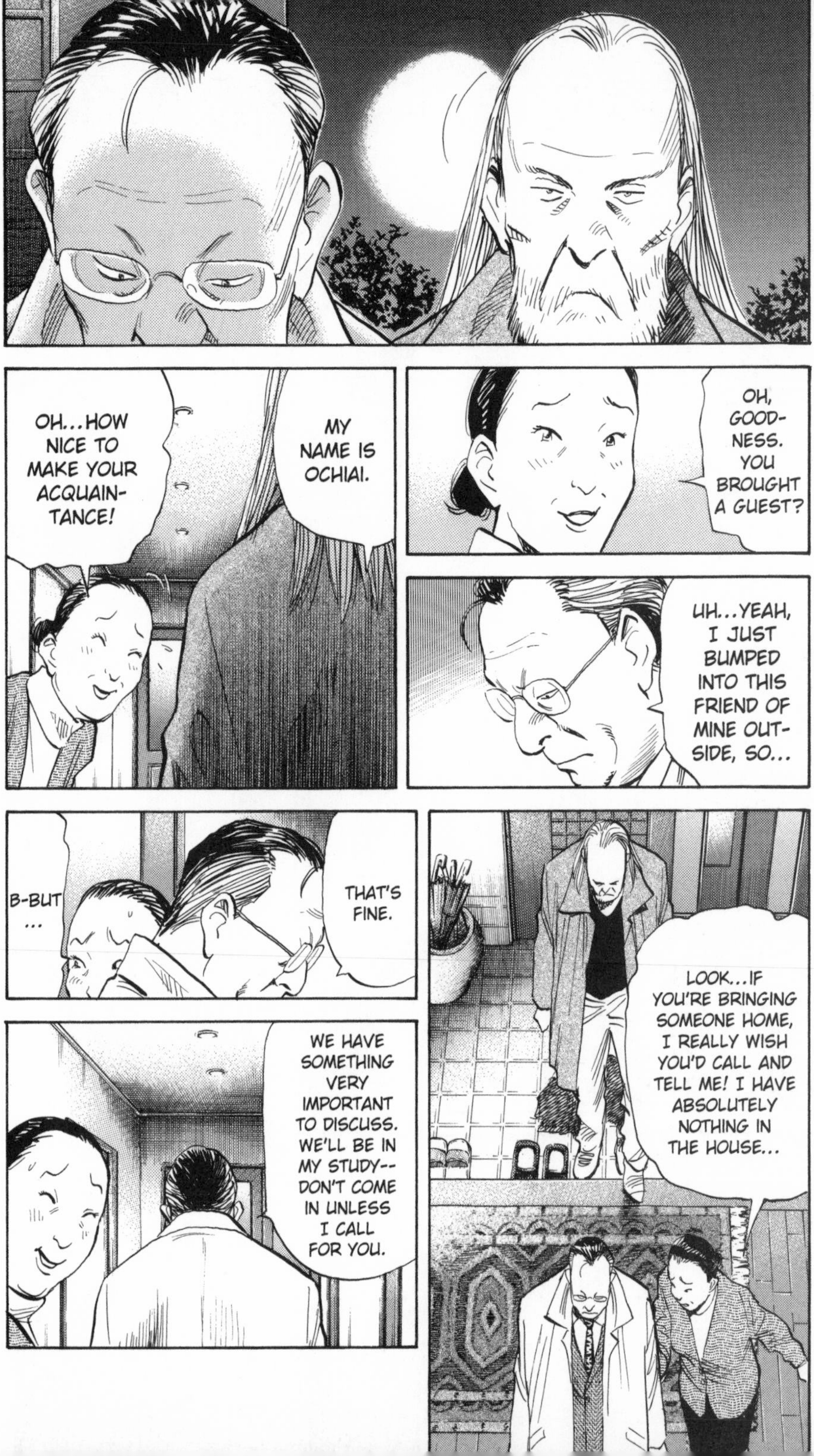
OH, GOODNESS. YOU BROUGHT A GUEST?
UH...YEAH, I JUST BUMPED INTO THIS FRIEND OF MINE OUTSIDE, SO...
MY NAME IS OCHIAI.
OH...HOW NICE TO MAKE YOUR ACQUAINTANCE!
LOOK...IF YOU'RE BRINGING SOMEONE HOME, I REALLY WISH YOU'D CALL AND TELL ME! I HAVE ABSOLUTELY NOTHING IN THE HOUSE...
THAT'S FINE.
B-BUT...
WE HAVE SOMETHING VERY IMPORTANT TO DISCUSS. WE'LL BE IN MY STUDY-- DON'T COME IN UNLESS I CALL FOR YOU.

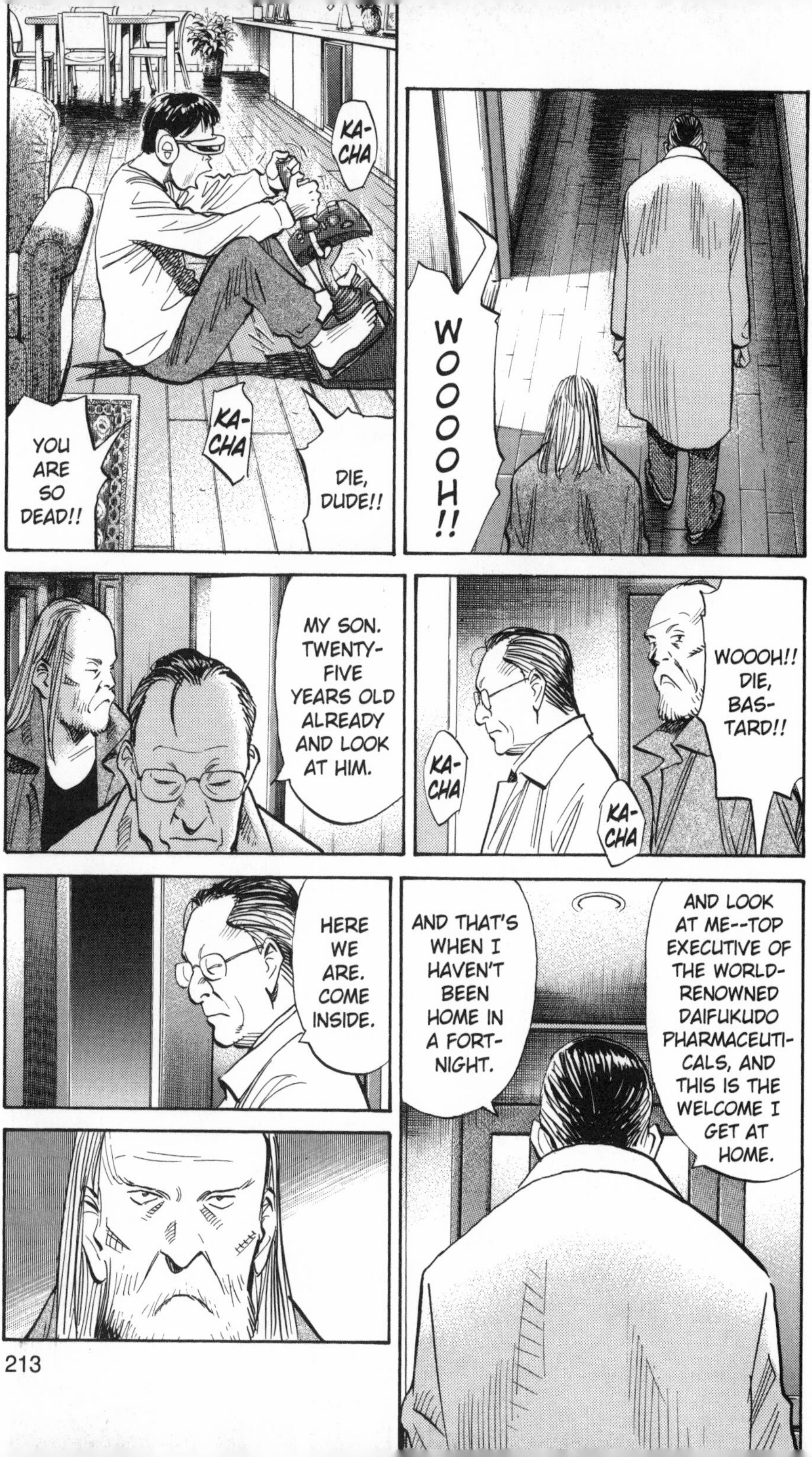
WOOOOOH!!
KA-CHA
DIE, DUDE!!
KA-CHA
YOU ARE SO DEAD!!
WOOOH!! DIE, BASTARD!!
KA-CHA
KA-CHA
MY SON. TWENTY-FIVE YEARS OLD ALREADY AND LOOK AT HIM.
AND LOOK AT ME--TOP EXECUTIVE OF THE WORLD-RENOWNED DAIFUKUDO PHARMACEUTICALS, AND THIS IS THE WELCOME I GET AT HOME.
AND THAT'S WHEN I HAVEN'T BEEN HOME IN A FORTNIGHT.
HERE WE ARE. COME INSIDE.

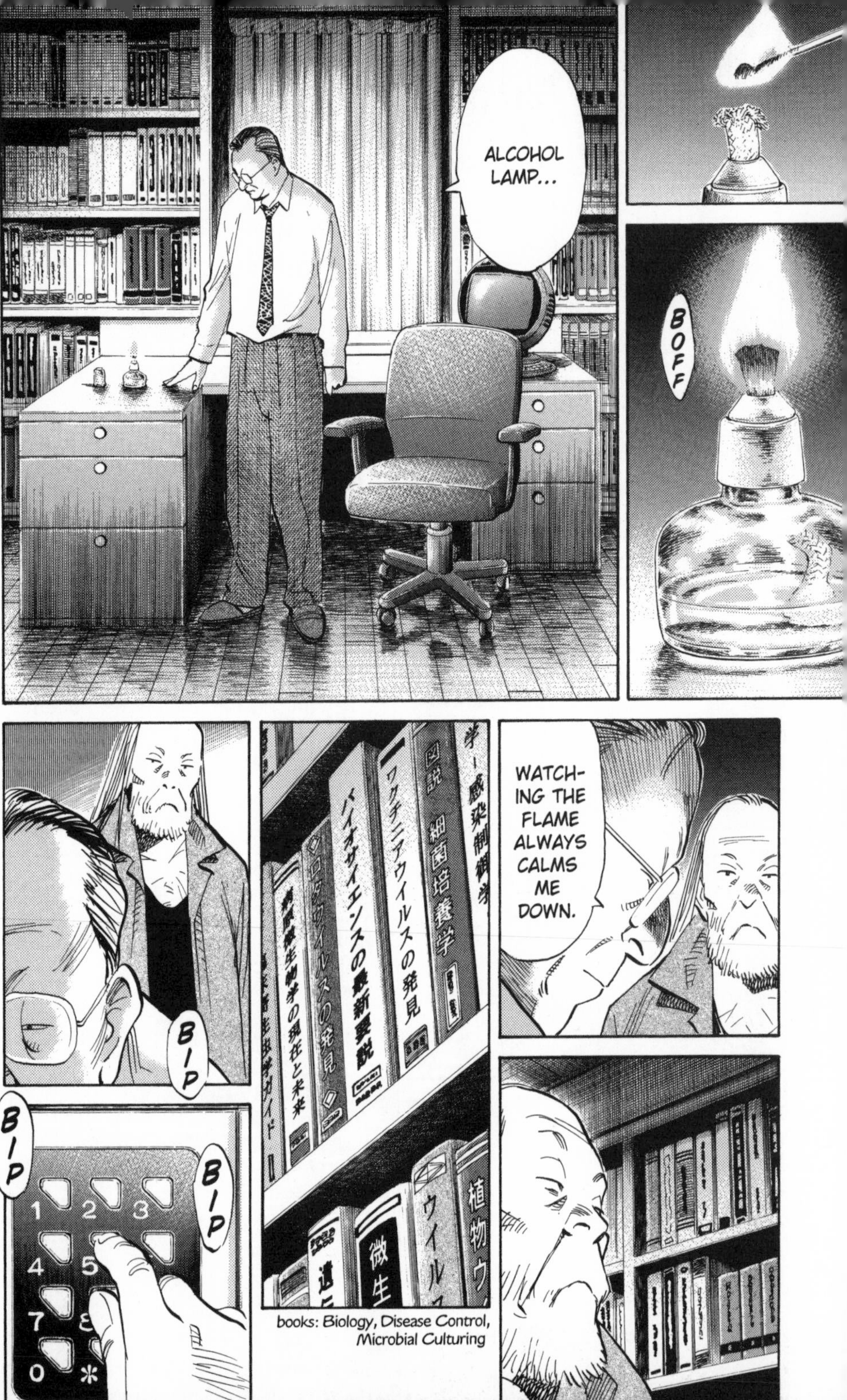
BOFF
ALCOHOL LAMP...
WATCHING THE FLAME ALWAYS CALMS ME DOWN.
感染制御学
図説 細菌培養学
ワクチニアウイルスの発見
バイオサイエンスの最新要説
ロタウイルスの発見
微生物学の現在と未来
books: Biology, Disease Control, Microbial Culturing
BIP
BIP
BIP
1 2 3
4 5
7 8
0 *

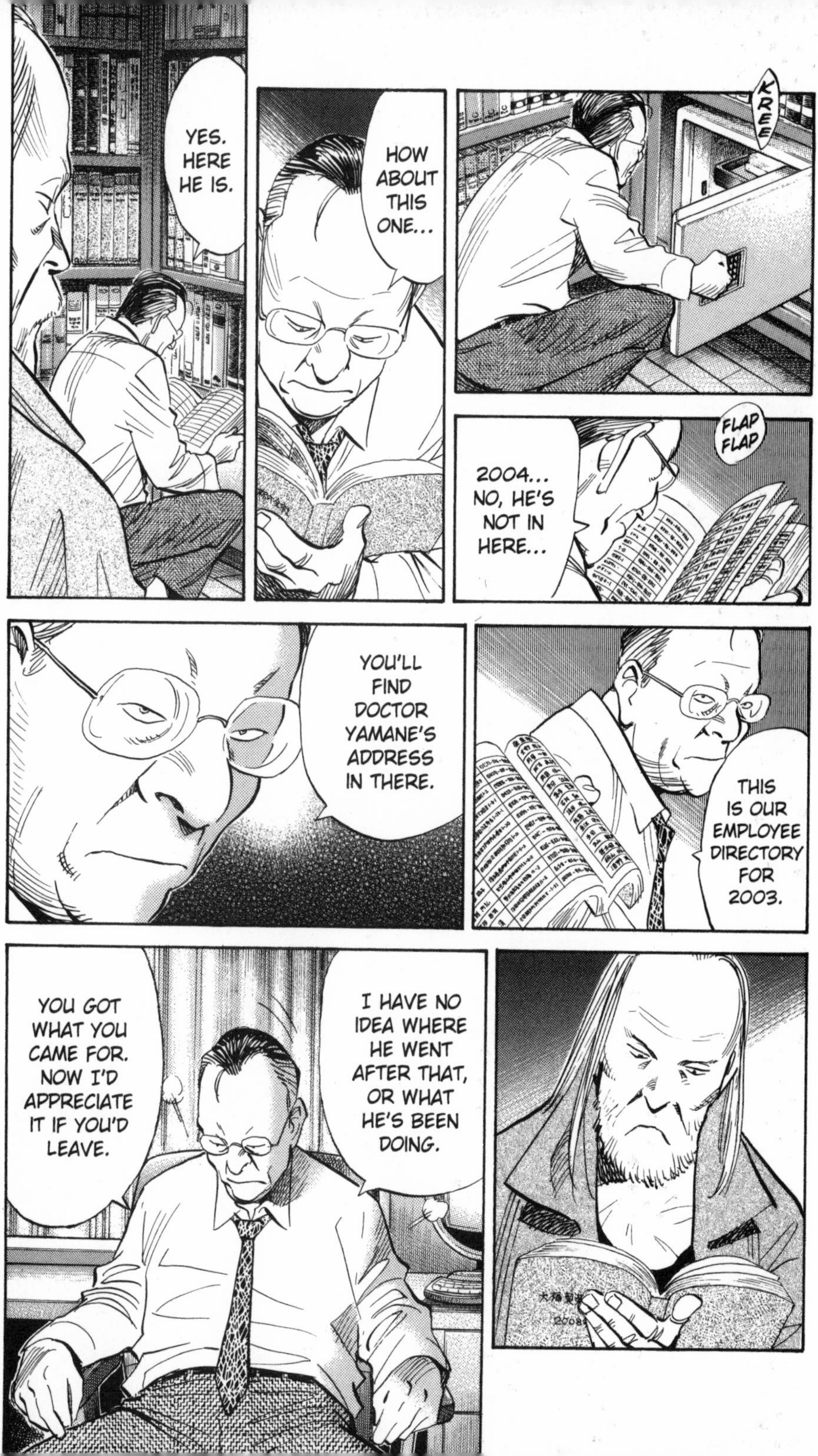
KREE
FLAP FLAP
2004... NO, HE'S NOT IN HERE...
HOW ABOUT THIS ONE...
YES. HERE HE IS.
THIS IS OUR EMPLOYEE DIRECTORY FOR 2003.
YOU'LL FIND DOCTOR YAMANE'S ADDRESS IN THERE.
I HAVE NO IDEA WHERE HE WENT AFTER THAT, OR WHAT HE'S BEEN DOING.
YOU GOT WHAT YOU CAME FOR. NOW I'D APPRECIATE IT IF YOU'D LEAVE.

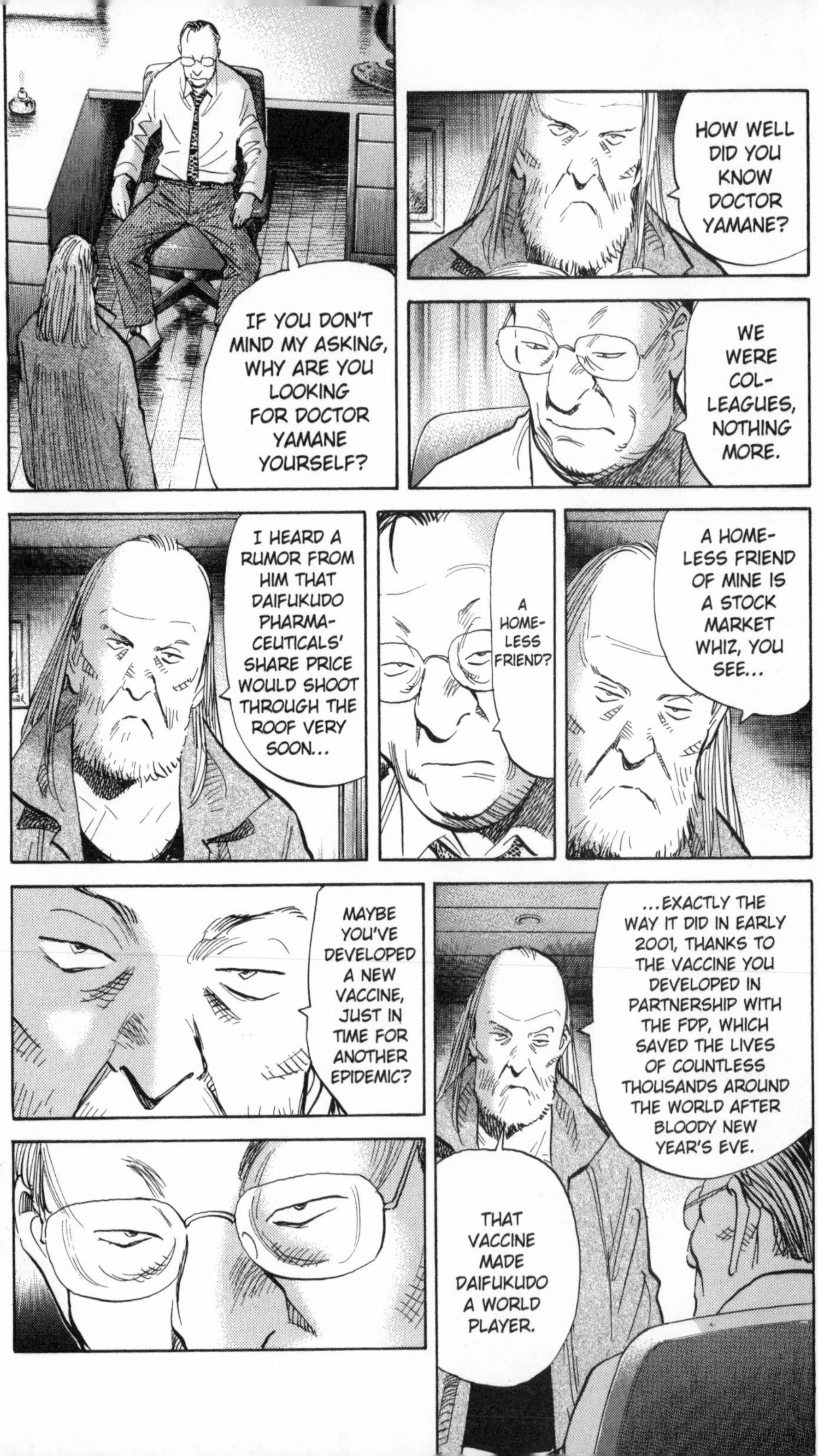
HOW WELL DID YOU KNOW DOCTOR YAMANE?
WE WERE COL-LEAGUES, NOTHING MORE.
IF YOU DON'T MIND MY ASKING, WHY ARE YOU LOOKING FOR DOCTOR YAMANE YOURSELF?
A HOME-LESS FRIEND OF MINE IS A STOCK MARKET WHIZ, YOU SEE...
A HOME-LESS FRIEND?
I HEARD A RUMOR FROM HIM THAT DAIFUKUDO PHARMA-CEUTICALS' SHARE PRICE WOULD SHOOT THROUGH THE ROOF VERY SOON...
...EXACTLY THE WAY IT DID IN EARLY 2001, THANKS TO THE VACCINE YOU DEVELOPED IN PARTNERSHIP WITH THE FDP, WHICH SAVED THE LIVES OF COUNTLESS THOUSANDS AROUND THE WORLD AFTER BLOODY NEW YEAR'S EVE.
THAT VACCINE MADE DAIFUKUDO A WORLD PLAYER.
MAYBE YOU'VE DEVELOPED A NEW VACCINE, JUST IN TIME FOR ANOTHER EPIDEMIC?

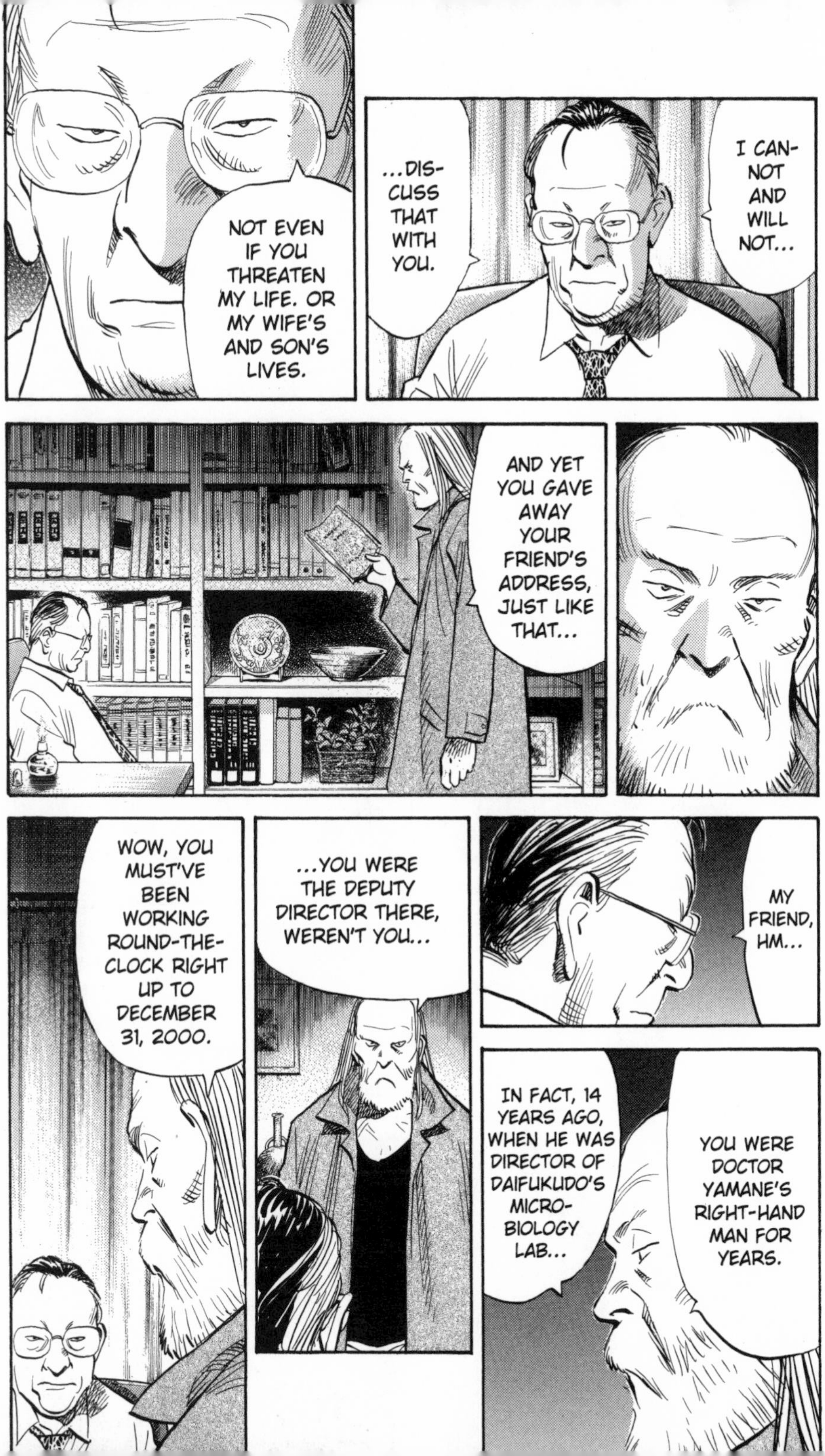
I CANNOT AND WILL NOT...
...DISCUSS THAT WITH YOU.
NOT EVEN IF YOU THREATEN MY LIFE. OR MY WIFE'S AND SON'S LIVES.
AND YET YOU GAVE AWAY YOUR FRIEND'S ADDRESS, JUST LIKE THAT...
MY FRIEND, HM...
YOU WERE DOCTOR YAMANE'S RIGHT-HAND MAN FOR YEARS.
IN FACT, 14 YEARS AGO, WHEN HE WAS DIRECTOR OF DAIFUKUDO'S MICROBIOLOGY LAB...
...YOU WERE THE DEPUTY DIRECTOR THERE, WEREN'T YOU...
WOW, YOU MUST'VE BEEN WORKING ROUND-THE-CLOCK RIGHT UP TO DECEMBER 31, 2000.

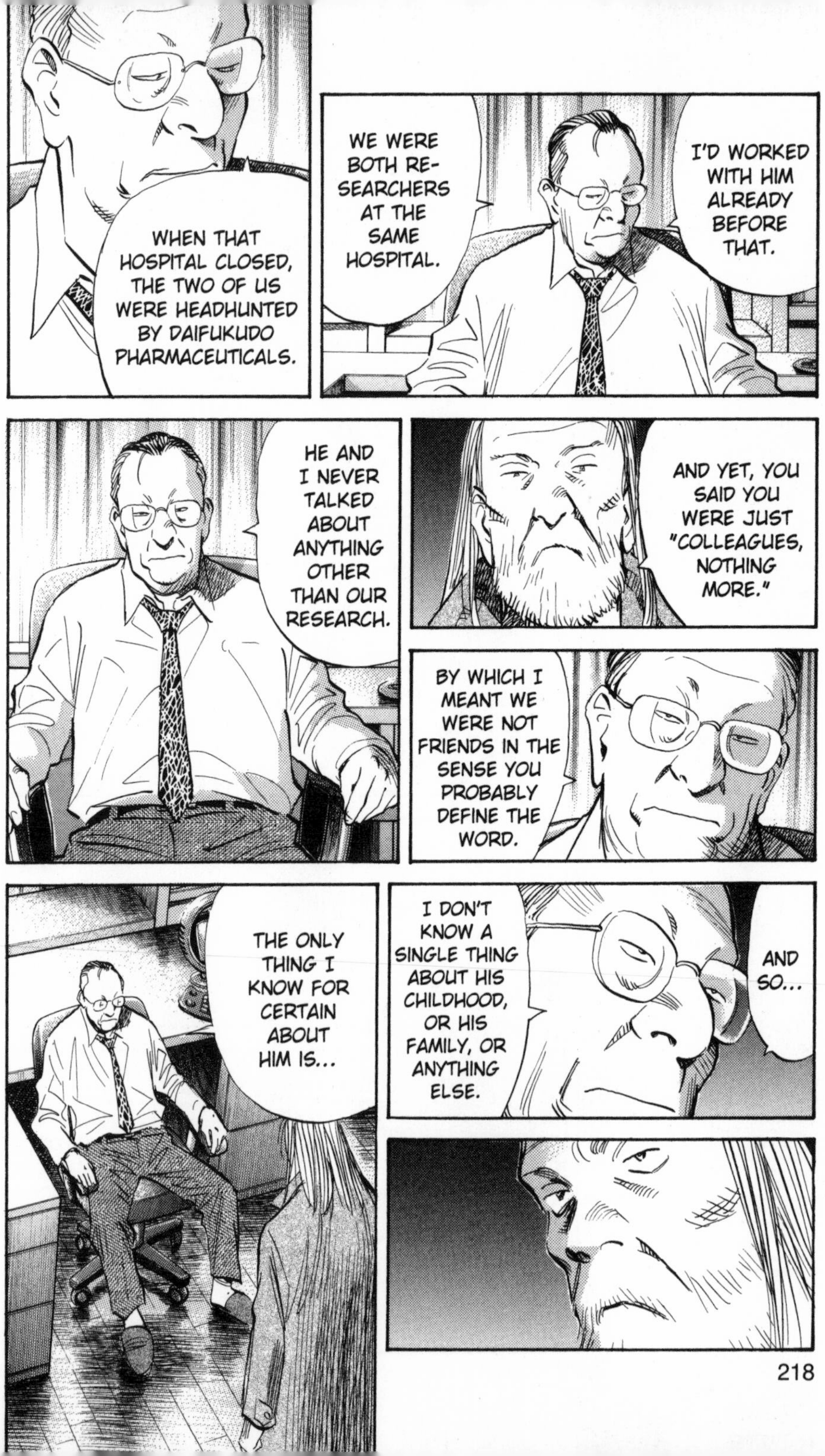
I'D WORKED WITH HIM ALREADY BEFORE THAT.
WE WERE BOTH RE-SEARCHERS AT THE SAME HOSPITAL.
WHEN THAT HOSPITAL CLOSED, THE TWO OF US WERE HEADHUNTED BY DAIFUKUDO PHARMACEUTICALS.
AND YET, YOU SAID YOU WERE JUST "COLLEAGUES, NOTHING MORE."
BY WHICH I MEANT WE WERE NOT FRIENDS IN THE SENSE YOU PROBABLY DEFINE THE WORD.
HE AND I NEVER TALKED ABOUT ANYTHING OTHER THAN OUR RESEARCH.
AND SO...
I DON'T KNOW A SINGLE THING ABOUT HIS CHILDHOOD, OR HIS FAMILY, OR ANYTHING ELSE.
THE ONLY THING I KNOW FOR CERTAIN ABOUT HIM IS...

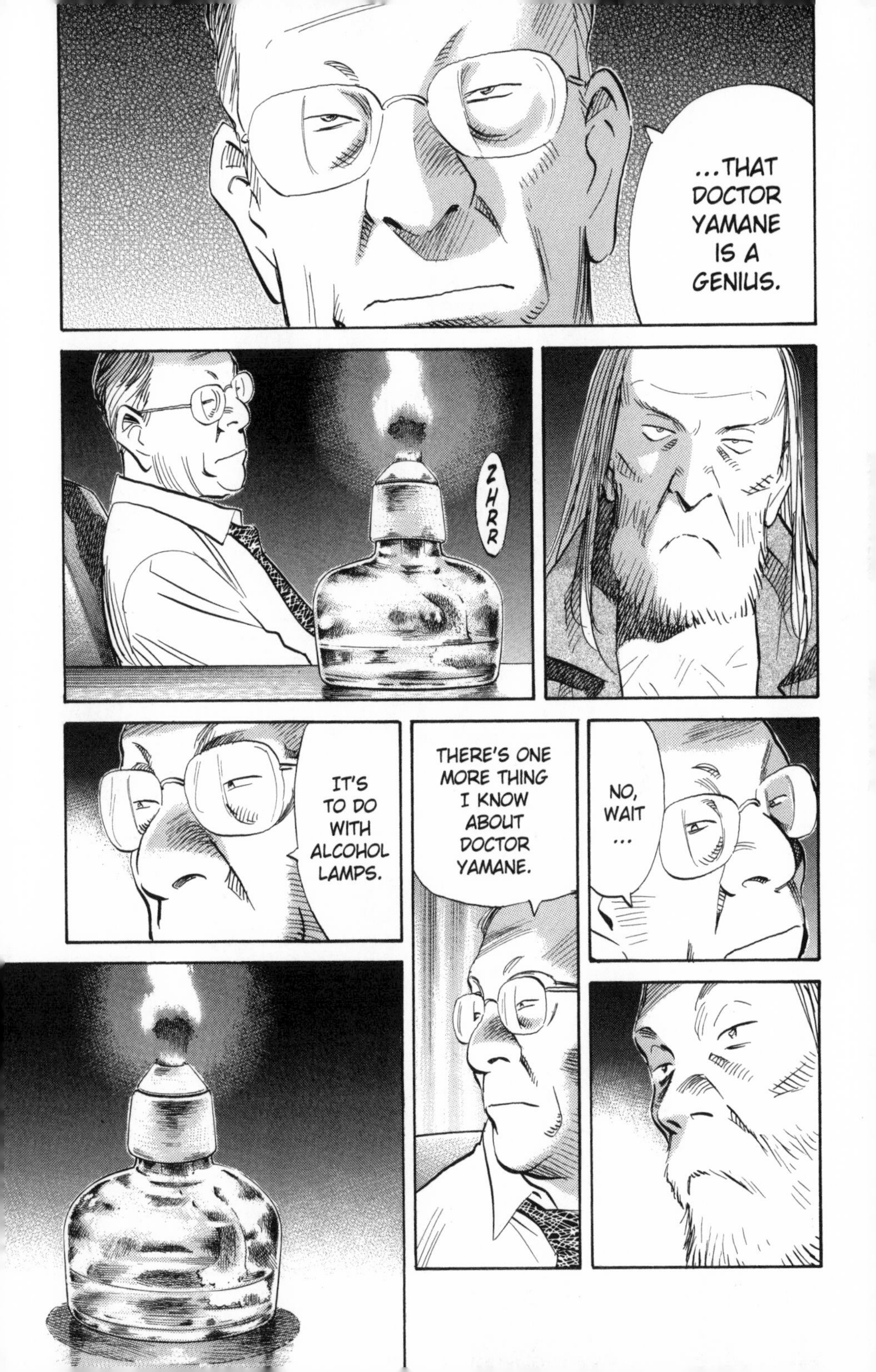
...THAT DOCTOR YAMANE IS A GENIUS.
ZHRR
NO, WAIT ...
THERE'S ONE MORE THING I KNOW ABOUT DOCTOR YAMANE.
IT'S TO DO WITH ALCOHOL LAMPS.

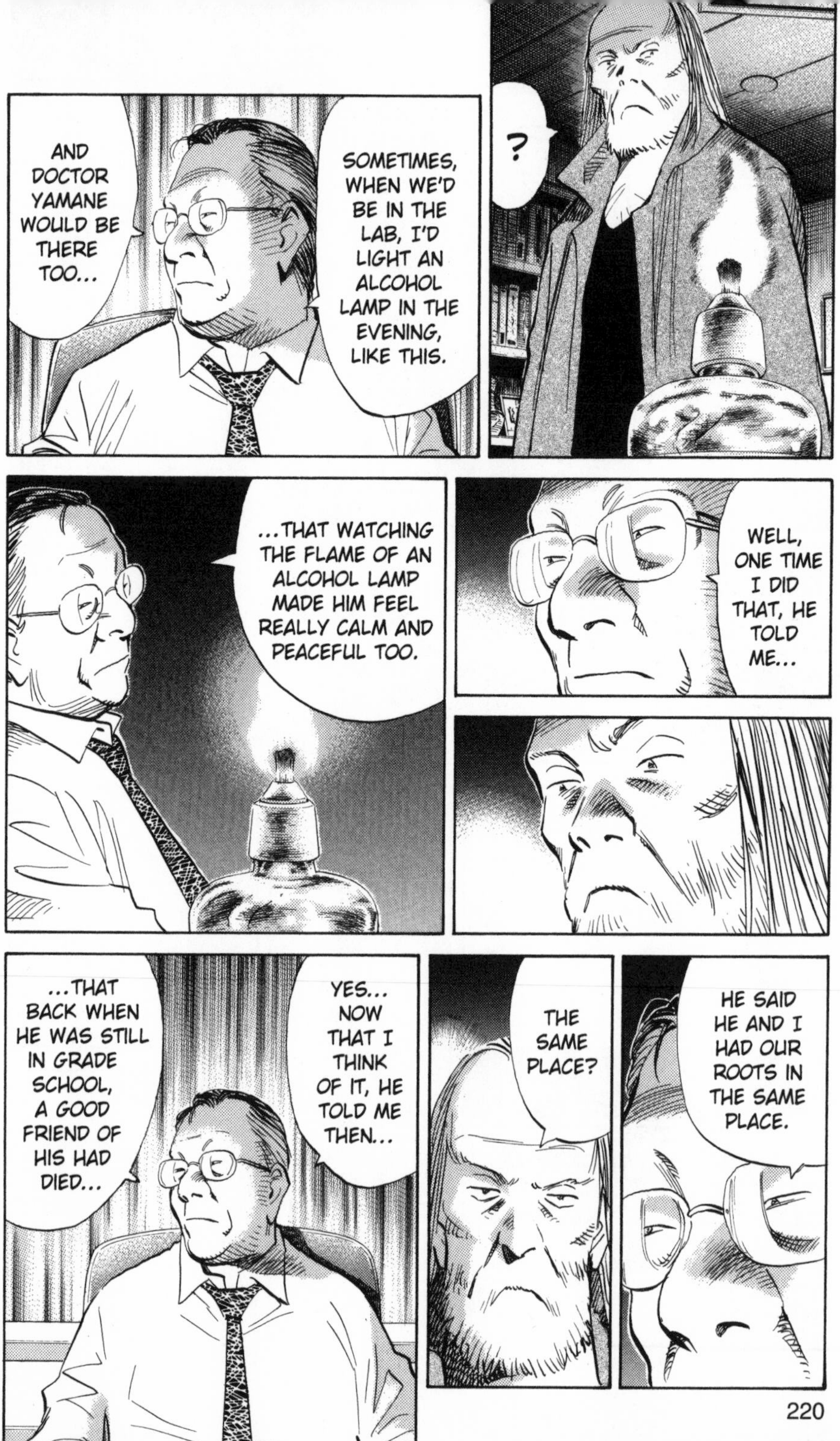
?
SOMETIMES, WHEN WE'D BE IN THE LAB, I'D LIGHT AN ALCOHOL LAMP IN THE EVENING, LIKE THIS.
AND DOCTOR YAMANE WOULD BE THERE TOO...
WELL, ONE TIME I DID THAT, HE TOLD ME...
...THAT WATCHING THE FLAME OF AN ALCOHOL LAMP MADE HIM FEEL REALLY CALM AND PEACEFUL TOO.
HE SAID HE AND I HAD OUR ROOTS IN THE SAME PLACE.
THE SAME PLACE?
YES... NOW THAT I THINK OF IT, HE TOLD ME THEN...
...THAT BACK WHEN HE WAS STILL IN GRADE SCHOOL, A GOOD FRIEND OF HIS HAD DIED...

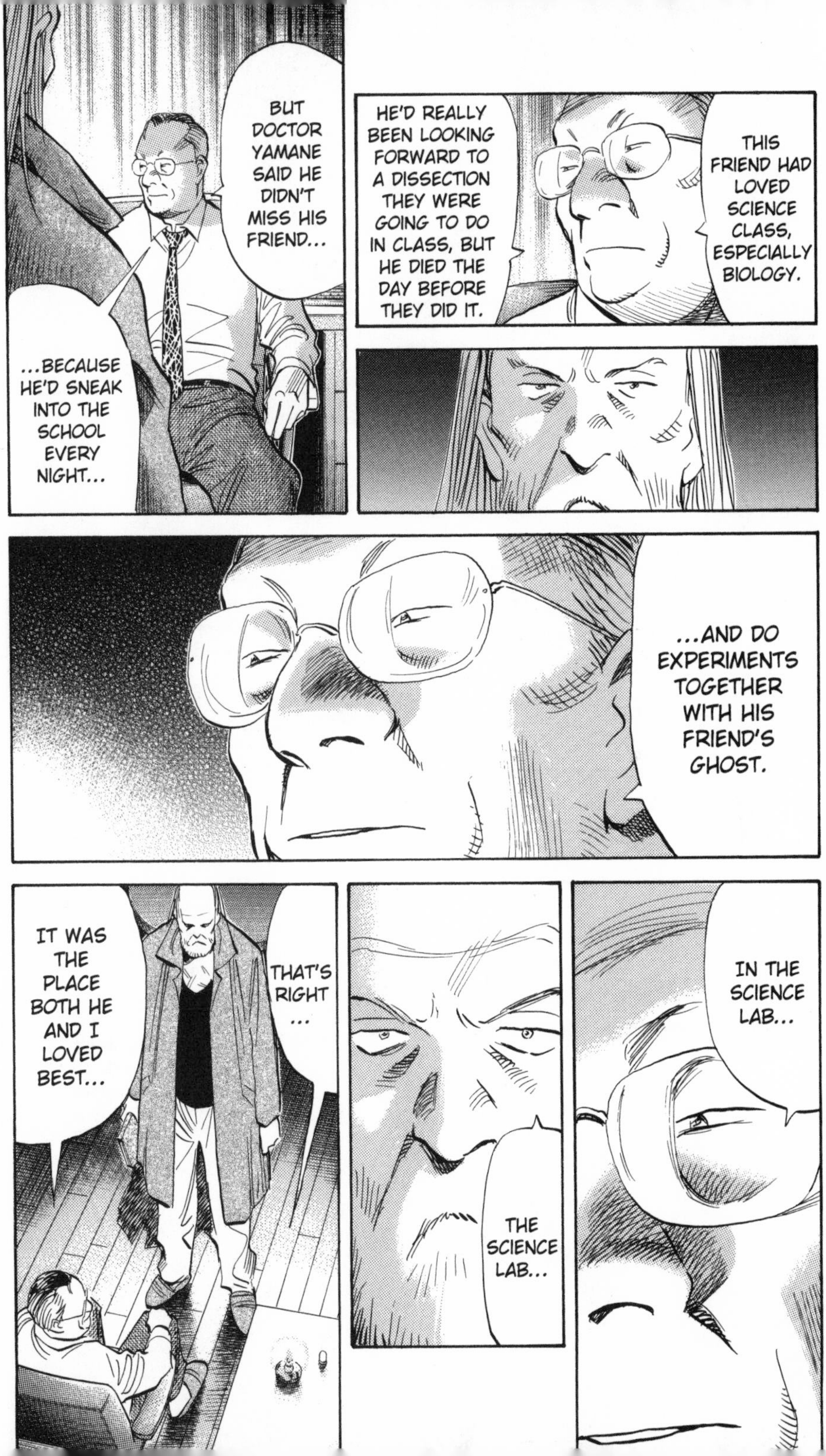
THIS FRIEND HAD LOVED SCIENCE CLASS, ESPECIALLY BIOLOGY.
HE'D REALLY BEEN LOOKING FORWARD TO A DISSECTION THEY WERE GOING TO DO IN CLASS, BUT HE DIED THE DAY BEFORE THEY DID IT.
BUT DOCTOR YAMANE SAID HE DIDN'T MISS HIS FRIEND...
...BECAUSE HE'D SNEAK INTO THE SCHOOL EVERY NIGHT...
...AND DO EXPERIMENTS TOGETHER WITH HIS FRIEND'S GHOST.
IN THE SCIENCE LAB...
THE SCIENCE LAB...
THAT'S RIGHT...
IT WAS THE PLACE BOTH HE AND I LOVED BEST...

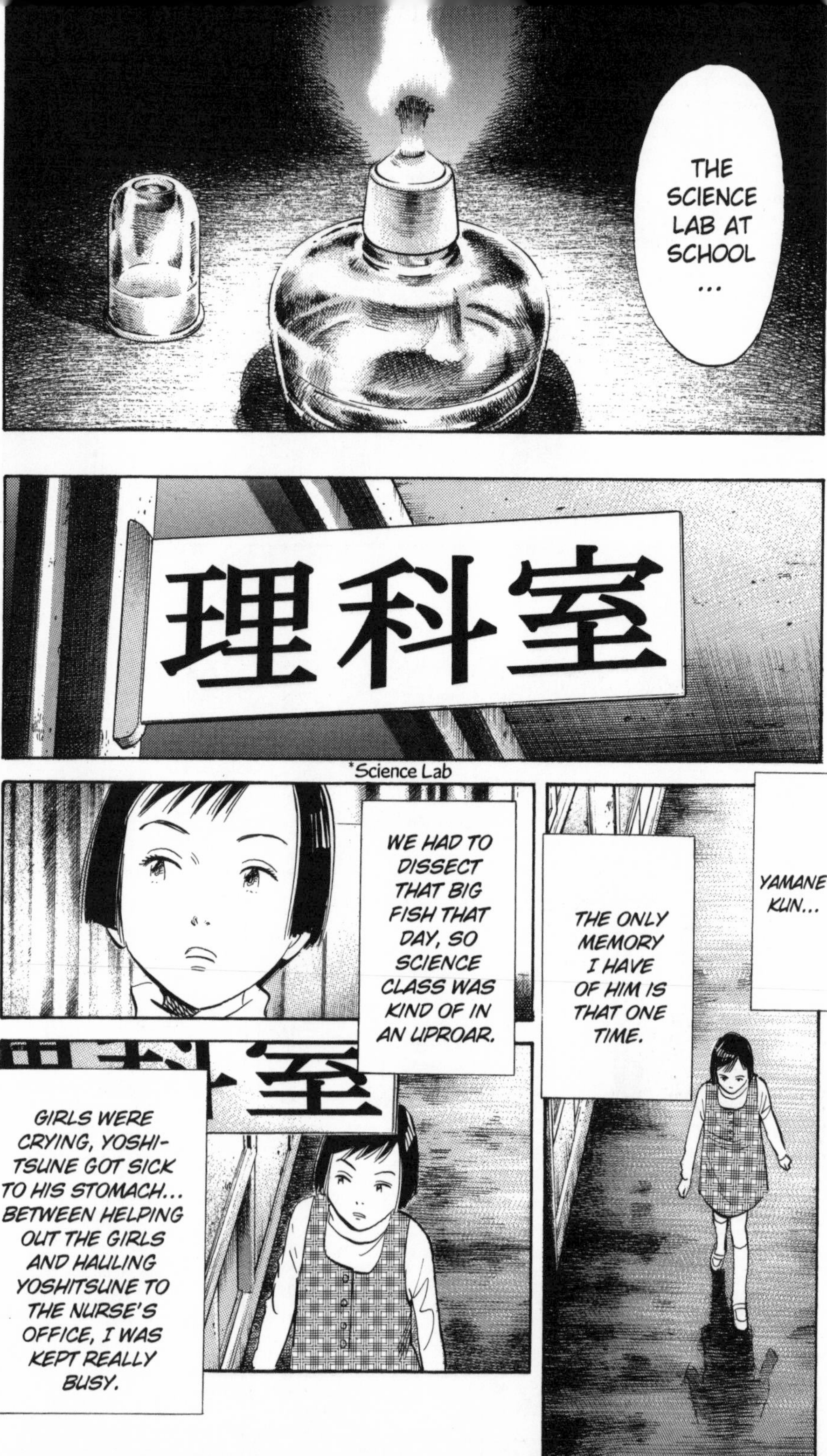
THE SCIENCE LAB AT SCHOOL ...
理科室
*Science Lab
YAMANE-KUN...
THE ONLY MEMORY I HAVE OF HIM IS THAT ONE TIME.
WE HAD TO DISSECT THAT BIG FISH THAT DAY, SO SCIENCE CLASS WAS KIND OF IN AN UPROAR.
GIRLS WERE CRYING, YOSHI-TSUNE GOT SICK TO HIS STOMACH... BETWEEN HELPING OUT THE GIRLS AND HAULING YOSHITSUNE TO THE NURSE'S OFFICE, I WAS KEPT REALLY BUSY.

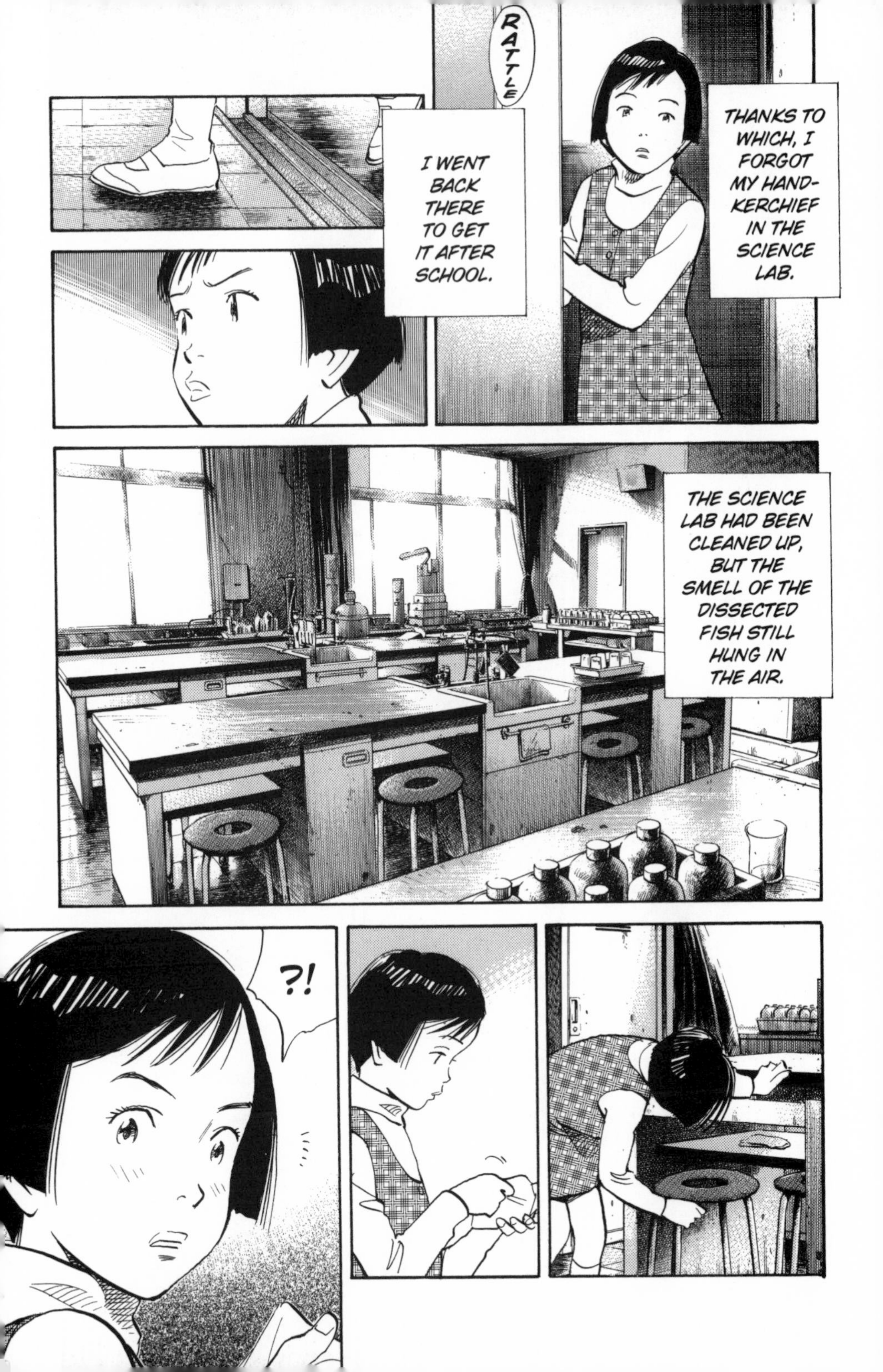
RATTLE
THANKS TO WHICH, I FORGOT MY HAND-KERCHIEF IN THE SCIENCE LAB.
I WENT BACK THERE TO GET IT AFTER SCHOOL.
THE SCIENCE LAB HAD BEEN CLEANED UP, BUT THE SMELL OF THE DISSECTED FISH STILL HUNG IN THE AIR.
?!

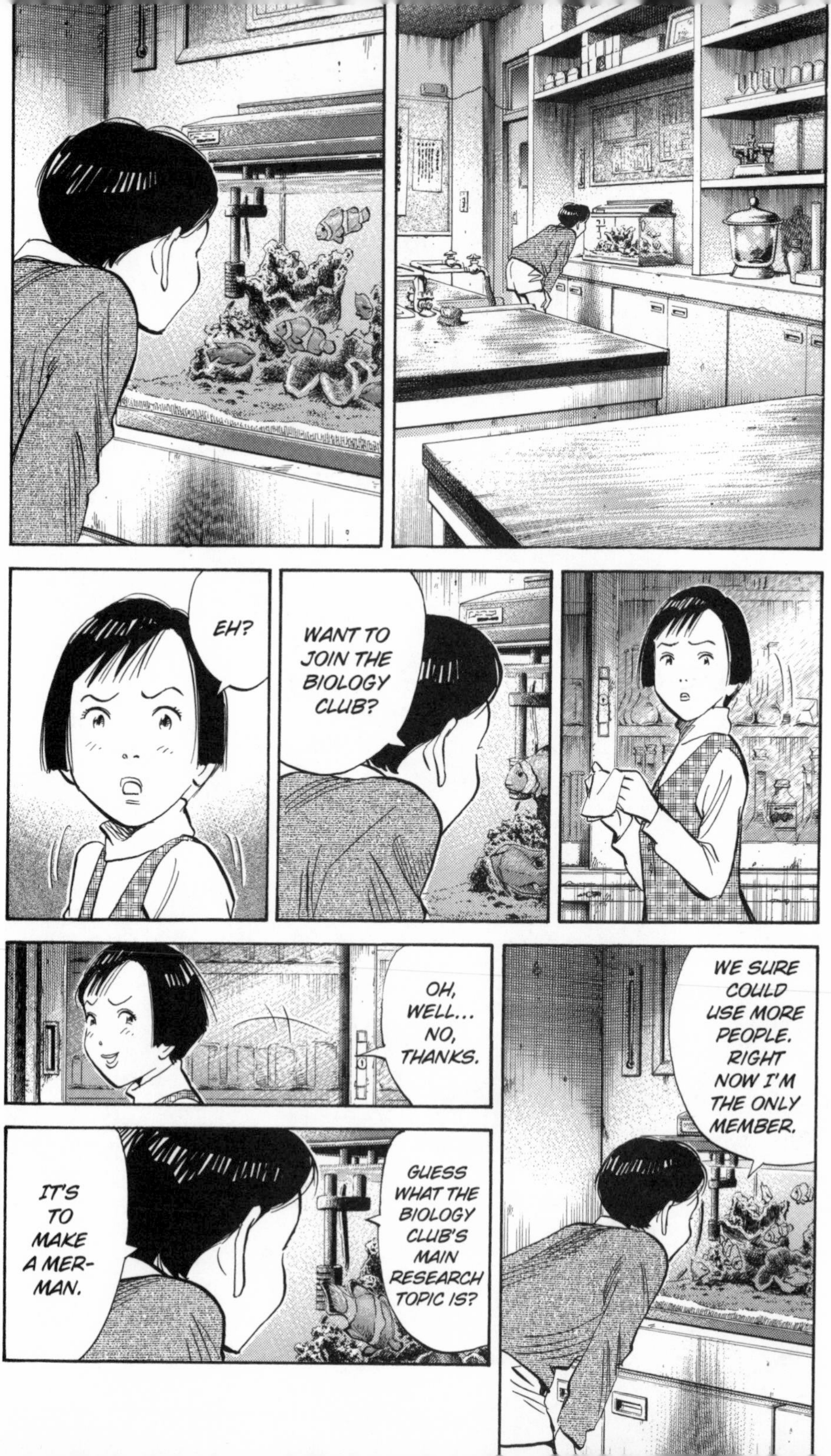
WANT TO JOIN THE BIOLOGY CLUB?
EH?
WE SURE COULD USE MORE PEOPLE. RIGHT NOW I'M THE ONLY MEMBER.
OH, WELL... NO, THANKS.
GUESS WHAT THE BIOLOGY CLUB'S MAIN RESEARCH TOPIC IS?
IT'S TO MAKE A MER-MAN.

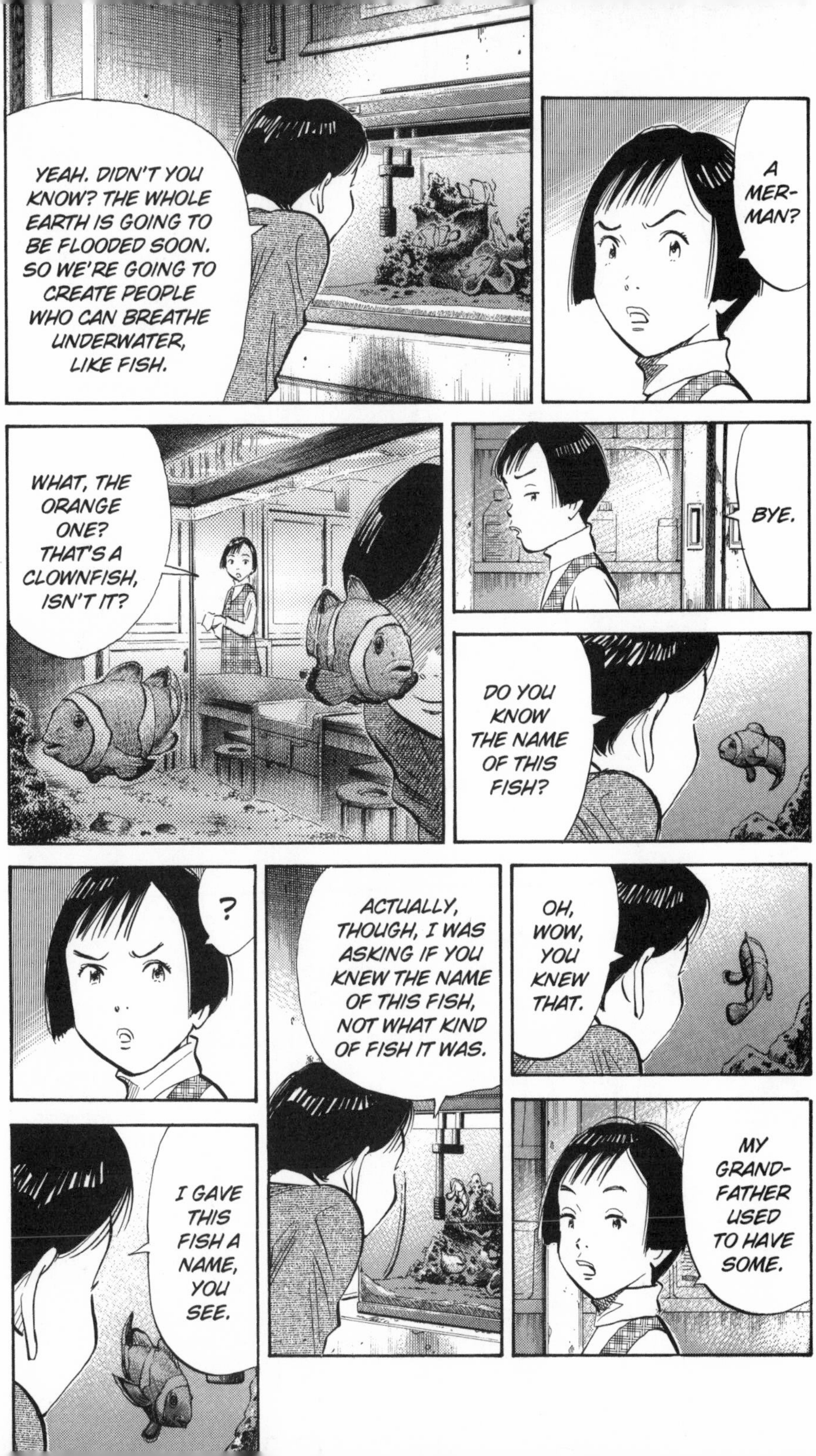
A MER-MAN?
YEAH. DIDN'T YOU KNOW? THE WHOLE EARTH IS GOING TO BE FLOODED SOON. SO WE'RE GOING TO CREATE PEOPLE WHO CAN BREATHE UNDERWATER, LIKE FISH.
BYE.
DO YOU KNOW THE NAME OF THIS FISH?
WHAT, THE ORANGE ONE? THAT'S A CLOWNFISH, ISN'T IT?
OH, WOW, YOU KNEW THAT.
MY GRAND-FATHER USED TO HAVE SOME.
ACTUALLY, THOUGH, I WAS ASKING IF YOU KNEW THE NAME OF THIS FISH, NOT WHAT KIND OF FISH IT WAS.
?
I GAVE THIS FISH A NAME, YOU SEE.

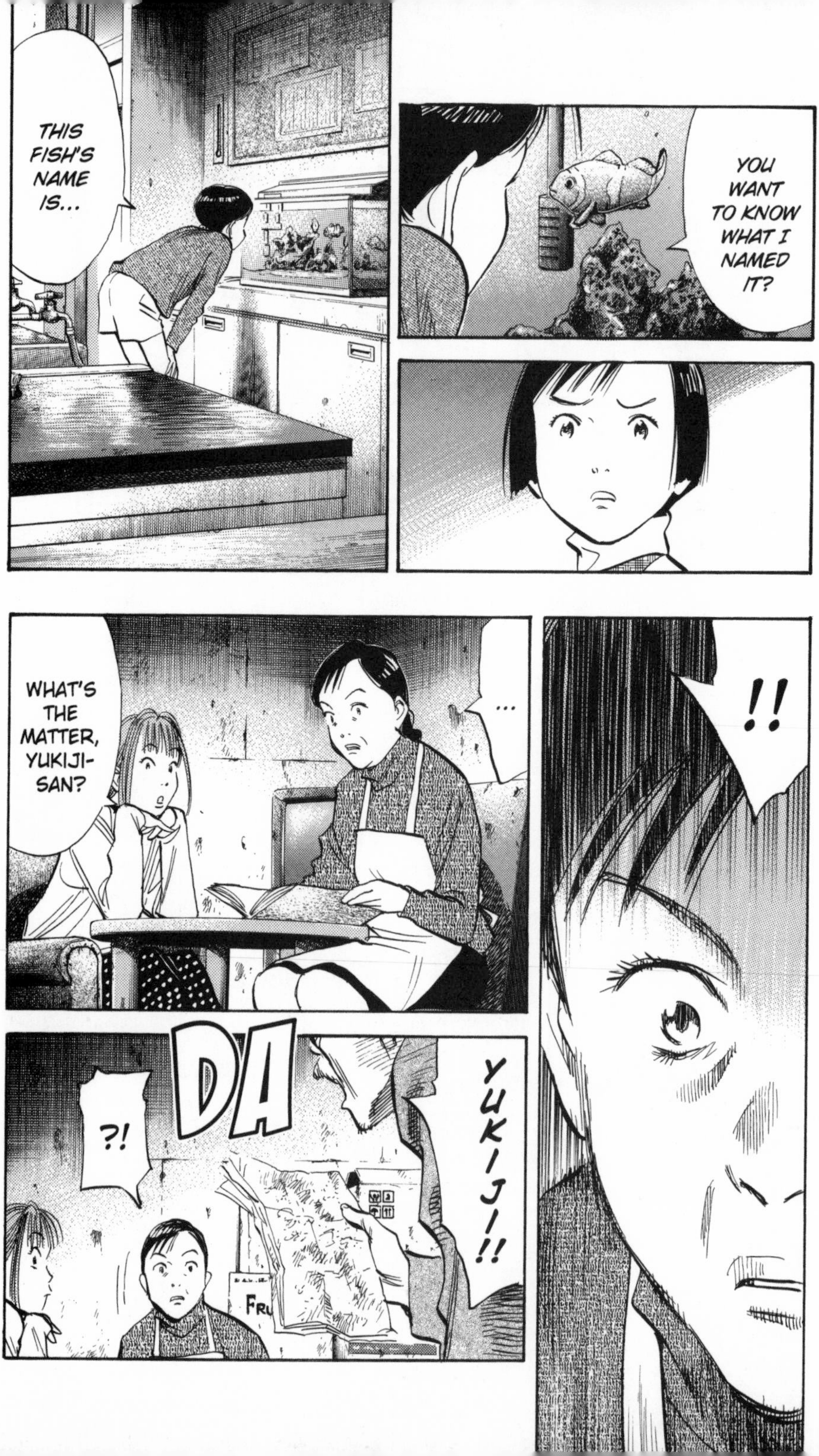

YOU WANT TO KNOW WHAT I NAMED IT?
THIS FISH'S NAME IS...
!!
...
WHAT'S THE MATTER, YUKIJI-SAN?
YUKIJI!!
DA
?!
FRU

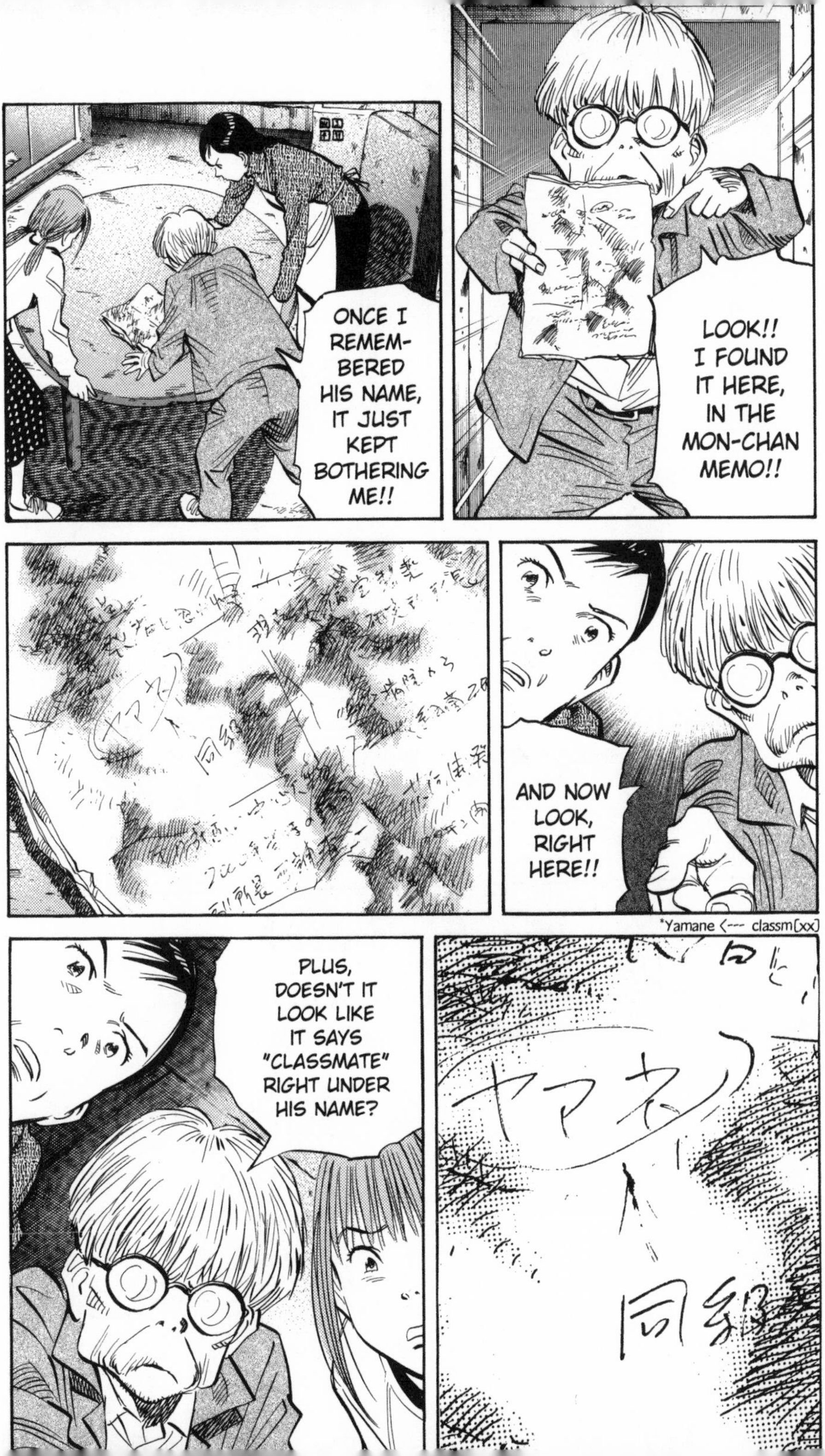
LOOK!! I FOUND IT HERE, IN THE MON-CHAN MEMO!!
ONCE I REMEMBERED HIS NAME, IT JUST KEPT BOTHERING ME!!
AND NOW LOOK, RIGHT HERE!!
*Yamane <--- classm[xx]
PLUS, DOESN'T IT LOOK LIKE IT SAYS "CLASSMATE" RIGHT UNDER HIS NAME?

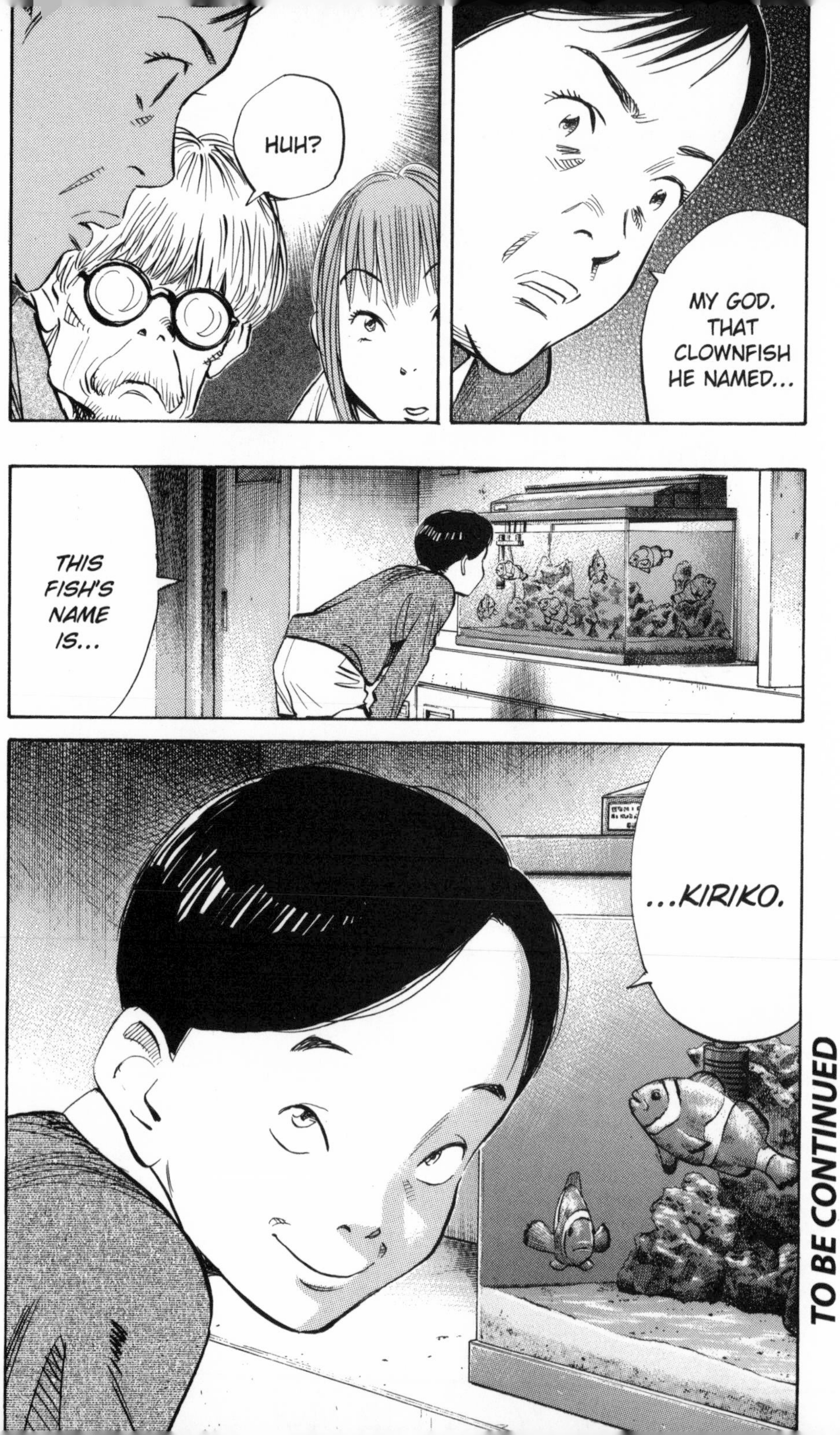
MY GOD. THAT CLOWNFISH HE NAMED...
HUH?
THIS FISH'S NAME IS...
...KIRIKO.
TO BE CONTINUED

NOTES FROM THE TRANSLATOR

This series follows the Japanese naming convention, with a character's family name followed by their given name. Honorifics such as -san and -kun are also preserved.

Page 21: *Dodonpa* is a genre of Japanese music. "Tokyo Dodonpa Musume" (Tokyo Dodonpa Girl) was a huge hit for singer Watanabe Mari in 1961.

Page 93: In Japan, drivers get points for infractions, and when a certain total is reached over a three-year period, they lose their license.

Page 129: *Menko* are cards with various pictures on them. They can be used for playing a card game that has been around since the Edo era.

Page 199: *Osechi ryori* is special food that is served at New Year's.

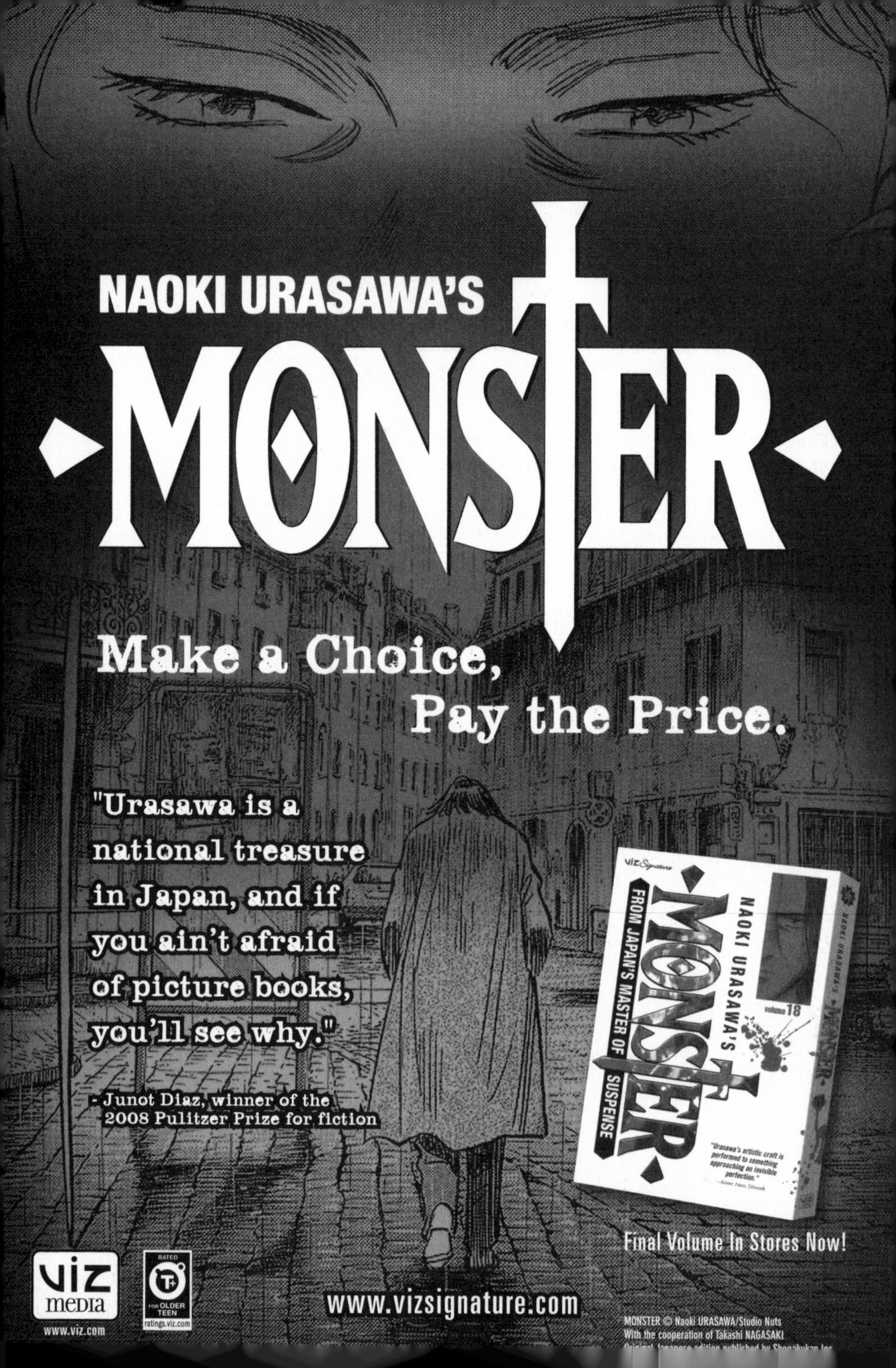

NAOKI URASAWA'S
MONSTER
Make a Choice,
Pay the Price.
"Urasawa is a national treasure in Japan, and if you ain't afraid of picture books, you'll see why."
- Junot Diaz, winner of the 2008 Pulitzer Prize for fiction
VIZ Signature
NAOKI URASAWA'S
MONSTER
FROM JAPAN'S MASTER OF SUSPENSE
volume 18
"Urasawa's artistic craft is performed to something approaching an invisible perfection."
—Anime News Network
Final Volume In Stores Now!
VIZ MEDIA
www.viz.com
RATED T+ FOR OLDER TEEN
ratings.viz.com
www.vizsignature.com
MONSTER © Naoki URASAWA/Studio Nuts
With the cooperation of Takashi NAGASAKI